THE POLICE AND INTERNATIONAL HUMAN RIGHTS LAW

THE POLICE AND INTERNATIONAL HUMAN RIGHTS LAW

Edited by

Marko Nikolić

SOCIETY Publishing

www.societypublishing.com

The Police and International Human Rights Law

Marko Nikolić

Society Publishing
2010 Winston Park Drive,
2nd Floor
Oakville, ON L6H 5R7
Canada
www.societypublishing.com
Tel: 001-289-291-7705
001-905-616-2116
Fax: 001-289-291-7601
Email: orders@arclereducation.com

ISBN: 978-1-77361-533-2 (Hardcover)

DECLARATION

ABOUT THE EDITOR

Marko obtained his Master's degree from University of Belgrade - Faculty of Law in 2014. He specialized in Criminal Law, Family Law and Environmental Law. He spent his Master year studying about international child abduction. He is currently employed in Ministry of Defense's Legal Department.

TABLE OF CONTENTS

LIST OF CONTRIBUTORS

Joseph J. Amon
Health and Human Rights Division, Human Rights Watch, New York, New York, United States of America
Johns Hopkins Bloomberg School of Public Health, Baltimore, Maryland, United States of America

Stefan D. Baral
Johns Hopkins Bloomberg School of Public Health, Baltimore, Maryland, United States of America
Center for Public Health and Human Rights, Johns Hopkins University, Baltimore, Maryland, United States of America

Chris Beyrer
Johns Hopkins Bloomberg School of Public Health, Baltimore, Maryland, United States of America
Center for Public Health and Human Rights, Johns Hopkins University, Baltimore, Maryland, United States of America

Nancy Kass
Johns Hopkins Bloomberg School of Public Health, Baltimore, Maryland, United States of America
Berman Institute of Bioethics, Johns Hopkins University, Baltimore, Maryland, United States of America

David McGrogan
Northumbria Law School, Newcastle upon Tyne, United Kingdom

Sabine C Carey
University of Mannheim

Neil J Mitchell
University College London

Will Lowe
University of Mannheim

Andrew Jakubowicz
University of Technology Sydney

Devaki Monani
Australian Catholic University

Magnus Mfoafo-M'Carthy
Lyle S. Hallman Faculty of Social Work, Wilfrid Laurier University, Kitchener, Ontario, Canada

Stephanie Huls
Lyle S. Hallman Faculty of Social Work, Wilfrid Laurier University, Kitchener, Ontario, Canada

Vanessa Johnston
Menzies School of Health Research and Institute of Advanced Studies, Charles Darwin University, Casuarina, NT 0811, Australia

Pascale Allotey
Centre for Public Health Research, School of Health Sciences and Social Care, Brunel University, West London, Uxbridge, UB8 3PH, UK

Kim Mulholland
Infectious Disease Epidemiology Unit, London School of Hygiene and Tropical Medicine, Keppel Street, London, WC1E 7HT, UK

Milica Markovic
School of Psychology, Psychiatry and Psychological Medicine, Monash University, Clayton, Victoria, Australia

Madelyn Hsiao-Rei Hicks
Health Service and Population Research Department, Institute of Psychiatry, King's College London, London, United Kingdom.

Michael Spagat
Department of Economics, Royal Holloway College, University of London, Egham, United Kingdom

Alina Potts
Program on Forced Migration and Health, Heilbrunn Department of Population and Family Health, Mailman School of Public Health, Columbia University, 60 Haven Ave B-4, Suite 432, New York, NY, USA

Kathleen Myer
Program on Forced Migration and Health, Heilbrunn Department of Population and Family Health, Mailman School of Public Health, Columbia University, 60 Haven Ave B-4, Suite 432, New York, NY, USA

Les Roberts
Program on Forced Migration and Health, Heilbrunn Department of Population and Family Health, Mailman School of Public Health, Columbia University, 60 Haven Ave B-4, Suite 432, New York, NY, USA

Tim Rhodes
Centre for Research on Drugs and Health Behaviour, London School of Hygiene and Tropical Medicine, University of London, London WC1E 7HT

Milena Simic
Centre for Research on Drugs and Health Behaviour, London School of Hygiene and Tropical Medicine, University of London, London WC1E 7HT

Sladjana Baros
Department of Ethnology and Anthropology, University of Belgrade, Serbia

Lucy Platt
Centre for Research on Drugs and Health Behaviour, London School of Hygiene and Tropical Medicine, University of London, London WC1E 7HT

Bojan Zˇikic
Department of Ethnology and Anthropology, University of Belgrade, Serbia

Corey S Davis
University of North Carolina, Gillings School of Global Public Health, Campus Box 7411, Chapel Hill, North Carolina 27599, USA

Leo Beletsky
Yale University, Center for Interdisciplinary Research on AIDS, 135 College

Street Suite 200, New Haven, CT 06510, USA

Helen McColl
International Rehabilitation Council for Torture Victims, Borgergade 13, 1022 Copenhagen K., Denmark

Craig Higson-Smith
South African Institute for Traumatic Stress, 302 Ideal Village, 30 Hannaben Street, Johannesburg 2198, South Africa

Sarah Gjerding
International Rehabilitation Council for Torture Victims, Borgergade 13, 1022 Copenhagen K., Denmark

Mostafa H Omar
El Nadim Centre for the Management and Rehabilitation of Victims of Violence, 3A Soliman El Halabi Street from Rasmis Street, Cairo, Egypt

Basma Abdel Rahman
El Nadim Centre for the Management and Rehabilitation of Victims of Violence, 3A Soliman El Halabi Street from Rasmis Street, Cairo, Egypt

Mona Hamed
El Nadim Centre for the Management and Rehabilitation of Victims of Violence, 3A Soliman El Halabi Street from Rasmis Street, Cairo, Egypt

Aida S El Dawla
El Nadim Centre for the Management and Rehabilitation of Victims of Violence, 3A Soliman El Halabi Street from Rasmis Street, Cairo, Egypt

Miriam Fredericks
Trauma Centre of Survivors of Violence and Torture, Cowley House, 126 Chapel Street, Woodstock 7925, Cape Town, South Africa

Nicole Paulsen
Trauma Centre of Survivors of Violence and Torture, Cowley House, 126 Chapel Street, Woodstock 7925, Cape Town, South Africa

Gugu Shabalala
Trauma Centre of Survivors of Violence and Torture, Cowley House, 126

Chapel Street, Woodstock 7925, Cape Town, South Africa

Carmen Low-Shang
Trauma Centre of Survivors of Violence and Torture, Cowley House, 126 Chapel Street, Woodstock 7925, Cape Town, South Africa

Fernando Valadez Perez
Collective Against Torture and Impunity, Pitágoras 1210, 16 Col. Del Valle, 03100 Mexico DF, Mexico

Liliana S Colin
Collective Against Torture and Impunity, Pitágoras 1210, 16 Col. Del Valle, 03100 Mexico DF, Mexico

Aurora D Hernandez
Collective Against Torture and Impunity, Pitágoras 1210, 16 Col. Del Valle, 03100 Mexico DF, Mexico

Eliomara Lavaire
Centre for Prevention, Treatment and Rehabilitation of Victims of Torture and their Relatives, Col. La Reforma, Calle Principal 109, Contiguo a Centro IDEAL, Tegucigalpa M.D.C., Honduras

Arely PA Zuñiga
Centre for Prevention, Treatment and Rehabilitation of Victims of Torture and their Relatives, Col. La Reforma, Calle Principal 109, Contiguo a Centro IDEAL, Tegucigalpa M.D.C., Honduras

Lucia Calidonio
Centre for Prevention, Treatment and Rehabilitation of Victims of Torture and their Relatives, Col. La Reforma, Calle Principal 109, Contiguo a Centro IDEAL, Tegucigalpa M.D.C., Honduras

Carmen L Martinez
Centre for Prevention, Treatment and Rehabilitation of Victims of Torture and their Relatives, Col. La Reforma, Calle Principal 109, Contiguo a Centro IDEAL, Tegucigalpa M.D.C., Honduras

Yasser Abu Jamei
Gaza Community Mental Health Programme, Sheikh Ejleen-El Rasheed

Zeyad Awad
Gaza Community Mental Health Programme, Sheikh Ejleen-El Rasheed

Edward J Mills
Programme in International Human Rights Law, University of Oxford, Oxford, UK
Department of Pharmacy, Rhodes University, Grahamstown, Eastern Cape, South Africa

Sonal Singh
Department of Pharmacy, Rhodes University, Grahamstown, Eastern Cape, South Africa
Bloomberg School of Public Health, Johns Hopkins University, Baltimore, USA
School of Medicine, Wake Forest University, Winston-Salem, USA

Cheryl Overs
Michael Kirby Centre for Public Health and Human Rights, School of Public Health and Preventive Medicine Monash University, Alfred Hospital Campus Melbourne, Victoria 3004, Australia

Kate Hawkins
Institute of Development Studies, University of Sussex, Brighton BN1 9RE, UK

Irene Messinger
Department for Political Sciences, Alumna University of Vienna, Vienna, 1090, Austria

Cody T. Ross
Department of Anthropology, University of California, Davis, Davis, California, United States of America

LIST OF ABBREVIATIONS

AIDS	Acquired Immune Deficiency Syndrome
CASAM	Center for Advocacy on Stigma and Marginalisation
CEDAW	Convention on the Elimination of Discrimination Against Women
DEVAW	Declaration on the Elimination of Violence Against Women
ECHR	European Convention on Human Rights Convention
ECtHR	European Court of Human Rights
EEA	European Economic Area
EMN	European Migration Network
EU	European Union
HIV	Human Immunodeficiency Virus
NGO	Non Governmental Organisation
NSWP	International Network of Sex Work Projects
PLRI	Paulo Longo Research Initiative
SRHR	Sexual and Reproductive Health and Rights
STI	Sexually Transmitted Infection
TCN	Third Country National
UN	United Nations
UNAIDS	Joint United Nations Programme on HIV/AIDS
UNFPA	United Nations Population Fund
US	United States

PREFACE

The behavior of the repressive authorities can often be on the border with the basic need for human rights protection. The violation of personal and collective freedoms can occur in a variety of possible situations. The police as an extended arm of the government cannot be viewed separately from the officials and the administration itself, regardless of the degree of autonomy that it has. However, offenses and crimes can occur in this domain under the control of the authorities, but they can also be the cause of the individual state of mind, the attitude of social groups, the reflection of powerless or weak state, etc. It is the spiritual and economic health of the nation that is the starting factor in the prevention of and the fight for the protection of human rights. A strong, democratic society will not lose control over the authorities, at the same time, it will be able to guide them in the right direction, to prevent behavior that can, in the long run, shake the very foundations of the community.

Before dealing with contemporary human rights issues, we will address a specific social group or a treatment of people with mental illnesses. Does legislation need to be modified?

Since this is one broad field with a lot of specifics, depending on the position and status of each country, we will deal with the problems of international students in Australia in the next part of our book. We take this example, as a reaction to the sudden emergence of a new social group, and the management of organs in such a situation.

We all know that torture in addition to physical harm devastate the psyche as well, but are the procedures similar to Australian asylum policies and practices, which are violating human rights, are associated with adverse health outcomes? What is the impact of police rudeness in situations when it acts in full compliance with the law?

The police is an authority not directly oriented to external activities, although the definition is different and it will often direct towards collaborative action with the army units. Therefore, in the next chapter, we will focus on the consequences of conflict related to civilians, alongside the effects of armed conflict on populations. And then we will immediately deal with the Measuring

Human Rights Violations in a conflict-affected country in Africa.

As we mentioned earlier, there are many potentially harmful situations and injuries. Since our space is limited, we will illustrate the variety of police influence through *Police violence and sexual risk among female and transvestite sex workers in Serbia: a qualitative study*.

Many problems can come from pure ignorance on the subject. Social dialogue can play a crucial role as well as continuous education. Therefore, we will also look at the issue of syringe access programs, and their reception by the police.

The outcomes of torture are always severe, whether committed by the other party in the conflict or during the police examination. That is why we also include the question of *Rehabilitation of torture survivors in five countries: common themes and challenges*. Closely linked with this issue is the topic of medical research on oppressed populations.

We have to deal with the issues of legislation, and the fact that police officers may be stressed and burdened with work. Could decriminalization in certain level help increase the quality of the work of law enforcement? In other words, would this way reduce the rate of human rights violations?

The next topic is the 'marriages of convenience' and the treatment of the Austrian police in this field as an introduction to the burning issue of migration policies.

In the end, we inevitably turn to the current topic of the American police's treatment of the African American population by observing the presence of Racial Bias in Police Shootings. We must not cover up the range of the problem. We must accept it in order to face it as a society and take measures to suppress such behavior!!!.

CHAPTER 1

HUMAN RIGHTS RESEARCH AND ETHICS REVIEW: PROTECTING INDIVIDUALS OR PROTECTING THE STATE?

Joseph J. Amon[1,2], Stefan D. Baral[2,3], Chris Beyrer[2,3], Nancy Kass[2,4]

[1] Health and Human Rights Division, Human Rights Watch, New York, New York, United States of America

[2] Johns Hopkins Bloomberg School of Public Health, Baltimore, Maryland, United States of America

[3] Center for Public Health and Human Rights, Johns Hopkins University, Baltimore, Maryland, United States of America

[4] Berman Institute of Bioethics, Johns Hopkins University, Baltimore, Maryland, United States of America

Citation: Amon JJ, Baral SD, Beyrer C, Kass N (2012) Human Rights Research and Ethics Review: Protecting Individuals or Protecting the State? PLoS Med 9(10): e1001325. https://doi.org/10.1371/journal.pmed.1001325

BACKGROUND

Human rights violations play an important role as determinants of, or structural barriers to, health [1]–[6]. Research, investigation, and documentation focused on human rights have led to the development of rights-based interventions [7],[8] and the promotion of human rights in the core strategies of international health organizations [9],[10].

At the same time, health and human rights investigations raise complex ethical and methodological challenges [11]. Key questions have emerged about the roles of ethical review and research ethics committees (RECs) when criminalized or marginalized populations are part of research or program efforts [12],[13]. Human rights researchers may also follow ethical codes and professional norms such as those of journalists or lawyers, for example, but these do not typically engage RECs and may in fact define their work differently than biomedical or epidemiologic definitions of "research" [14]–[16]. Furthermore, members of local (i.e., in country) RECs may have conflicts of interest when state actors have a role in or supervision over RECs and can exert their influence to limit the scope of or impede investigations into human rights abuses.

In some circumstances, interests other than ensuring the sound protection of research participants may come to dominate the decisions that RECs make, including whether they agree to review the research and/or allow the research to be conducted at all. Researchers aware of these decision-making processes may "self censor" the focus of their research or choose to conduct research elsewhere. As increasing amounts of research are conducted on the impact of human rights on health, more attention is needed on the roles of RECs and researchers to ensure genuine protection of the individuals involved in human rights investigations. Here we present examples of how human rights researchers can address complex ethical challenges by building the capacity of community-based organizations representing vulnerable populations and by adopting ethical operating principles. We illustrate our policy proposals using case studies of research involving men who have sex with men (MSM) in Africa, ethnic minorities in Myanmar, and individuals in compulsory drug treatment centers in Asia.

HUMAN PARTICIPANT PROTECTIONS

The protection of participants in health-related research has evolved into a well-articulated international framework supported by normative documents, conventions, and, in growing numbers of jurisdictions, laws. Key among these are the World Medical Association's 1964 *Declaration of Helsinki* [17], the US Department of Health and Human Services *Belmont Report* and regulations for the protection of research participants [18],[19], the Council for International Organizations of Medical Sciences international ethical guidelines [20], and the International Conference of Harmonisation of Technical Requirements for Registration of Pharmaceuticals for Human Use (http://www.ich.org/). All of these guidelines require prior review of research by an REC before research can be implemented. More recently, the World Health Organization published standards for such committees outlining key requirements for their structure, governance, and review standards [21].

Over the last ten years, there has been extraordinary growth in the numbers of RECs in low- and middle-income countries (LMICs). As new committees in LMICs have emerged, many countries have adopted a structure whereby local committees, affiliated with specific research institutions or organizations, are supported by a national committee. The national committee is in charge of creating policies, providing oversight, and, in some cases, performing an additional, final review.

Unfortunately, the methodology and intent of human rights research has not been fully considered in existing standards and guidelines on the ethical conduct of research. Similarly, RECs have traditionally been orientated to biomedical and epidemiologic research and have rarely considered human rights research. While principles such as autonomy, beneficence, non-malevolence, and justice are common to ethical codes in diverse disciplines [14]–[16],[18],[22], the definition of "research" and the requirement for REC review are not universal across different types of research.

DEFINING "RESEARCH"

The definition of research and the difference between health research (typically requiring ethics review) and monitoring, evaluation, or practice (typically exempt from review) are not straightforward [23]. For individuals engaged in rights research and RECs considering their jurisdiction over such research, the determination of whether a human rights investigation constitutes research can be contentious and may reflect differences in disciplinary training and professional norms.

Health and human rights investigations can often be considered "non-research" under the US Department of Health and Human Services and international definitions that define research as developing "generalizable knowledge" [19],[20]. Documentation of particular human rights abuses, factors that contribute to particular cases of human rights abuse, or human rights protections in particular situations are not usually considered "generalizable." While broader surveys determining the prevalence of abuses may be considered research, in some cases they may be considered monitoring, which, again, is commonly exempt from review. In addition, individuals who provide testimony or evidence of human rights abuses are not traditional research participants. Instead, these individuals have an important motivation for engagement in human rights investigations, that is, for seeing such investigations as perhaps their only means of achieving justice for themselves and their communities. Thus, their view of the balance of "risk" versus "benefit" may be substantially different from the view held by biomedical researchers or REC members.

CONDUCTING RESEARCH ON MSM AND HIV IN AFRICA

Recently identified HIV outbreaks among MSM in several African countries have revealed many neglected or hidden human rights abuses. These abuses include discrimination in access to HIV prevention and treatment, lack of access to justice, police abuse, arbitrary arrest and detention, and ill-treatment and torture. In nearly all African countries in which research has been conducted, HIV infection rates have been markedly higher among MSM than among other men of reproductive age [24]–[29]. These epidemics are occurring among largely hidden, stigmatized, and—in many countries—criminalized MSM communities, challenging research and service provision [30].

In some countries, police have specifically targeted outreach workers providing information and condoms to MSM [31],[32], and health-care workers have been complicit in efforts to "prove" homosexuality with forced anal exams [33]–[35]. In Uganda, conducting research on MSM, including investigations of possible human rights abuses, has become difficult or impossible. Reasons for this difficulty include proposed legislation to make sodomy a capital offense and to criminalize the failure to report individuals suspected of engaging in homosexual behaviors, and targeted violence against individuals identified as MSM, including murder [36],[37].

Nevertheless, MSM health service providers and gay service and rights organizations and activists in many African countries have been enthusiastic partners in HIV-related programs, including research, even though governments have been reluctant to support research on MSM. In several cases, governments have actively opposed research that would lend credence to the reality that lesbian, gay, bisexual, and transgender persons exist in their countries, and to the fact that MSM are at elevated risk for HIV infection [37],[38].

At one site of a multi-country study being conducted by two of the authors of this article (S. D. B. and C. B.), the head of the only university-based REC informed the research team that, since homosexuality was criminalized in the country, no research protocols related to MSM would be accepted for review. The REC chair told the researchers that the role of the REC included the protection of social and cultural values of the country. While RECs may legitimately reference social and cultural values in considering what constitutes risk to individual human participants, the REC in this case defined its role well beyond protection of human welfare to instead reinforce a political position of the state.

In response, researchers engaged community-based organizations serving MSM in the country to gauge the level of support for the study, and trained community leaders on research ethics [39]. The study protocol was then reviewed by community leaders, who suggested protocol changes based on further community consultation. At the same time, the protocols were also reviewed by a REC in the US that was informed that the in-country REC had refused to review the protocol. After approval by the US REC, the researchers decided that the final decision to proceed should be made by the community-based organizations in country based upon their assessment of the risks and benefits of the research. Community members also participated in validating research findings, and members of the community presented the results to their peers and in domestic and international forums.

INVESTIGATING HEALTH AND HUMAN RIGHTS IN MYANMAR

In democratic societies where government legitimacy has broad acceptance, and where ministries of health are seen as working to advance the health and well-being of the population, researchers rarely question whether academic or state entities have the right to form and oversee RECs. In contrast, in repressive societies, and where an REC is seen as not representative of, or legitimately protecting the interests of, a particular vulnerable group (e.g., prisoners, women, or an ethnic or religious minority), RECs may be understood as agents of the state: prioritizing the protection of state interests over those of research participants. In the case of Myanmar, decades of civil and ethnic conflict have left large areas of the country under contested political control. Several major ethnic nationalities, including the Karen, Kachin, Chin, Shan, Mon, and Wa, have been in open armed conflict with the ruling military-backed regime or have cease-fire agreements that allow them considerable autonomy. Most of these ethnic groups do not have formal relationships with the ruling government.

In working with ethnic populations in border zones since 1992, we (as well as collaborators from the University of California, Los Angeles, and other entities) have struggled with the question of who most legitimately represents these populations and specifically who should safeguard their rights and interests if researchers or investigators want to collect data. For individuals with no formal communication with the regime they are fighting, the concept that this regime could make decisions for their health and well-being is both absurd and offensive. However, popular support for the government in exile is strong among most of Myamnar's ethnic national organizations, and this exiled government has a well-established health and welfare committee. Consequently, we have helped to establish and build the capacity of an REC composed of Myanmar physicians and nurses in exile, community health workers, community members, and faith-based leaders. This group has now had several years of experience functioning as an REC and reviewing proposals, and their authority has been accepted by RECs at US institutions [40]–[42].

DOCUMENTING ABUSES IN COMPULSORY DRUG TREATMENT CENTERS

Between July 2007 and September 2011, Human Rights Watch conducted investigations of compulsory detention of drug users in China [43],[44], Cambodia [45], Viet Nam [46], and the Lao People's Democratic Republic [47]. In these countries, drug use is legal but drug users are subject to extrajudicial administrative detention for the purpose of compulsory treatment of drug dependency. The investigations conducted by Human Rights Watch included interviews with individuals recently detained in drug detention centers; key informant interviews with non-government organizations, funding entities, and, in some cases, government officials; review of relevant government laws and policies; and review of international donor policies and programs in drug detention centers. The investigators found that individuals in drug detention centers were routinely held without clinical determination of drug dependency or due process, and once detained were denied evidence-based drug treatment as well as other basic health services. Drug users were often forced to perform arduous physical exercise, military drills, or forced labor, and were subject to physical and sexual abuse.

While research on drug addiction, HIV virology, HIV prevalence, and HIV prevention has been routinely conducted inside detention centers with the approval of government-affiliated RECs and the authorization of the government-controlled detention centers, the specific ethical concerns of conducting research in institutions that violate due process protections have not been addressed. At a minimum, researchers should be expected to accurately characterize the research setting and status of participants. Yet, researchers have often ignored the conditions within and lack of judicial oversight of such centers, presenting them as legitimate treatment facilities [48],[49]. Researchers rarely report on the availability of evidence-based drug dependency treatment [48],[50]–[55] and have obscured the status of research participants (e.g., referring to detainees as "patients" [48] or vaguely alluding to their "complex legal needs" [55]). Published papers also often omit mention of the challenges of conducting independent research [48],[50]–[55]. One study acknowledged using detention center staff to witness consent [55], potentially increasing the risk of coercion. Researchers who do not have full, independent, or ongoing access to detention centers may be unable to assess negative consequences for research participants, and detainees who do not have access to legal counsel or the right to free speech may be unable to file a complaint alleging abusive research.

In response to these challenges, we chose to conduct research with individuals in the community who had been recently released from detention centers. However, human rights monitoring by independent international organizations is not allowed in China, Viet Nam, or the Lao People's Democratic Republic, and we did not feel that local RECs would approve research related to torture and ill-treatment. Therefore, a decision was made to proceed without local REC approval in order to protect both research participants and researchers, who we feared could be targeted by the state for proposing research that is viewed as sensitive to state security or disruptive of government goals of "social harmony." In place of local REC approval, and because we felt that there was no defined community of recently released drug users to formally consult with (and that community engagement in the context of ongoing persecution would not be safe regardless), researchers developed and followed specific ethical operating principles. In contrast to the typical approach of RECs, where review is limited to the research protocol, every step of the research, from the protocol review to implementation to dissemination of results to scientific, diplomatic, and media audiences included internal ethics review by technical and legal experts.

MITIGATING RISKS IN HUMAN RIGHTS INVESTIGATIONS

To address the possible conflicts investigators may face in protecting participants in the course of health and human rights investigations, local RECs are needed that can be considered truly independent. In addition, two distinct and complementary strategies—community-based review and the development of strong ethical operating principles—can help protect investigators and participants in health-related human rights research.

In the context of governments that persecute specific populations, actively limit free speech, and routinely punish criticism of the state, RECs are unlikely to be independent. Under these circumstances, using local RECs to safeguard the rights and interests of research participants may be counterproductive, putting both investigators and participants at risk. In these settings, researchers may need to actively engage communities and follow clear ethical operating principles in place of local REC review.

Community-based review and participatory research have a long history and were developed to address community members' concerns about neglect by and communities' mistrust of researchers, health-care systems, and government [56],[57]. Conducted correctly, community-based participatory research (including financial and technical support for community engagement and leadership) creates bridges between policy-makers, scientists, and communities; facilitates reciprocal learning; assists in the development of culturally appropriate measurement instruments and interventions; and establishes a level of trust that enhances both the quantity and the quality of data collected and programs delivered [39],[57]–[61]. While there is a well-established body of literature on engagement of marginalized populations in high-income settings and on some vulnerable populations in LMICs [57],[58], the issues faced by criminalized and violently stigmatized populations have less often been addressed.

One challenge of community-based review is that in many settings the "community" is not homogenous, organized, or able to participate in extensive consultation and review of proposed research. Research with migrants, prisoners, drug users, and criminalized populations is often conducted without a representative advocacy group. In other settings, it may not be clear who legitimately speaks for marginalized populations. In all settings, community-based review can be time-consuming and resource intensive.

In conducting human rights research, particularly in settings where safety may be of particular concern, a critical first step is to have standing procedures on investigator and participant protection. All Human Rights Watch staff who conduct interviews, for example, undergo security training and training on participants' protection and data safety. Researchers can also receive specialized training on how to sensitively interview people in such a way as to minimize risk of re-traumatization, including training on interviewing victims of sexual violence, children, persons in extreme pain, prisoners, and the mentally disabled. All researchers must participate in a security meeting prior to a research mission that establishes chains of communication so that security emergencies can be identified and handled once the mission is in progress. Post-mission meetings are held if security concerns arise, and the security of participants stemming from contact with researchers is monitored. Prior to publication of any findings from research (in the form of reports, journal articles, press releases, opinion pieces, photography, or other media), legal review is required and provides further assessment of research participant protection.

CONCLUSION

For individuals who experience human rights abuses, the consequences of reporting that abuse are often uncertain. Yet even when the risk of retaliation is judged to be high, many individuals may be willing to take such a risk in order to press for justice, despite the fact that justice may take years or even decades to be served. Individuals who are a part of communities that are systematically discriminated against, stigmatized, or criminalized may experience high levels of ongoing harm, and see participation in a human rights investigation as one of few means of challenging those abuses or demanding redress.

In the decade to come, RECs in LMICs will likely acquire increasing jurisdiction, resources, and authority over local research. These changes will offer a promise of greater protection for research participants who in the past have faced abuses with little opportunity for redress. But RECs may have little experience in evaluating the inherent risks faced by individuals vulnerable to human rights abuses as well as the risks and benefits from participation in a human rights investigation. RECs, which primarily review pre-research protocols, may also be poorly suited to the review of dynamic investigations using open-ended research methodologies where the risk to participants is less a result of research processes (e.g., questionnaires) than from post-research products (e.g., reports, legal processes, and media coverage). The use of RECs to limit health and human rights research for political, cultural, or other considerations is a misuse of the legitimate functions of RECs. Careful attention must be paid when local committees assert that their views represent local cultural norms, or that human rights are an illegitimate focus of research as they express foreign values. A critical distinction for researchers is understanding the difference between respecting cultural traditions that are "matters of etiquette, ritual, or religion," with little or no relation to ethics, from those cultural traditions with ethical (or human rights) implications, such as female genital mutilation or infanticide [62]. Cultural practices or government policies that either deliberately or incidentally serve to suppress or threaten the rights of certain people cannot be respected. RECs, charged specifically with upholding the rights and protection of individuals, should not use culture or "values" as a means to deny human rights. Increasing attention to human rights as a determinant of health will result in increasing requests to RECs to review research that investigates the role and complicity of state actors, government laws and policies, and social or cultural norms as they relate to health. Stronger, independent RECs trained in human rights may be better equipped to more adequately review this research. When RECs are unable to do so, or where research on human rights or criminalized or marginalized populations is expressly prohibited, researchers may need to rely upon alternative strategies, including engaging communities and following ethical operating principles, to ensure that research participants are protected and that research is ethically conducted. While such innovations do not eliminate all risks, and may be costly in terms of time and resources, the alternatives, which may include acceding to censorship or not conducting investigations at all, are unacceptable limits.

AUTHOR CONTRIBUTIONS

Wrote the first draft of the manuscript: JJA. Contributed to the writing of the manuscript: JJA SDB CB NK. ICMJE criteria for authorship read and met: JJA SDB CB NK. Agree with manuscript results and conclusions: JJA SDB CB NK.

REFERENCES

1. Amon JJ, Kasambala T (2009) Structural barriers and human rights related to HIV prevention and treatment in Zimbabwe. Glob Public Health 4: 528–545.
2. Beyrer C, Terzian A, Lowther S, Zambrano JA, Galai N, et al. (2007) Civil conflict and health information: the Democratic Republic of Congo. In: Beyrer C, Pizer H, editors. Public health & human rights: evidence-based approaches. Baltimore: Johns Hopkins University Press.
3. Nowrojee B (2005) Making the invisible war crime visible: post-conflict justice for Sierra Leone's rape victims. Harv Hum Rights J 18: 85–105.
4. Singh S, Dahal K, Mills E (2005) Nepal's war on human rights: a summit higher than Everest. Int J Equity Health 4: 9.
5. Todrys KW, Amon JJ, Malembeka G, Clayton M (2011) Imprisoned and imperiled: access to HIV and TB prevention and treatment, and denial of human rights, in Zambian prisons. J Int AIDS Soc 14: 8.
6. Lohman D, Schleifer R, Amon JJ (2010) Access to pain treatment as a human right. BMC Med 8: 8.
7. Barr D, Amon JJ, Clayton M (2011) Articulating a rights-based approach to HIV treatment and prevention interventions. Curr HIV Res 9: 396–404.
8. London L (2008) What is a human-rights based approach to health and does it matter? Health Hum Rights 10: 65–80.
9. Global Fund to Fight AIDS, Tuberculosis and Malaria (2011) The global fund strategy 2012–2016: investing for impact. Geneva: Global Fund to Fight AIDS, Tuberculosis and Malaria. Available: http://www.theglobalfund.org/documents/core/strategies/Core_GlobalFund_Strategy_en/. Accessed 15 August 2012.
10. Joint United Nations Programme on HIV/AIDS (2010) Getting to zero: 2011–2015 strategy. Geneva: United Nations. Available: http://www.unaids.org/en/media/unaids/contentassets/documents/unaidspublication/2010/JC2034_UNAIDS_Strategy_en.pdf. Accessed 15 August 2012.
11. Beyrer C, Kass NE (2002) Human rights, politics, and reviews of research ethics. Lancet 360: 246–251.
12. Burris S, Davis C (2009) Assessing social risks prior to commencement

of a clinical trial: due diligence or ethical inflation? Am J Bioeth 9: 48–54.

13. Lynch HF, Dawson L (2009) Adding insult to injury: reluctance to engage in clinical research with at-risk groups further disenfranchises these populations. Am J Bioeth 9: 62–64.
14. Society of Professional Journalists (1996) SPJ code of ethics. New York: Society of Professional Journalists. Available: http://www.spj.org/ethicscode.asp. Accessed 15 August 2012.
15. American Bar Association (2012) Model rules of professional conduct. New York: American Bar Association. Available: http://www.americanbar.org/groups/professional_responsibility/publications/model_rules_of_professional_conduct/model_rules_of_professional_conduct_table_of_contents.html. Accessed 15 August 2012.
16. O'Neill WG (2010) The statement of ethical commitments of human rights professionals: a commentary. In: O'Flaherty M, Ulrich G, editors. The professional identity of the human rights field officer. London: Ashgate.
17. World Medical Association (1964) WMA Declaration of Helsinki—ethical principles for medical research involving human subjects. Helsinki: World Medical Association. Available: http://www.wma.net/en/30publications/10policies/b3/. Accessed 15 August 2012.
18. The National Commission for the Protection of Human Subjects of Biomedical and Behavioral Research (1979) The Belmont report: ethical principles and guidelines for the protection of human subjects of research. Washington (District of Columbia): US Department of Health and Human Services. Available: http://www.hhs.gov/ohrp/policy/belmont.html. Accessed 15 August 2012.
19. (2009) US Code of Federal Regulations, Title 45: Public Welfare. Part 46: Protection of Human Subjects. Washington (District of Columbia): US Department of Health and Human Services. Available: http://www.hhs.gov/ohrp/humansubjects/guidance/45cfr46.html. Accessed 15 August 2012.
20. Rose S (2009) International ethical guidelines for epidemiological studies. Am J Epidemiol 170: 1451–1452.
21. World Health Organization (2011) Standards and operational guidance for ethics review of health-related research with human participants. Geneva: World Health Organization. Available: http://whqlibdoc.who.

int/publications/2011/9789241502948_eng.pdf. Accessed 15 August 2012.

22. Christakis NA (1992) Ethics are local: engaging cross-cultural variation in the ethics for clinical research. Soc Sci Med 35: 1079–1091.
23. Hodge JG, Gostin LO (2004) Public health practice vs. research: a report for public health practitioners including cases and guidance for making distinctions. Atlanta (Georgia): Council of State and Territorial Epidemiologists. Available: http://www.cste.org/pdffiles/newpdffiles/CSTEPHResRptHodgeFinal.5.24.04.pdf. Accessed 17 September 2012.
24. Baral S, Sifakis F, Cleghorn F, Beyrer C (2007) Elevated risk for HIV infection among men who have sex with men in low- and middle-income countries 2000–2006: a systematic review. PLoS Med 4: e339
25. Baral S, Adams D, Lebona J, Kaibe B, Letsie P, et al. (2011) A cross-sectional assessment of population demographics, HIV risks and human rights contexts among men who have sex with men in Lesotho. J Int AIDS Soc 14: 36.
26. Beyrer C, Trapence G, Motimedi F, Umar E, Iipinge S, et al. (2010) Bisexual concurrency, bisexual partnerships, and HIV among Southern African men who have sex with men (MSM). Sex Transm Infect 86: 323–327.
27. Beyrer C, Baral SD, Walker D, Wirtz AL, Johns B, et al. (2010) The expanding epidemics of HIV type 1 among men who have sex with men in low- and middle-income countries: diversity and consistency. Epidemiol Rev 32: 137–151.
28. Baral S, Trapence G, Motimedi F, Umar E, Iipinge S, et al. (2009) HIV prevalence, risks for HIV infection, and human rights among men who have sex with men (MSM) in Malawi, Namibia, and Botswana. PLoS ONE 4: e4997
29. Beyrer C, Baral SD, van Griensven F, Goodreau SM, Chariyalertsak S, et al. (2012) Global epidemiology of HIV infection in men who have sex with men. Lancet 380: 367–377.
30. Trapence G, Collins C, Avrett S, Carr R, Sanchez H, et al. (2012) From personal survival to public health: community leadership by men who have sex with men in the response to HIV. Lancet 380: 400–410.
31. Roscoe W, Murray S (1998) Boy-wives and female-husbands: studies in African homosexualities. London: Palgrave Macmillan. 336 p.

32. Poteat T, Diouf D, Drame FM, Ndaw M, Traore C, et al. (2011) HIV risk among MSM in Senegal: a qualitative rapid assessment of the impact of enforcing laws that criminalize same sex practices. PLoS ONE 6: e28760 doi:https://doi.org/10.1371/journal.pone.0028760.
33. Amon J (2010) HIV treatment as prevention—human rights issues. J Int AIDS Soc 13 (Suppl 4) O15.
34. Semugoma P, Beyrer C, Baral S (2012) Assessing the effects of anti-homosexuality legislation in Uganda on HIV prevention, treatment, and care services. SAHARA J In press.
35. Amon J (2010) Abusing patients: health providers' complicity in torture and cruel, inhuman or degrading treatment. In: Human Rights Watch, editor. Human Rights Watch world report 2010: events of 2009. New York: Seven Stories Press. pp. 49–59.
36. Baral S, Semugoma P, Diouf D, Trapence G, Poteat T, Ndaw M, et al. (2010) Criminalization of same sex practices as a structural driver of HIV risk among men who have sex with men (MSM): the cases of Senegal, Malawi, and Uganda [abstract]. XVIII International AIDS Conference 18–23 July 2010; Vienna, Austria.
37. Semugoma P, Nemande S, Baral SD (2012) The irony of homophobia in Africa. Lancet 380: 312–314.
38. de Gruchy J, Lewin S (2001) Ethics that exclude: the role of ethics committees in lesbian and gay health research in South Africa. Am J Public Health 91: 865–868.
39. The American Foundation for AIDS Research, the International AIDS Vaccine Initiative, Johns Hopkins University Center for Public and Human Rights, United National Development Program (2011) Respect, protect, fulfill: best practices guidance in conducting HIV research with gay, bisexual, and other men who have sex with men (MSM) in rights-constrained environments. Available: http://www.amfar.org/uploadedFiles/_amfar.org/In_The_Community/Publications/MSMguidance2011.pdf. Accessed 15 August 2012.
40. Mullany LC, Richards AK, Lee CI, Suwanvanichkij V, Maung C, et al. (2007) Population-based survey methods to quantify associations between human rights violations and health outcomes among internally displaced persons in eastern Burma. J Epidemiol Community Health 61: 908–914.
41. Thailand Burma Border Consortium (2011) Programme report:

January–June 2010. Bangkok: Thailand Burma Border Consortium.

42. Mullany LC, Lee CI, Yone L, Paw P, Oo EK, et al. (2008) Access to essential maternal health interventions and human rights violations among vulnerable communities in eastern Burma. PLoS Med 5: e242 doi:https://doi.org/10.1371/journal.pmed.0050242.
43. Cohen JE, Amon JJ (2008) Health and human rights concerns of drug users in detention in Guangxi Province, China. PLoS Med 5: e234
44. Human Rights Watch (2010) Where darkness knows no limits: incarceration, ill-treatment and forced labor as drug rehabilitation in China. Available: http://www.hrw.org/sites/default/files/reports/china0110webwcover.pdf. Accessed 15 August 2012.
45. Human Rights Watch (2010) "Skin on the cable": the illegal arrest, arbitrary detention and torture of people who use drugs in Cambodia. Available: http://www.hrw.org/sites/default/files/reports/cambodia0110webwcover.pdf. Accessed 15 August 2012.
46. Human Rights Watch (2011) The rehab archipelago: forced labor and other abuses in drug detention centers in southern Vietnam. Available: http://www.hrw.org/sites/default/files/reports/vietnam0911ToPost.pdf. Accessed 15 August 2012.
47. Human Rights Watch (2011) Somsanga's secrets: arbitrary detention, physical abuse, and suicide inside a Lao drug detention center. Available: http://www.hrw.org/sites/default/files/reports/laos1011webwcover_0.pdf. Accessed 15 August 2012.
48. Xue YX, Luo YX, Wu P, Shi HS, Xue LF, et al. (2012) A memory retrieval-extinction procedure to prevent drug craving and relapse. Science 336: 241–245.
49. Amon JJ (2012) Chinese addiction study and human rights. Science 337: 522–523.
50. Hien NT, Giang LT, Binh PN, Wolffers I (2000) The social context of HIV risk behaviour by drug injectors in Ho Chi Minh City, Vietnam. AIDS Care 12: 483–495.
51. Xiao L, Wu Z, Wang Y, Chen J (2009) [Comparison of quality of life for drug addicts in methadone maintenance treatment clinics, community and compulsory detoxification institutions in Sichuan Province.]. Wei Sheng Yan Jiu 38: 67–70.
52. Tran SD, Williams AB, Truong HT, Do NH (1998) Risk factors for HIV seropositivity in a sample of drug users in drug treatment in Ho Chi

Minh City, Vietnam. J Acquir Immune Defic Syndr Hum Retrovirol 17: 283–287.

53. Fozi K, Azmi H, Kamariah H, Azwa MS (2006) Prevalence of thiamine deficiency at a drug rehabilitation centre in Malaysia. Med J Malaysia 61: 519–525.
54. Zhu WX, Dong JQ, Hesketh T (2009) Preventing relapse in incarcerated drug users in Yunnan Province, China. Drug Alcohol Rev 28: 641–647.
55. Shen SY, Zhang ZB, Tucker JD, Chang H, Zhang GR, et al. (2011) Peer-based behavioral health program for drug users in China: a pilot study. BMC Public Health 11: 693.
56. Corbie-Smith G, Thomas SB, Williams MV, Moody-Ayers S (1999) Attitudes and beliefs of African Americans toward participation in medical research. J Gen Intern Med 14: 537–546.
57. Thomas SB, Quinn SC (1991) The Tuskegee Syphilis Study, 1932 to 1972: implications for HIV education and AIDS risk education programs in the black community. Am J Public Health 81: 1498–1505.
58. Marsh V, Kamuya D, Rowa Y, Gikonyo C, Molyneux S (2008) Beginning community engagement at a busy biomedical research programme: experiences from the KEMRI CGMRC-Wellcome Trust Research Programme, Kilifi, Kenya. Soc Sci Med 67: 721–733.
59. Boga M, Davies A, Kamuya D, Kinyanjui SM, Kivaya E, et al. (2011) Strengthening the informed consent process in international health research through community engagement: The KEMRI-Wellcome Trust Research Programme Experience. PLoS Med 8: e1001089
60. Schensul J (2005) Sustainability in HIV prevention research. In: Trickett EJ, Pequegnat W, editors. Community interventions and AIDS. New York: Oxford University Press. pp. 176–195.
61. Tindana PO, Singh JA, Tracy CS, Upshur REG, Daar AS, et al. (2007) Grand challenges in global health: community engagement in research in developing countries. PLoS Med 4: e273
62. Macklin R (1999) Against relativism: cultural diversity and the search for ethical universals in medicine. New York Oxford University Press.

CHAPTER 2

HUMAN RIGHTS INDICATORS AND THE SOVEREIGNTY OF TECHNIQUE

David McGrogan

Northumbria Law School, Newcastle upon Tyne, United Kingdom

ABSTRACT

Indicators are increasingly used in international human rights monitoring, and time, expertise and resources are being devoted in ever-growing quantities to the production of more apparently powerful and sophisticated ways to objectively measure human rights performance. However, there is a certain level of resistance and scepticism to the statistical measurement of human rights on the part of many practitioners and advocates, who argue that

Citation: David McGrogan, *European Journal of International Law*, Volume 27, Issue 2, 1 May 2016, Pages 385–408, https://doi.org/10.1093/ejil/chw020 Published: 25 July 2016

it is reductionist and disruptive to their work. This article uses the writing of Michael Oakeshott as a lens through which to examine the shift towards indicators and argues that it is a project that is strongly characterized by rationalism: a desire for certainty, uniformity and clarity that neglects the experiential, tacit, and conversational. This not only provides a method for analysing the dangers present in the phenomenon but also explains why the reliance on indicators and other measurement methods seems destined to grow despite the reservations held by practitioners and scholars alike.

INTRODUCTION

Mary Robinson once envisioned a 'science of human dignity' based on the use of statistics in monitoring human rights.[1] For good or ill, the quest to construct this science is well underway. The monitoring of human rights performance is increasingly dominated by a culture of indicators, benchmarks and statistical measurement. Perceived as a way to more accurately assess compliance, and to better elaborate the content of rights, indicators in particular have come to occupy a central role in the agenda of the United Nations (UN) treaty-based mechanisms. At the same time, there is a trend among human rights advocates to devote ever-increasing time and energy towards the creation of more powerful, useful and specifically tailored statistical methods for measuring human rights performance.

This effort marks a significant shift in emphasis away from what might be called the 'traditional' approach to human rights monitoring, which was largely (though by no means entirely) carried out as a discursive or narrative-based process. States parties would describe their efforts made towards the protection and promotion of human rights, and treaty body members would consider those efforts based on their own expertise and judgment alongside reports from local advocates and non-governmental organizations (NGOs). The better approach is increasingly seen as being a process resembling an audit, certifying that relevant indicators are produced – and produced in the correct disaggregated fashion – and assessing the accuracy of the data.

It would be an exaggeration to say that this shift signifies a rift in 'the human rights community', if such a thing exists. Most of those who support an increased role for indicators see them as simply another tool in the arsenal of human rights monitoring to go alongside existing mechanisms. Yet there is a concern that indicators are transforming 'from a tool to a paradigm' – that instead of being complementary to traditional methods, they could come to dominate or supplant them.[2] Indeed, there is a sense that this is already taking place, particularly given the developments within the Office of the High Commissioner for Human Rights (OHCHR) and its efforts to systematize and standardize the uses of indicators within the UN treaty body system. Likewise, developments in academia in the field of the statistical measurement of human rights have proliferated with, undoubtedly, an attendant opportunity cost regarding other varieties of research. Some scholars have expressed concern with this apparent shift towards audit-based procedures – a shift that marginalizes questions of human judgment and, instead, focuses on methods of verifying whether and how data is produced.

This article argues that this shift can be readily attributed to a strong rationalist propensity, as Michael Oakeshott would have described it, present within the move towards indicators. That is, the push for ever-more accurate and pervasive statistical measurement is strongly characterized by the application of technique – by ever-greater centralization, uniformity and certainty, which means that, as with all rationalist projects, it tends to grow increasingly rationalist over time, and its rationalism comes to dominate and crowd out other methods of thinking.

The move to indicators is ripe, then, for analysis from an Oakeshottian perspective. The analysis presented here not only encompasses existing concerns about the domination of human rights monitoring and discourse by indicators – the dangers of unanticipated consequences and the chilling effects that indicators have on conversation and dialogue – but also provides an explanation for why the project continues to grow; why it appears to represent not just a supplementary tool to traditional human rights monitoring but also the transformation of a tool into a paradigm that displaces other perspectives. The article begins by describing the shift towards the use of indicators in the monitoring of human rights, before explaining why this shift can be described as having a strong propensity towards rationalism. It then considers some of the pernicious consequences of this shift, before explaining why its rationalist propensity is so expansionist and transformative.

THE HUMAN RIGHTS INDICATOR PROJECT

It is difficult to think of areas in the public sphere in the developed world, or in international governance in general, that have not come to be characterized by the use of purportedly objective, mostly numerical, measures indicating achievement or performance and the resultant league tables and rankings. Some prominent examples listed in a recent collection on indicators[3] are the Programme for International Student Assessment, which measures the educational achievements of 15-year-old students across the Organisation for Economic Co-operation and Development;[4] the state fragility index used by the US Agency for International Development;[5] and the yardsticks for the quality of national laws regarding corporate bankruptcy used by the World Bank and the European Bank for Construction and Development when making decisions on lending.[6] In the domestic sphere, examples from the literature are the *US News and World Report*'s ranking of US law schools;[7]performance indicators used by the Audit Commission to produce national league tables for local authorities in England and Wales across various national indicators;[8]and the Research Assessment Exercise (now Research Evaluation Framework) used within the audit of British higher education institutions.[9]

The field of international human rights is no exception to the general trend towards the use of indicators and quantitative measurement. Indeed, in recent years, indicators have become something of a fad among advocates of economic, social and cultural rights and are commonly presented as a remedy to a perceived sense of those rights' marginalization.[10] The shift to indicators is often seen as having come into being alongside a broader move towards an improved conceptualization of economic, social and cultural rights over the past several decades.[11] This is not to say, however, that the realization and monitoring of civil and political rights has fallen outside of its purview.

Human rights indicators and benchmarks have been in use since at least the early 1990s, when the Special Rapporteur on the Realization of Economic, Social and Cultural Rights recommended considering how indicators might be used in measuring progression towards the realization of such rights.[12] Within the UN treaty body system, this largely took place in an ad hoc fashion as treaty bodies developed their working methods and interpretations of treaty provisions. For instance, in 1999, the Committee on Economic, Social and Cultural Rights (CESCR) issued its General Comment No. 13 on the Right to Education, in which it suggested that there was a minimum obligation for state parties to create a national education strategy allowing monitoring through the use of indicators and benchmarks.[13] At the same time, however, there have been efforts to make the production of indicators and their usage more systematic and widespread. A reader familiar with the literature on the quantitative measurement of human rights performance will be aware of a number of such projects. These include the SERF Index developed by Sakiko Fukuda-Parr and colleagues,[14] Todd Landman's concepts of rights in principle, practice and policy and their subdivision into indicators[15] and the project to develop a specific suite of indicators for the right to health.[16]

By far the most significant such effort, however, has been the project undertaken by the UN's OHCHR, initially at the behest of the chairs of the treaty bodies themselves, to systematize the production and usage of human rights indicators. Beginning in 2005 and culminating in the 2012 *Human Rights Indicators: A Guide to Measurement and Implementation*, this project has resulted in a conceptually unified approach that aims to produce a core set of 'universally relevant' human rights indicators and a generally applicable method for generating them.[17] This document has three main pillars. First, the preference is for the quantitative over the qualitative: '[F]act based or objective indicators, in contrast with judgement-based or subjective indicators, are verifiable and can be easier to interpret when comparing the human rights situation in a country over time and across populations.'[18] By the same token, qualitative indicators based on expert judgments are considered to be unreliable, unrepresentative, lacking in transparency and generally of a 'limited purpose'.[19] The guide subdivides indicators into four categories labelled A, B, C and D and considers A – indicators that are quantitative and objective – to be the most useful.[20] Even where intrinsically subjective phenomena are being measured, the preference is for quantitative data that might emerge through statistically representative surveys (one example being the 'percentage of individuals who feel safe walking alone at night').[21] Where indicators based on expert judgment are to be used, they are to be coded in the first place in order to convert them into numbers or symbols that can be tabulated and counted.[22]

Second, in order to 'concretize' the content of each right and make explicit the link between the normative standards of a given right and its indicators, it was decided that attributes – usually around four in number – ought to be identified within each right. The aim was to provide a way to break down the many different rights in a way that facilitated the easy selection and measurement of indicators. For the right to life, which is the main example given, these attributes were 'arbitrary deprivation of life', 'disappearances of individuals', 'health and nutrition', and 'death penalty'.[23]The same approach, it was suggested, should be taken with all rights, drawing from all of the nine international human rights treaties to determine a handful of attributes that could then be used as the basis on which indicators might be selected.[24] Third, it was made clear that the framework ought to revolve around Avedis Donabedian's model of structure-process-outcome,[25] which had originally been created in order to evaluate the quality of care in health services. The essential aim was to create a set of structural, process and outcome indicators for each attribute of each right, which would in effect measure a given state's commitment, effort and results respectively. This process would help 'unpackage the narrative on the normative content of a right', 'demystify the notion of human rights and take the human rights discourse beyond the confines of legal and justice sector discussions' and so on.[26]

The sample indicators on the right not to be subjected to torture or cruel, inhuman or degrading treatment serve as an illustration of the OHCHR's aim.[27] As usual, the right is divided into a handful of separate attributes: 'Physical and mental integrity of detained or imprisoned persons', '[c] onditions of detention', '[u]se of force by law enforcement officials outside detention' and '[c]ommunity and domestic violence'. Each of these has a common set of structural indicators, which include 'international human rights treaties relevant to the right … ratified by the State', '[d]ate of entry into force and coverage of the right not to be tortured in the constitution or other forms of superior law' and '[d]ate of entry into force and coverage of domestic laws for implementing the right not to be tortured, including code of conduct on medical trials and scientific experimentation on human beings'. The indicators then become subdivided into further structural, process and outcome indicators. Taking one of the attributes, '[c]ommunity and domestic violence', a structural indicator is '[d]ate of entry into force and coverage of specific legislation on community and domestic violence'; a process indicator is '[p]roportion of women reporting forms of violence … against themselves or their children initiating legal action or seeking help from police or counselling centres' and an outcome indicator is '[i]ncidence and prevalence of deaths and crimes related to community and domestic violence … in the reporting period'. For this single right, across the four attributes, there are 10 structural indicators, 19 process indicators and nine outcome indicators provided. This is broadly illustrative of the 14 rights that are examined in the guide.

The OHCHR's approach has now begun to be adopted across the UN treaty bodies, and the production of indicators and the collection and disaggregation of data with indicators in mind can only be expected to draw increasing time, attention and resources from governments, practitioners and academics alike. At the same time, however, there is a certain level of resistance against the move towards indicators, not least from some members of the treaty bodies themselves, who have been described as 'lukewarm'.[28] The quantitative measurement of human rights has been viewed as being problematic almost since its inception,[29] and just as the indicator project has gathered momentum, so have the concerns expressed about it. Indeed, it is rare to find an academic article written about the subject that has not acknowledged severe problems with, at the very least, the reliability of statistics, data collection and disaggregation.[30]

More seriously, some scholars have seen in the project a shift in focus towards auditing: a change in emphasis from judgment-based decision making to an exercise in verification and checking – in other words, a reconceptualization of the role of the treaty bodies away from the judgment-based, subjective assessments of state parties' performance and specific, contextual recommendations towards the objective evaluation of data collection methods and the verification of outcomes. This brings with it the concern that monitoring through indicators ignores the complexity of what human rights represent – that no level of quantitative measurement or benchmarking can displace the 'pesky, irreducible core of human judgment' that must always be the final arbiter of which policy is implemented, how resources are allocated and how choices are prioritized.[31] That is to say, both the nature of human rights monitoring and the nature of human rights practice is highly dependent on context and, hence, human judgment and expertise, and this cannot be replaced simply with the use of more and better indicators and benchmarks.

What explains the rise in the use of indicators, despite these concerns? And why should proponents of human rights view it with such caution? This article argues that all of these questions can be answered by considering the move towards indicators as a project characterized by a propensity towards rationalism.

OAKESHOTT AND RATIONALISM

Oakeshott defined rationalism by reference to a character – the rationalist. He describes this person as standing, at all times, for independent thought, free from obligation to any authority except for reason: 'He believes … in the open mind, the mind free from prejudice and its relic, habit. He believes that the unhindered human "reason" … is an infallible guide in political activity.'[32] This makes him, on the one hand, partially a sceptic because he never hesitates to subject any opinion, habit or belief to the power of his reason. He has no capacity or willingness to accept the 'mysteries and uncertainties of experience' or the traditional knowledge of his society at face value. Yet, on the other hand, he is also an optimist: he has absolute faith in the power of reason and rational argument to solve mankind's problems through the pursuit of universally valid answers.[33] His political activity consists in bringing the 'social, political, legal and institutional inheritance of his society before the tribunal of his intellect' – a project of innovation and construction; of solving problems and scrubbing clear the *tabula rasa* of the 'irrational scribblings of tradition-ridden ancestors'.[34] Nothing is to be accepted merely because it exists or has existed for generations but only because it passes the test of reason.

Oakeshott's rationalism has a number of different characteristics. First, it views all problems as being resolvable; it transforms the sphere of political action from the open-ended and conversational to 'something more like an argument, which demands a conclusion'.[35] Politics is that of 'felt need' – continuous resolution of crises through the application of reason.[36] It is not a project of making do or the careful amendment of traditional rules and practices but, rather, the use of rationality unclouded by 'the fumes of tradition' to construct new rules, new inventions and new solutions.[37] It is the politics of the blank slate: a preference at all times for the well-reasoned solution based on abstract rationality over the messy but tried and tested.

Second, rationalism has within it what Oakeshott calls a 'doctrine of human knowledge', the result of which (or perhaps the cause) is a preoccupation with certainty.[38] He examines this through an extended musing on knowledge and how it can be sorted into two separate categories that are akin to the ancient division between *techn* and *epist m* . That is, knowledge is generally divisible into two sorts: practical knowledge (knowledge that is generated by and contingent on practice) versus technical knowledge or technique (knowledge that is formulated into rules). The difference is that which lies between the craft of a chef and the recipes contained in a cookery book or between the skill of driving a car and the rules contained in the highway code. Nobody supposes that the knowledge a good cook has is confined to what can be contained in a book; he also has what Michael Polanyi would have referred to as 'tacit knowledge' – what one has learned through practice (how different tastes combine, how much salt to add to a particular dish, how to replace ingredients with others and many unspoken rules of thumb).[39] Essentially, all human activities – driving, cooking, painting, writing poetry, science – are comprised, according to Oakeshott, of both of these types of knowledge: the formal rules that must generally be learned and that compromise technique, and the informal, experiential, tacit understanding of the craftsman or practitioner. Moreover, the technical and practical can never be separated or used as a replacement for each other. Thus, a pianist acquires not only technique (how to read music and so forth) but also artistry; a chess-player learns style and insight a well as what the potential moves are; and a scientist acquires intuition about profitable avenues to explore as well as the theory of his field.[40]

The rationalist, according to Oakeshott, believes that all real knowledge is technical knowledge and, therefore, that practical knowledge is not really knowledge at all – it is rather a 'nescience, which would be negligible if it were not positively mischievous'.[41] While practical knowledge seems imprecise and uncertain – a matter of opinion – and therefore not to be trusted, technical knowledge is clear and absolute. The rationalist therefore holds reason sovereign; he believes in the 'sovereignty of technique'. Concomitantly, he believes in certitude: technical knowledge gives the appearance of being certain, in that it is self-contained and not predicated on prior knowledge, prejudice, preconceptions – or traditions. In its certainty, it is complete and providing of 'order and distinctness'.[42] It is the reduction of the 'tangle and variety of experience' to a 'set of principles' that can be assessed upon rational grounds.[43]

Third, as a result of both its capacity to provide final resolutions and its certainty, and likewise its scepticism of tradition and its suspicion of practical knowledge, rationalism tends to have as one of its goals the purging of habit and prior prejudice. Since technical knowledge has the appearance of being self-contained, and since the rationalist believes in the supremacy of technical knowledge, other forms of knowledge can be ignored. Indeed, this is desirable to avoid being governed by 'nescience'. In other words, the rationalist expects and desires certainty, believes that technical knowledge is the only kind of knowledge that can provide it and, hence, requires the expurgation of anything that may hinder it – like the desire of Voltaire to have good laws by burning all existing laws and starting afresh.[44] Thus, the rationalist, as well as viewing problems as being permanently resolvable, also believes in the certainty of technical knowledge to provide such resolutions and, as a result, believes in the scrubbing out of what comes before it.

Readers sometimes come to the conclusion that Oakeshott is developing something of a straw man in his portrayal of the rationalist[45] (or, worse, is simply using the figure as a kind of stand-in for socialists, progressives or liberals).[46] Others view his theories as being outdated – a reaction against the world in which Oakeshott lived, with its recent history of domineering ideologies and its reformative, progressive post-war fervour.[47] Others still construe his position as being nihilistic – a refutation of reason itself.[48]

However, Oakeshott was keen to emphasize that rationalism was not merely a phenomenon of the era in which he was living and writing. This is because, far from referring specifically to a doctrine or a philosophy, Oakeshott's description of the rationalist is really a personification of a certain conception of knowledge.[49] His essay is not to be understood, then, as a polemic against a certain class of people or ideas but, rather, against a certain method of thinking. It is a propensity rather than a person. Moreover, it is a propensity present in everyone and everything. In politics, rationalism has 'come to colour the ideas, not merely of one, but of all political persuasions, and to flow over every party line', and it is discernable in all fields of human activity.[50] At the same time, however, it is nowhere absolute or complete, and the propensity can only ever be partially embraced – the rationalist is a non-existent extreme. Or, rather, 'the Rationalist is no-one, and yet he is everyone'.[51] Oakeshott's critique is not of a person, a political persuasion or a movement but, rather, of a tendency that we all share to some degree or other. Oakeshott's description of the rationalist and rationalism provides us with a compelling account for the international human rights system's move towards the use of indicators, as the next section makes clear.

THE PROPENSITY TO RATIONALISM IN THE INDICATOR PROJECT

The rationalist character of the use of indicators to measure human rights performance is uncontroversial, if we use the word 'rational' in its ordinary meaning. Indeed, it seems unlikely that any of those engaged in the advocacy or production of indicators would disagree. The language of the OHCHR is of systematization, objectivity and science, and a prominent recent volume on the measurement of human rights is almost explicit in stating the case for a neutral, empirical approach that sets to one side foundational, philosophical or normative concerns.[52] Using the term in its dictionary meaning, the approach is self-consciously rational or purportedly so.

Oakeshott's rationalism, however, has certain important characteristics. He did not simply mean by 'rationalism' to refer to anything that purported to be objective or scientific. He was referring to a more specific mode of thinking that was constructed around the use of reason unfiltered by tradition or habit to provide resolutions to problems and 'felt needs'; the preoccupation with certainty, finality and uniformity that comes from the sovereignty of technique; and the desire to expurgate prior prejudice and override the practical, traditional and experiential. It is the application of abstract and universal technical knowledge to any and all problems – or the use of premeditated principles to arrange a political community.[53] Put this way, the move towards indicators clearly has something of the character of Oakeshottian rationalism about it.

In the first instance, and most prosaically, the use of statistical indicators can certainly be conceptualized as the application of technical knowledge to a single, big, perceived problem – what Landman and Edzia Carvalho refer to as the 'large and variable gap between the expectations for human dignity outlined through human rights standards and the reality of the precariousness of those rights as they are variously enjoyed around the world'.[54] That is, there is one large and pressing issue in the field of international human rights law – the disparity between agreed obligations and actual performance – and this can be resolved, it is argued, by the use of objective measurement. As Judith Welling puts it, in a passage that neatly summarizes this view:

> By improving the accuracy and comprehensiveness of data relating to the status quo, international indicators assist states parties in better understanding the current situation ... By providing feedback on the outcomes of state policy, international indicators can inform decision making and suggest areas for future policy change at the governmental level … Illuminating the current conditions will thus help state members to better understand the consequences of their policy decisions as well as how they might improve their ability to satisfy ESCR commitments.[55]

That is, objective measures supposedly allow for making objective judgments about progress, which can only be to the good since it will provide information on what has been achieved and what remains to be achieved and, thus, equip relevant parties with the necessary knowledge to make progress. A set of other advantages logically follow from this given and are summarized in Landman and Carvalho's book as allowing contextual description and documentation, classifying and categorization, monitoring of compliance, mapping and pattern recognition, secondary analysis and advocacy.[56] Such advantages would all have the general ancillary benefit of making the work of the monitoring bodies more efficient and streamlined.[57] Many of these benefits are mentioned in the OHCHR guidelines,[58] and it is not unusual to see advocated in the literature a fostering of a 'culture of statistics' within the international human rights system in general, with many of these benefits in mind.[59]Even where scepticism is raised about the possibility of measuring human rights performance empirically, and the underlying assumptions behind the production of indicators, there usually remains a sense that what are needed are simply better indicators used in different ways.

The usefulness of indicators in this respect, however, is even greater from a purposive perspective. Indicators 'link the conceptual discussion about human rights compliance to implementation practices'.[60] They do not merely measure human rights compliance in the abstract; they also instigate movement in pre-determined directions and supply ready-made policy goals. Implicit in any indicator is a final destination or, at the very least, a direction of travel. The indicator 'proportion of women reporting forms of violence … against themselves or their children initiating legal action or seeking help from police or counselling centres' has within it an implied goal of improving this proportion and the ultimate target of increasing it to 100 per cent. However, it also readily lends itself to benchmarks – increasing the proportion from 5 per cent to 10 per cent and so on – and, indeed, the OHCHR guide makes great play of benchmarking not merely in human rights monitoring but also in the performance monitoring of development programs and government policy interventions as a whole. The use of human rights indicators in governance, then, is not merely a method of measuring compliance but also a measure of building certain human rights targets and goals – and, indeed, norms – into government policy. For human rights advocates, this is clearly something that is intrinsically desirable.

At the same time, indicators imply the existence of ideals.[61] The World Bank makes their normative character explicit: 'In a sense, they are also *communicative instruments*.'[62] They are not merely data but also statements of what is desirable, which means that they can express values: the adoption of a set of universal indicators 'would be a high-profile reinforcement of the claim that those human rights set out in international law are indeed universal'.[63] This gives indicators a certain political usefulness. Human rights indicators, especially if standardized and universalized, give substance to the normative position that human rights are available to all individuals on the basis of interrelatedness, interdependence and indivisibility.[64] But, of course, individual indicators also have a normative function in expressing not only a purportedly empirical measure of compliance or performance regarding a certain right but also a vision of what that right ought to mean and what its functions ought to be. The indicator 'proportion of women reporting forms of violence … against themselves or their children initiating legal action or seeking help from police or counselling centres', for instance, makes a clear statement about the content of the right being measured. It makes explicit that this right is not merely concerned with the traditional focus on the judiciary and the criminal justice system but also includes the prevention or punishment of domestic violence. It also makes explicit, through a structural indicator, that specific legislation on community and domestic violence is a desirable mechanism for doing so. Irrespective of whether this interpretation is to be welcomed, it illustrates the power of an indicator to make statements about the width and scope of a given right. Of course, this can be done as much through state-specific indicators as it is through universal ones, though it may be noted that the setting of 'attributes' by the OHCHR has much of this character. In defining the attributes of a given right, the OHCHR is not merely expressing empirically what it considers the nature of that right to be but is also implicitly including and excluding areas of public and private life from its scope.

It is apt, then, to think of the indicator project as being a response to a set of 'felt needs' – whether they are for more information and measurement *per se*, for the goal of human rights 'mainstreaming' in policy and budgeting generally, for clarification and elaboration on the nature and content of rights or, indeed, for expressing normative values. In turn, these serve the larger felt need of bringing states' behaviour in line with their obligations and of expressing certain standards and ideals. Moreover, it is a response that attaches great importance to the rationalist principles of certainty and uniformity.

Of course, no UN body has taken the view that a universal standardized set of indicators that applies always and everywhere is required. While the OHCHR's stated position is that the 'core content' of human rights ought to be monitored through the use of universal indicators, its desire is not for a complete and concrete suite of indicators for every single human right in every single state party to every treaty.[65] Yet while there may never be a complete set of universal indicators, it is nonetheless the case that what has been advocated is the universal use of indicators and a universal framework guiding their use. Uniformity and certainty, in other words, manifest themselves not at the level of direct implementation but, rather, at the level of conceptualization – it is in the overarching structure of the international human rights system in which uniformity and certainty appear.

The desire for certainty most clearly finds its expression in the emphasis on objectivity. As Sally Engle Merry puts it, much of the power of indicators lies in their capacity to 'convert complicated contextually variable phenomena into unambiguous, clear, and impersonal measures'.[66] The objective transforms the nebulous into the concrete. Much of the indicator literature advances the argument that all forms of data – qualitative and quantitative, subjective and objective – are in some respect mutually reinforcing, but there is generally an implied or express preference for the quantitative and the objective. While qualitative and quantitative data may be viewed as complementary, the qualitative and the subjective is often represented as being in some sense inferior in usefulness, primarily because it is lacking in certainty and, thus, in need of reformulating in such a way that it can be numerically measured – repackaged so the subjective becomes less so. The OHCHR's guide, with its four quadrants of indicators ranked A–D, puts this most starkly, but a similar implicit hierarchy is present elsewhere – for instance, in Gauthier de Beco's 2008 article, which seems to place household perception data below socio-economic data and events-based data in terms of its usefulness for monitoring human rights performance and places expert judgments lowest of all,[67] or Craig Mokhiber's desire to bring subjective measures within the rubric of data such as opinion polls and other more 'objective' measures of public confidence.[68] As well as being more accurate and clear, a crucial element cited as an advantage of using quantitative indicators is that they provide consistency. Unlike the subjective opinion of an expert, an indicator allows close tracking of performance over time, permitting the accurate assessment of improvement or failure.[69]

Yet the desire for uniformity and certainty also manifest themselves as broader guiding principles, both within the initial impetus towards the wider use of indicators and their continuing expansion. Obviously, the OHCHR's efforts are straightforwardly an attempt to systematize and universalize the production and use of indicators – if not to achieve uniformity at the level of individual indicators used, then to achieve it in the form of a 'common approach'.[70] However, there is also an aspect of the drive towards indicators that seeks not merely to measure but also to map; if not to definitively set out in concrete terms where the limits of each right lie and what their respective characteristics are, then at least to rationalize the process by which this could be determined.

THE CONSEQUENCES OF THE RATIONALIST PROPENSITY

The indicator project, then, can be aptly described as possessing a strong propensity towards rationalism. This analysis now turns to the potential consequent pernicious effects that, indeed, have been identified by scholars who are sceptical of the move to indicators. The first of these – the production of unintended consequences – is obvious and something that Oakeshott dealt with briefly. This is not the concern that rationalist endeavours will necessarily result in bad outcomes (although this certainly may be the case[71]), but it is rather that, being weighted towards only half of the available sphere of knowledge (the technical), rationalist projects can only at best be half right. Therefore, they must result in unforeseen effects. While Oakeshott did not use this language, he was clearly alluding to something similar to Robert Merton's 'unanticipated consequences of purposive social action'[72] – a theme that scholars have subsequently teased out of Oakeshott's work.[73] That is to say, an approach that is at best half right will also be at best half wrong and often in such a way that its proponents cannot recognize.

Unanticipated consequences must manifest themselves in the indicator project because both the measured and the users of measures have the tendency to change their behaviour as a result of the measurement concerned. Measures 'create social worlds' by causing people to think and act differently.[74] Michael Power, in his work on auditing, divided such reactions into decoupling and colonization. In the first instance, there is a strong incentive for the subjects of an audit to attempt to render the process 'ceremonial' – to produce comfort in the auditing body through ritualized compliance and the production of 'auditable form' rather than actual substance.[75] In other words, states may simply 'buffer away' the monitoring process by going through an ineffectual, but apparently exhaustive, set of checking and measurement, issuing of technical guidance, production of measures and metrics and so forth.[76] As Power argues, while such efforts can never be completely successful, they shift the focus away from the proper moral concern (in the case of human rights, the protection of individual human beings) to something altogether more abstract and ultimately often meaningless: the creation of auditable outputs to satisfy external monitors as an end in itself.[77] To this might be added the opportunity cost of diverting resources and time towards the creation of auditable performance (indicators, standards, measures and associated data collection and disaggregation) as opposed to the actual protection of individual citizens' human rights.

In the second approach, precisely the opposite concern is that the values and practices of audit permeate an organization – or a state – to such an extent that it creates new mentalities, new strategies and new goals that interact in hitherto unknowable or unpredictable ways. Actors change their behaviour and activities in the name of these new values, and they do so in complex ways that may result in unintended and undesirable outcomes. Power uses the example of the Research Assessment Exercise in United

Kingdom (UK) universities, which caused academics to prefer publishing in journals to books and to prefer not to spend time doing activities that were not measured, such as editing books and reviewing publications.[78] While these effects are not catastrophic for higher education or research in the UK, they are certainly different from what was desired or intended. We can expect similarly unpredictable effects to take place wherever an audit takes place, with the danger not that they are necessarily negative but, rather, that they are unknown and unknowable *ex ante*.

As Power puts it, decoupling and compartmentalization are inevitable because individuals are 'infinitely more complex and adaptable than normalizing attempts to measure and control them',[79] but at the same time, colonization through auditing must also always be expected, because motivations will always tend to become aligned with targets. At its worst, this produces an indicator culture that simply creates a game-playing mentality for the audited and 'reverse effects', in which the production of auditable performance actually undermines the initial aim.[80]

Of greater concern to Oakeshott, however, was that the twin desires of the rationalist – for, on the one hand, uniformity and certainty and, on the other, the application of principle distilled from experience – would diminish and displace discourse; that they would close conversation through the application of reason to finding the best or correct course. And, indeed, this danger is immanent in the human rights indicator project. In the first place, if the content of rights has been determined through attributes, and delineated through specific indicators, then there must be a chilling and finalizing effect on conversation and dialogue. For if a set of indicators and attributes defines a given right's content, then what need is there to discuss alternative visions of that right? There are merely numerical measures by which to assess performance. This, indeed, was foremost among Oakeshott's concerns. Whereas unintended consequences are almost mentioned as an aside, he was particularly anxious that the aim of rationalist projects was to provide finality and certainty rather than a continual making do.

The capacity for indicators to reduce and close off conversation has been widely acknowledged. Ann-Janette Rosga and Margaret Satterthwaite, for instance, identify the dangers associated with internationally agreed indicators 'artificially [closing] the gap between international law and domestic policy', whereby national political discourse and contestation about rights is simply bypassed through the manifestation of apparently neutral and objective indicators, agreed in supra-national fora, in domestic policy.[81] Indeed, the OHCHR's guide is explicit about this in its advocacy of the introduction of indicators into national human rights action plans, development strategies and budgeting.[82] National budgets being fixed in line with internationally agreed targets, whether one agrees with a given target or not, indisputably terminates or sublimates political conversation surrounding the use of public funds.

Yet in a sense, the closing-off of dialogue and conversation is a much more subtle and pervasive process, associated not with the outright and absolute introduction of human rights indicators wholesale into domestic policy but, rather, with the creation of a technique of global governance, to paraphrase Benedict Kingsbury and colleagues. It has been persuasively suggested that indicators are part of what Nikolas Rose refers to as a method of 'governing at a distance'[83] – a representation of how political power becomes reconfigured so as to provide for the autonomy of individual actors while, at the same time, governing their conduct through supposedly neutral measures – 'the instrumentalization of a regulated autonomy'.[84]Governing at a distance, in other words, is governance that does not regulate actors directly but, rather, attempts to link their behaviour to political objectives and is particularly useful – or, indeed, crucial – where systems are decentralized. Indicators in the sphere of international human rights, it seems, are a mechanism for achieving this. They allow state actors to have autonomy within a largely decentralized system while, at the same time, aligning their behaviour towards certain political goals (that is, predetermined conceptions of human rights) through the use of apparently apolitical measures and standards.[85]

Thus, the cloak of neutrality is of particular usefulness to the marketing of indicators. It is precisely because they depoliticize what would otherwise be highly contested choices that they are most useful. As Rosga and Sattherthwaite point out, indicators purport to offer technical answers to what would otherwise be extremely difficult questions, and this makes indicators presentable as a kind of neutral exercise that ought to be voluntarily accepted, rather than an assertion of authority and power.[86] This is useful in securing voluntary compliance on the part of what are commonly referred to as 'human rights stakeholders' and in persuading states to submit to the supervision of treaty bodies and the OHCHR on the basis that this supervision is merely technical and therefore non-threatening. However, by extension, this can only have the effect, and, indeed, is often designed to have the effect, of removing human rights from the sphere of domestic conversation and debate, which, in turn, distances human rights from the very stakeholders who have most at stake – ordinary citizens.[87]

The language and mentality of auditing reinforces this denuding of discourse. For debate is not, of course, entirely ended by the adoption and creation of indicators. Rather, much remains to be discussed both in their creation and in the application of the broader conceptual framework. But this discussion, taking place as it does away from domestic politics in the realm of international experts and technicians, submerges political questions in technical arguments surrounding how and what to measure, how to collect data and so forth.[88] While political considerations are immanent in the process, they are left unexplored. Moreover, because quantitative measurement produces a sense of definitiveness and objective reality in the indicators it produces, it conceals the underlying socio-political claims the indicators may represent.[89] That is, in deciding what to include or exclude in a given indicator, the producer is making decisions, implicitly, about what is or is not desirable, and such a decision can only be a political, value-based process, especially in a field such as human rights. Depoliticizing what would ordinarily be politically contested, through the application of technical standards, may provide a sense of neutrality and objectivity, but it is a false sense. It removes socio-political values from the public realm and embeds them in the construction of indicators, which shifts the balance of power towards the experts engaged in that process.[90] The scope of influence of politicians and politics is correspondingly reduced, and the focus moves away from the ethical towards manner – from content to form.[91]

Thus, technique replaces the difficult process of moral and political education that Oakeshott held so important: 'The morality of the Rationalist is the morality of the self-conscious pursuit of moral ideals, and the appropriate form of moral education is by precept, by the presentation and explanation of moral principles.'[92] This can be seen very clearly in the way in which indicators are intended to transform the administration of human rights law at the domestic level into, essentially, an exercise in discourse-free checking. Once the indicators have been agreed, human rights performance can apparently be assessed objectively, with quantitative improvements across the various metrics demonstrating that compliance is taking place and the human rights situation is improving. The questions of whether it actually is improving, and what this means, are sublimated beneath the auditing process, but, more importantly, so are questions of morality and the field of moral education. Rather than the slow, flexible evolution of the moral traditions and habits of a community through political conversation, there is instead simply the blunt application of the precept. Rather than a concept of a given right developing organically within the society in question, there is instead the displacement of localized rights and rights dialogue,[93] and the suffocation of local idioms.[94] Instead of injustice being framed around the individual, it is framed around the failure to perform against targets or the mere failure to produce auditable performance itself. Instead of being a discourse about establishing what is right and wrong – or just – in given cases or in a given policy, the matter of enshrining and protecting human rights instead becomes a task for management.[95]

Ultimately, this also has the effect – and, as has been often seen, the stated intention – of diminishing the role of the subjective, experiential and practical in the protection of human rights and the assessment of its performance. It represents the reduction, as Oakeshott put it, of 'the tangle and variety of experience to a set of principles'.[96] The rationalist view of experience is a limiting one. It accepts only experience that has been converted into a formula, not the wider sense of experience cumulating within a society into traditions and habits that, though mysterious or opaque, contain its accumulated practical knowledge. This leads the rationalist to cut himself off from tradition and, in turn, become 'apt to attribute to mankind a necessary inexperience in all the critical moments of life';[97] to paternalistically ignore local and contextual wisdom in the name of certain and uniform objective measurement – to seek to extract knowledge from its context and its history.[98] The power of indicators to reduce and submerge the complexities of contextual phenomena into standards and categories is a ready example of the capacity for rationalism to act in this way, as is the reduction of subjective, expert narrative into quasi-objective measures through coding into numerical representations or through the reduction of lived experience to survey data, which transforms the rich tapestry and complexity of communities and individuals into quantitative measures such as 'percentage of individuals who feel safe walking alone at night'. It is the imposition of the simplicity of principles onto the 'tangle and variety' of lived experience. It is to ignore how matters are currently 'attended to' and, instead, to approach matters as a social engineer.[99]

Removing moral discourse from the sphere of human rights and driving it into 'what is measurable instead of what matters' then has the effect of depriving the human rights movement of its power as a mechanism for justice, and diminishing its potential by focusing on what is measurement friendly.[100] The unpredictable, ungovernable, chaotic nature of changing social norms, which may seem dormant for decades before undergoing dramatic shifts, is lost amid the need to demonstrate structure, process and outcome. Denuding the human rights movement of discourse by shifting the emphasis towards verification and auditing strips away its political power. The end result is the draining away of its spirit. Instead of Immanuel Kant's moral politician, the 'genuine republican' seeking to act in the right way based on the context of the society in which he lived, there is instead simply the development and application of professional technique.[101] Instead of narrative, the telling of stories 'that keep alive and strengthen the ideas of freedom, equality and universality', there is a managerial sensibility that sees its role as the verification of performance towards outcomes agreed among a caste of international experts, rather than justice.[102]

THE TRANSFORMATION FROM TOOL TO PARADIGM

Yet most advocates of the use of quantitative data in the measurement of human rights see a continued role for the subjective and experiential complemented by the use of indicators. The OHCHR's guide itself describes indicators as a 'tool to support' narrative or judicial assessments, and this perspective is fairly common.[103] As Nancy Thede describes it, the majority 'see the usefulness of a combination of analysis and quantified data, the latter being a useful complement to the former but never under any circumstances being able to stand on its own.'[104] And there are, indeed, alternative visions for the use of indicators that suggest how the technical knowledge provided by statistical measures can supplement the intuitive and tacit practical knowledge of the practitioner, rather than supplant it.

An extensive example of such a process is provided by Christopher Stone in the form of 'locally usable near real time "active indicators"', used by the Jamaican Constabulary Force to mine data regarding raids and searches in order to establish best practices, or by the Attorney General of Lagos State to establish how many prisoners were on pre-trial detention in prisons and for how long in order to focus resources on the elimination of bottlenecks.[105] Here, quantitative data in the form of indicators is used in a decentralized fashion by local professionals and experts to notice patterns and find hidden discrepancies or misallocations of resources in order to improve their work. Stone contrasts this with the many 'carcasses of failed indicator projects' littering developed countries – the results of resistance to the exercising of external power on the part of local agencies ('those in positions of immediate and legitimate authority', as Stone puts it) and of constant shifting priorities forced by new indicators demanded by governmental ministers, donors or UN agencies.[106] Rather, Stone describes the use in Jamaica and Lagos of indicators that are designed specifically for use by an official with formal authority over those expected to produce the outcome being measured – for instance, the commissioner of the Jamaican Constabulary Force.[107] This design enables close, responsive, timely measurement for a clear purpose, improving the effectiveness and efficiency of police raids and, crucially, ensuring that data is examined at the level of operational responsibility by those in positions of legitimate authority, not national or international figures who are far away from the actual practice in question (both literally and figuratively) and who lack accountability and, hence, legitimacy in the eyes of those working 'on the ground'. Other examples from the Philippines and Colombia demonstrate how human rights indicators can be developed and used locally, even when they are created in response to international standards or principles, to provide information about local needs.[108]

These, it seems, could be examples of Oakeshott's description of the combination of the technical and the practical made real: the tacit, intuitive, experiential nature of the practitioner supported and enhanced by the application of statistical tools in a bottom-up, contextual process carried out at the most decentralized level possible – and the approach certainly holds promise in the field of human rights. Given this possibility, then, it seems churlish, even disingenuous, to describe the move towards indicators as being in danger of crowding out less technical methods of monitoring human rights. Construed as simply being supplementary to, and supportive of, judgment-based, subjective assessments, where is the harm in an increased use of indicators, moderated by common sense?

The danger is that the rationalist tendency is always at risk of becoming dominant. Perhaps the greatest concern is simply that the desire for ever greater acquisition of technique will accelerate and that it will consequently come to subvert the experiential, practical knowledge, analysis and assessments of the locally embedded expert. Despite best intentions – in other words, despite human rights practitioners taking the view that quantitative measures and indicators are simply complementary to human judgment about how to best protect human rights in a given context – it may be that the rationalist tendency will nonetheless turn monstrous (not least because of financial considerations, which will always prioritize measureable 'impact'). Merry describes in compelling terms how, at the treaty body level, 'indicator culture' has come to be the default mode of monitoring human rights performance,[109] and in the UK, the Equality and Human Rights Commission's work has come to revolve heavily around the use of indicators in a 'measurement framework'.[110] At a recent workshop organized by the

International Council on Human Rights Policy, the participants expressed the concern that 'evaluation methods and frames of impact assessment [are] exerting a disproportionate pressure on the narratives and practices of human rights work, distorting priorities, objectives and processes'.[111] Or, as Paul Gready puts it, '[f]or human rights, there is a real danger that its reference point may shift too radically from international human rights law to the requirements of evaluation and donors'.[112]

Why should this be so? Oakeshott's final, and most pressing, concern was that rationalism would perpetuate itself – that the field of morality and moral education would become more and more a matter of the acquisition of technique – primarily because of the view the rationalist had towards practical knowledge. Since he saw it as being inferior to technical knowledge, he begins to neglect it, if not to attempt actively to extirpate it. And because of this, he 'dries up [his] mind' – he sees the only solutions to perceived problems as the application of yet more technique: 'All the Rationalist can do when left to himself is to replace one rationalist project in which he has failed by another in which he hopes to succeed'.[113] The political content of human rights – the goal of justice for the individual against the power of the State – becomes stripped away by the need for better measurement and better performance based on what can be measured.[114]

The concern, then, is not that anybody advocates for the replacement of judgement-based assessment by the use of purely objective-seeming statistical measures, indicators and benchmarks. Rather, it is that the rationalist propensity sees the resolution of problems as purely being a matter for the application of technique, rather than for the more difficult, time-consuming and decentralized – uncontrolled – method of developing practical knowledge. Instead of the slow, steady, quiet evolution of moral principle and of the tacit, experiential knowledge of the expert, the default position becomes that quantitative measurement provides the cure for all ills. Once the culture of statistics and indicators enters the mainstream, it becomes difficult to reverse. Where practical knowledge is seen as 'nescience', the only solutions postulated will be technical in nature, and the only cure for rationalist failures will be more rationalism. And this describes with great accuracy the response to the problems associated with the indicator project, which are characterized by, if anything, an even greater tendency towards rationalism than the project itself.

Indeed, it seems that the temptation towards centralization and certitude in the production and use of indicators is almost inescapable once the indicator culture has taken hold. The rationalist tendency, unable or unwilling to leave too much space for the practical, for the experiential and for the tacit, always prefers the application of technique. This is most evidently the case for those who view the use of globally determined quantitative measures as being essential to the realization of human rights. 'While the criticisms and challenges to the creation of international indicators for ESCR are informative', as Welling rather revealingly puts it, 'they do not justify allowing the international community to remain uninformed about the deficiency of ESCR protection and access around the world.'[115] In other words, indicators may have their flaws, but the solution can only be the generation of more data that the 'international community' can utilize. The cure is only ever technical in character; it is the production of frameworks and systems by which techniques of indicator creation and usage can come to be implemented. The alternative is for the 'international community' to be *uninformed*.

Thus, the first step in the next stage of rights-based development is identified as 'the compilation of an internationally agreed and scientifically adequate list of core development indicators for civil and political rights, based on international standards';[116] the solution to conceptual problems surrounding economic, social and cultural rights is presented as being the development of more detailed suites of indicators by the CESCR so as to give 'concrete meaning' to those rights,[117] and the solution to discrepancies between agreed minimum standards for humanitarian relief due to differing local contexts is presented as '[describing] the gap between the standards and indicators listed in the handbook and the ones reached in actual practice … [and explaining] what needs to be changed'.[118] The OCHCHR's guide, which acknowledges the limitations of the use of indicators in its opening pages, argues that the solution is stronger involvement of human rights stakeholders in their production.[119] The problems associated with being half right are often resolved, that is, through the application of technique; through ever more rationalistic responses.

The tendency of rationalism to perpetuate itself is also apparent even where the entire indicator project is viewed with scepticism. Thede, for instance, while acknowledging the dangers of 'statistical mystique', the value-laden nature of indicators, the difficulty or impossibility of capturing values in numerical form and the prospect of a 'productivist' approach undermining human rights themselves, still comes to the conclusion that what is required is to 'establish what are the component aspects of each right, what the relationship of each component is to the overall respect of that right and, finally, what are the indicators that can generate meaningful information about one or the other of the components of that right' – in short, a 'theory to link concept to indicator'.[120] In other words, these issues are to be resolved with the application of reason to reach solutions, which is precisely the type of effort undertaken by the OHCHR to centralize and systematize a conceptual framework for determining and measuring the attributes of each and every human right.

Merry, meanwhile, in a careful and considered analysis of the problems associated with human rights indicators (noting that they are unrepresentative, dependent on the cooperation of states parties to the treaties, dependent on ranking to have any effect, decontextualized and ahistorical and lacking a sanction mechanism for failures of implementation) comes to the apparent conclusion that what is required is simply more 'powerful' indicators permitting ranking, punishment for lack of achievement and, above all, 'clear theory embedded in the indicator' – in other words, more simplification, more clarity and more streamlining.[121] The problems associated with the application of technique are cured by the application of yet more of it.

And despite an extensive and considered critique of the development of the indicator project, Rosga and Satterthwaite similarly propose a solution that boils down to the production of a set of outcome indicators produced by the treaty bodies, the OHCHR and NGOs, to be applied universally. Here, the approach adopted by Fukuda-Parr and colleagues, that is, 'ranking countries by measuring the relationship between the extent to which a population enjoys fundamental economic and social rights and the resource capacity of the state to fulfil ESR obligations' is cited as promising, though how this approach avoids the pitfalls identified by the authors is not made clear.[122]Political conversation at the domestic level is to continue, but only if it is framed around the universally applicable Donabedian model, with the power to determine structural and process indicators devolved to the national level – outcome indicators having been centrally mandated. In addition, indicators must be created to measure political participation so as to avoid the bypassing of political discourse in domestic politics.[123] The solution to the pitfalls of governmentality, it turns out, is more of it. What is required is the utilization of indicators to permit global governance to interface with the governed more directly.[124]

The rationalist propensity's tendency to propose rationalist solutions is well illustrated by the fact that even Stone is still tempted, ultimately, to suggest that what is required is an 'iterative method' for the construction of global indicators. That is, since he is unwilling to entirely leave the production and use of indicators to practitioners or experts, whether liaising across borders or otherwise, Stone eventually comes to the proposition that there ought to be a 'system or framework of indicators that can be used across countries, in very different national contexts'.[125]While this ought to be produced from the 'bottom up', the character of the rationalist still lurks in the background in that the end result seems to remain a globally produced and universally applicable system. The rationalist propensity is unsatisfied with any approach that does not, ultimately, lead to the uniform and certain application of principle, however this is produced. While there is promise, then, in the notion of indicators produced and consumed by those in positions of legitimate authority, as Stone suggests, there must come with it a wariness of rationalist tendencies towards uniformity and certainty in different guises.

CONCLUSION

Describing the indicator project, and the indicator culture that surrounds it, as 'rationalist' gives us a fruitful method for understanding not only its flaws but also its growth. What, then, is to be proposed? One obvious critique of Oakeshott's position is that, as elsewhere in his work, he seems to present a bleak scenario in which matters have progressed too quickly and too far in the wrong direction to ever be reversed.[126] He appears to present us with a vision of a rationalist tendency that grows ever more pronounced until there is space for nothing else. This article considers that vision to be compelling but, at the same time, recognizes that there is considerably more nuance both to Oakeshott's position and to the current status of human rights monitoring. In fact, there always remains the possibility of a reversal so long as there is the 'positive power' of defence against overweening rationalism.[127]

First, this must take the form of a greater awareness of the importance of balance between technical and the practical knowledge. There must be a greater acknowledgement of the importance of the role that the 'pesky, irreducible core of human judgment' has to play in monitoring human rights performance. Human societies are complex, and their niceties in many ways defy quantitative measurement. The necessity for the kind of tacit, practical knowledge that only comes about through deep familiarity with the subject matter cannot be overstated. Attempting to monitor performance through technique, especially if technical methods come to dominate the landscape, will always fall foul of the tendency to be, at best, half right – ignorant of the intuitive, tacit, subjective understanding of what is best that comes about only from experience and practice and, hence, leading to poor decisions and unintended consequences.

Second, there must be a greater level of scepticism about solutions to the problems associated with rationalism, which themselves hold technique to be sovereign. It is tempting, when faced with concerns about the misuse of statistics, the growth of technocracy and international governmentality, and the denuding of moral discourse associated with the turn to human rights auditing, to propose – as amply illustrated by the examples in the previous section – even more technocratic solutions that cede yet more power to the processes in question. This temptation must be resisted, or at the very least questioned: the pitfalls of a preoccupation with technique will not be avoided by the application of more of it.

And third, this article has summarized some of the dangers associated with indicator projects constructed at the international level, divorced both from domestic and local political discourse and the work of local human rights practitioners. In particular, it has expressed strong concerns with the notion that either indicators themselves, or systems for producing and utilizing them, should become universal and uniform – that the rationalist desire for certainty, centralization and the application of precept should come to dominate. Rather, the preference must surely be for human rights indicators that are used in a manner similar to that which Stone describes, namely created by and for local actors who have operational responsibility and accountability for what is being measured. This may go against the prevailing tendency among those interested in the international monitoring of human rights, which finds it deeply unsatisfactory and, indeed, even dangerous to see the conceptualization and measurement of human rights as something in need of decentralization. Yet this article demonstrates why such a rebalancing is needed. Otherwise, the risk is of diminishing moral discourse in human rights and thus removing discussion about what rights are, and what they protect, from the conversation of human societies – a prospect that cannot but be detrimental to their realization.

REFERENCES

1. M. Robinson, speech at the launch of the American Association for the Advancement of Science's Science and Human Rights Coalition (2009), available at www.aaas.org/page/mary-robinson (last visited 25 March 2015).
2. International Council on Human Rights Policy (ICHRP), Report on Workshop – No Perfect Measure: Rethinking Evaluation and Assessment of Human Rights Work (January 2012), at 3.
3. K. Davis *et al.* (eds) *Governance by Indicators: Global Power through Quantification and Rankings* (2012).
4. Bogdany and Goldmann, 'Taming and Framing Indicators: A Legal Reconstruction of the OECD's Programme for International Student Assessment', in Davis *et al.*, *supra*note 3, 52.
5. Bhuta, 'Governmentalizing Sovereignty: Indexes of State Fragility and the Calculability of Political Order', in Davis *et al.*, *supra* note 3, 132.
6. Halliday, 'Legal Yardsticks: International Financial Institutions as Diagnosticians and Designers of the Laws of Nations', in Davis *et al.*, *supra* note 3, 180.
7. See, e.g., Espeland and Sauder, 'Rankings and Reactivity: How Public Measures Recreate Social Worlds', 113(1) *American Journal of Sociology* (2007) 1.
8. Discussed in Tsoukas, 'The Tyranny of Light', 29(9) *Futures* (1997) 827, at 837–838.
9. See, e.g., Strathern, 'The Tyranny of Transparency', 26(3) *British Educational Research Journal* (2000) 309, at 309–321.
10. See, e.g., Welling, 'International Indicators and Economic, Social and Cultural Rights', 30 *Human Rights Quarterly* (*HRQ*) (2008) 933.
11. *Ibid*, at 936–937.
12. UN GAOR World Conference on Human Rights, Report of the Secretariat: Report of the Seminar on Appropriate Indicators to Measure Achievement in the Progressive Realization of Economic, Social and Cultural Rights, UN Doc. A/CONF.157/PC/73 (1993).
13. Committee on Economic, Social and Cultural Rights (CESCR), General Comment No. 13, UN Doc. E/C.12/1999/10 (1999), para. 52.
14. SERF Index, available at www.serfindex.org/about/ (last visited 14 April 2016).

15. Landman, 'Comparative Politics and Human Rights', 24(4) *HRQ* (2002) 890; see also Landman, 'Measuring Human Rights: Principle, Practice and Policy', 26 *HRQ* (2004) 906.
16. See, e.g., Backman *et al.*, 'Health Systems and the Right to Health: An Assessment of 194 Countries', 372(9655) *The Lancet* (2008) 2047.
17. Office of the High Commissioner for Human Rights (OHCHR), *Human Rights Indicators: A Guide to Measurement and Implementation* (2012).
18. *Ibid.*, at 17.
19. *Ibid.*, at 67–68.
20. *Ibid.*, at 19.
21. *Ibid.*
22. *Ibid.*, at 66.
23. OHCHR, Report on Indicators for Promoting and Monitoring the Implementation of Human Rights, UN Doc. HRI/MC/2008/3 (2008), para. 7.
24. *Ibid.*
25. See, e.g., Donabedian, 'The Quality of Care: How Can It Be Assessed?', 260(12) *Journal of the American Medical Association* (1988) 1743.
26. OHCHR, *supra* note 23, para. 9.
27. OHCHR, *supra* note 17, at 91.
28. S. Merry, *Chapter 4: The Problem of Human Rights Indicators* (2012), at 46 (unpublished), available at www.law.uvic.ca/demcon/2012%20readings/Chapter%203%20Problem%20of%20HR%20indicators.pdf (last visited 25 March 2015).
29. See, e.g., Barsh, 'Measuring Human Rights', 15 *HRQ* (1993) 87.
30. See, e.g., the otherwise relatively uncritical articles by Felner, 'A New Frontier in Economic and Social Rights Advocacy? Turning Quantitative Data into a Tool for Human Rights Accountability', 5 *Sur. Revista Internacional de Direitos Humanos* (2008) 109, at 131–132; de Beco, 'Human Rights Indicators for Assessing State Compliance with International Human Rights', 77 *Nordic Journal of International Law* (2008) 23.
31. Rosga and Satterthwaite, 'UN Indicators in Critical Perspective', in Davis *et al.*, *supra*note 3, 297.
32. Oakeshott, 'Rationalism in Politics', in M. Oakeshott (ed.), *Rationalism*

in Politics(1962) 1, at 4.

33. *Ibid.*, at 1–3.
34. *Ibid.*, at 5.
35. Candreva, *The Enemies of Perfection* (2005), at 28.
36. Oakeshott, 'Rationalism in Politics', *supra* note 32, at 5.
37. *Ibid.*, at 4–7.
38. *Ibid.*, at 7–13.
39. M. Polanyi, *Personal Knowledge* (1958).
40. Oakeshott, 'Rationalism in Politics', *supra* note 32, at 7–13.
41. *Ibid.*, at 11.
42. *Ibid.*, at 6.
43. *Ibid.*
44. *Ibid.*, at 5.
45. See, e.g., Kettler 'The Cheerful Discourses of Michael Oakeshott', 16 *World Politics*(1964) 483, at 488.
46. See, e.g., citations in Candreva, *supra* note 35, n. 3, 4, 5.
47. See, e.g., Franco, 'Review of *The Politics of Faith and the Politics of Skepticism*', 91 *American Political Science Review (APSR*) (1997) 439.
48. See, e.g., Berns, 'Rationalism in Politics (Review)', 57(3) *APSR* (1963) 670.
49. Candreva, *supra* note 35, at 53.
50. Oakeshott, 'Rationalism in Politics', *supra* note 32, at 6.
51. Gee and Webber, 'Rationalism in Public Law', 76(4) *Modern Law Review* (2013) 708, at 712.
52. Landman and Carvalho, *Measuring Human Rights* (2010), at 1.
53. See Oakeshott, 'Political Education', in Oakeshott, *Rationalism in Politics*, *supra* note 32, 111.
54. Landman and Carvalho, *supra* note 52.
55. Welling, *supra* note 10, at 944.
56. See Landman and Carvalho, *supra* note 52, at 4–5.
57. See Welling, *supra* note 10, at 942.
58. See OHCHR, *supra* note 17.
59. See, e.g., Thede, 'Human Rights and Statistics: Some Reflections on

the No-Man's Land between Concept and Indicator', 18 *Statistical Journal of the United Nations*(2001) 259, at 271.

60. S. McInerney-Lankford and H. Sano (eds), *World Bank Study: Human Rights Indicators in Development* (2010), at 14.
61. Kingsbury, 'Introductory Remarks: Panel on Indicators in International Law', 106 *American Society of International Law Proceedings* (2012) 243, at 243.
62. McInerney-Lankford and Sano, *supra* note 60 (emphasis in original).
63. Raworth, 'Measuring Human Rights', in S. Gruskin *et al.* (eds), *Perspectives on Health and Human Rights* (2005) 393, at 403.
64. See, e.g., OHCHR, *supra* note 17, at 10.
65. See OHCHR, Report on Indicators for Monitoring Compliance with International Human Rights Instruments, 18th Meeting of Chairpersons of the Human Rights Treaty Bodies, UN Doc. HRI/MC/2006/7 (2006), para. 28.
66. Merry, 'Measuring the World: Indicators, Human Rights and Global Governance', 52(3) *Current Anthropology* (2011) 583, at 584.
67. de Beco, *supra* note 30, at 34–38.
68. Mokhiber, 'Toward a Measure of Dignity: Indicators for Rights-Based Development' Conference on Statistics, Development and Human Rights, International Association for Official Statistics, 2000.
69. See Malhotra and Fasel, 'Quantitative Human Rights Indicators: A Survey of Major Initiatives' Expert Meeting on Human Rights Indicators, Turku, Finland, March 2005, available at www.gaportal.org/sites/default/files/Quantitative%20Human%20Rights%20Indicators.pdf (last visited 14 April 2016).
70. OHCHR, *supra* note 17, at 30.
71. See, e.g., Barsh, *supra* note 29; S. Morse, *Indices and Indicators in Development: An Unhealthy Obsession with Numbers* (2004); Bhuta, 'Governmentalizing Sovereignty: Indexes of State Fragility and the Calculability of Political Order', in Davis *et al.*, *supra*note 3, 132, at 147–149.
72. Merton, 'The Unanticiated Consequences of Purposive Social Action', 1(6) *American Sociological Review* (1936) 894.
73. See, e.g., Teles and Kaliner, 'The Public Policy of Skepticism', 2(1) *Perspectives on Politics* (2004) 39.

74. Espeland and Stevens, 'Rankings and Reactivity: How Public Measures Recreate Social Worlds', 113 *American Journal of Sociology* (2007) 1.
75. M. Power, *The Audit Society* (1997), at 96.
76. See also Meyer and Rowan, 'Institutionalised Organisations: Formal Structure as Myth and Ceremony', in W. Powell and P. DiMaggio (eds), *The New Institutionalism in Organizational Analysis* (1991) 41.
77. Power, *supra* note 75, at 121.
78. *Ibid.*, at 100.
79. *Ibid.*, at 120
80. *Ibid.*
81. Rosga and Satterthwaite, *supra* note 31, at 308.
82. OHCHR, *supra* note 17, at 103–132.
83. See, e.g., Davis *et al.*, 'Indicators as a Technology of Global Governance', 46(1) *Law and Society Review* (2012) 71, at 81.
84. See Rose, 'Governing "Advanced" Liberal Democracies', reproduced in P. Miller and N. Rose, *Governing the Present* (2008) 199, at 212–213.
85. On this point, see also Satterthwaite, 'Indicators in Crisis: Rights-Based Humanitarian Indicators in Post-Earthquake Haiti', 43 *New York University Journal of International Law and Politics* (2010) 865.
86. Rosga and Sattherthwaite, *supra* note 31, at 311.
87. See, e.g., Felner, *supra* note 30, at 133–134.
88. See Merry, *supra* note 66, at 588.
89. See Davis *et al.*, *supra* note 83, at 87.
90. *Ibid.*
91. See Jacobsson, 'Standardization and Expert Knowledge', in N. Brunsson and B. Jacobsson (eds), *A World of Standards* (2002) 41, at 46–48.
92. Oakeshott, *Rationalism in Politics*, *supra* note 32, at 35.
93. See, e.g., Mazzone, 'The Rise and Fall of Human Rights: A Sceptical Account of Multilevel Governance', 3(1) *Cambridge Journal of International and Comparative Law*(2014) 929.
94. See, e.g., Hafner-Burton and Ron, 'Seeing Double: Human Rights Impact through Qualitative and Quantitative Eyes', 61(2) *World Politics* (2009) 360, at 393–394.

95. See Koskenniemi, 'International Law: Constitutionalism, Managerialism and the Ethos of Legal Education', 1 *European Journal of Legal Studies* (2010) 1.
96. Oakeshott, 'Rationalism in Politics', *supra* note 32, at 2.
97. *Ibid*., at 3.
98. Merry, 'Measuring the World: Indicators, Human Rights and Global Governance', 52 *Current Anthropology* (2011) 84.
99. See Oakeshott, 'Scientific Politics', 1 *Cambridge Journal* (1947–1948) 347, at 355.
100. ICHRP, *supra* note 2, at 4.
101. Koskenniemi, *supra* note 95.
102. ICHRP, *supra* note 2, at 3, describing how donors typically adopt the view that human rights practitioners have 'too broad a justice perspective'.
103. OHCHR, *supra* note 17, at 4.
104. Thede, *supra* note 59, at 270.
105. Stone, 'Problems of Power in the Design of Indicators of Safety and Justice in the Global South', in Davis *et al*., *supra* note 3, 282.
106. *Ibid*., at 281–283.
107. *Ibid*., at 285.
108. See Santos, Decentralisation and Human Rights: A Philippine Perspective on the Feasibility of Their Interface in Policy and Practice, International Council on Human Rights Policy Working Paper (2001), available at www.ichrp.org/files/papers/39/116_-_The_Philippines_-_Linking_Local_Government_and_Human_Rights_Santos__Soliman__2001.pdf(accessed 14 April 2016); Urueña, 'Internally Displaced Population in Colombia: A Case Study on the Domestic Aspects of Indicators as Technologies of Global Governance', in Davis *et al*., *supra* note 3, 249.
109. Merry, *supra* note 28.
110. Equality and Human Rights Commission, available at www.equalityhumanrights.com/about-us/our-work/key-projects/equality-measurement-framework (last visited 25 March 2015).
111. ICHRP *supra* note 2, at 3.
112. Gready, 'Reasons to Be Cautious about Evidence and Evaluation: Rights based Approaches to Development and the Emerging Culture

of Evaluation', 1(3) *Journal of Human Rights Practice* (2009) 380, at 383.

113. Oakeshott, *Rationalism in Politics*, *supra* note 32, at 32.
114. ICHRP, *supra* note 2, at 4.
115. Welling, *supra* note 10, at 958.
116. Mokhiber, *supra* note 68, at 9.
117. de Beco, *supra* note 67, at 40.
118. Humanitarian Charter and Minimum Standards in Disaster Response, Sphere Project (2004), at 8–9.
119. OHCHR, *supra* note 17, at 4.
120. Thede, *supra* note 59, at 268.
121. Merry, *supra* note 28.
122. S. Fukuda-Parr, T. Lawson-Remer and S. Randolph, Measuring the Progressive Realization of Human Rights Obligations: An Index of Economic and Social Rights Fulfillment, Economics Working Paper No. 200822 (2008), available at http://digitalcommons.uconn.edu/econ_wpapers/200822 (last visited 14 April 2016).
123. See Rosga and Satterthwaite, *supra* note 81, at 312–314.
124. *Ibid.*, at 315.
125. *Ibid.*, at 292–294.
126. See, in particular, Oakeshott, 'The Tower of Babel', in Oakeshott, *Rationalism in Politics*, *supra* note 32, 59.
127. Oakeshott, *Rationalism in Politics*, *supra* note 32, at 35.

CHAPTER 3

STATES, THE SECURITY SECTOR, AND THE MONOPOLY OF VIOLENCE: A NEW DATABASE ON PRO-GOVERNMENT MILITIAS

Sabine C Carey[1], Neil J Mitchell[2] and Will Lowe[3]

[1]University of Mannheim

[2]University College London

[3]University of Mannheim

ABSTRACT

This article introduces the global Pro-Government Militias Database (PGMD). Despite the devastating record of some pro-government groups,

Citation: Sabine C Carey, Neil J Mitchell, and Will Lowe , Journal of Peace Research Vol 50, Issue 2, pp. 249 - 258 . First Published March 19, 2013 , https://doi.org/10.1177/0022343312464881

there has been little research on why these forces form, under what conditions they are most likely to act, and how they affect the risk of internal conflict, repression, and state fragility. From events in the former Yugoslavia, Iraq, Sudan, or Syria and the countries of the Arab Spring we know that pro-government militias operate in a variety of contexts. They are often linked with extreme violence and disregard for the laws of war. Yet research, notably quantitative research, lags behind events. In this article we give an overview of the PGMD, a new global dataset that identifies pro-government militias from 1981 to 2007. The information on pro-government militias (PGMs) is presented in a relational data structure, which allows researchers to browse and download different versions of the dataset and access over 3,500 sources that informed the coding. The database shows the wide proliferation and diffusion of these groups. We identify 332 PGMs and specify how they are linked to government, for example via the governing political party, individual leaders, or the military. The dataset captures the type of affiliation of the groups to the government by distinguishing between informal and semi-official militias. It identifies, among others, membership characteristics and the types of groups they target. These data are likely to be relevant to research on state strength and state failure, the dynamics of conflict, including security sector reform, demobilization and reintegration, as well as work on human rights and the interactions between different state and non-state actors. To illustrate uses of the data, we include the PGM data in a standard model of armed conflict and find that such groups increase the risk of civil war.

Keywords: armed groups, conflict, dataset, pro-government militias

INTRODUCTION

The activities of pro-government militias have been a feature of recent uprisings, as illustrated by events in Libya, Bahrain, and Syria. Pro-government militias have been active in many different contexts around the globe, but research has not kept pace with this development, largely due to lack of systematic data. The Pro-Government Militias Database (PGMD) intends to fill this gap by identifying these militias and irregular armed groups that are linked to government authorities between 1981 and 2007.

The PGMD enables research on state capacity, human rights, and civil war to address new questions. While we know of the impact of poverty, natural resources, terrain, regime type, and ethnicity on armed conflict (e.g. Collier & Hoeffler, 2004; Fearon & Laitin, 2003; Hegre & Sambanis, 2006), less attention has been paid to agents and organizations that carry out the violence – although the importance of the organization of the security sector is recognized (Toft, 2009). Recent research has examined the fragmentation of rebel groups (e.g. Bakke, Cunningham & Seymour 2012; Cederman & Gleditsch, 2009; Cunningham, 2011), but the government usually is assumed to be a unitary actor. Case evidence suggests that this conceptualization is often misleading. Despite the effect that pro-government militias can have on the political, economic, and social stability and security of civilians, with the notable exception of Ahram's (2011a) analysis of Janowitz's (1977) data, there is little quantitative research on these groups. This research lags behind the case study literature in analyzing the impact of these groups with, for example, studies of death squads in El Salvador (Stanley, 1996) and paramilitary groups elsewhere in Latin America (Centeno, 2002;Mazzei, 2009), the military's arming of political party organizations in Indonesia (Cribb, 2001: 233; see also Robinson's (1995: 228) discussion of 'semi-official armed gangs'), or the use of the Bakassi Boys by a state governor in Nigeria (Reno, 2002).[1]There are currently no systematic measures of these informal violent organizations that act on behalf of the government.

To evaluate the conditions under which these groups form, to understand the relationship between them and the governments of the countries in which they operate, to know what is case specific and what is more general about them, and to analyze their consequences for the nature of conflict and for the prospects for peace, we need such measures. The PGMD allows researchers to examine under what conditions these informal actors form and operate. It provides a missing element useful for the study of state strength, violence and human rights violations, security sector issues and the prospects for peace, and possibly political cleavages and electoral violence. As case researchers (Staniland, 2012: 23) note, there are 'daunting' challenges to collecting such data. The data collection is an observational process designed to capture the variety of informal armed groups across continents while organizing knowledge of them in a coordinated and systematic way. A complete listing of all such groups would be ideal, as would comprehensive listings of all episodes of political violence or human rights violations (see Morrow, 2007: 563). Our data provide a basis for examining patterns and associations and a platform for further observations. In this article we give an overview of the theoretical argument that initiated the project, the data collection procedure and its challenges, and the features and limitations of the database. We show how the data can usefully be added to standard models of armed conflict.

PRO-GOVERNMENT MILITIAS (PGMS)

The project stems from the puzzle of why governments with regular forces delegate to informal groups. Governments face more severe agency problems with militias, yet may be tempted to use these groups to add numbers or local knowledge, or to evade accountability for strategically useful violence as in the Sudan. The question is whether governments *can't control* or *won't control* these groups (Mitchell, 2004). This logic offers a general explanation of these groups beyond cultural explanations or Weberian accounts of militias as constitutive of state failure (Bates, 2008). We distinguish the formation of these groups from a particular condition of a country, such as disorder, civil war, or state failure. If there are general incentives to delegate to these groups (e.g. increasing deployed forces or avoiding accountability) we expect them to work across cultural, geographical, and even political systems and these groups to be more numerous and more widely distributed than Weberian conceptions of states seeking to monopolize violence would suggest. Our data collection supports this assumption. We have identified 332 pro-government militias distributed around the world between 1981 and 2007. The relationship between these groups, disorder, civil wars, and state failure are empirical questions that can be evaluated with this new dataset.

We define a PGM as a group that

- is identified as pro-government or sponsored by the government (national or subnational),
- is identified as not being part of the regular security forces,
- is armed, and
- has some level of organization.

Criterion 1: The group is identified by the media source, which is discussed in more detail below, as pro-government or sponsored by the government, either on the national or subnational level. There are a variety of possible links between the group and the government, including information sharing, financing, equipping, training, and an operational link. We adopt a conservative approach. Simply sharing an enemy with the government or evidence that a group does not oppose the government or is simply tolerated by the government is insufficient for the group to be considered as pro-government. Depending on the available information, the data include more details on the nature of the link to government.

Criterion 2: The group is not part of the regular state security force. However, the PGM may operate with the regular forces, or even be composed of members of the security forces organized clandestinely as an unofficial or informal group (e.g. death squads). This relationship with the regular forces might include, in addition to sharing of personnel, information sharing, joint operations or training.

Criterion 3: The group is equipped for violence, but does not have to commit violence to be included. This criterion is not limited to firearms; some groups are equipped with machetes or clubs.

Criterion 4: The group has some evidence of organization, for example an identifiable leader, name, or a geographical, ethnic, religious or political basis. We exclude 'flash' or spontaneous mobs.

We do not select groups on how long they are pro-government, but only on these four criteria. When a group fails to fulfil these, then the group is coded as terminated as a PGM according to our definition. This includes the disarmament or banning of the group by the government or its integration into the regular security forces. If a president or party ceases to be in government, then the PGMs affiliated with them also cease to be PGMs. Groups can also cease to be classified as PGMs as a result of a border change. For example, armed groups linked to the Indonesian government were active in East Timor, fighting the independence movement. These pro-Indonesia groups end in our dataset with the transition government that was put in place in East Timor in December 1999, although some of these groups were still active within Timor-Leste after 1999. But they were then linked to the Indonesian government, so no longer fitted our definition of a domestic pro-government militia.

AFFILIATION WITH GOVERNMENT: INFORMAL AND SEMI-OFFICIAL PGMS

While all groups in the database are pro-government, their affiliation with government varies. In some instances the government tries to keep the group at arm's length, while in other cases governments openly create, train, and pay such groups. For example, village defense forces that have been created by governments fall under this second category, where the link to the PGM is far more open and institutionalized than in the case of the Janjaweed. As an initial effort to capture affiliation with the government we use two categories, informal and semi-official PGMs.

Informal PGMs are armed, supported by or act on the side of the government and are described as pro-government, government militia, linked to the government, government-backed, or government-allied. Examples include the Young Patriots in Cote d'Ivoire, the Ansar-e Hezbollah in Iran, and the Interahamwe Militia in Rwanda during the early 1990s. 'Death squads', even when closely linked to the government, are normally informal and clandestine, and are categorized as informal PGMs.

A semi-official PGM has a recognized legal or semi-official status, in contrast to the looser affiliation of informal PGMs. A semi-official PGM is separate from the regular forces and identified as a distinct organization. Examples of semi-official PGMs include Village Defence Committees in India, the Revolutionary Committees in Libya under Gaddafi, and the Rondas Campesinas in Peru. In many countries, the term 'paramilitary' refers to regular forces, or police units with some military status which are not included in the PGM dataset.

OVERVIEW OF THE PGMD

The PGMD contains open source information about pro-government armed groups obtained from LexisNexis searches of news sources from around the world. The sources include transcripts translated into English in BBC World Summaries of local news, Agence France Presse, Xinhua General News Service, and major international newspapers. Search terms included 'government militia', 'paramilitary', 'government death squads', 'government irregular forces', and 'vigilante', and returned numerous documents, many of them off-topic. While this broad search strategy was heavily labour-intensive, we reduced the risk of missing information. Users of the data have access to over 3,500 key sources that informed the coding decisions. The dataset covers 178 countries for the time period from 1981 to 2007, and for 88 countries we found evidence of at least one PGM during this time period.[2] We focus on pro-government groups active within their own borders. Acknowledging the scope of the dataset, the dynamic nature of the relationship between groups and governments, and the complicated task of imposing a uniform coding scheme on disparate open source information on a global scale, researchers made a concerted effort to cross-check the information to ensure consistency. The coding has been checked independently by at least three researchers, more in most cases. But no further claims are made about the accuracy of this information.

The PGMD consists of a relational data structure that links 16 tables representing aspects of the data, from armed groups themselves and their membership and target characteristics, to group actions, to the documentary evidence researchers used to create the dataset. Although we focus here on combinations of groups, countries, and years as units of analysis, the relational structure allows separate data matrices to be constructed for any combination of our 16 tables of information. The data structure is realized as a Sqlite database.[3] The database supports distributed web-based coding and a searchable website that can be used to browse and download the PGM data.

In the following, we discuss the key variables and provide details on specific datasets drawn from our database. The data that use the pro-government militia as the unit of analysis include variables on their links to their government and membership characteristics. The database contains information on the alleged targets and purpose of the PGMs, as well as other information discussed below.

ORIGIN AND TERMINATION

For each PGM we recorded formation and termination dates. When no such date was given in the sources, we recorded the date the group was first mentioned.[4] As a termination date we coded the date when a group ceased to be a pro-government militia according to our definition. One difficulty was patchy information on termination. In many instances, the groups simply ceased to be mentioned in the news reports. Therefore, there is often missing data on group termination. This problem of establishing group 'life-cycles' is not a problem particular to PGMs, but extends to research on groups more generally (e.g. Berkhout & Lowery, 2008).

PGM CHARACTERISTICS

As outlined above, we distinguished between informal and semi-official PGMs. Furthermore, we identify how the PGM is linked to the government, for example to the state or military institution, an individual person, such as the president or a minister, a political party, or the subnational government. We recorded all links that are identified in the sources.

The database includes variables that capture various other characteristics including the sources of support for the groups, such as a foreign government, landowners, or being self-maintained through plunder and looting. We recorded the geographical location of the activities of the groups as precisely as possible and include a minimum and maximum headcount of each group where the sources provide these kinds of information. We recorded membership characteristics, for example whether it was ethnic or ideology-based, whether the group recruits children or adolescents, or whether their membership was urban or rural-based. We also coded alleged targets, such as armed and unarmed political opposition, criminals, and civilians, as well as group purposes, such as fighting insurgents, intimidating civilians, or gathering intelligence.

PROCEDURES AND MISSING DATA

Some countries or groups receive more attention than others in the news media. But we expect that the range of sources used and the length of the period for which data are collected reduce the problem of overlooking groups in less prominent countries or conflicts. Nevertheless, we expect that the dataset underrepresents PGMs, which is partly a function of differences in the availability of sources across the time period.

As we rely on news sources to describe the link of a group to government, another difficulty is the potential misspecification of a PGM's relationship to the government. Using multiple sources through LexisNexis across time is likely to reduce this problem. If the source is ambiguous about the relationship between the national government and the group, or if different sources contradict each other in their classification of the link between the government and the group, more information is sought from country-specific sources and academic research. In cases where we could not establish the status of the group as separate from regular forces, we noted the group in the codebook but did not include it in the database.

Table I. PGM types

Type	*Freq.*	*Percentage*
Informal PGMs	218	66
Semi-official PGMs	114	34
Total	332	100

Table II. Links to government

Government link	*Freq.*	*Percentage*
State or military institution	211	64
Individual state official	117	35
Political party	54	16
Subnational government	34	10
Unclear	4	1
No information	4	1

The Data

For the period between 1981 and 2007 we have coded 332 PGMs. As shown in Table I, about two-thirds are classified as informal PGMs, which are loosely affiliated with and linked to the government, while one-third are identified as semi-official PGMs.

In Table II we identify four possible links between the militias and the government: to an institution of the state or the military, to individual members of the state apparatus, to the governing political party, or to a subnational government. Groups can have more than one link to government. For 64% of PGMs the link was to an institution, either to the state or to the military. About one-third of PGMs are linked to an individual, such as the president, prime minister or another government minister. In 16% of cases the PGM is connected to the political party in power and in only 10% to the subnational government. More localized groups may be less easy to observe using our search procedure.

Tables III and IV show common membership characteristics as well as the most frequently reported targets. Members of PGMs have a range of characteristics, without one characteristic being particularly dominant. Member characteristics were drawn inductively from the available sources. The most common characteristic, although applying to less than one-third of the groups, was belonging to an ethnic group. For 20% of the groups the sources reported that 'volunteers' had joined the government militias, while 18% of PGMs were made up of villagers, 17% were ideology-based and 17% of PGMs had adolescent members. Other membership groups include former soldiers or former rebels. Staniland (2012) analyzes insurgents defecting to the government, and such groups are also included in the database from the time they become pro-government.

Table III. Most common member characteristics

Member characteristic	*Freq.*	*Percentage*
Ethnicity	95	29
Volunteers	68	20
Village/rural areas	58	18
Ideology	55	17
Adolescents	55	17
Religion	42	13
Security forces	40	12
Party activists	40	12

Table IV. Most common PGM targets

Target	*Freq.*	*Percentage*
Armed opposition	201	61
Unarmed opposition	122	37
Civilians	116	35
Ethnic group	54	16

For alleged targets, we coded one or more mentions of any alleged target. Just over 60% of PGMs targeted armed opposition groups. In most cases, governments use informal armed groups to counter a threat to their rule in the form of armed opposition. At some distance, unarmed opposition, such as members of opposition parties or outspoken government critics (in 37% of cases) and civilians (in 35% of cases) emerged as the next most common targets of PGMs. Our data collection also shows that ordinary civilians were often targeted by PGMs. Ethnic groups were also frequently identified as targets, but at 16%, ethnic groups appear to be a less frequent target. It may be that opposition groups have an ethnic dimension that is not picked up in the reporting of the conflict.

In addition to the data that use the group as the unit of analysis, we provide datasets with the country-year as unit of analysis, containing basic information on the number of active PGMs and the number of countries with at least one PGM in a particular year between 1981 and 2007. To capture the duration of the militias, we used the information on origin and termination as discussed above. To circumvent the problem of missing data on termination, we recorded the years during which these groups have been found to be active. Examples of such activities could include anything from training exercises to operations and acts of violence. Whenever we were unable to identify a termination date for a militia, we used the last year of recorded activity as a proxy for termination.[5] In these cases, the militia group is assumed to exist for all years between the date of origin and last year of recorded activity.

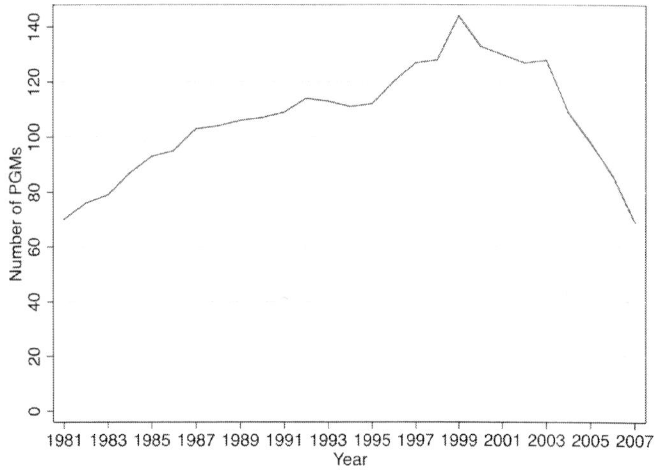

Figure 1. Number of PGMs worldwide, 1981–2007.

Figure 1 presents the total number of active groups annually from 1981 to 2007. The figure shows a general upward trend throughout the 1980s and 1990s. The number of pro-government militias peaks in 1999 and then drops off substantially. We are not yet sure of the reasons behind the sharp decline of PGMs. In part this pattern could be a result of lagged reporting. Sometimes news reports published several years after the event provide further details on PGMs and their activities in earlier years.

Figure 2 graphs the total number of countries with at least one PGM per year. As for the data presented in Figure 1, groups with unspecified dates of dissolution are estimated to have ended in the year of their last recorded activity. Our data show a slight downward trend in the number of countries with PGMs during the 1980s, and a drop after a small increase in 2004. Again the decline towards the end of the data collection could partly be due to limited information available for the most recent time period. Countries with the highest number of PGMs are Indonesia with 37, Sudan with 21, and the Philippines with 19, possibly suggesting an 'archipelago effect' where difficult terrain induces a government to rely on local forces.

Table V shows the correlation of PGMs with civil war, using the 25 battle-related deaths threshold from the UCDP/PRIO Armed Conflict Dataset (ACD) (Gleditsch et al., 2002). Using country-years as the unit of analysis, 43% of PGMs are present in countries experiencing civil war. Most of the time PGMs are found outside of armed conflict. Focusing on civil wars, most civil wars are characterized by the presence of militias (81%

of civil wars). In short, accounting for militias fighting on the government side is likely to be important for capturing the dynamics of internal conflict and the prospects for peace, but these groups cannot be treated as simply epiphenomenal to civil wars.

USEFULNESS OF THE DATA

To illustrate uses of the data, we analyze civil war, adding our PGM measure to a standard model of armed conflict. We expect PGMs to increase the risk of armed conflict because they offer governments a low-cost response to insurgents while complicating the incentive structure on which a settlement of the conflict might be built.

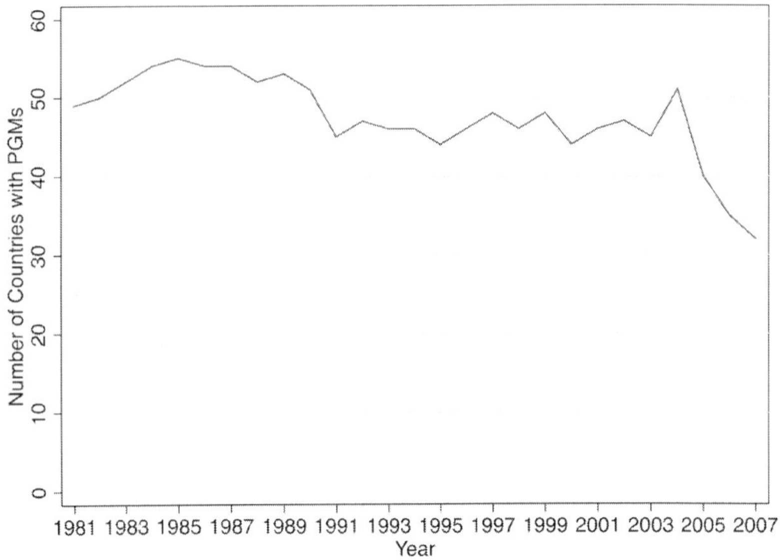

Figure 2. Number of countries with at least one PGM, 1981–2007.

Based on the large quantitative literature (e.g. Fearon & Laitin, 2003; Hegre & Sambanis, 2006; Ross, 2006; Wimmer, Cederman & Min 2009), the model includes mountainous terrain, ethnic exclusion, natural resources, democracy, economic development, and population size. We model the incidence of civil war, not onset, due to the extremely small number of onsets in our dataset, which is restricted to start in 1981. We operationalize incidence with the ACD measure mentioned above.

Table V. PGMs and armed conflict

PGMs	*Uppsala/PRIO Armed Conflict*		
	0	*1*	*Total*
0	2,489	143	2,632
	94.57%	5.43%	100%
	75.84%	18.99%	65.23%
1	793	610	1,403
	56.52%	43.48%	100%
	24.16%	81.01%	22.68%
Total	3,576	753	4,035
	81.34%	18.66%	100%
	100%	100%	100%

The data on terrain come from Fearon & Laitin (2003), resources are measured with oil production figures from Ross (2011), and GDP per capita and population size are taken from the World Bank. For ethnicity, we use the ethnic exclusion measure from Wimmer, Cederman & Min (2009) and for democracy the *xpolity* measure (Vreeland, 2008).[6] We use a logit model with robust standard errors, clustered on countries. Similar to Ross's (2006) study on civil war, we include a counter for the peace years and three cubic splines to correct for serial correlation (Beck, Katz & Tucker, 1998). Due to data availability, our analysis covers 1981 to 2005. The first model in Table VI analyzes civil war with the standard set of explanatory variables. In the second model we add the PGM dummy variable indicating whether a country in a particular year had at least one pro-government militia (coded 1) or not (coded 0). In the third model we separate this PGM variable into two separate indicators, distinguishing between informal and semi-official pro-government militias. The findings of the first model match current research on civil war with the exception of *Mountainous terrain* and *Oil production*, which are statistically insignificant, perhaps due to the restricted time period of the analysis. The fit of the model with the PGM variable appears to be better, given the larger Wald χ^2 and pseudo R^2 statistics. The PGM dummy variable is highly statistically significant and positive. Converting the logit coefficient gives an odds ratio of 4.172; the risk of civil war occurrence is almost five times larger when PGMs are present. When distinguishing between informal and semi-official PGMs in the third model, again both militia variables are statistically significant at $p < 0.001$. Converting the coefficients into odds ratios, the probability of civil war is just over 2.5 times greater in countries with informal PGMs and 3.7 times greater with semi-official PGMs.

Table VI. Logit estimates on the incidence of intrastate conflict, 1981–2007

	Standard model	*PGM variable*	*Two PGM types*
Pro-government militias		1.428***	
		(0.227)	
Informal PGMs			0.969***
			(0.235)
Semi-official PGMs			1.309***
			(0.231)
GDP per capita[a]	–0.533***	–0.601***	–0.564***
	(0.151)	(0.141)	(0.141)
Population size[a]	0.260**	0.107	0.037
	(0.098)	(0.106)	(0.104)
Regime type	0.058*	0.040	0.039
	(0.026)	(0.025)	(0.025)
Oil production[a]	0.012	0.016	0.014
	(0.018)	(0.017)	(0.017)
Size of excluded population[a]	0.155***	0.126***	0.121**
	(0.036)	(0.035)	(0.035)
Mountainous terrain[a]	0.089	0.047	0.074
	(0.075)	(0.079)	(0.079)
Peace years	–2.414***	–2.223***	–2.136***
	(0.200)	(0.192)	(0.190)
Spline 1	–0.201***	–0.158***	–0.176***
	(0.023)	(0.023)	(0.023)
Spline 2	0.040***	0.037***	0.035***
	(0.006)	(0.006)	(0.006)
Spline 3	–0.004*	–0.003	–0.003
	(0.002)	(0.002)	(0.002)
Constant	2.846*	3.932**	4.150**
	(1.350)	(1.321)	(1.309)
Pseudo R-squared	0.56	0.58	0.59
Wald Chi-squared	433.15***	434.92***	555.63***
Pseudo Log-Likelihood	–672.96	–630.88	–618.84
Number of clusters	142	141	141
Number of observations	3093	3087	3087

Values are coefficients with robust standard errors in parentheses, clustered on countries. *$p < 0.05$, **$p < 0.01$, ***$p < 0.001$.
[a] The natural log was taken of these variables, with 0.5 being added to all values beforehand.

There are further issues to investigate including likely endogeneity between PGMs and conflict, yet this brief analysis of intrastate conflict suggests that information on PGMs may provide valuable insights beyond the standard models. For conflict scholars, informal actors are likely to influence the nature and duration of conflict. They may have incentives to act as 'spoilers' and prolong the conflict. The consequences of governments deciding to use these sorts of groups may be assessed in terms of their impact on the well-being of civilian populations and on human rights protection using the new PGM dataset. For scholars interested in the well-being of the state, ethnic and political cleavages, and the institutional bases of collective action, party politics and election violence, these groups provide an opportunity for theory development and empirical analysis.

CONCLUSION

Despite the sometimes highly visible activities of pro-government militias in Europe, Latin America, Asia and Africa, there has been no large-scale systematic comparative research on why these forces form and how they affect the risk of internal conflict, civil war and harm to civilians. Because of the increasing role of non-state actors generally, and the significant presence that they have had in conflicts across countries, it is important to collect information on these groups and to seek to improve transparency on their links to governments, assuming that governments that back these groups have a responsibility for their actions. The PGMD enables the academic community to investigate the conditions under which these groups are formed and dismantled and what impact they have on the security and stability of their host countries. The data will likely be useful to scholars working on state capacity and control, conflict and repression and collective action more broadly. Given the span across time and space, we expect our database to be more useful for making cross-country and cross-time comparisons than for carrying out in-depth qualitative case studies for specific countries – although given the amount of information we have gathered on the groups, we hope that our database will provide a useful starting point for such endeavours. We anticipate that the PGMD will also be of interest to policymakers, the media, and non-academic users concerned with conflict and human rights related issues. By focusing on these organizations, these data allow researchers and policymakers to obtain a more comprehensive estimate of the repressive apparatus of a country than that provided by relying on the size of formal security forces alone. Beyond the problem of theories focusing attention on state actors rather than non-state actors, there is simply a lack of available data on these groups. The Pro-Government Militias Database addresses this deficit.

ACKNOWLEDGEMENTS

We are particularly grateful to our research assistants, Jonathan Sullivan, Tim Veen, Bronia Flett, Catriona Webster, Damaris Veen, Martin Ottmann, Anke Roexe, Philip Hultquist and Adam Scharpf and to Anita Gohdes for database maintenance. We would like to thank Chris Butler, University of New Mexico, and the late Elinor Ostrom and Mike McGinnis, at a presentation at the Workshop in Political Theory and Policy Analysis, Indiana University (October 2010), for their valuable contributions.

Funding

This project has been funded by the Economic and Social Research Council (ESRC), UK, RES-062-23-0363. Additional support has come from the Centre for the Study of Civil War (CSCW) at the International Peace Research Institute Oslo (PRIO).

Notes

[1]For a historical discussion of pirates and mercenaries see Thomson (1996). For a discussion of death squads see Campbell & Brenner (2000). For a discussion of Indonesia, Iraq and Iran see Ahram (2011b).

[2]We have excluded Lebanon and Somalia due to difficulties in identifying governments over the time period.

[3]See http://www.sqlite.org. Sqlite is free relational database system that may be queried using SQL, for example via R or directly. The software necessary to query Sqlite databases directly is built into computers running Mac OSX and Linux, and is available for Windows. Sqlite databases are contained in a single file that can be easily transported between different operating systems and requires no complicated installation procedures.

[4]Whenever we found evidence for groups preceding or succeeding other PGMs, we have recorded such links and possible name changes.

[5]When neither date was available the group was considered to exist until the end of the reporting period.

[6]We transformed the three transitional codes –66, –77, and –88 in line with the transformation done in the *polity2* measure (Marshall, Gurr & Jaggers, 2010).

REFERENCES

1. Ahram, Ariel I (2011a) Origins and persistence of state-sponsored militias: Path dependent processes in third world military development. Journal of Strategic Studies 34(4): 531–555.
2. Ahram, Ariel I (2011b) Proxy Warriors: The Rise and Fall of State-Sponsored Militias. Stanford, CA: Stanford University Press.
3. Bakke, Kristin M, Cunningham, Kathleen Gallagher, Seymour, Lee JM (2012) A plague of initials: Fragmentation, cohesion, and infighting in civil wars. Perspectives on Politics 10(2): 265–283.
4. Bates, Robert (2008) When Things Fell Apart: State Failure in Late-Century Africa. New York: Cambridge University Press.
5. Beck, Nathaniel, Katz, Jonathan N, Tucker, Richard (1998) Taking time seriously: Time-series–cross-section analysis with a binary dependent variable. American Journal of Political Science 42(4): 1260–1288.
6. Berkhout, Joost, Lowery, David (2008) Counting organized interests in the European Union: A comparison of data sources. Journal of European Public Policy 15(4): 489–513.
7. Campbell, Bruce, Brenner, Arthur, eds (2000) Death Squads in Global Perspective: Murder with Deniability. New York: Palgrave Macmillan.
8. Cederman, Lars E, Gleditsch, Kristian Skrede (2009) Introduction to special issue on 'Disaggregating civil war'. Journal of Conflict Resolution 53(4): 487–495.
9. Centeno, Miguel Angel (2002) Blood and Debt: War and the Nation State in Latin America. University Park, PA: Penn State University Press.
10. Collier, Paul, Hoeffler, Anke (2004) Greed and grievance in civil war. Oxford Economic Papers 56(4): 563–595.
11. Cribb, Robert (2001) Genocide in Indonesia, 1965–1966. Journal of Genocide Research 3(2): 219–239.
12. Cunningham, Kathleen Gallagher (2011) Divide and conquer or divide and concede: How do states respond to internally divided separatists? American Political Science Review 105(2): 275–297.
13. Fearon, James D, Laitin, David D (2003) Ethnicity, insurgency, and civil war. American Political Science Review 97(1): 75–90.
14. Gleditsch, Nils Petter, Wallensteen, Peter, Eriksson, Mikael, Sollenberg, Margareta, Strand, Håvard (2002) Armed Conflict 1946–2001: A new

dataset. Journal of Peace Research 39(5): 615–637.

15. Hegre, Håvard, Sambanis, Nicholas (2006) Sensitivity analysis of empirical results on civil war onset. Journal of Conflict Resolution 50(4): 508–535.
16. Janowitz, Morris (1977) Military Institutions and Coercion in the Developing World. Chicago, IL: University of Chicago Press.
17. Marshall, Monty G, Gurr, Ted Robert, Jaggers, Keith (2010) Polity IV Project: Dataset Users' Manual. Center for Systemic Peace, George Mason University (http://www.systemicpeace.org/inscr/p4manualv2010.pdf).
18. Mazzei, Julie (2009) Death Squads or Self-Defense Forces: How Paramilitary Groups Emerge and Challenge Democracy in Latin America. Chapel Hill, NC: University of North Carolina Press.
19. Mitchell, Neil (2004) Agents of Atrocity: Leaders, Followers and Violation of Human Rights in Civil Wars. New York: Palgrave Macmillan.
20. Morrow, James D (2007) When do states follow the laws of war? American Political Science Review 101(3): 559–572.
21. Reno, William (2002) The politics of insurgency in collapsing states. Development and Change 33(5): 837–858.
22. Robinson, Geoffrey (1995) The Dark Side of Paradise: Political Violence in Bali. Ithaca, NY: Cornell University Press.
23. Ross, Michael (2006) A closer look at oil, diamonds, and civil war. Annual Review of Political Science 9: 265–300.
24. Ross, Michael (2011) Oil and Gas Production and Value, 1932–2009 (http://dvn.iq.harvard.edu/dvn/dv/mlross;jsessionid=4093c9a83111a0af9cde52b38824).
25. Staniland, Paul (2012) Between a rock and a hard place: Insurgent fratricide, ethnic defection, and the rise of pro-state paramilitaries. Journal of Conflict Resolution 56(1): 16–40.
26. Stanley, William (1996) The Protection Racket State: Elite Politics, Military Extortion, and Civil War in El Salvador. Philadelphia, PA: Temple University Press.
27. Thomson, Janice E (1996) Mercenaries, Pirates, and Sovereigns: State-Building and Extraterritorial Violence in Early Modern Europe. Princeton, NJ: Princeton University Press.

28. Toft, Monica Duffy (2009) Securing the Peace: The Durable Settlement of Civil Wars. Princeton, NJ: Princeton University Press.
29. Vreeland, James Raymond (2008) The effect of political regime on civil war: Unpacking anocracy. Journal of Conflict Resolution 52(3): 401–425.
30. Wimmer, Andreas, Cederman, Lars-Erik, Min, Brian (2009) Ethnic politics and armed conflict: A configurational analysis of a new global data set. American Sociological Review 74(2): 316–337.

CHAPTER 4

MAPPING PROGRESS: HUMAN RIGHTS AND INTERNATIONAL STUDENTS IN AUSTRALIA

Andrew Jakubowicz[1], **Devaki Monani**[2]

[1]University of Technology Sydney
[2]Australian Catholic University

ABSTRACT

The rapid growth in international student numbers in Australia in the first decade of the 2000s was accompanied by a series of public crises. The most important of these was the outbreak in Melbourne Victoria and elsewhere of physical attacks on the students. Investigations at the time also pointed to cases of gross exploitation, an array of threats that severely compromised their human rights. This paper reviews and pursues the outcomes of a report

Citation: Cosmopolitan Civil Societies Journal 2015, 7(3): 4473, - http://dx.doi.org/10.5130/ccs.v7i3.4473

prepared by the authors in 2010 for Universities Australia and the Human Rights Commission. The report reviewed social science research and proposed a series of priorities for human rights interventions that were part of the Human Rights Commission's considerations. New activity, following the innovation of having international students specifically considered by the Human Rights Commission, points to initiatives that have not fully addressed the wide range of questions at state.

INTRODUCTION

International Students and the Crisis in Human Rights

One of the most controversial areas of global human rights debates lies in that area where state actors are called on to defend rights and prosecute breaches associated with non-citizens. Nowhere is this more apparent than in the case of international students studying in a country in which they do not have citizenship. Furthermore all the most difficult issues are intensified in circumstances where international education is a significant industry, and international students are perceived in practice as sources of income for financially-stressed universities, colleges and schools. In many cases the students are recruited in an attempt by profit making institutions to optimise income flow. These institutions may subordinate their educational and pastoral responsibilities to the economic interests of their shareholders. In the first decade of the century, Australia became very adept at developing educational programs and recruitment strategies that would attract many hundreds of thousands of students, a significant number of whom came from India. They were destined, at the 'high end', for post-graduate research study of great value to their countries of origin and Australia, while at the less qualified level many began in secondary school, or undertook low-level English language acquisition programs, or trade qualifications.

The year 2008 exemplified the rate of change and the size of the pressures on the system (Australian Government, 2008). In that year there were 544,000 international students in Australia, about 3% of the population, a year on year increase of 21%. The largest single group, from China, had risen 20% to a total of 130,000. Students from India, at number two, had increased by 54%, approaching 100,000. None of the institutions or the communities in which they were located had made any real provision for such a meteoric increase. Issues like human rights and the implications of the changing population make-up were not on the agenda of the Human Rights

Commission, nor of interest to government bodies at the state level charged with the wellbeing of students, local or international. The enrolment of foreign students peaked in 2009, with China supplying 155,000 (up another 18%), and India 121,000 (up another 25%) (Australian Government, 2009). Indian students became the focus of public attention in 2009, when there were reports of widespread attacks on them, and a number of students or ex-students were murdered. Discussing this phenomenon, Dunn *et al.*(2011a) reported evidence of a 'curry-bashing' subculture in parts of Melbourne that clearly fits ideas of racism.

Singh (2011) shows that Indian students and their families were involved in nearly $3 billion of transfers to Australia in December 2010. They had a strong expectation of gaining permanent residence (PR) and were using education for planned migration outcomes. When the Indian student crisis reached its crescendo in Australia in 2009, the Australian Human Rights Commission arrived at a rather late awareness that the rights of students should be a central issue for resolution and progress. As with many temporary residents, the Australian human rights debate had essentially passed international students by. Occasionally they were referenced in discussion of racism, but for the most part, they had not been considered within the civil rights debate in Australia. Consequently, the major agencies for the protection of human rights were poorly prepared when the bashings, murders and other intimidation and exploitation of international students surfaced in 2008. The circumstances had long been known to some local and state agencies, but there was no real discourse available to draw on for the students, their advocates and agencies, who were anxious to engage with government, universities and colleges.

It took the racialisation of the debate, as media and political focus intensified on Indian (and particularly Punjabi students), to demonstrate how deeply embedded racialism was in public policy assumptions. Xenophobic, rather than specifically racial, dynamics may have been at work, given the all-encompassing and indiscriminate nature of the key human rights complaints. Indians were by no means the only targets (or in some cases they were also perpetrators) in the events under review. The complaints, when they appeared, were drawn out of generally wary students from a range of countries. The range of issues included experiences of racialised violence, housing exploitation, lack of transport access, employment exploitation and racial and sexual harassment.

Student Responses

In this article we want to present an overview of the responses that emerged at the advent of the student crisis. The article argues for the need for universities in Australia to adopt if not all at least in part the human rights principles when dealing with international students. The 2010 debates were fuelled by three key concerns – the projections on the increasing population of Australia and the impact of these projections on the student population; the Baird report on state and federal governments' management of the international student industry1 (2010); and the decisions of the Council of Australian Governments (COAG, 2010) on the presence of international students2.

Universities Australia (UA), the sector's umbrella and representative body, soon identified a serious lack of empirical knowledge as a major factor in its rather slow response to the issues as they affected the sector. UA approached the Human Rights Commission (HRC), who together with the Academy of the Social Sciences in Australia as the peak group for social science research, developed a series of symposia to identify and workshop what data there was about the international students' plight. The HRC role was crucial, as it framed the issues within a human rights perspective, and would therefore press for human rights relevant outcomes and programs. The symposia provided the first sustained occasions where scholars and policy-makers were asked to locate the international students crisis within a human rights paradigm. Social science insights predisposed analysts to examine to what extent and in what forms Australian institutional racism might play a role in perpetuating and tolerating situations of violence, exploitation and discrimination towards international students. The first step in any analysis of racist institutions that might condone racist practices lies in having them acknowledge that those types of question be asked of them.

The Indian student crisis, as it became known, triggered widespread soul-searching and some hard-headed policy reviews in Australia. The broad dimensions of these reviews included the revamping of visas, changes to permanent residency criteria, tighter controls on college and university enrolments, improved consumer rights, and the mapping out of a human rights charter of sorts covering international students. The intersection of economic issues and human rights issues has ensured that the crisis and its continuing aftermath remain pressing questions for diplomatic, trade, education, justice, health and housing portfolios of government, at national, state and local levels in Australia.

Development of the Principles to Promote and Protect the Human Rights of International Students

Public media attention has focused on the Indian students at the centre of well-publicised violence and exploitation, yet the issues continue to affect international students from many different backgrounds. Moreover, problems of urban violence and corrupt exploitation of vulnerable people are features of Australian society, rather than being generated by the characteristics of the national cultures of the students. The interaction of culture, opportunity, expectations and institutional practices suggests that a range of analytical approaches needs to be deployed to help develop longer-term strategies in public policy. This article draws on a Report prepared by the authors (Jakubowicz and Monani, 2010) for three of the key stakeholders in the development of evidence-based policy, namely Human Rights Australia (HRA), Universities Australia (UA), and the Academy for Social Sciences in Australia (ASSA). The previous report set the parameters for interrogating how the university sector should understand the issues for the sector and the wider society, and how social science research could contribute to both understanding and responding to the negative experiences of some international students in Australia. While rapidly overtaken by events as government inquiries, delegations and crisis responses proliferated, the report underpinned what became the *Principles to Promote and Protect the Human Rights of International Students*, launched in Adelaide in October 2012 (https://www.humanrights.gov.au/news/stories/new-international-students-guidelines-launched). A recent 2015 review of the AHRC principles in action has once again placed racism and racial discrimination as one of the top three human rights issues facing international students, alongside employment and accommodation challenges (AHRC, 2015, p.10).

Our discussion paper (Jakubowicz and Monani, 2010), submitted to the Academy of Social Sciences Australia, contributed to shaping the parameters of the policy debate on international students' human rights principles developed by the Australian Human Rights Commission. Here, we wish to revisit the international students' human rights principles and present the current policy mandate on international students and human rights. This article is divided into two sections. The first describes and lays out the key features of the Indian student revolt and the lived experience of international students. The second section revisits the international student debate within a human rights paradigm as adopted by the Australian Human Rights Commission.

Racism and the Lived Experience of International Students: Issues Remain Unaddressed

From the moment that visuals of the Indian student protest began to unfold on television here in Australia and across Asia, panic set in in the minds of the Australian people. The protest was conducted in the wake of the screwdriver stabbing of a 25- year old Indian student, Sravan Kumar Theerthala, in May 2009. Students demanded safety and urged police authorities in Victoria to recognise the increase in race based hate crimes particularly towards Indian students. Indian students as 'foreigners' had managed to stage a revolt never seen before by the Australian public.

Nearly 2000 students chanted as they marched down Melbourne's streets, carrying signs which read 'I pay fees, I pay tax', 'I get stabbed in Oz' and' Racism is more dangerous than swine flu'. Gautam Gupta, a spokesman for the Federation of Indian Students of Australia (FISA), said that the protesters had issued a series of demands, which the State Government needed to meet.

We want a multicultural police section and we want crime statistics made public so that we know the extent of the problem. We want blanket cover for all international students, covering them for accidents and assaults and the government should run an ad campaign highlighting the positive influence that migrants and international students have made to this country. My advice to every Indian student now who wants to come to Australia is, Please don't come (Millar& Doherty, 2009).

Criticism was mounted against the Indian students by the police and the media for suggesting that Indian students were victims of racial crime. Instead, the Victorian police downplayed the issue of racism, and suggested that Indian students tended to carry expensive gadgets such as mobile phones and laptops thereby attracting unnecessary attention on public transport. Others, such as the vice-president for international students in 2009 at Victoria University in Melbourne, Andrew Holloway, blamed statistics instead. He stated that:

It just happens to be coincidental that there's a large number of South Asian students travelling on their own late at night time and if you look at it, the work patterns of Indian students are somewhat different from other students. They tend to work at 24/7 conveniences, petrol stations, late-at-night shops, and therefore are more likely to be on the public transport network late at night time (Waters and Macbean, 2009). In contrast, the Islamic Council of Victoria suggested that it seemed to be an ill-conceived idea and, in particular, Nazeem Hussein expressed his disappointment:

I think it's one thing to help the victims look less like victims, sorry to look less Indian, but I think it's another thing to really attack the core issue here which is racism. And we're seeing not as much from the police that we would have probably expected. It's only a particular type of crime that is on the rise and that's crimes against people that look Indian. So really that statistic means not very much given that this particular crime is on the increase (Waters and Macbean, 2009).

The education industry in Australia was the hardest hit by the Indian student events and Australia gained a reputation for being an unsafe student destination. Suddenly the 'invisible international student' was now 'visible' and actively speaking out.

There is a gap in leadership around the issue of international students and more specifically around the tolerance of cultural diversity in Australia. Australia lacks a strong research base about cultural diversity and racism on which to build good policy. International students' lives, and the lives of their families in their home countries, need to be presented in the Australian media in order to give locals a realistic perspective on international students and their journey to Australia. Instead, the media has focused on the destruction of the glass windows of the historic clocks around Flinders Street Station. Stories about student vandalism during the protests continued to be broadcast on Australian television (Millar, *The Age*, 31st May 2009) while in India, images of Indian students being stabbed and robbed were being repeatedly telecast (*Press Trust of India*, 15th June, 2009). Both countries have had to grapple with the reality of the violent nature of the racist crimes. For Australia, it has been a matter of shame, and for Indians, one where fear prevails even today about Australians and their attitudes towards Indians.

Two discourses emerged simultaneously in the academic literature about international students' experience in Australia. The first focused on the discriminatory interracial conflicts amongst international students and the locals. The second emphasised the rapid commercialisation of international education in Australia (Nyland, Forbes-Mewett & Hartel, 2013) as being one of the major causes for the discontent generated amongst international students (Jakubowicz & Monani, 2010). Nelson (2013), in her research on denial of racism and its implications for local action in Australia, reminds us of former Prime Minister Kevin Rudd's visit to India, where he denied racism was a factor in the attacks, portraying Indian students as victims solely of criminal intent by emphasising the 'opportunistic' nature of the attacks (Nelson, 2013, p. 92). Other studies conducted by Dunn *et al.* (2011b) note that when some attacks were described as racist, political leaders continued to oscillate back and forth between acknowledgement and denial of racism. Mason (2012 a), when analysing Australian politicians' responses3, examined an interwoven discourse of avoidance, nationalist rhetoric, and deflection. She expresses some disappointment at the strategy adopted by Australian Federal parliamentarians, one that neither acknowledges nor denies, whilst placing the racial attacks within a nationalist and crime-control rhetoric. This refusal to acknowledge the racial element in the attacks may have done serious harm to the victim community, and may have been a major barrier to effective intervention aimed at prevention of a recurrence of such events, while also rendering it less likely that authorities would successfully complete investigations if victims withheld co-operation (Mason, 2012a, pp. 13-19).

The police faced a number of constraints in making available to the public declarations of crimes possibly motivated by racism, often seeking to confine their comments to the evidence at hand (Mason 2012b). The police's refusal to take the racist intent seriously was problematic. Some Indian students interpreted this as an active sidelining of what they identified as major life-threatening events emerging during their stay in Australia4. As Mason (2012b) concludes, this was perhaps one of the main reasons for a May 2009 international student rally at Flinders Street station in downtown Melbourne. Mason (2012b) draws on the frustration expressed by the Federation of Indian Students Association's president, Gautam Gupta, in his statement to the press: 'How can they say that none of these attacks were racist when we hear criminals saying terms like "Curry bashing"?' (Mason, 2012b, p. 46). Baas (2009) suggests 'curry bashing' is a relatively new epithet (imported from the UK perhaps) and is significantly linked to the 'disgust' expressed towards Indians by some white Australians. He draws from the blogosphere in Australia during 2005-2009 which sent out strong signals of hate towards the perceived 'hordes' of Indian students arriving in Australia. One blogger remarked that Indians are incapable of moving out of anyone's 'bloody way' when they walk around in groups in the city: 'so many of these 'f…ng Indians have crowded the streets of Melbourne' (Baas, 2009, p. 39). Racist language keeps evolving in Australia according to the groups that migrate to Australia; however the intent remains the same. In this case, the group happened to be fee-paying international students of Indian origin.

Robertson (2008) suggests that between 1997 and 2009, the Australian education market was the third largest export after iron ore and coal. During this twelve-year period, four million international students were educated in Australia. Robertson (2008) maintains that, despite the high levels of profitability international students brought to Australia, academics such as Birrell, Healy and Kinnaird (2007) continued to express resentment that students were not readily integrating into the labour market on completion of their degrees and that they were not capable of gaining the necessary skills required to remain in Australia. Robertson (2013) criticises the way international students were characterised in both the literature and the media discourse in Australia. In her most recent article, Robertson (2013) claims students and student-migrant activism have been completely overlooked and overshadowed by more dominant discourses with racist undertones of international students wanting to permanently migrate to Australia. Nyland *et al.* (2013) urge 'education suppliers' to examine and enhance student needs and academic values. The authors send out a warning that discontent amongst international students can only make institutions further vulnerable, and pose challenges that can be potentially 'income damaging' (Nyland *et al.*, 2013, p. 37).

The lack of quality institutions in the home countries of the international students was not adequately picked up during the international student crisis in Australia. Rather, international students were blamed for taking away opportunities from local students through the admission processes for certain courses because of their ability to pay higher fees. Students were blamed for the rise in the rental market since Australian landlords preferred international students who were willing to pay higher prices for housing close to universities. This was despite research in Melbourne, showing students chose to live in suburbs that offered affordable rental options, most of which were also identified by locals as crime hubs (Babacan, Pyke, Bhathal, Gill, Grossman, and Bertone, 2010).

Nevertheless, 'international students' in Australian society began to be looked on as 'invaders', as young people who were here to stay, particularly as several degrees offered pathways to permanent residency in Australia. This debate left many in the Australian community incapable of viewing international students as lonely and vulnerable individuals who were often unable to speak the local language, had no local social connections and were indebted to financial institutions in their home countries or their families for the only opportunity they might ever have to receive a quality education such as that offered in Australia5. Anecdotal evidence available through media transcripts reveals that the single biggest factor for Indian international students feeling vulnerable was the lack of empathetic response from their own communities. For instance, the president of the Federation of Indian Associations of Victoria, Vasan Srinivasan, stated:

I have been living here for the last 23 years … but have never experienced any racial slur from the Australians. I have two young daughters; if they were racist, do you think I would have stayed in this country? (Sharma, 2010).

These sorts of comments were problematic for Indian students, because Mr. Vasan Srinivasan received significant funding for the Federation of Indian Association of Victoria to deliver an international student helpline (Indian express, 2009). In doing so, the Australian authorities rewarded those organisations that sided with the Australians. Students who were victims of racist attacks felt that by denying the racist nature of these attacks the individuals running the helpline were refusing to empathise with them. The gap between the Indian students and more established Indian community members widened6 further when some members publicly attended forums and described themselves as the Friends of the Liberal Party of Australia. International students themselves cannot affiliate with political parties as they are not entitled to vote, even though some doctoral students could remain in Australia on an international student visa for over 10 years. When the more established communities of their country of origin flag political loyalties, the international student feels vulnerable, marginalised and under-represented.

In his election policy speech in 2001, Prime Minister John Howard declared a strict policing of immigration (Howard, 2001). He asserted that 'we' would decide how, when, and who came to Australia, and the circumstances in which they arrived. International students from Asia need to present family bank account statements, land and property details, and are usually required to pay a full fee prior to arriving in Australia. These policies demonstrate the desire to accept only wealthier students from developing countries. Like other developed countries, Australia has not extended education support to the most poor or financially needy students. However, because of the high dollar rate, even the wealthier Asian and Indian students can find it difficult to maintain the standards of living to which they were accustomed in their home countries. The students that Australia attracts from developing countries belong to wealthy families and hence are less likely to tolerate and accept discrimination. Many Indian and Chinese students held notions of implicit superiority, and thus, when the news broke out in many parts of the world of Australia's explicit racism, there was an instant downturn in numbers for the simple reason that students influenced their peers back in their home country with their experiences in Australia. Much of the 2010 debate was framed by the national strategy for international education, and was subsequently adopted by the Council of Australian Governments (COAG). During this period the Australian Human Rights Commission (AHRC) identified various limitations in the National Students Strategy by COAG (see Jakubowicz and Monani, 2010, p. 19). These included:

- no strategic goals associated with combating racism (except through an undefined community engagement process that places the onus on the students to become engaged);
- no discussion of access to affordable transport;
- no discussion of access to affordable and appropriate accommodation;
- no affirmation of human rights.

However, on a closer review it was clear that the strategy focused on Australia's bureaucratic, political and economic context, overlooking the international students' needs and interests. For example, provider closure taskforces were to be established in each state to ensure rapid and coordinated support for students in the event of provider closure. Yet to what extent students would be able to get full compensation for the sudden closures of private colleges was uncertain. Anecdotal evidence suggests that some students remained in a limbo about their future in Australia since their visas were linked to their courses of study. The issues are many, and the challenge is to ensure that there is a mechanism in place to ensure that student rights are protected; and by the same token, students also become aware of their own responsibilities. In our previous report we recommended these issues be considered at state and national policy levels (Jakubowicz and Monani, 2010).

Revisiting Human Rights for International Students in Australia

Australia is one of the first countries to bring the international student human rights framework into the forefront of the human rights and public policy agenda. Australia is also the first country to have experienced an international student revolt in 2009, hence bringing about a human rights approach to international student education in Australia is an ongoing priority. On 4th October 2012 the Australian Human Rights Commission (AHRC) issued a policy document entitled *Principles to Promote and Protect the Human Rights of International Students*. Along with other colleagues, we advocated the inclusion of various aspects of the *Racial Discrimination Act 1975* into this document. In doing so, the AHRC has affirmed that 'Everyone is entitled to their human rights without discrimination' (AHRC, 2012, 9). International students are now able to access their rights through the *Racial Discrimination Act* irrespective of their visa status. In 2014, a review of the impact of the principles was conducted; the AHRC published the impact statement in January 2015. This review is timely for inclusion and discussion in this paper.

When introducing the *Principles to Promote and Protect the Human Rights of International Students*, the Race Discrimination Commissioner declared that:

Australia has a responsibility to protect the human rights of everyone in the country, which includes international students. This responsibility comes from a number of international human rights treaties that Australia has agreed to uphold. Some international students also experience discrimination, exploitation, or harassment because of their race, colour, culture, religion, language or sex. This can happen in their dealings with, amongst others, health providers, migration agents, real estate agents and employers. In many instances, international students are not aware of their human rights, how their rights are protected under Australian law and what options exist for them to take action when their rights are breached (AHRC, Helen Szoke, Race Discrimination Commissioner, 2012, p. 3).

The *Principles* promotes equality and non-discrimination by establishing four operational frameworks.

- *Enhancing the Human Rights of International Students* – covers equal access to health, accommodation, safe and affordable public transport, crisis-management and support opportunities for issues arising in the home country of the students.
- *Ensuring all international students have access to human rights and freedom from discrimination* – includes information on the complaint process, governing bodies, tenancy rights and responsibilities, and access to appropriate legal advice.
- *Understanding the diverse needs of international students* – involves ethical research with international students to develop appropriate and responsive policy, research focusing on the narratives of international students' experience of discrimination and racially motivated crime, and publicly reporting on how

information about the numbers and causes of international student deaths is being utilised to ensure the safety and well-being of international students.

- *Empowering international students during their stay in Australia* – recommends engaging with international students and various stakeholders to improve study outcomes, using social media portals and websites such as 'Study in Australia' for presenting information on resources and services, creating awareness about sexual health and well-being, increasing cultural competency, and establishing ongoing engagement opportunities between international students and mainstream local communities.

Several areas identified in Sections 6.3 and 6.4 of our previous report have now been interwoven into this in-depth policy document. In particular, the aspect of developing a strong research base about cultural diversity and racism (Jakubowicz and Monani, 2010, p. 21) has now been addressed through the third human rights principle.

Reading the current human rights issues facing international students in Australia today, 'racism and racial discrimination' emerges as one of the top three human rights issues alongside employment and accommodation. In particular, Indian, Sri Lankan and Nepalese students used the AHRC platform to make formal race-related complaints (AHRC, 2015, p.10). It is clear that the mechanism of a complaints process through the AHRC has now revealed that extent, nature and ethnic backgrounds of the international students. Prior to the AHRC principles in action there was no real way of knowing and managing data on the international student community. Hence a fully informed evidence-based approach is now being utilised by the AHRC which will ultimately impact the way in which international students are supported in Australia.

The *Principles* has helped to deal with the complexity of the relationship between the state (Australia) and the international student as a potential international aid recipient, citizen, consumer and exporter. Marginson interviewed students about their hostile information exchanges with immigration authorities, involving significant delays on extension of student visas, administrative inefficiency and inconsistent and incorrect advice (Marginson, 2012, p. 505). The main intention of the *Principles* has been to assist students by ensuring that they have the right to take action where they have experienced profound distress. Racially based exclusion was a key dimension of foreign and immigration policy until the 1970s, and the residues of a racialised worldview remain prevalent in some parts of Australian society. In Section 2.1 of our report, dealing with the Colombo Plan and the end of White Australia in the 1950s, we provide an overview of the invitation extended to international students in Australia. The end of White Australia occurred in a series of steps. In 1958 the old dictation test was removed and in 1965 the residency requirement for Asians to apply for citizenship was reduced. In 1966 Australian signed the *International Convention on the Elimination of All Forms of Racial Discrimination* (ICERD), and in 1967 Australians voted to include Indigenous people as full citizens and assign responsibility for their wellbeing to the Commonwealth. By 1973 the racial preferences contained in the *Migration Act* were removed. In 1976 the *Racial Discrimination Act* outlawed (but did not make criminal) discrimination on the basis of race, reflecting both the ICERD implementation and the Australian reservation, which rejected the criminalisation of either discrimination or hate speech. This reservation continues to affect policy and government and police capacities to prosecute racism. The UN CERD Committee expressed serious concern about this continuing reservation during the Australian Government appearance before it in August 2010. Despite this, the sequence of both international and national acts, often extended by state-based legislation, cemented into policy discourse the recognition that the racialised worldview of White Australia, with its implicit hierarchies of colour and unchangeable barriers of cultural difference, was no longer acceptable. Australia was becoming a country that acknowledged a racist past, but was now intent on building a non-racist egalitarian future (Jakubowicz 1997/2010, as cited in Jakubowicz and Monani, 2010, p. 6). The *Principles* (AHRC, 2012) is now another successful milestone in these series of initiatives.

The *Principles* clarifies that international student rights are not linked to the visa status of the student. In our 2010 report, we argued for a national compact between students, institutions and government that could require sign on, performance and review. The main premise of the AHRC is to work in collaboration with several stakeholders responsible for addressing the issues and concerns faced by international students. The *Principles* offers a national compact model that consults, engages and reviews student needs on an ongoing basis along with the students and a number of stakeholders (AHRC, 2012, p. 14). More importantly, the AHRC is currently struggling to 'elevate the importance of principles to people overseas such as education agents', and much of their work in the area of wide adoption of the principles by universities has remained largely stagnant (AHRC, 2015).

According to Nyland *et al.* (2013), the efficacy of the Overseas Student Ombudsman (OSO) remains doubtful. The OSO has refused to critically evaluate the international education industry (Nyland, *et al.*, 2013, p. 26). Unlike the OSO, the AHRC provided scholars and stakeholders with a platform to bridge the gap with international students. The AHRC engagement strategy was a multi-tiered and collaborative approach. It did not shy away from acknowledging and accepting the flawed export education market and the humiliation that its victims experienced. Marginson (2012) points out that international students are systematically excluded from entitlements available to local students, such as subsidised transport, free medical care, student loans, and higher degree scholarships. Indeed there are no minimum benchmarks in relation to service quality, either for local or for international students. Thus international students pay more for the same education than local students and are more vulnerable to under-provision (Marginson, 2012, p. 503).

Universities and colleges need to engage with local radio to develop programming that can respond to international student issues. One example of good practice is 2SER Radio, which is a joint initiative between the University of Technology Sydney and Macquarie University. At the start of the student protests in Melbourne, one of the authors of this paper, Devaki Monani, launched 'Humaari Awaarz' (Our Voice) in Hindi on the not-for-profit, community radio station 3CR. This program covered topics of racism amongst Indian and Australian cricketers in Melbourne, as well as the student protests, and gave representation to the voices of many Indians in Melbourne. Unfortunately, once the producer relocated, the show could not be continued, because Indian students with limited resources did not have the time or financial support to carry it forward. Programs like this have great potential for Indian students as they give them the opportunity to express themselves in a non-judgemental environment with a pure, not for profit intent. They can add to the stream of shows supported by the Special Community Broadcasting Service (SBS)7.

In addition to radio content development, we also argued in our 2010 report for local Facebook and Twitter sites to become ways of building community, developing networks and keeping information flowing. The AHRC has now implemented this recommendation in its fourth principle of 'Empowering international students during their stay in Australia by using social media' as a key component of information sharing and promotion. This move is particularly appropriate for engaging with youth as it provides a more interactive platform for students to give feedback on the information they have received. The AHRC have currently not considered working with broadcast media. In our previous report we recommended a reality TV show on international students that follows them across the world, explores their experiences, and tracks their fights against scams and exploitation, as well as showing them enjoying the benefits of international education. We would like to see this production take place with a rights focus, and see a commercial channel or an international production house taking this plan forward. Hopefully, this show would do more than show Indians how 'dumb, drunk and racist' Australians are considered (see the ABC show, 2012). Ideally it would reflect the marginalisation of international students and challenge bureaucracy and corruption in relation to higher education opportunities for international students. The movement behind the *Principles* is still in its infancy. However, it is bringing us closer to achieving a more humane understanding of engaging with international students.

CONCLUSION

International students remain a whole-of-society challenge, because they not only generate a whole-of-society benefit, but also reflect an intense vulnerability. They often carry a burden of expectation and emotional and financial investment from family that renders them wary of testing the capacity of the Australian justice and human rights system to protect them. So while there are some representative bodies that can articulate their situations, often, individual students have little if any contact with them, while experiencing a deep reluctance to use them. The dynamic around the human rights of students illuminates the critical importance of the institutions of state and civil society recognising and reflecting their specific circumstances and needs, and ensuring that the structures that citizens may take for granted are in fact pro-active in ensuring the rights of student sojourners.

Policy determination requires open conversations, stakeholder engagement and social change policies. Australian governments need to ensure that international students continue to experience opportunities in Australian society as active participants in learning and social interaction. Given Australia's history, whole-of-government, cross-society, collaborative action can ensure optimum outcomes for Australia, specific stakeholders, and the students themselves. The *Principles* and the commitment reflected by the AHRC and individual scholars are designed to bring this about. Brand Australia in international student markets will need to reflect quality, diversity, justice and rights, not just 'fun in the sun' or a ticket to play and stay (Jakubowicz, 2010).

Footnotes

[1] Australia's education system encompasses four diverse sectors: English language intensive courses for overseas students (ELICOS) which deals with preparing students with English language competency and providing pathways to other more sophisticated courses; schools, both government and non-government; vocational education and training (VET), which consists of technical colleges, dual sector universities and private colleges providing technical and apprenticeship training programs; and higher education, which is the largest sector for international students, enrolling predominantly in universities (IEAC, 2013, p. 10).

[2] Because the VET courses in some cases gave maximum points to migrate to Australia, many Indian and Chinese students between 2005 and 2009 chose to enrol in those courses. The courses were run and managed by the TAFE sector as well as the private colleges. Section 2.2 of the Jakubowicz and Monani (2010, p. 6) report discusses the creation of the international industry in greater depth.

[3] The Australia India Institute (AII) was officially launched in New Delhi on 1 September 2009 by the then Deputy Prime Minister, Julia Gillard. In late 2009, the Australian Government Department of Education, Employment and Workplace Relations (DEEWR) provided just over $8 million to the Australia India Institute over three years. The University of Melbourne contributed $1.75 million in cash and in kind. The Australia India Institute aims to establish collaborative research projects on topics of mutual interest, to increase the professional linkages between Australia and India and to help Australians better understand contemporary India (AII, Annual Report, 2010).

[4] *The Age* newspaper reports that the helpline set up by Mr Vasan Srinivasan of the Federation of Indian Association of Victoria (FIAV) remains unattended. The Federation of Indian Association of Victoria receives funding to support students, because they are the peak community organisation in Victoria. The FIAV continues to deny that the attacks had any racist elements. See: http://www.theage.com.au/national/indian-students-fearful-after-murder-20100105-lras.html. This article also lists the names of students who lost their lives in the Melbourne attack.

[5] By early 2009, the resentment and anger amongst Indian students in

Victoria rose, and on 31 May 2009 an estimated crowd of 5000 gathered on the streets of Melbourne. The placards expressed the extreme vulnerability of Indian students in Australia with slogans such as 'unite against racism' and 'safety down under'. Taxi drivers had been expressing their distress and safety concerns since 2008 (Robertson, 2013, p. 1468). Indian student taxi drivers were looked on as problematic elements responsible for taking jobs away from Australian permanent resident taxi drivers.

[6] Devaki Monani attended a meeting for the welfare of international students in collaboration with the Australia India Solidarity Group, Bharat Times and Victorian Multicultural Commission, on 14 June 2009 at West Footscray. The meeting also had Labor MP Marsha Thompson as an observer. The support for Indian students at the meeting was lacking. The majority of the attendees was of the opinion that Australia is not a racist country.

[7] There has recently been an increase in everyday Hindi radio live streaming of Indi Pop Bollywood music and news from India through SBS, Pop Desi (SBS, 2013). However, SBS Hindi radio programming only reports on local news and brings music from home to listeners in Australia. What continues to remain absent is an Indian radio program that offers critical perspectives about the issues faced by Indian migrants to Australia, particularly the more recent and ongoing arrivals of international students.

REFERENCES

1. ABC 2012, 'Dumb, drunk and racist', available at: www.abc.net.au/tv/**dumbdrunkracist**/episodes/. Accessed 17 March 2013.
2. Australian Government 2008, 'International student data 2008' available at https://internationaleducation.gov.au/research/International-Student-Data/Pages/InternationalStudentData2008.aspx#1 Accessed 1 November 2015.
3. Australian Government 2009, 'International student data 2009' available at https://internationaleducation.gov.au/research/International-Student-Data/Pages/InternationalStudentData2009.aspx#1 Accessed 1 November 2015.
4. Australian Human Rights Commission, AHRC 2015, 'International Students Human Rights: a review of the principles and the issues', https://www.humanrights.gov.au/sites/default/files/document/publication/2015_IS_ReviewReport%20.pdf, Accessed on 17 September, 2015.
5. Australian Human Rights Commission, AHRC 2012, 'The principles to promote and protect the human rights of international students' www.**humanrights**.gov.au/racial.../international_students_**principles**.pdf, Accessed 17 October 2012.
6. Australia India Institute (AII), 2010, Annual Report, www.aii.unimelb.edu.au/sites/.../aus**india**%20**annual**%20**report**_0.pdfAccessed 17 March 2013.
7. Baas, M. 2009, 'Curry bashing: Racism, violence and alien space invaders', *Economic and Political Weekly*, vol. 44, no. 34, pp. 37-42.
8. Babacan, H., Pyke, J., Bhathal, A., Gill, G., Grossman, M., and Bertone, S. 2010, 'The Community Safety of International Students in Melbourne: A Scoping Study', Institute for Community, Ethnicity and Policy Alternatives (ICEPA), Victoria University, February 2010. Available at: http://vuir.vu.edu.au/15491/1/The_Community_Safety_of_International_Students_in_Melb_A_Scoping_Study.pdf, Accessed 25 September 2010.
9. Baird, B. 2010, 'Stronger, simpler, smarter ESOS: supporting international students: review of the Education Services for Overseas Students (ESOS) Act 2000: final report, February 2010'. Available at: https://internationaleducation.gov.au/Regulatory-Information/Education-Services-for-Overseas-Students-ESOS-Legislative-

Framework/ESOSReview/Documents/ESOS_REview_Final_Report_Feb_2010_pdf.pdf Accessed 1 November 2015.

10. Birrell, R.J., Healy, E.J., and Kinnaird, R.T. 2007, 'Cooks galore and hairdressers aplenty', *People and Place*, vol. 15, no. 1, pp. 30-44.
11. Council of Australian Governments (COAG); 2010, International Students Strategy for Australia 2010-2014, available at: https://www.coag.gov.au/node/307, Accessed 25 September, 2010.
12. Dunn, K. M., Gandhi, V., Pelleri, D., & Maeder-Han, K. 2011a, 'Racism in the tertiary education sector : a case of Indian student attacks in Australia', *Geography Bulletin*, vol. 43, no. 3, pp. 7-16.
13. Dunn, K.M., Pelleri D. and Maeder-Han K. 2011b, 'Attacks on Indian students: The commerce of denial in Australia', *Race & Class*, vol.52, no. 4, pp.71–88. doi: http://dx.doi.org/10.1177/0306396810396603
14. Federation of Indian Associations of Victoria 2009, 'Violence, Against International Students and finding ways to deal with it: Brain Storming Luncheon Session-Where to from here?' Unpublished Notes, Forum organised with the support of Australia Indian Solidarity Group Inc. Bharat Times and Victorian Multicultural Commission.
15. Howard, J. 2001, Election Policy Speech for the 2001 Federal Election held on the 28 October 2001, available at: http://www.abc.net.au/lateline/content/2001/s422692.htm Accessed 17 March, 2013.
16. IEAC 2013, Advice from the International Education Advisory Council on Australia-Educating Globally, available at: https://aei.gov.au/IEAC2/theCouncilsReport/Documents/Australia%20%E2%80%93%20Educating%20Globally%20FINAL%20REPORT.pdf, Accessed 2 April 2013.
17. The Indian Express 2009, 'Helpline launched to protect Indian students in Australia', *The Indian Express*, http://archive.indianexpress.com/news/helpline-launched-to-protect-indian-students-in-australia/459963/
18. Jakubowicz, A. 2010, 'On the beach: Selling Australia as a land or as a people' available at: http://andrewjakubowicz.com/publications/on-the-beach-selling-australia-as-a-land-or-as-a-people/ Accessed 2 April 2013.
19. Jakubowicz, A. and Monani, D. 2010, 'International Student Futures in Australia: A Human Rights Perspective on Moving Forward to Real Action', Occasional Paper 6/2010, The Academy of Social Sciences in Australia, Canberra 2010.

20. Marginson, S. 2012, 'Including the other: regulation of the human rights of mobile students in a nation-bound world', *Higher Education*, vol.63, no.4, pp.497-512. doi: http://dx.doi.org/10.1007/s10734-011-9454-7
21. Mason, G. 2012a, "I am tomorrow': Violence against Indian students in Australia and political denial', *Australian & New Zealand Journal of Criminology*, vol.45, no. 1, pp. 4–25. doi: http://dx.doi.org/10.1177/0004865811431330
22. Mason, G. 2012b, 'Naming the 'R' word in racial victimization: Violence against Indian students in Australia', *International Review of Victimology*, vol. 18, no. 1, pp. 39–56. doi: http://dx.doi.org/10.1177/0269758011422474
23. Millar, P. 2009, 'Indian Student March in Protest Against the Attacks', *The Age* 31 May 2009, available at: http://www.theage.com.au/national/indian-students-march-in-protest-against-attacks-20090531-brhj.html, Accessed 17 March, 2013.
24. Millar, P. and Doherty, B. 2009, 'Indian Anger Boils over', *TheSydney Morning Herald*, 1st June, http://www.smh.com.au/national/indian-anger-boils-over-20090531-brrm.html, Accessed 29 September 2015.
25. Nelson, J. K. 2013, 'Denial of racism and its implications for local action', *Discourse & Society*, vol.24, no. 1, pp.89-109. doi: http://dx.doi.org/10.1177/0957926512463635
26. Nyland, C., Forbes-Mewett, H. and Hartel, C. 2013, 'Governing the international student experience: Lessons from the Australian international education model', *Academy of Management Learning and Education*, vol. 12, no.4, pp. 656-673. doi: http://dx.doi.org/10.5465/amle.2012.0088
27. Press Trust of India 2009, 'Yet Another Indian Attacked in Australia', available at: http://www.ndtv.com/article/diaspora/yet-another-indian-attacked-in-australia-4667, Accessed 17 March 2013.
28. Robertson, S. 2013, 'Campus, city, networks and nation: Student-migrant activism as socio-spatial experience in Melbourne', Australia, *International Journal of Urban and Regional Research*, vol.37, no.3, pp. 972-988. doi: http://dx.doi.org/10.1111/j.1468-2427.2012.01204.x
29. Robertson, S. 2008, 'Residency, citizenship and belonging: choice and uncertainty for students-turned-migrants in Australia', *International Journal of Asia-Pacific Studies*, vol.4, no.1, pp.97-119.

30. SBS 2013, Announcement of the new SBS Radio Schedule, on-air 29th April 2013, http://www.sbs.com.au/shows/popdesi/ available at: http://www.sbs.com.au/radio/schedule2013 accessed 1 April 2013.
31. Sharma, P. 201, 'Do you Speak Australian', available at: http://www.outlookindia.com/article/do-you-speak-australian/264016, Accessed 12 October 2015.
32. Singh, S. 2011, 'Indian students in Melbourne: Challenges to multiculturalism' *Journal of Intercultural Studies*, Vol. 32, No. 6, pp. 673-689. Available at: https://researchbank.rmit.edu.au/eserv/rmit:14041/n2006029271.pdf Accessed 1 November 2015. doi: http://dx.doi.org/10.1080/07256868.2011.618110
33. Waters, J. and Macbean, N. 2009, 'Anger grows over Indian student bashings', *Sydney Morning Herald*, 29th April, available at: http://www.abc.net.au/news/2009-05-29/anger-grows-over-indian-student-bashings/1697904, Accessed 29 September 2015.

CHAPTER 5

HUMAN RIGHTS VIOLATIONS AND MENTAL ILLNESS: IMPLICATIONS FOR ENGAGEMENT AND ADHERENCE

Magnus Mfoafo-M'Carthy and Stephanie Huls

Lyle S. Hallman Faculty of Social Work, Wilfrid Laurier University, Kitchener, Ontario, Canada

ABSTRACT

The literature review identifies and examines human rights violations experienced by individuals with mental illness on a global level. In addition, the intent is to explore how current legislation either reinforces or supports these violations. The authors conducted an extensive review of the existing literature on mental health and human rights violations. Keywords were used to exhaust databases on this subject matter and to collect data, interpretations,

Citation: Magnus Mfoafo-M'Carthy and Stephanie Huls *SAGE Open* https://doi.org/10.1177/2158244014526209 First Published March 10, 2014

and government publications on mental health and human rights. Individuals with mental illness are experiencing human rights violations on a global scale both within and outside of psychiatric institutions. These violations include denial of employment, marriage, procreation, and education; malnutrition; physical abuse; and negligence. This information was reviewed and compiled into the following article, along with interpretations of current implications and suggestions for future research. It is evident that more supports need to be instilled, especially within the context of low- and middle-income countries lacking adequate staffing and accessible services. Furthermore, legislation needs to be modified, updated, or created with relevant systems in place to make these laws enforceable.

Keywords: psychiatry, behavioral sciences, rights, criminology, social sciences, sociology of health and illness, sociology, sociology of mental health, social work

INTRODUCTION

It is estimated that approximately 500 million individuals globally are affected by mental illness (International Labour Organisation, 2000). The World Health Organization (WHO; 2012) speculates that depression alone will rank second highest in the global burden of disease by 2020. In Canada, it is believed that mental illness will affect approximately 20% of the population in their lifetime (Regehr & Glancy, 2010). According to recent figures, the direct and indirect economic cost of mental illness is estimated to range from 48 to 50 billion dollars (Lim, Jacobs, Ohinwaa, Schopflower, & Dewa, 2008). This significant expense is not expected to decrease, but rather increase over time and moreover affect the labor force while straining the world economy (International Labour Organisation, 2000). Given the inherent vulnerability of those with mental health issues and the stigma of being a burden on society, it is essential that human rights are acknowledged for this population and also that human rights violations are globally recognized and curtailed. Reports show that individuals with mental health issues are maltreated and marginalized due to the nature of their illness. This trend is attributed to a number of factors including culture, ethnicity, religion, language, and poverty.

Although there are ongoing discourses over the treatment of individuals diagnosed with mental illness and those exhibiting mental health symptoms around the world, it is important to note that the severity of abuse varies from one culture to another based on inherent beliefs. For instance, just as in certain cultures, women are not accorded equal rights and are relegated to the background, some cultures perceive the mentally ill as not being part of normal society; therefore, those with mental illness are subjected to varying forms of abuse. The maltreatment and abuse of the mentally ill have been widely captured in literature (Awad & Voruganti, 2008).

The focus of this study was to explore the literature on how mental health issues affect the rights of individuals with mental illness. The rationale for this literature review is to examine globally the human rights abuses of mental health issues and shed light on its impact on economies worldwide. Furthermore, this review intends to explore options to enhance the treatment adherence to practices that will improve the conditions of individuals marginalized due to their mental health condition.

Simply put, the question to be explored will be to "examine how human right abuses/violations affect the mentally ill globally." The study will review the literature as a foundation to our findings and then give recommendations.

LITERATURE REVIEW

Mental health embodies the integration of psychological, emotional, and social harmony. It encompasses ones quality of life and general well-being. Culture, language, ethnicity, and religion play a significant role in the interpretation of mental health causes. Studies show that being diagnosed with or exhibiting symptoms of mental health issues exposes a person or community to labeling. Such people are branded as socially inadequate and are associated with resulting shame, humiliation, and loss of face. In most cultures, groups with low positions in hierarchical social structure experience high rates of mental health problems (Rosenfield, 2012). In modern society, connection with mental illness exposes a person to levels of medicalization and marginalization.

In certain cultures, mental illness is perceived as a sign of weakness or curse. This negative connotation results in family members distancing themselves from or maltreating those who are ill. Furthermore, those with mental illness are deemed unproductive and perceived as not contributing to the upkeep of the family. It is also argued that the lack of resources in African countries as well as in other developing countries makes it difficult for governments to enhance the treatment or improve the conditions of the mentally ill, which inevitably exposes many to abuses.

Over the years, research has shown that stigma plays a significantly debilitating role in the treatment of the mentally ill (Barke, Nyarko, & Klecha, 2011; Link et al., 2001). The literature on stigma describes how individuals with disabilities, including mental illness, often find themselves on the periphery of society. This circumstance is deemed "an attribute that is deeply discrediting" (Goffman, 1963, p. 3). Such individuals are marginalized, mistreated, and often stigmatized in society. Individuals with mental illness are often viewed as "strangers" where this characteristic of "strangeness" frequently results in social distancing (Baumann, 2007). Unfortunately, as this treatment is prevalent in both the industrial and developing countries, the argument could be made that governments are failing to put in place measures or systems to enhance the treatment of the mentally ill. Thus, very limited progress has been made to improve the lot of the mentally ill who are ostracized in society.

METHOD

The intent of the study was to review the global literature on the subject and examine how different cultures respond to this topic. The search criteria included papers on the treatment of the mentally ill in various countries throughout the world. The major databases used to identify the articles were PubMed, PubMed Central Canada, , African Journals Online, Scholars Portal, EBSCOHost, ProQuest, PsycINFO, and . The WHO database was also examined for the purpose of this venture. Only papers published in English were allowed for consideration in this review. The review examined peer-reviewed published articles, policy papers, as well as government publications since 2000. Keywords or statements of combinations of these terms were included in the search along with librarian assistance. Keywords (and a combination of these words) included mental health*, mental illness*, rights, human rights*, psychiatry*, human rights violations and mental illness, colonial psychiatry, and deprivation of liberty. This method yielded numerous articles related to mental illness and human rights.

In the process of searching the literature, keywords (rather than titles and abstracts) were used to examine the documents for matches. All of the references were recorded and stored electronically using refworks. Tracking was conducted after reading the papers and bibliographies were reviewed for further documents. The criteria for inclusion included both qualitative and quantitative articles on human rights and mental illness. For the purpose of this study, literature reviews and meta-analyses were not included. In the event that the same data were reported by two different papers, only the first report has been included. Papers published in peer-reviewed journals and gray literature were included.

Given this study's objective on mental health and human rights violations, certain articles were excluded from review, in cases where it was determined that the study, article topic, or demographic lay outside of the purview of this article. Information was recorded down in the form of notes, entered into a literature table, and categorized by themes which are represented in the following "Results" section.

In total, approximately 1,000 articles, book chapters, and dissertations were found. Of these, 200 papers were reviewed because they either focused or had some discussions on mental health and human rights abuses. Articles were excluded for numerous reasons including the following: reported the same data as other papers, did not explore issues being looked at, literature reviews and meta-analysis. Nevertheless, the most significant were those that focused on mental health and human rights or articles that reflected research conducted internationally. Of the resulting articles, book chapters, and theses elicited from the search, 37 articles were deemed appropriate and utilized for the purpose of adequately addressing human rights and mental illness. Thus, from the 200 papers reviewed, a preliminary review narrowed the findings to 37 articles and government publications—31 articles and 6 government documents. Articles that did not specifically focus on human rights and mental illness were excluded. Theses and book chapters that did not directly address the issues of human rights and mental illness were excluded as well.

RESULTS

Illiteracy and Mental Health

The findings emphasized the importance of taking note of the co-morbidity of illiteracy and mental illness. This has been linked to an increased likelihood of experiencing human rights violations, as illiteracy can adversely affect the ability to reach out for formal supports. In India, illiteracy has a greater influence on women than men, where despite free education, women are less likely to be encouraged to attend school (Vijayalakshmi, Ramachandra, Reddemma, & Math, 2012).

Stigmatization may also play a role in the educational opportunities for those with mental health issues as reflected by the high incidence of dropouts. Students with mental illness can face teasing, harassment, and prejudice from their peers, and arguably, their teachers (WHO, 2010).

Development Programs and Mental Health

Despite the creation of development programs intended to improve the lives of the world's most vulnerable populations, such programs exclude, often intentionally, the mentally ill as part of their recipients. A striking example is the Bangladesh Vulnerable Group Development Program, which stipulates that service users needed to be "mentally and physically sound" to access the program (WHO, 2010, p. 3). UN Secretary-General Ban Ki-moon clarifies the implications of this exclusion:

The rate of mental disorders and the need for care is highest among disadvantaged people—yet these are precisely the groups with the lowest access to appropriate services. At the same time, fear of stigma leads many to avoid seeking care. The consequences are enormous in terms of disability, human suffering and economic loss. We have a pressing obligation to scale up care and services for mental disorders, especially among the disadvantaged, while stepping up efforts to protect the human rights of those affected. (WHO, 2010, p. 7)

This inequality even extends to emergency and disaster situations. After Hurricane Katrina in the United States, Federal Emergency Management Agency (FEMA) allegedly discriminated against those with mental health issues based on the belief that these individuals were dangerous (WHO, 2010).

Furthermore, the unemployment rate for mentally ill individuals is approximately 70% to 90%; yet, development programs that create job opportunities often omit these individuals in their planning and enactment of projects (WHO, 2010).

Prison Settings and Mental Health Court

In fact, individuals with mental illness who are receiving care in psychiatric institutions suffer greater human rights violations than individuals who are in correctional facilities. While those in psychiatric care may not have committed a crime, they are subjected to a similar removal of rights and liberties as with a criminal offender. Comparable with their criminal counterparts, individuals with mental illness are perceived as "more dangerous [and] less competent"; two qualities that are not welcome within general society (Diseth & Hoglend, 2011, p. 393).

An additional area of concern regards individuals determined to be not criminally responsible and therefore detained either in the psychiatric section within a prison or in a designated wing within a hospital setting. According to Fellner (2006), the majority of incarcerated individuals in the United States of America are struggling with mental health issues:

Indeed, one of the primary roles of prisons in the United States today is to house the mentally ill. Prisoners have rates of mental illness that are two to four times greater than the rates of members of the general public. (p. 1)

Housing of the mentally ill in prisons can be partially attributed to the lack of community-based services that were to be developed as a result of hospital closures (Fellner, 2006).

Regardless of the environment, the intent is to provide psychiatric treatment to accommodate the unique needs of the prison population. However, issues arise, such as the cohabitation of varying degrees of mental health severities, lack of appropriate professional training for staff members (Naudts et al., 2005), disciplining individuals instead of providing psychiatric support, verbal abuse and neglect from staff, and the exacerbation of mental illness due to confinement (Fellner, 2006). As symptoms of mental illness may be viewed by untrained prison staff as behavioral issues, these prisoners can build lengthy disciplinary records, which could potentially negatively affect their release time (Fellner, 2006; Matejkowski, Caplan, & Cullen, 2010). Reintegration into society and the opportunity for parole are often contingent upon program participation; yet, these classes infrequently consider the additional support that individuals with mental illness may require. In addition, programs may not address certain life skills that are unique to those with mental illness such as compliance with medication (Matejkowski et al., 2010).

Szasz (as cited in Breeding, 2006) suggests that those with mental illness who have been involuntarily admitted may be treated worse than their criminal counterparts:

A prisoner will be released after he completes his sentence, and possibly before. A mental patient may be required to undergo a change in his "inner personality"—a change that may be induced by measures far more intrusive than anything permitted in a jail—before the psychiatric authorities let him go. And they may never let him go. Commitment, unlike a sentence, is for an indefinite period. (p. 252)

Breeding (2006) further highlights the contradiction of justice: Individuals in mental health court are guilty until proven innocent. The added danger is that an individual's refutation of a diagnosis can be interpreted as a symptom of their mental illness.

Physical Health and Mental Health

The gap in service provon for those with mental illness transfers into the health care system as well. Those with mental illness are at a higher risk of acquiring considerable physical health problems, which potentially shortens their lifespan (WHO, 2010). Human rights violations occur frequently within health care settings, if these services are available to those with mental health issues at all (P. Hunt & Mesquita, 2006). An example of this neglect can be found in a shelter in Indonesia that houses individuals with mental illness. During a 7-month time period, 181 of the 644 individuals died of diarrhea or lack of nourishment (WHO, 2010).

Tarantola (2007) points out a cyclical relationship between physical and mental health. Those who experience human rights violations are at an increased risk of experiencing physical health concerns. Poor health, in turn, increases individuals' susceptibility to human rights violations (Tarantola, 2007).

Decon-Making Ability and Mental Illness

Callaghan and Ryan (2012) review the practices of compulsory treatment in Australia and stated that this form of treatment should only concern individuals who are unable to make independent decons. While this could equally result in a human rights violation, the authors suggest the following criteria for an individual who is able to make decons: ability to comprehend, recall, repeat, and utilize the information presented to them (Boyle, 2011; Callaghan & Ryan, 2012). In 2004, the European Court of Human Rights emphasized that temporarily detaining an individual who does not offer consent, nor has the capacity to do so, could be considered a deprivation of liberty. In response, the Deprivation of Liberty Safeguards was implemented to ensure the rights of individuals in this position (Boyle, 2011).

Social/Cultural Stigmatization of Mental Illness

While medical conditions typically have tests, lists of symptoms, and clear treatment methods, mental illness are not as "tangible" and can therefore be viewed as less credible, which only furthers stigmatization (Loo, Trollor, Alonzo, Rendina, & Kavess, 2010, p. 423). This lack of understanding of mental illness conducted through a biomedical lens rather than from the perspective of "social justice, quality of life, human rights and human security" (Giacaman et al., 2011, p. 547). This also raises the concern of applying Western standards and mental health techniques in countries where there are alternative understanding of mental illness, descriptive language, and treatment techniques. Some countries continue to rely on traditional and/or faith healers, family, and community to remedy their mental health issues (Giacaman et al., 2011; Vijayalakshmi et al., 2013). Davar (2008) suggests that the West's insistence that medication is more effective than counseling in low-income countries may be influenced by underlying tones of colonialism or even as a means to create further profit for the pharmaceutical industry.

Further to not knowing their rights, individuals with mental health concerns are often stigmatized by societal and cultural views. From "not . . . a human being at all" to being seen as "facing punishment for their past actions," individuals struggle to find support within their community, not to mention on a higher systemic level (Drew et al., 2011, p. 1669). The occurrence of stigmatization is exacerbated with the viewpoint that the cause of mental illness is internal and not something that can be addressed from a social or systemic shift (Kogstad, 2009). In India, the principle of karma can impede those with mental illness from reaching out for support due to its implied culpability (Vijayalakshmi et al., 2013). Society also stereotypes those with mental illness as feeble, aggressive, of lower intelligence, or even victim to paranormal influences (WHO, 2010).

As evident throughout this review, it is important to consider culture when studying the types of treatments offered in different communities. For example, out of the 25 nations reviewed by the World Health Organization's Assessment Instrument for Mental Health Systems (WHO-AIMS), Korea ranked third in terms of involuntary admissions to hospital. This has created concern regarding forcible admission; however, it is suggested that these numbers must be viewed through a cultural lens. Bola, Park, and Kim (2011) indicate that these numbers can be attributed to the fact that stigma prevents individuals from voluntarily accessing treatment; also, these services may not be adequately supported financially for individuals.

Addressing Stigma

Given the scope of individuals who are affected and how this relates to national levels of success and accountability, implementing education and awareness programs is essential to decreasing stigmatization (Mwanza et al., 2011). However, it should also be noted that stigmatization is a primary cause of human rights violations and that labeling individuals can in fact cause further harm to this population. This gap seems to have been addressed on a grassroots level by nongovernmental organizations (NGOs) and community efforts through support groups and implementation of traditional healing practices (Dhanda & Narayan, 2007).

The concept of spreading awareness is imperative to normalizing a stigmatized population, as lack of infrastructure and monitoring in psychiatric institutions leaves the public unaware of the aforementioned human rights violations (P. Hunt & Mesquita, 2006). However, the notion of education surrounding mental health standards faces a financial barrier, as this agenda is much more accessible to countries that are recognized as high income. Through their research, Drew et al. (2011) identify that the majority of low-income and middle-income countries were not adequately equipped to support those needing to access mental health services.

Violations

Violations of individuals diagnosed with mental health disorders vary from one culture/country to another. These violations may be dependent on the cultures of the country in question or the resources available to those countries. For instance, more resources are allotted to the treatment of mental illness in high-income countries than in low-income countries. In high-income countries, it is ensured that trained professionals are available to treat individuals diagnosed with mental illness. To be specific, the income level of the world based on its Gross Domestic Product (GDP) is divided in categories. According to the World Bank, economies are measured by their gross national income (GNI). According to the 2011 GNI, a lower income country was considered USD $1,025 or less; a lower middle-income country was $1,026 to $4,035; an upper middle-income country was $4,036 to $12,475; and a high-income country was $12,476 or more (World Bank Data, 2013). High-income countries are often developed countries; middle-income countries as well as some developing countries contain emerging markets; and low-income countries mostly consist of developing countries.

The violation and stigmatization of individuals diagnosed with mental illness include discrimination surrounding employment, marriage, parenting, and family planning; access to health services; sexual violence; access to housing; entitlement to vote; and access to basic education (Drew et al., 2011; Vijayalakshmi et al., 2013; WHO, 2010). While it may be presumed that these violations are specific to underdeveloped countries, the inability to marry exists in Bulgaria, Russia, Thailand, and India. In Switzerland, though known for its neutrality, applications of nationality can be declined if an individual struggles with intellectual disabilities. In addition, only Canada, Ireland, Italy, and Sweden (out of 63 countries assessed) do not place legal limitations on voting for individuals with mental illness (WHO, 2010).

The violation of the mentally ill has been reported as occurring in a variety of settings ranging from home life to schools, prisons, work environments, and social services (Drew et al., 2011). The traits of the mental health care system are regularly identified as inadequate and emotionally or physically abusive (Cooper, Ssebunnya, Kigozi, Lund, & Flisher, 2010). Individuals are often institutionalized for long periods of time without appropriate cause and are then subjected to conditions that include violence, substandard nutrition and cleanliness, torment, unconsented treatment as extensive as electroconvulsive therapy (ECT; P. Hunt & Mesquita, 2006), loss of dignity (Kogstad, 2009), and sedation as a control method (Mayers, Keet, Winkler, & Flisher, 2010). Violations in Zambia have included denial of food, restriction of movement, poverty due to cost of treatment, and being brought to hospital in chains or in the company of armed officials (Mwanza et al., 2011). Treatment can also fail to involve basic social communication, as some believe that this would not be helpful to an individual with mental health concerns (Kogstad, 2009).

While the Cochrane Review highlights the lack of empirical evidence for the effectiveness of isolation and use of restraint, these practices, along with sedation, are frequently implemented within institutions. The review also references that within the literature, certain qualitative studies have in fact pointed to negative outcomes. Another concern that is equal to the use of possibly nonbeneficial practices is the intent behind the use, as sedation can be implemented for purposes of control rather than as a means of support for the individual (Mayers et al., 2010).

Further violations can be witnessed in a number of different countries. As described by Yamin and Rosenthal (2005), in Accra, Ghana, 300 mentally ill men were housed in a space that was built for 50 individuals and were not provided with treatment. In Hungary, individuals were administered obsolete medication and kept in beds that were caged, thereby limiting their movement. In Turkey, Peru, and Bulgaria, institutions engage in the dangerous practice of unmodified ECT, which does not utilize anesthesia. Certain countries perpetuate human rights violations due to the lack of appropriate and accessible staffing. Less than 50% of hospitals in Bangalore, India, have psychologists available to their patients. Some of these violations occur due to a long-standing history of cultural or faith-based practice regarding treatment of the mentally ill (WHO, 2010). For example, in Somalia, an individual may be placed in a hollow with hyenas. The intent is to scare the "dijinns, or evil spirits" from the person, and therefore the symptoms of mental illness (WHO, 2010, p. 12). Other faith-based or traditional practices can involve restriction of movement through chains or attempts to remove spirits by whipping the mentally ill person (Doku et al., 2011).

These violations extend to accessing of justice, civil, and political rights. In England and Wales, a report by Mind discovered that 60% of individuals with mental illness who approached police regarding a crime felt that the authorities did not treat the report with severity. In certain instances, reports are not documented due to the belief that individuals with mental illness are unreliable (WHO, 2010).

Within the population of individuals with mental disorders, there are subgroups who are at an increased risk of violation. For example, those of varying ethnicities and race are more likely to experience prejudice and women are more likely to be sexually abused and even sterilized without consent (P. Hunt & Mesquita, 2006). Kastrup (2011) notes the disparity between mental health support for those within marginalized populations, as well as the lack of human rights fulfillment.

In 1993, the slogan "Human Rights Are Women's Rights" became a prominent message. During the World Conference on Human Rights in Vienna (Jansen, 2006), it was agreed that violence against women was considered a human rights issue. This practice is most notably seen during times of war, when sexual violence against women can increase and be used as a tool of war. This violence can lead to fear or mental health issues that deter women from being active community members, which further exacerbates the issue of human rights (Jansen, 2006). Violations can also be seen within the very institutions that are meant to support women with mental health issues, such as in Kosovo, where incidents were reported in which women were raped in psychiatric institutions while the violence was witnessed by staff and humanitarian workers (Yamin & Rosenthal, 2005).

Legislation

Despite the issues of mental health violations documented in the literature, it has also been observed that significant legislations are documented pertaining to the treatment of individuals with disability including those with mental disorders. *The Universal Declaration of Human Rights* (UDHR) encompasses 30 articles; however, no articles identify the need for rights around mental health concerns, and only one article (Article 25) alludes to the importance of social service access (The United Nations, n.d.). Instead, information about mental health can be found in the *United Nations Convention on the Rights of Persons with Disabilities*. As defined here, disabilities include "long term . . . mental . . . impairments . . . which in interaction with various barriers may hinder their full and effective participation in society on an equal basis with others" (The United Nations, 2006, Article 1).

To ensure that human rights are honored in relation to mental health, WHO developed the *Mental Health and Human Rights Project*, which focuses on mental health legislation within a global context (WHO, 2006). This project was supplementary to the *United Nations Principles for the Protection of Persons With Mental Illness and the Improvement of Mental Health Care*, which was established in 1991 and created a minimum level of human rights required in mental health practice (WHO, 2005). However, the principles (known as the Mental Illness [MI] Principles) have been critiqued as being ineffective and contrary to the UDHR. It is noted that the MI Principles are not legally binding and fail to institute any form of international supervon (Weissbecker, 2009). The UN Secretary-General stated that they "offer in some cases a lesser degree of protection than that offered by existing human rights treaties, for example, with regard to the requirement for prior informed consent to treatment" (WHO, 2005, p. 14). P. Hunt and Mesquita (2006) indicate that "several international human rights instruments allow for exceptional circumstances in which persons with psychiatric disabilities can be involuntarily admitted to a hospital or other designated institution" (p. 344). However, such vague terms protect the regular occurrence of human rights violations (Kogstad, 2009). The case of *Harry v. Mental Health Review Board* in Australia illustrates an example of improper use of mental health law to alleviate embarrassment from family or communities (Freckelton & McGregor, 2010).

These statements call into question the voice of the service user and whether human rights in regard to mental health are indeed being honored. This concern is exacerbated by the fact that individual countries are able to enact their own regulations, definitions of mental health disorders, and principles. As a result, more than 40% of countries lack a mental health policy and more than 30% of countries lack a mental health program (P.

Hunt & Mesquita, 2006). In some countries such as Zambia, policies exist but are antiquated, offensive, and based on colonial eras (Mwanza et al., 2011). The lack of legislation can also be attributed to the use of traditional and faith-based practices, which often go unregulated (Doku et al., 2011).

In addition, legislation may be put in place to manipulate social participation. According to WHO (2005), "In many countries a diagnosis of personality disorder has been used against vulnerable groups, especially young women, whenever they do not conform with the dominant social, cultural, moral and religious standards" (p. 21). This method of mental health diagnoses is also used for political purposes to attribute personality disorders to those who may be viewed as a nonconformist (WHO, 2005). In addition, in India, women viewed as oppositional can be branded as insane (Davar, 2008). To create uniformity among the concept of mental health, Tarantola (2007)suggests a more holistic understanding, which would include emotional, social, and cultural influence and welfare.

While the intention of establishing universal guidelines such as UDHR, UNCRPD (UN Convention on the Rights of Persons with Disabilities), and MI Principles is important for those within the government and legislative context, this does little to provide information to those who are directly affected. A survey participant from Jordan stated that "the most important right is my right to have the knowledge of all of my rights and to be empowered to [confront] violations against my rights" (Drew et al., 2011, p. 1666). This right to knowledge relies heavily, however, on the assumption that the legislation in fact supports those with mental health issues. Uganda's mental health system is an example of a legislation that is in accordance with international policy; yet, it is criticized for its perpetuation of stigmatization and violation of human rights for those with mental health concerns (Cooper et al., 2010). These guidelines additionally rely heavily on agreement, commitment, compliance, and mutual understanding of the issues of mental health and human rights.

DISCUSSION

Human rights violations not only affect the physical, psychological, emotional, and spiritual well-being of service and nonservice recipients with mental disorders but also significantly influence potential service recipients' access to mental health services, thereby creating a dynamic where not receiving any form of treatment or support may become more desirable (Loo et al., 2010).

Furthermore, culture, religion, and traditional practices play a role regarding which type of mental health treatment is sought out by individuals. Some individuals do not believe that mental illness exists or that only the physical symptoms need to be addressed (McDaid, Knapp, & Raja, 2008). This view can be partially attributed to lack of professional and public knowledge, resulting in the stigmatization of this population.

Absence of resources may be symptomatic of an overlying cause of lower socioeconomic status. While dedication to mental health and humane treatment of these individuals is a noble cause, this may not be feasible in certain countries. Ethiopia is home to 77 million people but only 18 psychiatrists, who are all employed in one hospital, located in the capital city (Alem, Jacobson, & Hanlon, 2008). Even if legislation were put into place, what would be enforced in the rural areas where individuals are not receiving formal care? Bruckner et al. (2011) estimate that 239,000 full-time employees would be required in low- and middle-income countries just to have adequate staffing. A proposed solution is to increase staff presence and emphasize community-based care, which would increase access and honor the human rights of individuals. According to Yamin and Rosenthal (2005),

From a human rights perspective, people are entitled to live in and receive care in the community not because it is more efficient, but because all human beings develop their identities within social contexts, and have rights to work and study, as well as be with friends and family. (p. 297)

Research into *why* human rights violations occur may be beneficial in creating a comprehensive plan to better ensure human rights of those with mental health issues. A psychiatrist in Ghana presents the following dilemma:

. . . people are trying to do their best to help people with mental illness, but when there is inadequacy and all those things set in, we don't intentionally try to violate people's rights. But when you keep someone in the mental hospital and you can't provide for the person, you then of course, you are violating that person's rights. (Doku et al., 2011, p. 18)

Furthermore, it is evident that legislation needs to be created which honors human rights, as there is a clear disparity between experiences of those with mental health concerns and the intent of human rights (Kogstad, 2009). However, it is also clear that these movements be considered within the contextual framework of culture and religion. P. Hunt and Mesquita (2006) suggest that legislation should consider the following when making decons surrounding human rights and mental health: "participation, autonomy, dignity, inclusion, monitoring, and accountability" (p. 332). In response to this need for individual voice, the *International Diploma on Mental Health Law* was conceived, it comprised of an interdisciplinary team including service users and aiming to provide education, awareness, and reform on a country-wide basis (Drew et al., 2011). The Mental Health and Poverty Project (MHaPP) is an initiative focusing on the cyclical nature of poverty and mental health in Ghana, Zambia, South Africa, and Uganda (Mwanza et al., 2011). While more integrated, this initiative solely focuses on African countries, which possibly negates the presence of human rights violations in more "developed" countries and creates further stigmatization for a continent that is already branded by poor global opinion.

Clearly, the prevalent issue of human rights violations in the context of mental health can no longer be ignored. However, given the additional factors and barriers of income status, accessibility, culture, religion, and traditional practices, it will be a challenge to create an understanding and enforcement of universal human rights. To completely dismiss cultural tradition would only contradict another set of human rights, thereby exchanging one form of violation for another. Thus, discussion is necessary regarding how one can balance the rights of traditional or faith-based practice with the UN's view of human rights. This therefore creates the need for both advocates and researchers to continue challenging and embarking on studies that will improve the lot of the mentally ill. For progress to enhance mental health treatment in numerous countries, serious intervention and engagement from governmental bodies are necessary.

Despite these arguments, one should not lose sight of the fact that programs have been introduced in the Western world to improve the treatment of the mentally ill. For example, the work of Winick and others on therapeutic jurisprudence has been designed to shift the treatment of the mentally ill from the medical model to a more collaborative approach. This shift in direction commenced in the 1980s as an interdisciplinary scholarly approach to enhance the treatment of the mentally ill (Winick, 2002, 2006). Since then, a number of interventions have been introduced in the treatment of the seriously mentally ill in the Western world, including Community Treatment Orders (CTOs) or Mandated Outpatient Treatment which legally compels individuals diagnosed with mental illness to follow through with a proposed treatment or else risk being hospitalized (A. M. Hunt, da Silva, Lurie, & Goldbloom, 2007; Kisely, Campbell, Scott, Preston, & Xiao, 2007; Mfoafo-M'Carthy & Williams, 2010). In addition, it should be noted that the study adds to the literature on issues of human rights abuses of the mentally ill and contributes to the discourse. Also, it continues to bring attention to the stigmatization of the mentally ill and the need for more education and understanding of the needs of this marginalized community.

LIMITATION

This review may not be considered exhaustive due to the fact that the literature reviewed were only English language articles, this eliminates the cross-cultural perception of the study as articles in other languages were excluded. Also, all the articles reviewed focused solely on Westernized perception or definition of mental illness, which does not enhance the diversity of the discourse.

CONCLUSION

Based on the findings of this review, the literature clearly articulates the importance of creating a system that will curtail the marginalization and stigmatization of individuals diagnosed with mental disorders. The review identified legislations intended to limit the human rights violations of individuals with mental health issues, yet not much has been achieved. Even in the Western world, programs including the work of Winick on therapeutic jurisprudence and other treatment options such as CTOs aimed at enhancing treatment to limit mental health violations have not made a significant impact. A major factor to improving the conditions of the marginalized is to curb violations against the mentally ill through meaningful engagement and political will on the part of governments. The observation is that, despite laws governing the treatment of those with mental health issues, much has not been done to address stigmatization of individuals diagnosed with serious mental illness. In developing countries and other parts of the world, family members with mental health issues continue to be marginalized, medicalized, and ostracized, hence exposing them to human right abuses.

Declaration of Conflicting Interests

The author(s) declared no potential conflicts of interest with respect to the research, authorship, and/or publication of this article.

Funding

The author(s) received no financial support for the research and/or authorship of this article.

REFERENCES

1. Alem, A., Jacobson, L., Hanlon, C. (2008). Community-based mental health care in Africa: Mental health workers' views. World Psychiatry, 7, 54-57.
2. Awad, G., Voruganti, L. (2008). The burden of schizophrenia on caregivers: A review. PharmacoEconomics, 26, 149-162.
3. Barke, A., Nyarko, S., Klecha, D. (2011). The stigma of mental illness in Southern Ghana: Attitudes of the urban population and patients' views. Social Psychiatry & Psychiatry Epidemiology, 46, 1191-1202.
4. Baumann, A. E. (2007). Stigmatization, social distance and exclusion because of mental illness: The individual with mental illness as a "stranger." International Review of Psychiatry, 19, 131-135.
5. Bola, J. R., Park, E. H., Kim, S. Y. (2011). Reassessing the high proportion of involuntary psychiatric hospital admissions in South Korea. Community Mental Health, 47, 603-606.
6. Boyle, G. (2011). Early implementation of the Mental Capacity Act 2005 in Health and Social Care. Critical Social Policy, 31, 365-387.
7. Breeding, J. (2006). The case of Sohrab Hassan: Assault on liberty in the Texas mental health courts. Journal of Humanistic Psychology, 46, 243-254.
8. Bruckner, T. A., Scheffler, R. M., Shen, G., Yoon, J., Chisolm, D., Morris, J., . . .Saxena, S. (2011). The mental health workforce gap in low- and middle-income countries: A needs-based approach. Bulletin of the World Health Organization, 89, 184-194.
9. Callaghan, S., Ryan, C. J. (2012). Rng to the human rights challenge in compulsory treatment—New approaches to mental health law in Australia. Australian and New Zealand Journal of Psychiatry, 46, 611-620.
10. Cooper, S., Ssebunnya, J., Kigozi, F., Lund, C., Flisher, A. (2010). Viewing Uganda's mental health system through a human rights lens. International Review of Psychiatry, 22, 578-588.
11. Davar, B. V. (2008). From mental illness to disability: Choices for women users/survivors of psychiatry in self and identity constructions. Indian Journal of Gender Studies, 15, 261-290.
12. Dhanda, A., Narayan, T. (2007). Mental health and human rights. The Lancet, 370, 1197-1198.

13. Diseth, R. R., Hoglend, P. A. (2011). Potential legal protection problems in the use of compulsory commitment in mental health care in Norway. International Journal of Law and Psychiatry, 34, 393-399.

14. Doku, V., Ofori-Atta, A., Akpalu, B., Osei, A., Read, U., Cooper, S., & MHaPP Research Programme Consortium . (2011). Stakeholders' perceptions of the main challenges facing Ghana's mental health care system: A qualitative analysis. International Journal of Culture and Mental Health, 4, 8-22.

15. Drew, N., Funk, M., Tang, S., Lamichhane, J., Chavez, E., Katontoka, S., . . .Saraceno, B. (2011). Human rights violations of people with mental and psychosocial disabilities: An unresolved global crs. The Lancet, 378, 1664-1675.

16. Fellner, J. (2006).Conundrum for Corrections, a Tragedy for Prisoners: Prisons as Facilities for the Mentally Ill. Washington University Journal of Law & Policy, 22, 135-144.

17. Freckelton, I., Mcgregor, S. (2010). Human rights and review of the involuntary status of patients with a mental illness: Kracke after Momcilovic. Psychiatry, Psychology and Law, 17, 173-186.

18. Giacaman, R., Rabaia, Y., Nguyen-Gillham, V., Batniji, R., Punamaki, R. L., Summerfield, D. (2011). Mental health, social distress and political oppression: The case of the occupied Palestinian territory. Global Public Health, 6, 547-559.

19. Goffman, E. (1963). Stigma: Notes on the management of spoiled identity. New York, NY: Simon & Shcuster.

20. Hunt, A. M., da Silva, A., Lurie, S., Goldbloom, D. (2007). Community Treatment Orders in Toronto: The emerging data. Canadian Journal of Psychiatry, 52, 647-656.

21. Hunt, P., Mesquita, J. (2006). Mental disabilities and the human right to the highest attainable standard of health. Human Rights Quarterly, 28, 332-356.

22. International Labour Organisation . (2000). Mental health and work: Impact, issues and good practices. Geneva, Switzerland: World Health Organization.

23. Jansen, G. G. (2006). Gender and war: The effects of armed conflict on women's health and mental health. Affilia: Journal of Women and Social Work, 21, 134-145.

24. Kastrup, M. C. (2011). Gender, human rights and cultural diversity:

Reflections on a career in transcultural psychiatry. Transcultural Psychiatry, 48, 66-78.

25. Kisely, S., Campbell, L. A., Scott, A., Preston, N., Xiao, J. (2007). Randomized and non-randomized evidence for the effect of compulsory community and involuntary out-patient treatment on health service use: Systemic review and meta-analysis. Psychological Medicine, 37, 3-14.
26. Kogstad, R. (2009). Protecting mental health clients' dignity—The importance of legal control. International Journal of Law and Psychiatry, 32, 383-391.
27. Lim, K., Jacobs, P., Ohinwaa, A., Schopflower, D., Dewa, C. S. (2008). A new Population based measure of the economic burden of mental illness in Canada. Chronic Disease in Canada, 28(3), 92-98.
28. Link, B., Struening, E., Neese-Todd, S., Asmussen, S., Phelan, J. (2001). Stigma as Barrier to Recovery: The Consequences of Stigma for the Self-Esteem of People With Mental Illnesses. Psychiatric Services. 52, 1621-1626
29. Loo, C., Trollor, J., Alonzo, A., Rendina, N., Kavess, R. (2010). Mental health legislation and psychiatric treatments in NSW: Electroconvulsive therapy and deep brain stimulation. Australasian Psychiatry, 18, 417-425.
30. Matejkowski, J., Caplan, J. M., Cullen, S. W. (2010). The impact of severe mental illness on parole decons: Social integration within a prison setting. Criminal Justice and Behavior, 37, 1005-1029.
31. Mayers, P., Keet, N., Winkler, G., Flisher, A. J. (2010). Mental health service users' perceptions and experiences of sedation, seclusion and restraint. International Journal of Social Psychiatry, 56, 60-73.
32. Mcdaid, D., Knapp, M., Raja, S. (2008). Barriers in the mind: Promoting an economic case for mental health in low- and middle-income countries. World Psychiatry, 7, 79-86.
33. Mfoafo-M'Carthy, M., Williams, C. C. (2010). Coercion and Community Treatment Orders (CTOs): One step forward, two steps back? Canadian Journal of Community Mental Health, 29(1), 69-80.
34. Mwanza, J., Cooper, S., Kapungwe, A., Sikwese, A., Mwape, L., & MHaPP Research Programme Consortium (2011). Stakeholders' perceptions of the main challenges facing Zambia's mental health care system: A qualitative analysis. International Journal of Culture and Mental Health, 4, 39-53.

35. Naudts, K. H., Cosyns, P., Mcinnery, T., Audenaert, K., Van Den Eynde, F., Van Heeringen, C. (2005). Belgium and its internees: A problem for human rights and a stimulus for service change. Criminal Behaviour and Mental Health, 15, 148-153.

36. Regehr, C., Glancy, G. (2010). Mental health social work practice in Canada. Toronto, Ontario, Canada: Oxford University Press.

37. Rosenfield, S. (2012). Triple Jeopardy? Mental health at the intersection of gender, race and class. Social Science & Medicine, 74, 1791-1801.

38. Tarantola, D. (2007). The interface of mental health and human rights in indigenous peoples: Triple jeopardy and triple opportunity. Australasian Psychiatry, 15, 10-17.

39. The United Nations . (2006). Convention on the rights of persons with disabilities. Retrieved from http://www.un.org/disabilities/convention/conventionfull.shtml

40. The United Nations . (n.d.). The Universal Declaration of Human Rights. Retrieved from http://www.un.org/en/documents/udhr/

41. Vijayalakshmi, P., Ramachandra, Reddemma, K., Math, S. B. (2012). Perceived human rights violations in persons with mental illness: Role of education. International Journal of Social Psychiatry, 59, 351-364.

42. Weissbecker, I. (2009). Mental health as a human right in the context of recovery after disaster and conflict. Counselling Psychology Quarterly, 22, 77-84.

43. Winick, B. (2002). Therapeutic jurisprudence and problem solving courts. Fordham Urban Law Journal, 30, 1055-1103.

44. Winick, B. (2006). Therapeutic jurisprudence: Enhancing the relationship between law and psychology. Law and Psychology, 9, 1-48.

45. World Bank Data . (2013). How we Classify Countries. Retrieved from http://worldbankdata.org/about/country-classifications

46. World Health Organization . (2005). Resource book on mental health, human rights and legislation: Stop exclusion. Dare to care. Geneva, Switzerland: Author.

47. World Health Organization . (2006). WHO Mental Health and Human Rights project. Retrieved from http://www.who.int/mental_health/policy/mental_health_and_human_rights_october_2006.pdf

48. World Health Organization . (2010). Mental health and development: Targeting people with mental health conditions

as a vulnerable group. Retrieved from http://whqlibdoc.who.int/publications/2010/9789241563949_eng.pdf

49. World Health Organization . (2012). Depression. Retrieved from http://www.who.int/mental_health/management/depression/en/

50. Yamin, A. E., Rosenthal, E. (2005). Out of the shadows: Using human rights approaches to secure dignity and well-being for people with mental disabilities. PLoS Medicine, 2(4), e71; 0296-0298.

CHAPTER 6

MEASURING THE HEALTH IMPACT OF HUMAN RIGHTS VIOLATIONS RELATED TO AUSTRALIAN ASYLUM POLICIES AND PRACTICES: A MIXED METHODS STUDY

Vanessa Johnston[1], Pascale Allotey[2], Kim Mulholland[3] and Milica Markovic[4]

[1]Menzies School of Health Research and Institute of Advanced Studies, Charles Darwin University, Casuarina, NT 0811, Australia

[2]Centre for Public Health Research, School of Health Sciences and Social Care, Brunel University, West London, Uxbridge, UB8 3PH, UK

[3]Infectious Disease Epidemiology Unit, London School of Hygiene and Tropical Medicine, Keppel Street, London, WC1E 7HT, UK

Citation: Vanessa Johnston, Pascale Allotey, Kim Mulholland and Milica Markovic, BMC International Health and Human Rights 20099:1 https://doi.org/10.1186/1472-698X-9-1 © Johnston et al; licensee BioMed Central Ltd. 2009

[4]School of Psychology, Psychiatry and Psychological Medicine, Monash University, Clayton, Victoria, Australia

ABSTRACT

Background

Human rights violations have adverse consequences for health. However, to date, there remains little empirical evidence documenting this association, beyond the obvious physical and psychological effects of torture. The primary aim of this study was to investigate whether Australian asylum policies and practices, which arguably violate human rights, are associated with adverse health outcomes.

Methods

We designed a mixed methods study to address the study aim. A cross-sectional survey was conducted with 71 Iraqi Temporary Protection Visa (TPV) refugees and 60 Iraqi Permanent Humanitarian Visa (PHV) refugees, residing in Melbourne, Australia. Prior to a recent policy amendment, TPV refugees were only given temporary residency status and had restricted access to a range of government funded benefits and services that permanent refugees are automatically entitled to. The quantitative results were triangulated with semi-structured interviews with TPV refugees and service providers. The main outcome measures were self-reported physical and psychological health. Standardised self-report instruments, validated in an Arabic population, were used to measure health and wellbeing outcomes.

Results

Forty-six percent of TPV refugees compared with 25% of PHV refugees reported symptoms consistent with a diagnosis of clinical depression ($p = 0.003$). After controlling for the effects of age, gender and marital status, TPV status made a statistically significant contribution to psychological distress ($B = 0.5$, 95% CI 0.3 to 0.71, $p \leq 0.001$) amongst Iraqi refugees. Qualitative data revealed that TPV refugees generally felt socially isolated and lacking in control over their life circumstances, because of their experiences in detention and on a temporary visa. This sense of powerlessness and, for some, an implicit awareness they were being denied basic human rights, culminated in a strong sense of injustice.

Conclusion

Government asylum policies and practices violating human rights norms are associated with demonstrable psychological health impacts. This link between policy, rights violations and health outcomes offers a framework for addressing the impact of socio-political structures on health.

Keywords: Psychosocial Stressor, Asylum Seeker, Personal Wellbeing Index, Temporary Protection, Iraqi Refugee

BACKGROUND

Perhaps most notable in the evolution of the health and human rights paradigm is the recognition that many human rights violations (HRVs) have adverse consequences for health. The health effects of blatant violations are obvious, such as those arising from torture [1]. Additionally, there are more subtle but nonetheless important right violations that may impact on health, such as the absence of basic health care systems or tolerance of discrimination against minority groups [2].

While the link between HRVs and health seems intuitive, beyond the obvious health effects of torture [3, 4], the empirical assessment of the health impacts of HRVs is in its infancy [5]. Put simply, we are yet to understand fully the nature of these relationships, how they interact and their importance for public health practice [6]. More research is required to assess the broad health impact of HRVs and to identify the pathways by which violations become embodied as poor health outcomes.

Over recent years, the asylum policies of successive Australian governments have generated much controversy; namely the mandatory detention of undocumented asylum seekers while their refugee claims are processed, and the introduction of a time limited (3–5 years) Temporary Protection Visa (TPV) to asylum seekers despite the verification of their claim for refugee status under the 1951 UN Refugee Convention. The temporary protection regime was introduced in 1999 and until very recently was a core component of Australia's policy approach to asylum seekers. However, in 2008, a newly elected Labour government announced it would abolish the temporary visa scheme and would revert to issuing permanent protection status to bonefide refugees. Additionally, under new detention arrangements, asylum seekers will be detained only as a last resort (e.g. if they are shown to pose a risk to the community) and for the least practicable time [7].

Under the TPV policy refugees were excluded from or had limited access to a range of federal government funded benefits and services such as full income support benefits, free English language tuition, government supported university places, interpreting and settlement services [8]. Additionally, TPV refugees were barred from family reunion programs. By contrast, individuals entering via Australia's offshore humanitarian program have their refugee status established and permanent humanitarian visa (PHV) issued prior to arrival in Australia. This entitles them to the full range of services afforded to permanent residents.

Australia has ratified several human rights treaties, including the *International Covenant on Civil and Political Rights (ICCPR)*, the *International Covenant on Economic, Social and Cultural Rights (ICESCR)*, the *1951 Convention Relating to the Status of Refugees* and the *Convention on the Rights of the Child*. The Australia government, as a party to these treaties, is obliged under customary international law to protect the human rights of all persons within its territory and subject to its jurisdiction [9]. The detention and temporary protection of asylum seekers, as practiced in Australia, are widely believed to have violated human rights norms under international law [10, 11] (see Table 1 for a summary of the key policies and practices that have received the most scrutiny in relation to their impact on human rights [11, 12, 13, 14, 15, 16, 17]).

Table 1: Human rights implications of Australian asylum policies and practices

Australian asylum policies and practices	**Human rights implications**
Detention of asylum seekers	Arbitrary detention of asylum seekers is prohibited by Article 9(1) of the ICCPR. For the lawful detention of asylum seekers to be considered non-arbitrary, it should only be administered for the shortest time possible and be a reasonable, necessary and proportionate means to achieving a legitimate outcome, while giving due regard to alternative means which are less imposing on an individuals' rights [12]. Australia's history of automatic, mandatory detention of asylum seekers until their claims are finalised may be categorised as arbitrary in practice (in almost all cases, except those detained for a brief period), as the deprivation of liberty for an indeterminate period is difficult to justify on the grounds that it is a reasonable means of achieving a legitimate aim (i.e. for the purpose of granting a visa or removal from the territory) [13].

Temporary protection of refugees	Under the Refugee Convention, a signatory State is not required to provide permanent residence to refugees to meet its Convention obligations. However, temporary protection, as outlined by the United Nation High Commissioner for Refugees (UNHCR) should in general, only be applied to large groups of asylum seekers, who come en masse into a receiving country and threaten to overwhelm the administrative capacity of that country [14]. By applying a blanket temporary protection policy to all undocumented asylum seekers, it is arguable that Australia was "overly restrictive in its interpretation and application of this key element of the Convention." [15, para. 4] As such, the legitimacy of the policy under international law is questionable, as it is contrary both to the spirit of the Refugee Convention as well as accepted international standards [15, 16].
Restricted entitlements of TPV refugees	Article 34 of the Refugee Convention requires host States 'as far as possible' to 'facilitate the assimilation and naturalization of refugees'. By denying TPV holders certain social and welfare rights, the Australian policy dismissed those sections of the Refugee Convention, which are aimed towards assisting refugees, an already vulnerable group, to return to a "situation of national protection in a new country, if not their own, as soon as possible" [11]. To assist in this process, the Refugee Convention affords refugees "the most favorable treatment" accorded foreign nationals in the resettlement country, with respect to employment (Refugee Convention, 1951, Article 17). It is arguable that the restrictions on TPV refugees in accessing services to assist them with employment opportunities were not in keeping with this obligation. In relation to public relief (Article 23) and social security (Article 24), refugees are to be given equal access as nationals [17], by stark contrast to the restricted welfare entitlements offered to TPV refugees in Australia. Finally, the Australian temporary protection regime was not consistent with UNHCR policy and the practice of other States (e.g. in the European Union) whereby full Refugee Convention rights should be granted if return remains impossible after a few years [11].

Two previous cross-sectional studies have investigated the impact of asylum policies on the health of refugees in Sydney, Australia. These studies reported that both negative detention experiences (e.g. prolonged detention or stressful events whilst in detention, such as exposure to violence) and temporary protection were associated with adverse mental health outcomes for refugees subjected to this regime [18, 19]. Separate qualitative research has highlighted that restricted access to settlement services combined with the persistent uncertainty about their residency status have impacted negatively on the integration of TPV holders into the community [20]. In particular, psychosocial stressors, such as social isolation, a lack of control over life circumstances and a collective sense of injustice appear to be salient in the experience of TPV holders [20, 21].

Drawing from this earlier research, we aimed to further explore the relationship between health and human rights in this specific context and investigate the mediating pathways which link the two. Our underlying premise was that the Australian asylum policies and practices were a violation of human rights. To address the study aim, we designed the first mixed methods study with this population. Specifically, we posed two research questions:

Are Australian asylum policies and practice of detention and temporary protection associated with adverse health outcomes?

Are psychosocial stressors experienced by TPV refugees associated with adverse health outcomes amongst this group?

METHODS

Participants

Data were collected between November 2004 and October 2005. The study group comprised of adult (≥ 18 years) TPV and PHV Iraqi refugees who arrived in 1999 (when the TPV was introduced) or later and were living in four adjacent local geographical areas in the northern suburbs of Melbourne, Australia. The study site was chosen because of the concentration of newly arrived Iraqi refugees in these areas [22]. Participants were excluded if they could not speak Arabic or English, did not hold a humanitarian visa, and/or had been living in the community (i.e. outside of detention) for less than six months.

The study used quantitative and qualitative methods. A cross sectional survey included both TPV and PHV refugees. The qualitative arm involved semi-structured interviews but was restricted to TPV refugees and a purposive sample of local service providers.

Sampling

The lack of a community sampling frame (i.e. TPV holders were not represented on any publicly accessibly database) constrained the sampling strategy for the survey. Based on community profiles from both the Department of Immigration and Citizenship (DIAC) settlement database (which collects data on PHV refugees) and local service providers, which have informally gathered data on TPV refugees [23], non-probalistic sampling techniques described by De Vaus [24] were used to purposively select participants who characterised the diversity of the Iraqi refugee population in Melbourne. Thus, recruitment targeted women and men of varying ages, educational backgrounds and family compositions (e.g. intact and non-intact nuclear families). It was not possible to systematically match TPV and PHV participants on demographics such as sex or age because of the "hard to reach" nature of refugee populations [25]. Participants were recruited through community organisations such as Migrant Resource Centres and non-government organisations providing services to refugees in the study site. Community health centres were not included as points of contact in order to avoid over-representation of 'patients'. Refugees who did not utilise these community services were accessed by snowballing within established community networks.

A sample size estimate was calculated based on prevalence data from then preliminary results of a community-based study with Iraqi refugees in Sydney. The provisional findings from this study found a prevalence rate of self-reported depression of approximately 70% in the TPV group and 40% in the PHV group (pers. comm., Dr Steel [University New South Wales], 24 May 2004). Taking a conservative estimate based on this prevalence data, we calculated that 60 subjects per group would have 80% power to achieve a statistically significant result at a 2-sided 5% level, if the true proportions were 55% and 25% for the TPV and PHV groups respectively [26].

The survey sample provided a sampling frame for the nested interviews that were conducted with 16 TPV holders. Using theoretical sampling, we drew on previous research, that suggested that age, gender, education and marital status influence post-migration mental health [27, 28] and sampled to reflect the diversity across these factors. The grounded theory approach influenced sampling, data collection and analysis for these in-depth interviews [29].

Outcome Measures

The questionnaire for the survey was designed to collect basic sociodemographic data and to assess socioeconomic and psychosocial stressors and general health outcomes. Socioeconomic stressors were defined as obstacles in accessing core social determinants of health, such as employment and training, language tuition, housing, health and welfare services and relate directly to the entitlements of migrants under international human rights and refugee law. The standardized instruments used to assess the three psychosocial constructs tested were: the *Medical Outcomes Study Social Support Scale* (MOS-SS) [30], the *Perceived Constraints* subscale of the Lachman and Weaver [31]*Sense of Control Scale*, and the *State-Trait Anger Expression Inventory* (*STAXI*) [32], respectively. The STAXI scale was chosen as a 'proxy' measure of injustice because empirical research has demonstrated that anger is the most consistent emotional reaction elicited by perceived injustice within and between cultures [33, 34]. We posed an open ended question to assess the experience of personal and family trauma. The decision to avoid more established scales such as the Harvard Trauma Questionnaire was based on ethical concerns that administration of the questionnaire may cause distress in the context of possible repatriation of TPV refugees back to Iraq (i.e. at the expiry of their temporary visa).

Health outcomes were measured for self-reported physical health (*SF-36 General Health Scale* [35]; *SF-36 Physical Functioning Scale*[35]), psychological health (*Hopkins Symptom Checklist-25; HSCL-25* [36]) and personal wellbeing (*Personal Wellbeing Index; PWBI* [37]). All self-rated health measures had previously been validated in an Arabic population. The survey was presented in English and in Arabic and was self-administered in the presence of the first author (VJ) and a bilingual, bicultural project worker. We applied Brislin's [38] translation and back-translation method using two bilingual professionals; the original and back-translated versions were assessed for meaning equivalence. The questionnaire was pilot tested, which after some amendments (e.g. reconciling some minor semantic differences), demonstrated good face validity.

Semi-structured interviews with refugees aimed to explore in greater depth the perceived socioeconomic and psychosocial stressors associated with Australian migration policies and the impact of these on their health and wellbeing.

Data Analysis

Preliminary univariate analyses were performed to test for differences across the two visa groups in relation to sociodemographic characteristics, the experience of socioeconomic and psychosocial stressors, and self-rated health outcomes. The proportion of the sample that reported symptoms consistent with a diagnosis of clinical depression on the HSCL-25 scale was calculated, according to an established DSM-IV derived algorithm [39]. The HSCL-25 scale was also used as a continuous measure in multivariate analyses. A Personal Wellbeing (PWB) score was calculated as the average of the items, converted into units of Percentage Scale Maximum (%SM) (using the formula: mean PWB score/10 × 100) [40].

Where normal probability plots of continuous data indicated a normal distribution, we used parametric statistical tests in our analyses. Nonparametric measures of association were used to ascertain group differences across categorical variables or where normality assumptions of continuous variables could not be strictly met. Where possible, data that were skewed were log transformed to achieve a normal distribution to enable analyses using t-tests and regression [41].

Standard linear regression models were used to asses the impact of visa status on selected self-rated mental health outcomes, after controlling for potential confounding factors. To investigate the association of independent variables with self-rated health outcomes amongst TPV holders, variables were simultaneously entered into a linear regression model for participants in this visa category. Analyses were undertaken with Statistical Packages for Social Sciences (SPSS) for Windows.

The first author (VJ) employed thematic coding to explore the qualitative data. This involved identifying themes and sub themes in the data, refining and reducing these initial themes, building hierarchies and linking themes into a broader theoretical framework [42]. Pseudonyms were used in the reporting of verbatim quotations from participants. Qualitative data were managed using the computer software program, Atlas-ti (Version 5).

Ethics

The study received ethics approval from the University of Melbourne Human Research Committee.

RESULTS

Survey Results

Seventy-one TPV refugees and 60 PHV refugees completed questionnaires. Table 2presents the key sociodemographic characteristics of participants in the two different visa categories. These characteristics were broadly representative of the wider Iraqi refugee population in the study site according to available data from the DIAC and service providers located in the area. These sources indicated that the average age for Iraqi refugees is mid-adulthood, the majority are married, Arabic and generally well educated [23].

Table 2: Summary of key sociodemographic characteristics of study sample by visa status

Characteristic	**TPV refugees n = 71**	**PHV refugees n = 60**	**p-value**
Age, years mean, (SD)	35.1 (11.0)*	34.5 (12.2)	0.76
Female	31 (44)	33 (55)	0.26
Married/de facto	39 (55)	36 (61)	0.60
Ethnicity – Arabic	59 (83)	49 (82)	0.73
Completed secondary education	50 (73)	45 (76)	0.77
Personal and/or family experience of persecution	37 (52)	23 (38)	0.16
Time in Australian community, months mean, (SD)	42.6 (8.6)	38.7 (20.4)	0.14
Separation from spouse and/or child in Australia	11/37† (30)	5/36 (14)	0.18
Received welfare payments in the last 6 months	53 (73)	54 (90)	0.04

* Number of participants with positive responses, % in parentheses

† Denominator is number of participants with spouse and/or children

There was no statistically significant difference between TPV and PHV Iraqi refugees with regard to their sociodemographic and cultural backgrounds and in broad terms, had similar pre-arrival refugee experiences. Where the two groups differed substantially was in their post arrival experiences and entitlements under Australia's migration legislation.

Experience of Socioeconomic and Psychosocial Stressors

The effects of the asylum policies were reflected in the socioeconomic stressors reported by refugees. A significantly greater proportion of TPV refugees reported obstacles with 'access' to services and other settlement-related resources compared with the PHV group, across all service categories except for health, where the proportions were similar in the two groups (see Table 3). The main reason that TPV refugees gave for the problems they had in accessing tertiary education, English classes and welfare, was their limited entitlements to these services (Results not shown), which was a core part of the TPV policy.

Table 3: Comparison of socioeconomic stressors by visa status

Socioeconomic stressor	TPV refugees n (%)	PHV refugees n (%)	p-value
Obstacles accessing accommodation	41/71* (58)	22/60 (37)	0.03
Obstacles accessing education/job training	43/68 (63)	11/52 (21)	< 0.001
Obstacles finding employment	40/61 (66)	8/34 (24)	< 0.001
Obstacles accessing English language tuition	39/67 (58)	8/59 (14)	< 0.001
Obstacles accessing health services	24/70 (34)	21/56 (38)	0.85
Obstacles accessing welfare services	18/68 (27)	2/58 (3)	0.001
Number of obstacles to 'access' reported – 3 or more†	42/70 (60)	10/58 (17)	< 0.001
At any time under current visa been unable to afford:			
Food	10/71 (14)	2/60 (3)	0.07
Clothing	16/71 (23)	9/60 (15)	0.38
Accommodation	24/71 (34)	8/60 (13)	0.01
Medications	16/71 (23)	2/60 (3)	0.003
Number of essential items (food, clothing, accommodation, medication) unable to afford – 1 or more	28/71 (39)	13/60 (22)	0.05

* The data in this table include only those refugees who had attempted to access these services as the denominator

† Questions related to 'access' to six services/settlement-related resources: accommodation, education/job training, employment, English language tuition health and welfare services.

The results also indicated a significant difference between the two visa categories in their experience of psychosocial stressors, with TPV refugees reporting, on average, less social support, more life constraints and higher state anger scores (see Table 4).

Table 4: Comparison of psychosocial stressors by visa status

	TPV refugees (n = 70)	**PHV refugees (n = 60)**	**p-value**
Medical Outcomes Study Social Support (MOS-SS) score [0–100 scale] (median)	28.1	45.3	0.01
Perceived constraints (PC) score [1–7 scale] mean, (SD)	4.6 (1.3)	4.0 (1.2)	0.003
STAXI score			
State-Anger score [10–40 scale] (median)	18.5	11.5	≤ 0.001
Trait-Anger score [10–40 scale] mean, (SD)	21.8 (7.1)	20.7 (5.2)	0.3
STAXI State/Trait Anger Ratio (geometric mean)*	0.90	0.64	≤ 0.001

* Original STAXI State/Trait Anger Ratio scale was analyzed in logarithmic scale

Self-rated Health Outcomes

While there was no significant difference between the two groups in the assessment of their 'general health' (GH) and their 'physical functioning' (PF), there was a highly significant difference between the groups in their reporting of psychological distress and their wellbeing (see Table 5).

Table 5: Comparison of self-rated health outcomes by visa status

	TPV refugees (n = 70)	PHV refugees (n = 60)	p-value
SF-36 General Health (GH) score mean, (SD)	55.5 (26.5)	59.0 (21.9)	0.41
SF-36 Physical Functioning (PF) score mean, (SD)	70.5 (30.4)	72.0 (28.5)	0.77
Psychological distress (HSCL-25) mean, (SD)	2.1 (0.7)	1.6 (0.5)	< 0.001
Depression (HSCL-25) %	46	25	0.003
Personal Wellbeing Index (PWBI) % SM mean, (SD)	53.2 (22.2)	67.0 (17.2)	< 0.001

Mean psychological distress scores were higher among TPV refugees compared with PHV refugees. Forty-six percent (46%) compared with 25% of permanent refugees reported symptoms consistent with a diagnosis of clinical depression. Self-rated personal wellbeing was lower among TPV refugees (mean PWBI of 53% SM), compared with PHV refugees (67% SM).

Contribution of Visa to Psychological Distress

Standard linear regression modelling was used to assess the contribution of visa category to the HSCL-25 scores, when the variance explained by other relevant variables was controlled for (see Table 6). The additional variables included in the regression equation were age, gender, and marital status; factors previously identified as predictors of psychological health amongst resettling refugees. A history of persecution was originally included in the model but contributed little to the variance in HSCL-25. When it was removed from the model, there was no effect on the regression coefficients for all of the other included variables, indicating that it was a redundant variable in the model. Previous research has found an association between exposure to trauma and psychological health amongst refugees [3, 4]. In the present study the proportions of participants in both groups reporting persecution were not significantly different, so there is no reason to suspect that pre-migration trauma played an important role in explaining differences in health outcomes between the temporary and permanent refugee groups.

Table 6: Standard linear regression model assessing predictors of psychological distress (HSCL-25) (n = 130)

Variable	B*	95% Confidence interval	p-value
Visa			
TPV (cf PHV)	0.50	0.30, 0.71	≤ 0.001
Gender			
Female (cf Male)	0.21	-0.01, 0.42	0.06
Marital Status			
Never married (cf Divorced/Widowed)	-0.72	-1.19, -0.25	0.003
Married (cf Divorced/Widowed)	-0.63	-1.04, -0.24	0.003
Age (for 10 years difference)	0.04	-0.07, 0.15	0.43

*Unstandardised regression coefficients (B) are provided with 95% confidence intervals.

The regression model explained an estimated 27.4% of the variance in HSCL-25 scores (R squared = 0.274) amongst Iraqi refugees [F (5,123) = 9.22, p = ≤ 0.001]. Visa and marital status made a significant independent contribution to variation in HSCL-25 scores.

Determinants of Psychological Health Amongst TPV Holders

Initially, the relationship between self-rated psychological distress (HSCL-25) of TPV refugees, and 12 independent variables was assessed. The range of variables chosen was based on prior research that had suggested a relationship with mental health outcomes or was hypothesised in this study to show a correlation. These were: age, gender, education, marital status, history of persecution, months in detention, separation from spouse and/or child in Australia, number of difficulties accessing services, number of essential items of daily living unable to afford, perceived life constraints, social support and anger.

A regression model was fitted to assess the contribution of five independent variables that demonstrated significant univariate associations. These were perceived life constraints, social support, anger, gender, marital status and 'number of daily essential items' refugees were unable to afford since arriving in Australia (see Table 7 for correlation matrix). The results of analysis of the regression model are presented in Table 8.

Table 7: Correlations among variables in regression model to assess determinants of psychological distress (HSCL25) amongst TPV holders

	HSCL25	Gender	No. essential items unable to afford	MOS-SS score	PLC score
Gender	0.34 (0.002)*				
No. essential items unable to afford	0.37 (0.001)	0.16 (0.09)			
MOS-SS score †	-0.41(< 0.001)	0.21 (0.04)	-0.20 (0.05)		
PC score ‡	0.39 (< 0.001)	0.19 (0.06)	0.32 (0.004)	-0.25 (0.02)	
STAXI S/T Anger Ratio §	0.41 (< 0.001)	0.02 (0.43)	0.19 (0.06)	-0.28 (0.01)	0.34 (0.02)

* p values in parentheses

† Medial Outcomes Study Social Support (MOS-SS) score

‡ Perceived Constraints (PC) score

§ STAXI State/Trait Anger Ratio. Original state/trait ratio scale has undergone logarithmic transformation

Table 8: Standard linear regression model to assess determinants of psychological distress (HSCL-25) amongst TPV refugees (n = 70).

Variable	B	95% Confidence interval	p-value
Gender			
Female (cf Male)	0.50	0.18, 0.81	0.002
No. essential items unable to afford			
One or more (cf Zero)	0.24	-0.06, 0.53	0.11
Marital Status			
Divorced/widowed (cf Never married)	0.27	-0.29, 0.84	0.34
Married (cf Never married)	-0.05	-0.35, 0.25	0.73

MOS-SS score (for 20 points difference)	-0.16	-0.24, -0.06	0.003
PC score	0.05	-0.07, 0.17	0.42
STAXI S/T Anger Ratio (for 0.1 point difference)	0.15	0.03, 0.28	0.02

This regression model explained an estimated 42.8% of the variance in HSCL-25 scores (adjusted R squared = 0.428) amongst Iraqi TPV refugees [$F (7, 60) = 8.17, p \leq 0.001$]. Three variables made a statistically significant contribution to HSCL-25 (psychological distress) scores. They were gender, social support and anger.

Qualitative Results

The quantitative data highlighted the specific psychosocial variables (e.g. social support) that were associated with adverse mental health outcomes. However, the qualitative data were critical in exploring the antecedents of these stressors, and how they impacted on health. Interviews with TPV refugees revealed that they felt socially isolated owing to policy restrictions on reuniting with family members, and the structural barriers that prevented them from fully participating in society (e.g. not being able to access government-funded English tuition). While their mainstay of support were other TPV refugees, most admitted that giving and getting support from other TPV holders could be emotionally draining and a burden some wished to avoid at various times. This was particularly evident during the period when Iraqi TPV refugees were applying for permanent protection and many felt additional anxiety about the outcome of their claims:

Q: During this difficult time in your life, who can you turn to for some support for you?

A: Who am I going to talk with? I cannot talk to anyone. Everyone is feeling hopeless because eighty percent of Iraqis they being refused [permanent protection]. It is hard to get support from people who have all these problems. It is hard to talk to other TPV holders...If there were some percentage of people that are accepted and they are happy, then they can support the smaller percentage of people who are struggling. But now – the situation – most of the people they are in a bad situation and so they cannot support each other. (Kadar – male, aged 43)

Additionally, some interviewees were particularly sensitive to not wanting to overburden important social ties. This was particularly the case with women, many of whom expressed the desire not to contribute additional stress to their children and husbands:

...I am the woman who supports everybody else and I can't speak to anybody about my feelings. I have to keep it inside. I can't talk. I cannot speak my feelings to my children, because they get upset. I have to keep my feelings because of the children. (Alima – female, aged 48)

In part, women's predilection to keep their 'worries' to themselves stems from their gendered roles, whereby Iraqi women are largely responsible for the rearing of children and are traditionally seen as the keepers of harmony in the home [43]. Consistent with this, the qualitative interviews revealed that women generally viewed their migration experiences through the lens of the family, with particular reference to their children for whom they felt ultimately responsible. Equally, when they talked about the future, the burden of anxiety was layered with not only fears for themselves, but also fears for their children:

For me, I want the permanent visa not to travel or go to another place but just to make sure that my children have a safe place for their future. My son he forgot Arabic, now he speaks like a baby in Arabic...He likes the school here and the teachers and his friends. How can I take him back to Iraq at this time? I always worry so much for my children. I am driving my family crazy with my worry. (Falak – female, aged 25)

Men on the other hand, generally presented themselves more autonomously. The family context was not a major theme in their migration narratives; rather loss of personal status and professional identity were more the norm:

Maybe if I got permanent visa, I will start my life here again. Maybe I can make my own job, my own business in the future and I can take a place here in Australia I think I still have the time to do something for Australia if I get the permanent visa. (Husam – male, aged 45)

The qualitative data also revealed that TPV holders perceived that they had little agency over their lives and they expressed anger at the lack of control over the refugee determination process, be that in detention or later when applying for a permanent protection visa. Their anger and frustration were compounded when after gaining refugee status, the policies in place imposed further barriers to achieving otherwise 'normal' resettlement goals. Family reunion, access to language facilities, education and employment remained out of their reach:

You feel like a person moving around in circles. I can't take a step forward, I can't help myself, and I can't help with this community. (Mahir – male, aged 40)

It's hard because of TPV. Makes you feel frustrated and you can't develop yourself. You feel insecure and so you stay like frozen. (Emir – male, aged 43)

Perception of injustice was another key precipitant of anger. Interestingly, one of the more common reasons the participants gave as to why they felt the policies were unjust related to human rights. Although only one specified an international treaty (the Refugee Convention) as a source of rights that *should* be afforded refugees, several outlined specific rights that are contained in binding international law, and which they were being denied as a result of the Australia's policies and practices. As highlighted in the following excerpt, these included the right to not be detained arbitrarily and the right to religious freedoms (Article 9 and 18 respectively of the ICCPR):

Q: What are your feelings about this policy of detention?

A: This is such an unfair policy, especially for children. They come here looking for a safe place; they are not criminals. We are just normal people looking for a safe place...There are no human rights coming to us here...

Q: What human rights do you think you were missing in [the detention centre]?

A: They treat the women disrespectfully. [The women] are desperate and nobody listen to them. You know our tradition, we are Muslim and the women can't go to male doctors, she needs a female and we can't find this is in [detention]...We are all people looking just for freedom but when they put us in this jail, they take the most important thing for us; our freedom (Alima – female, aged 48)

The qualitative data also revealed some insights into how these refugees' anger and sense of injustice were expressed. For a few, this was expressed outwardly in the form of political action or individual protest and mostly this approach was described as beneficial for wellbeing, insomuch as it was an affirmative demonstration of personal agency and assertion of dignity. By contrast, the experience of anger for other interviewees was more likely to be directed inward at themselves, rather than expressed externally. Some internalised the dominant stereotype of asylum seekers as being 'undeserving,' or interpreted their experiences as god's punishment for previous wrongdoings, while others felt diminished by the treatment they had received by the Australian government. This was more often the case with interviewees with poor language skills, and who lacked education, were unemployed and had diminished family and other supports. This reaction was illustrated by one participant who spent over one in an immigration facility on Nauru. He was interviewed just prior to his voluntary repatriation to Iraq, the prospect of another two years here without his wife and children intolerable. He stated:

I hate myself that I am a refugee because I have seen myself like a miserable person in front of the Australian government...some people they put you down because you are a refugee. (Emir – male, aged 40)

DISCUSSION

In this study, TPV refugees suffered a higher prevalence of symptoms consistent with clinical depression, higher mean psychological distress and lower sense of wellbeing compared with PHV refugees. Temporary visa status was a significant determinant of psychological distress amongst Iraqi refugees in Melbourne, after controlling for gender, age and marital status. Socioeconomic stressors arising from the denial of core economic and social rights to TPV refugees were significantly more prevalent for TPV versus PHV refugees. However, amongst TPV refugees, psychosocial stressors were more predictive of poor psychological health (i.e. low reported social support and perceived injustice (using anger as a proxy measure). Gender, too, made a significant unique contribution to psychological distress amongst TPV holders. The qualitative data corroborated the survey results. The interview data revealed that female TPV refugees were particularly vulnerable to mental distress, at least in part arising from the emotional burden they shouldered in caring for children and the cultural expectation that they will nurture harmonious relations in the home. The qualitative data also indicated that the psychosocial impact of rights violations in this context predominate over the socioeconomic. While surveyed TPV refugees reported significantly more difficulties in accessing education, English language tuition and welfare, compared with PHV refugees, their narratives were more focused on the pervasive and detrimental impact of the interminable uncertainty about their future, social isolation, anger and sense of injustice.

There are some limitations to the study. In particular, the use of a non-random sampling frame runs this risk of bias in comparing these two groups of refugees. For example, it may be possible that Iraqi refugees with the poorest health were more interested in partaking, perhaps motivated by self-interest. However, prior research suggests it is generally harder to engage such individuals in research projects [44, 45] and consequently, it is more likely that the results are an under, rather than an overestimate of the measured health outcomes. It is also notable that the rates of depression found in this study (using a standardised self-report measure) fall within the boundaries of prevalence data previously reported for Iraqi asylum seekers in Australia and Iraqi refugees in the international literature [18, 46].

Another source of bias may arise from TPV refugees exaggerating their plight in the hope that this might advance their claims when they applied for permanent protection. While this cannot be completely discounted, the anonymous nature of data collection (i.e. no identifying information was collected) and the clear statement contained in the Information Sheet, which emphasized that the research was independent of DIAC, should have diminished this risk. Additionally, because decisions about ongoing protection are based around risk of future persecution in Iraq, issues relating to living difficulties in Australia, the subject of this research, bear little relevance. The generalisability of the study may also be questioned owing to the sampling methods. In countering this argument, it is noteworthy that the sociodemographic characteristics of the sample were broadly comparable (across age, gender, education and ethnicity) to those of the wider Iraqi refugee community living in the study site according to available data from the DIAC settlement database and other community providers. The extent to which the results are generalisable to other ethnic groups remains uncertain. Finally, transcultural measurement issues are a potential source of measurement error, although considerable effort was invested in the translation and implementation of the survey to guard against this.

Despite these limitations, the study results are broadly confirmatory of a growing body of evidence that Australian asylum policies have been associated with adverse mental health outcomes amongst refugees who have been subject to this regime. Like the two cross-sectional studies preceding this one, temporary visa status was predictive of adverse mental health outcomes amongst refugees. It is noteworthy; however, that length of time in detention was not a significant contributor in this current study, as it was in the study by Steel and colleagues [18]. This may be related to the fact that our study included few participants who had been in detention for a notably prolonged period (e.g. no one over 12 months), which may be more predictive of mental health impact in the long-term (i.e. several years after release). In a similar comparative cross-sectional study with Persian-speaking refugees, it was not length of time in detention but 'stressful' experiences in detention (e.g. exposure to acts of violence, not receiving adequate medical attention etc.) that contributed to PTSD (but not depression) [47]. This suggests that more research may be required to elucidate further the association of length of time in detention and long-term mental illness in this population.

While this study is valuable in adding confirmatory evidence of the adverse health impact of temporary protection of refugees, the originality of this research, is that it extends empirical knowledge about the health impact of human rights violations and the pathways through which rights violations are embodied as poor psychological health outcomes; evidence which has to date been scant. Notably, the results underscore the importance of psychosocial determinants of health, such as social support and sense of injustice, and access to other underlying determinants, such as food and accommodation. That is, the key determinants of the health and wellbeing of TPV refugees cannot be narrowly defined in relation to individual access to health care, but rather are associated with the psychosocial and socioeconomic ramifications of the denial of their human rights. This supports the work of Burris and colleagues [5], who state that "law may be an enormously important pathway along which social structure becomes health destiny in individual lives."

Perhaps most important, is the finding that policies that violate human rights are associated with adverse health outcomes. This link between policy, rights violations and health outcomes offers a framework for addressing the impact of socio-political structures on health. The message for governments is that creating the social conditions for realizing health requires, among other things, that human rights of individuals and collectives be upheld [6, 48]. While it is true that many States continue to be remiss in their legal and moral obligations to uphold human rights, there are notable exceptions, like South Africa (with a legally enforceable bill of rights), who have demonstrated that respect for rights can result in improved health outcomes [49].

CONCLUSION

Human rights matter for health. In light of this and other corroborative research the Australian federal government needs to be accountable, not only for its legal obligations to uphold human rights, but also for the adverse health consequences arising from policies that violate those rights. To this end, recent Australian migration policy changes to abolish the temporary protection regime and reform immigration detention practices are welcome developments.

Detention of asylum seekers and temporary protection are already used to varying degrees in the US and across some countries in the European Union (EU). Currently in the EU, there are moves towards instituting such practices as standard practice [50]. This study should give pause to States wishing to follow Australia's example.

DECLARATIONS

Acknowledgements

This research was supported by an Australian National and Medical Research Council PhD Scholarship (N. 251782) and a Victorian Health Promotion Foundation research grant (No. 2002-0280). The sponsors of the study had no role in study design, data collection, data analysis, data interpretation, or writing of the report. The corresponding author had full access to all the data in the study, and had final responsibility for the decision to submit for publication. We would like to acknowledge Professor John Carlin and Professor Ian Gordon for their assistance with the statistical analyses and to the Al Amel TPV Association and staff at the Northern Migrant Resource Centre for their support of the project. We are also grateful to Professor Daniel Reidpath for reading a revised version of the manuscript and for his helpful comments. Finally, we acknowledge the refugees who participated in this project.

Competing Interests

The authors declare that they have no competing interests.

Authors' Contributions

VJ developed the study protocol, designed the analysis plan, collected and interpreted the data, and wrote the paper. She will act as guarantor for the paper. PA, KM and MM contributed to the development of the protocol, analysis plan and data interpretation and provided field supervision for the study. They also provided critical feedback on the draft of the paper. All authors read and approved the final manuscript.

REFERENCES

1. Mollica RF, McInnes K, Poole C, Tor S: Dose effect relationships of trauma to symptoms of depression and post-traumatic stress disorder among Cambodian survivors of mass violence. Br J Psychiatry. 1998, 173: 482-488. 10.1192/bjp.173.6.482.
2. Gruskin S, Mills EJ, Tarantola D: History, principles, and practice of health and human rights. The Lancet. 2007, 370 (9585): 449-455. 10.1016/S0140-6736(07)61200-8.
3. Mollica RF, Donelan K, Tor S, Lavelle J, Elias C, Frankel M, Blendon RJ: The effect of trauma and confinement on functional health and mental health status of Cambodians living in Thailand-Cambodia border camps. JAMA. 1993, 270 (5): 581-586. 10.1001/jama.270.5.581.
4. Shrestha NM, Sharma B, Van Ommeren M, Regmi S, Makaju R, Komproe I, Shrestha GB, de Jong JT: Impact of torture on refugees displaced within the developing world: symptomatology among Bhutanese refugees in Nepal. JAMA. 1998, 280 (5): 443-448. 10.1001/jama.280.5.443.
5. Burris S, Kawachi I, Sarat A: Integrating law and social epidemiology. J Law Med Ethics. 2002, 30 (4): 510-521. 10.1111/j.1748-720X.2002.tb00421.x.
6. Braveman P, Gruskin S: Poverty, equity, human rights and health. Bull World Health Organ. 2003, 81 (7): 539-545.
7. Labor unveils new risk-based detention policy. [http://www.minister.immi.gov.au/media/media-releases/2008/ce08072.htm]
8. Taylor J, Stanovic D: Services and entitlements: refugees, migrants and asylum seekers. Migration Action. 2004, XXVI (2): 32-35.
9. Refugees and their human rights. Refugees Studies Programme Working Paper No.17. [http://www.rsc.ox.ac.uk/PDFs/workingpaper17.pdf]
10. Edwards A: Tampering with refugee protection: the case of Australia. Int J of Refugee Law. 2003, 15 (2): 192-211. 10.1093/ijrl/15.2.192.
11. "By Invitation Only": Australian Asylum Policy. [http://www.hrw.org/]
12. HRC: Communication No. 560/1993 Australia (1997): 03/04/97 UN Doc. CCPR/C/59/D/560/1993 (A v Australia). Human Rights Committee. 1997
13. A Report on visits to Immigration Detention Facilities by the Human Rights Commissioner 2001. [http://www.hreoc.gov.au/Human_

RightS/idc/index.html]

14. UNHCR: A thematic compilation of Executive Committee Conclusions (second edition). 2005, Geneva: Office of the United Nations High Commissioner for Refugees, Department of International Protection
15. Sengchanh V: Refugees – Two lifetimes in one. 2001, Murdoch University Electronic Journal of Law, 8:
16. Human Rights Watch commentary on Australia's Temporary Protection Visas for refugees. [http://www.hrw.org/backgrounder/refugees/australia051303.htm]
17. Cholewinski R: Enforced destitution of asylum seekers in the United Kingdom: the denial of fundamental human rights. Int J of Refugee Law. 1998, 10 (3): 462-498. 10.1093/ijrl/10.3.462.
18. Steel Z, Silove D, Brooks R, Momartin S, Alzuhairi B, Susljik I: Impact of immigration detention and temporary protection on the mental health of refugees. Br J Psychiatry. 2006, 188: 58-64. 10.1192/bjp.bp.104.007864.
19. Momartin S, Silove D, Manicavasagar V, Steel Z: Dimensions of trauma associated with posttraumatic stress disorder (PTSD) caseness, severity and functional impairment: a study of Bosnian refugees resettled in Australia. Soc Sci Med. 2003, 57: 775-781. 10.1016/S0277-9536(02)00452-5.
20. Marston G: Temporary Protection, Permanent Uncertainty. The experience of refugees living on Temporary Protection Visas. 2003, Melbourne: Centre for Applied Social Research RMIT University
21. Mansouri F, Cauchi S: The psychological impact of extended temporary protection. Refuge. 2006, 23 (2): 81-95.
22. Top 10 local government areas in Victoria for Iraqi humanitarian entrants 1999–2003. [http://www.immi.gov.au/living-in-australia/delivering-assistance/settlement-reporting-facility/]
23. BSL: Closing the gap for TPV refugees in Victoria: A State-wide Action Plan. 2005, Melbourne: Ecumenical Migration Centre, Brotherhood of St Laurence
24. De Vaus DA: Surveys in social research. 2002, Crows Nest, Ausralia: Allen and Unwin
25. Spring M, Westermeyer J, Halcon L, Savik K, Robertson C, Johnson DR, Butcher JN, Jaranson J: Sampling in difficult to access refugee and immigrant communities. J Nerv Ment Dis. 2003, 191: 813-819.

10.1097/01.nmd.0000100925.24561.8f.

26. Dobson AJ, Gebski VJ: Sample sizes for comparing two independent proportions using the continuity-corrected arc sine transformation. Statistician. 1986, 35: 51-53. 10.2307/2988298.
27. Hinton WL, Tiet Q, Tran CG, Chesney M: Predictors of depression among refugees from Vietnam: A longitudinal study of new arrivals. J Nerv Ment Dis. 1997, 185 (1): 39-45. 10.1097/00005053-199701000-00007.
28. Porter M, Haslam N: Predisplacement and postdisplacement factors associated with mental health of refugee and internally displaced persons. JAMA. 2005, 294 (5): 602-612. 10.1001/jama.294.5.602.
29. Glaser BG, Strauss A: The discovery of grounded theory: strategies for qualitative research. 1967, New York: Aldine
30. Sherbourne CD, Stewart AL: The MOS Social Support Survey. Soc Sci Med. 1991, 6: 705-714. 10.1016/0277-9536(91)90150-B.
31. Lachman ME, Weaver SL: The sense of control as a moderator of social class differences in health and well-being. J Pers Soc Psychol. 1998, 74: 763-773. 10.1037/0022-3514.74.3.763.
32. Spielberger CD: State-Trait Anger Expression Inventory. Professional Manual. 1991, Tampa, Florida: Psychological Assessment Resources Inc
33. Mikula G, Schere KR, Athenstaedt U: The role of injustice in the elicitation of differential emotional reactions. Pers Soc Psychol Bull. 1998, 24 (7): 769-784. 10.1177/0146167298247009.
34. Scherer KR: Profiles of emotion-antecedent appraisal: testing theoretical predictions across cultures. Cognition and Emotion. 1997, 11 (2): 113-150. 10.1080/026999397379962.
35. Ware JE, Snow KK, Kosinski M, Gandek B: SF-36 Health Survey. Manual and interpretation guide. 1993, Boston, MA: The Health Institute, New England Medical Centre
36. Mollica R, Caspi-Yavin Y, Lavelle J, Tor S, Yang T, Chan S, Pham T, Ryan A, Marnaffe D: Hopkins Symptom Checklist (HSCL-25): manual for Cambodian, Laotian and Vietnamese versions. Torture. 1996, 6 (Suppl 1): 35-42.
37. Australian Unity Wellbeing Index: Cumulative Psychometric Record. [http://acqol.deakin.edu.au/index_wellbeing/index.htm]
38. Brislin RW: Translation and content analysis of oral and written

material. Handbook of cross-cultural psychology. Edited by: Triandis HC, Berry JW. 1980, Boston: Allyn and Bacon, 2:

39. Mollica RF, Sarajlic N, Chernoff M, Lavelle J, Vukovic IS, Massagli MP: Longitudinal study of psychiatric symptoms, disability, mortality, and emigration among Bosnian refugees. JAMA. 2001, 286 (5): 546-554. 10.1001/jama.286.5.546.
40. Personal Wellbeing Index. [http://www.deakin.edu.au/research/acqol/instruments/wellbeing_index.htm]
41. Bland JM, Altman DG: Statistics Notes: Transforming data. BMJ. 1996, 312 (7033): 770-
42. Ryan A, Bernard HR: Techniques to identify themes. Field Methods. 2003, 15 (1): 85-109. 10.1177/1525822X02239569.
43. al-Khayyat S: Honour and shame: women in modern Iraq. 1990, London: Saqi Books
44. Pirzada A, Yan LL, Garside DB, Schiffer L, Dyer AR, Daviglus ML: Response rates to a questionnaire 26 years after baseline examination with minimal interim participant contact and baseline differences between respondents and nonrespondents. Am J Epidemiol. 2004, 159 (94–101):
45. Slymen DJ, Drew JA, Elder JP, Williams SJ: Determinants of non-compliance and attrition in the elderly. Int J Epidemiol. 25 (411–419):
46. Laban CJ, Gernaat HBPE, Komproe IH, Schreuders BA, De Jong JTVM: Impact of a long asylum procedure on the prevalence of psychiatric disorders in Iraqi asylum seekers in The Netherlands. J Nerv Ment Dis. 2004, 192 (12): 843-851. 10.1097/01.nmd.0000146739.26187.15.
47. Momartin S, Steel Z, Coello M, Aroche J, Silove DM, Brooks R: A comparison of the mental health of refugees with temporary versus permanent visas. Med J Aust. 2006, 185 (7): 367-361.
48. Mann J: Medicine and public health, ethics and human rights. The Hastings Centre Report. 1997, 27 (3): 6-13. 10.2307/3528660.
49. Singh JA, Govender M, Mills EJ: Do human rights matter to health?. The Lancet. 2007, 370 (9586): 521-527. 10.1016/S0140-6736(07)61236-7.
50. Hatton TJ: European asylum policy. National Institute Economic Review. 2005, 106-119. 10.1177/0027950105061503. 194.

CHAPTER 7

THE DIRTY WAR INDEX: A PUBLIC HEALTH AND HUMAN RIGHTS TOOL FOR EXAMINING AND MONITORING ARMED CONFLICT OUTCOMES

Madelyn Hsiao-Rei Hicks[1], Michael Spagat[2]

[1]Health Service and Population Research Department, Institute of Psychiatry, King's College London, London, United Kingdom.
[2]Department of Economics, Royal Holloway College, University of London, Egham, United Kingdom

Documentation, analysis, and prevention of the harmful effects of armed conflict on populations are established public health priorities [1–5]. Al-

Citation: Hicks MH-R, Spagat M (2008) The Dirty War Index: A Public Health and Human Rights Tool for Examining and Monitoring Armed Conflict Outcomes. PLoS Med 5(12): e243. https://doi.org/10.1371/journal.pmed.0050243

though public health research on war is increasingly framed in human rights terms [6–13], general public health methods are typically applied without direct links to laws of war. Laws of war are international humanitarian laws and customary standards regarding the treatment of civilians and combatants, mainly described in the four Geneva Conventions of 1949 and their Additional Protocols I and II regarding international and civil conflicts [14]. With notable exceptions [11,15–17], absolute numbers are usually reported (e.g., number of persons killed), without systematic description of the proportional effects of armed conflict, thereby limiting the utility of findings and scope of interpretation.

In this paper, we introduce the "Dirty War Index" (DWI): a data-driven public health tool based on laws of war that systematically identifies rates of particularly undesirable or prohibited, i.e., "dirty," war outcomes inflicted on populations during armed conflict (e.g., civilian death, child injury, or torture). DWIs are explicitly linked to international humanitarian law to make public health outcomes directly relevant to prevention, monitoring, and humanitarian intervention for the moderation of war's effects. After choosing the particular outcome to be measured, a DWI is calculated as:

$$\text{DWI} = \frac{\text{Number of "dirty," i.e., undesirable or prohibited cases}}{\text{Total number of cases}} \times 100$$

Summary Points

- War, a major public health problem, is a situation where the interests of public health, human rights, and humanitarian law intersect.
- The DWI is a data-driven public health tool that identifies rates of particularly undesirable or prohibited, i.e., "dirty," outcomes inflicted on populations during war (e.g., civilian death, child injury, or torture).
- A DWI is calculated as: (Number of "dirty," i.e., undesirable or prohibited cases/Total number of cases) × 100.
- DWIs are designed for direct, easy translation of war's public health outcomes into the human rights, policy, and interdisciplinary work needed to address war's practice.
- DWIs support monitoring, deterrence, and humanitarian intervention by explicit links to international humanitarian laws and by exposing rates of unacceptable combat outcomes (DWI values) from different weapons or combatant groups.

For example: In Table 1, we measure the DWI ratio of "Number of civilians killed/Total number of civilians and opponent combatants killed" using a casualty dataset for Colombia's civil conflict [18]. Table 2 links this DWI to relevant laws of war. DWI values of 99 for illegal paramilitaries, 46 for guerrillas, and 45 for government forces show that paramilitaries are "dirtiest" in terms of proportion of civilians constituting their victims of unopposed attacks (chi-square = 5,010, degree of freedom [df] = 2, $p < 0.001$). 99% of paramilitary victims were civilians and only 1% were military opponents. This finding, combined with the paramilitaries' methods (execution by close-range gunfire in massacres), suggests intentional targeting of civilians that requires recognition in Colombia's paramilitary demobilization, disarmament, and reintegration process [19].

Table 1. Dirty War Index for Attacks by Actors in the Colombian Civil Conflict, 1988–2005: Civilian Versus Opponent Combatant Mortality

ents killed	41	2,946	659
ent combatant mortality al no. of civilians and ; killed, times 100	6,944/6,985 = 0.99 × 100 = 99	2,498/5,444 = 0.46 × 100 = 46	539/1,198 = 0.45
100)	99	46	45
	Paramilitaries rank highest in killing the greatest absolute number of civilians. Their DWI value of 99 ranks "dirtiest," approaching the "dirtiest" theoretically possible (100). Civilians comprised 99% of victims killed and legitimate targets only 1%. The high number and high DWI suggest systematic civilian targeting.	Guerrillas rank 2nd in killing absolute numbers of civilians. Their DWI of 46 shows that civilians comprised 46% of victims killed in their attacks, a proportion that needs to be substantially lowered.	Government for killing absolute r However, as wit DWI of 45 indica lower substantia civilians killed in

Table 2. DWIs Suggested for Measuring Rates of Undesirable or Prohibited Outcomes from Aggression in Armed Conflict

DWI	Pertinent Laws of War [14]	Example DWI Calculations (Numerator/Denominator) × 100
Mortality to civilians versus combatants	Fourth Geneva Convention and APs I & II prohibit direct targeting of civilians. AP I prohibits indiscriminate weapon use, indiscriminate weapons, and incidental civilian casualties disproportionate to the advantage gained in attacking a military target [22].	No. civilians killed/Total no. civilians and combatants killed
Injuries to civilians versus combatants	As above	No. civilians injured/Total no. civilians and combatants injured [15]
Lethality to civilians	As above	No. civilians killed by weapon(s)/Total no. civilians killed or injured by weapon(s) [15,17,18]
Torture of civilians or combatants	Prohibited by Fourth Geneva Convention (re: civilians). APs I & II. Prohibited by Third Geneva Convention (re: prisoners of war).	No. captured combatants tortured/Total no. captured combatants
Rape of civilians or combatants	As above	No. raped by combatant group/Total no. having face-to-face contact with combatant group [32]
Sexual humiliation or indecent assault of civilians or combatants	As above	No. captured males sexually assaulted/Total no. captured males
Mutilation of civilians or combatants	As above	No. mutilated by combatant group/Total no. having face-to-face contact with combatant group

Kidnapping or hostage-taking	As above	No. kidnapped/Total relevant population
Disappearances	As above	No. households with disappeared member/Total no. households
Summary execution of captured prisoners	Third & Fourth Geneva Conventions and APs I & II prohibit targeting civilians and prisoners of war for harm and require fair trials before penalties.	No. captured combatants executed/Total no. captured combatants
Terrorist attacks	Prohibited by Fourth Geneva Convention, APs I & II.	No. terrorist attacks/Total no. attacks
Assassination of civilian leaders (e.g., union leaders, mayors, teachers, religious leaders)	As above	No. teachers killed/Total no. teachers
Attacks on medical and religious personnel and on medical units	Prohibited by the four Geneva Conventions, APs I & II.	No. attacked medical workers/Total no. medical workers
Use of particularly undesirable (e.g., indiscriminate) weapons or prohibited weapons	AP I prohibits weapons of a nature to cause superfluous injury or unnecessary suffering [48]. Convention on the Use of Certain Conventional Weapons prohibits weapons deemed to be excessively injurious or to have indiscriminate effects. Protocol I to the Convention on Conventional Weapons prohibits weapons with fragments undetectable by X-rays. Protocol II to the Convention on Conventional Weapons prohibits or restricts mines and booby-traps. Protocol III to the Convention on Conventional Weapons prohibits or restricts incendiary weapons. 1925 Geneva Protocol and 1972 Convention prohibit toxic gas and chemical and biological weapons. 1997 Ottawa Convention on the Prohibition of the Use, Stockpiling, Production and Transfer of Anti-Personnel Mines and on their Destruction [5]. 2008 Dublin Convention on Cluster Munitions prohibits and restricts the use of cluster munitions.	• No. child deaths from a weapon type/Total no. deaths from the weapon type; or • No. casualties from a prohibited weapon/Total no. casualties
Suicide bombers disguised as civilians	AP I prohibits feigning civilian status. AP I requires combatants to distinguish themselves during military operations by uniforms, marks, or carrying arms openly [22].	No. casualties by disguised suicide bombs/Total no. casualties
Child mortality or injury	Third and Fourth Geneva Conventions and APs I & II grant general civilian protection and special protection to children [49]. Children may be more vulnerable to some weapons. High rates of direct child mortality suggest indiscriminate warfare or targeting; both prohibited.	No. child casualties/Total no. casualties
Female civilian mortality or injury	Fourth Geneva Convention and APs I & II grant general civilian protection and special protection to women. High rates of direct mortality to women civilians suggest indiscriminate warfare or targeting; both prohibited.	No. women civilians killed/Total no. all adults killed
Elderly civilian mortality or injury	Elderly civilians may be vulnerable. High rates of direct elderly civilian mortality suggest indiscriminate warfare or targeting; both prohibited.	No. elderly civilians killed/Total no. all civilians killed [50]
Violence to noncombatant indigenous groups	Can be a targeted or vulnerable group in conflict.	No. indigenous group member casualties/Total indigenous population

As ratios, DWIs complement absolute numbers and lend themselves to comparisons over time, between wars, between weapons, and between warring combatant groups to identify better versus worse performers. Noncombatant wounded-to-killed ratios can provide evidence of war crimes [16]. Proportional "atrocity statistics" [20] from a Darfur survey substantiated US Secretary of State Colin Powell's declaration of genocide and the referral of Darfur's situation to the International Criminal Court [20,21]. By facilitating clear, systematic comparisons, DWIs can help analyze and expose how combatants engage in war and affect populations, thereby increasing the accountability of military and political leaders. This paper describes the theoretical basis and practical applications of the DWI, with brief examples from armed conflicts. More detailed DWI analyses of specific conflicts are planned for future papers.

CALCULATING AND USING DWIS

A DWI can be easily used and understood, facilitating interdisciplinary communication and research on war's effects. DWIs can measure rates of undesirable outcomes from accepted methods (e.g., civilian casualties from aerial bombing of military targets). They can also measure rates of using prohibited, illegitimate methods (e.g., torture), and rates of applying illegitimate methods to especially vulnerable populations (e.g., torturing children) to describe rates of exceptional atrocity. However, the mere application of DWI analysis to a combatant group does not indicate that it is "dirty": a DWI ratio simply identifies how often, if at all, the group is linked with the particular undesirable outcome being measured, facilitating comparisons. To illustrate, we draw on data from B'Tselem (http://www.btselem.org/english/statistics/Index.asp), a nongovernmental organization that monitors casualties from the Israeli-Palestinian conflict. We apply a "female mortality DWI" (Number of females killed/Total number killed) to conflict-related killings from September 29, 2000 to April 30, 2007: Israeli security forces killed 213 females among 4,057 Palestinians (DWI = 5). Palestinians killed 283 females among 705 Israeli civilians (DWI = 40). Palestinians killed 10 females among 317 Palestinians (DWI = 3). Comparison of actors' DWIs shows significantly higher discrimination of female from male targets by Israeli security forces and by Palestinian actors when targeting Palestinians, and lower discrimination of female from male targets when Palestinian actors target Israeli civilians (chi-square = 833, df = 2, $p < 0.001$).

The best possible DWI value is 0, indicating that the objectionable outcome is identified in no measured cases. The worst possible DWI value is 100, indicating that the objectionable outcome is identified in 100% of measured cases. Any rate above 0 for prohibited actions or war crimes is unacceptable, and eliminating violations is imperative. DWIs for undesirable outcomes are less straightforward. The highly undesirable outcome of civilian harm is not prohibited by laws of war if combatants do everything feasible to distinguish between civilians and military targets (the principle of distinction), if they attempt to minimize incidental harm to civilians, and if they intend to avoid harming civilians in excess of anticipated military goals (the principle of proportionality) [1,22,23]. Civilian harm is also balanced against the "military necessity" of objectives [24]. Though what is feasible, proportional, or necessary is highly subjective [22–24], clearly the lowest possible rates should be sought for undesirable outcomes such as "incidental" civilian death. High DWI values for undesirable outcomes indicate extreme destruction, signal the need for close scrutiny, and may suggest war crimes.

Tables 2 and 3 list specific DWIs, their pertinent laws of war, and example calculations. Table 2lists DWIs for undesirable or prohibited aggression in armed conflict. DWIs can be analyzed by demographic subgroup for indiscriminate warfare, disproportionate effects of targeting, or particular vulnerability to weapons. For example, with "casualties" defined as injuries or deaths, a "child casualty DWI" (Number of child casualties/ Total number of casualties) applied to weapons-casualty data from Chechnya [25] gives the following child casualty ratios for different explosive devices: antitank landmines (34/223, DWI = 15), antipersonnel landmines (223/1,004, DWI = 22), booby traps (65/214, DWI = 30), and other unexploded ordnance (UXO) (255/892, DWI = 29). DWIs indicate that in Chechnya, UXO and booby traps are more dangerous to children than landmines and significantly "dirtier" in this respect (chi-square = 25.0, df = 3, $p < 0.001$).

Table 3. DWIs Suggested for Measuring Rates of Unacceptable Endangerment in Armed Conflict

DWI	Pertinent Laws of War [14]	Example DWI Calculations (Numerator/Denominator) × 100
Use of child soldiers	APs I & II, and the 1989 Convention on the Rights of the Child, prohibit recruiting or deploying in hostilities children under 15. 1990 African Charter on the Rights and Welfare of the Child prohibits recruiting or deploying in hostilities children under 18. 1998 Rome Statute of the International Criminal Court makes it a war crime to enlist or deploy in hostilities children under 15. Optional Protocol to the Convention on the Rights of the Child prohibits compulsory recruitment of children under 18 [49].	No. child combatants/Total no. child and adult combatants
Use of human shields	Prohibited by AP I [22,23].	No. events using human shields/Total no. events
Initiating weapons fire from among civilians	AP I prohibits using human shields and requires combatants to protect civilians from dangers of military operations to the maximum extent feasible [22,23,26].	No. events where combatant group attacks from among civilians/Total no. attacks
Locating headquarters or weapons storage among civilians	AP I requires combatants to avoid locating military objectives within or near densely populated areas to the maximum extent feasible [22,23,26].	• No. military sites located among civilians/Total no. military sites: or • No. households near military sites/Total no. households
Combatants taking civilian appearance during military operations (not wearing uniforms)	AP I prohibits feigning civilian status [22,23,26].	No. combat events where combatants do not wear uniforms or distinguishing marks/Total no. combat events
Combatants disguised as humanitarian, peacekeeping, or medical workers	AP I prohibits feigning noncombatant status [22,23].	No. of events of disguise/Total no. events
Leaving landmines or UXO	Protocol V to the Convention on Conventional Weapons on Explosive Remnants of War requires removing explosive remnants to reduce civilian risk [5]. 1997 Ottawa Convention prohibits anti-personnel mines and calls for their destruction. 2008 Dublin Convention on Cluster Munitions requires clearance and destruction of cluster munitions.	• Meters-squared of land with UXO/Total meters-squared of land; or • No. households with landmine injury/Total no. households [11]
Destroying infrastructure essential for civilian survival (e.g., food, water sources, hospitals)	Prohibited by Fourth Geneva Convention, APs I & II.	No. households with destroyed food source/total no. households [11]

AP, Additional Protocol.
doi:10.1371/journal.pmed.0050243.t003

Table 3 lists DWIs for unacceptable endangerment in armed conflict [14,23,24]. To illustrate, we apply the last DWI listed, "Destroying infrastructure essential for civilian survival (food, water, hospitals)," to survey data from eastern Burma where the Burmese military junta is in conflict with ethnic minority groups. The Burmese military regime destroyed or stole food from 472 of 1,813 surveyed households [11]. The Burmese military's DWI of 26 indicates a 26% rate of committing the humanitarian violation of destroying civilian food sources, associated in the study with significantly greater odds of household landmine injury (perhaps due to foraging for food), child malnutrition, and death [11].

In Table 4 we analyze the Northern Ireland conflict for two complementary DWIs: aggressive acts (killing civilians) and endangerment to civilians (by not wearing uniforms). Combatants who blur distinctions between themselves and civilians transfer their risk onto civilians [23,24]. Endangerment of noncombatants can be a byproduct of a method, as when guerrilla forces hide "among the people," taking the battlefield to civilians [23,24,26]. Endangerment can also be a direct goal. As described by Viet Cong leaders [27] and American soldiers [23] in the Vietnam War, Viet Cong forces trained children to throw grenades at South Vietnamese and American soldiers, partly to provoke opponents to shoot children and bring shame to themselves and their force. Child soldiers are more often killed or injured than adult soldiers, being deployed at the front line, to lay or clear mines, or as suicide bombers because they provoke less suspicion [3,28,29]. To illustrate the issue of variable access to valid data for DWI applications, precise data for calculating child solider DWIs (Table 3) may be difficult to obtain for some conflicts. However, DWIs for using child soldier suicide bombers (Tables 2 and 3) could be highly accurate due to extensive media coverage of suicide attacks.

Table 4. The Northern Ireland Conflict, 1969–2001: Complementary DWI Analyses for Unacceptable Aggression and Endangerment by Actors

DWI	British Security Forces	Irish Republican Paramilitaries	Loyalist Paramilitaries
No. civilians + civilian political activists killed [51]	190	738	873
Total no. persons killed [51]	362	2,056	1,020
Civilian mortality DWI calculation	190/362 = 0.52 × 100 = 52	738/2,056 = 0.36 × 100 = 36	873/1,020 = 0.86 × 100 = 86
Civilian mortality DWI value[a]	52	36	86
Combatants not wearing uniforms or distinguishing marks in attacks	Extremely low rate; British forces routinely wear uniforms in attacks.	Extremely high rate; Republican paramilitaries routinely dress as civilians in attacks.	Very high rate; Loyalist paramilitaries frequently dress as civilians during attacks.
Attacks without uniform DWI value	Approaches 0	Approaches 100	Approaches 100
Interpretation	British forces rank second dirtiest in terms of civilians constituting half their victims (DWI = 52), yet killed the lowest number of civilians (n = 190). British forces have a low, i.e., "clean" DWI value for attacks without uniform.	Republican paramilitaries have a high "attacks without uniform DWI" approaching 100. They thereby probably increase British forces' civilian mortality DWI by decreasing distinction between civilians and Republican combatants. Republican paramilitaries killed a high number of civilians (n = 738), but relative to their high number of total victims were least dirty in their civilian mortality ratio (DWI = 36). That their military opponents (British forces) wear uniforms increases their ability to distinguish civilians from combatants and to achieve a lower civilian mortality DWI.	Loyalist paramilitaries are dirtiest in terms of the civilian mortality DWI, with civilians constituting 86% of victims (DWI = 86). Loyalists also killed the highest absolute number of civilians (n = 873).

[a]Chi-square = 675, df = 2, $p < 0.001$.
doi:10.1371/journal.pmed.0050243.t004

DWI analysis can use any data source (media reports, epidemiological surveys, coroners' reports) as long as the data are adequately valid, accurate, and comprehensive. DWI analysis can be applied to event-based data or to aggregated data covering, for example, a year, a phase, or a whole conflict. Analysis of all DWIs supported by good data provides fuller description of a conflict and combatant behavior. A qualitative understanding of a conflict's nature and context is necessary for DWI application and interpretation. When possible, analysis should recognize when combatants avoid inflicting dirty outcomes, i.e., "clean" combat. DWIs suggest valuable data for prospective inclusion in conflict monitoring.

CONSIDERATIONS

When DWIs are used to compare combatant groups or methods, it should not be assumed that those with the highest values are simply the dirtiest. Nor should it be assumed that lower DWI values "don't count." A group may have a low DWI for recorded civilian mortality, but high DWIs for assassinating civilian leaders and disappearances. Another group may have low DWIs generally, and a very low DWI for torturing prisoners, but torture breaches the precepts of humanity utterly so that to have a measurable rate at all is deplorable.

DWIs reflect, in part, local conditions. For example, the lethality of civilian injuries reflects local treatment technology and access. It may therefore seem incorrect to compare DWIs for civilian lethality when health services differ. Similarly, it may seem unfair to compare child mortality DWIs between a conflict where children comprise a large proportion of the population and so are more likely to be killed and a conflict where children are few. However, researchers should not adjust for such factors when comparing DWIs across settings. This is because actors in armed conflict know, or are morally obliged to know, local resources and demographics and their implications for civilian harm. Combatants are obliged to take proportionately more care not to kill children when waging war in a child-dense population. Responsibility for dirty outcomes is not ameliorated by local conditions.

As for any conflict analysis [2,3,30], DWI selection, application, and interpretation must recognize the potential, varied biases of data sources and of particular DWIs. Conflicts are highly politicized, and combatants, supporters, and detractors have always tried to manipulate reports of war outcomes. Combatants may attempt to construct more favorable DWIs not only by decreasing dirty combat, but by concealing dirty outcomes, or by misrepresenting or provoking opponents' dirty outcomes. For example, a group might attempt to raise an opponent's child mortality DWI by using child soldiers or children as human shields.

Some DWI outcomes, such as injuries, may tend to be under-reported [16]. War-associated rape may be difficult to measure due to stigma and under-reporting, though substantial reports exist [21,24,31,32]. Although bias can affect DWI values, as ratios DWIs are relatively less affected by under- or over-counting than absolute numbers. For example, if a population generally under-reports war-related rape by 40%, this does not bias comparing rates between different combatant groups.

DWIs, complemented by absolute numbers, can suggest strategic aspects of actors' methods. For example, systematic civilian targeting is suggested by combined findings of: many events killing or injuring civilians; high ratios of civilian versus combatant mortality; frequent use of methods causing high civilian casualties; frequent use of methods causing high civilian lethality; and high rates of civilian harm from methods that are inherently "targeted" (handguns, machetes). Such proportional and numerical findings on civilian casualties have been used as evidence in International Criminal Court trials to establish systematic patterns indicating war crimes [33].

DWIS MEASURE OUTCOMES, NOT JUSTIFICATIONS OR INTENTIONS

DWIs focus on whether the practice of war is just (*jus in bello*) and ignore whether the reason for war is just (*jus ad bellum*), separating two logically distinct moral issues in war [23]. We focus on practical outcomes because justifications for war are contested, are used to legitimize dirty combat, and can bias examination of war's impact [24,27,34–36]. Combatants and their supporters may believe or describe methods as just, whether the method is suicide bombing [24,37,38] or the World War II targeting of civilians by Germany and by the Allies with carpet bombing, fire-bombing, and atomic bombs directed at cities [23,24,26,27].

Although intentions affect combat outcomes, such as civilian mortality rates [16,27,34,35], we separate DWIs from intentionality for the following reasons. Intentions are contested, obscured, and distorted [3,35]. Dirty outcomes can result from malicious intent, beneficent intent, or recklessness (lack of intent to take due care). Frequently, combatant violence that appears wanton, sadistic, or vengeful (e.g., rape, mutilation) is mobilized by political actors for hidden strategic aims [24,27,35,39,40]. Combatants' intended effects may be disrupted by targets or adversaries [41]. Individual combatant behavior reflects overriding goals and sociocultural aspects of larger groups [34,35,38].

Accommodating intentions or justifications in DWIs would imply that good intentions or a "just war" attenuate responsibility for bad outcomes; an implication that is morally and legally refuted [36]. DWIs therefore only recognize the crucial matter of outcomes: the killing, injury, or abuse of individuals and populations who should be protected from war.

POTENTIAL DETERRENT EFFECT OF THE DIRTY WAR INDEX

We choose the term "Dirty War Index" for three reasons. First, it unites moral, humanitarian, and scientific values inherent to most armed conflict research. Second, it avoids euphemisms that sanitize descriptions of war-induced public harm [12,13,27,42]. Third, emotional and cultural implications of "dirty" versus "clean" may heighten the sensitivity of combatant groups to the index, increasing its potential deterrent effect. No nation or combatant group wants to be considered "dirty" or described as dirtier than others.

Increased accountability can have a deterrent effect in armed conflict and encourages adherence to international humanitarian law; an important element in preventing violence towards noncombatants [1,24]. DWIs increase scrutiny and accountability specifically for dirty war methods. DWIs are analogous to corruption and bribery indices used by nongovernmental organizations and the World Bank to improve international governance through public monitoring and ranking governments by corruption [43,44]. In *Better: A Surgeon's Notes on Performance* [45], Atul Gawande describes how systematic analysis of war casualties reveals problems and suggests solutions, and how identifying exemplary performers can improve general performance. The DWI is developed for systematic, data-driven identification of relatively good versus bad performance, heightening its potential to stimulate positive change.

Military and political leaders not only want to win wars. They also seek superior moral authority [23]. Moral authority has social currency, creating better access to material resources, support, and security within local and international communities. To improve behavior in combatants and politicians insufficiently motivated by altruism, harnessing such self-interest is crucial. Exposure of atrocities through DWIs can put reputation, legitimacy, future resources, threat of retaliation, or power itself at stake [24].

As comparative rates, DWIs evoke the potential for change. The possibility of becoming "cleaner" may appeal to some offenders [24]. Actors may compete for better outcomes relative to military opponents, relative to in-group political competitors, or relative to themselves over time. A DWI's potency can be increased by engagement with social, cultural, and religious values of actors and their communities: honor versus dishonor [24], gaining versus losing "face," shame versus pride, dignity versus humiliation [37,46], sacred versus profane [37], and valuing mercy and the lives of innocents [47]. Terms other than "Dirty War Index," e.g., the "Dishonorable War Index," could be used to greater effect in different contexts.

War and its destruction trigger emotions and self-interests that can obscure analysis by threatening us so that we revert to familiar prejudices, reactions, and cognitive frameworks. Through a public health approach using valid, precise proportional rates as outcomes, DWIs can help us and our audiences to detach from political biases and break through psychological denial when considering actors or methods in war. DWIs can present conflict data from a new perspective, thereby encouraging actors in war to reassess their combat methods, accountability, and interests.

ACKNOWLEDGMENTS

We thank Hamit Dardagan of Iraq Body Count for suggesting the mistreatment of captured combatants as Dirty War Indices and the term "Dishonorable War Index," and for his helpful comments.

REFERENCES

1. Krug EG, Dahlberg LL, Mercy JA, Zwi AB, Lozano R, editors. (2002) World report on violence and health. World Health Organization. Available: http://www.who.int/violence_injury_prevention/violence/world_report/en/. Accessed 4 November 2008.
2. Murray CJL, King G, Lopez AD, Tomijima N, Krug EG (2002) Armed conflict as a public health problem. BMJ 324: 346–349.
3. Mack A, editor. (2008) Human Security Brief 2007. Human Security Report Project. Available: http://www.humansecuritybrief.info/access.html. Accessed 4 November 2008.
4. Coupland R (2007) Security, insecurity and health. Bull World Health Organ 85: 181–184.
5. Cobey JC, Raymond NA (2001) Antipersonnel land minds: A vector for human suffering. Ann Intern Med 134: 421–422.
6. Annas GJ (1998) Human rights and health—The Universal Declaration of Human Rights at 50. N Engl J Med 339: 1778–1781.
7. Flanagin A (2000) Human rights in the biomedical literature: The social responsibility of medical journals. JAMA 284: 618–619.
8. Levy BS, Sidel VW, editors. (2008) War and public health. 2nd edition. New York: Oxford University Press. 486 p. editors.
9. (2002) Addressing human rights violations: A public mental health perspective on helping torture survivors in Nepal. In: de Jong J, editor. Trauma, war, and violence: Public mental health in socio-cultural context. New York: Kluwer Academic. pp. 259–281. editor.
10. Thoms ONT, Ron J (2007) Public health, conflict and human rights: Toward a collaborative research agenda. Confl Health 1: 11.
11. Mullany LC, Richards AK, Lee CI, Suwanvanichkij V, Maung C, et al. (2007) Population-based survey methods to quantify associations between human rights violations and health outcomes among internally displaced persons in eastern Burma. J Epidemiol Community Health 61: 908–914.
12. McDonnell SM, Bolton P, Sunderland N, Bellows B, White M, et al. (2004) The role of the applied epidemiologist in armed conflict. Emerg Themes Epidemiol 1: 4.
13. Nathanson V (2000) Preventing and limiting suffering should conflict break out: The role of the medical profession. International Review of

the Red Cross 839: 601–615. Available: http://www.icrc.org/Web/Eng/siteeng0.nsf/html/57JQQ5. Accessed 4 November 2008.

14. International Committee of the Red Cross (2008) International humanitarian law. Available: http://www.icrc.org/Web/Eng/siteeng0.nsf/htmlall/ihl?OpenDocument. Accessed 4 November 2008.
15. Coupland RM (2001) Armed violence. Med Glob Surviv 7: 33–37.
16. Coupland RM, Meddings DM (1999) Mortality associated with use of weapons in armed conflicts, wartime atrocities, and civilian mass shootings: Literature review. BMJ 319: 407–410.
17. Taback N, Coupland R (2005) Towards collation and modeling of the global cost of armed violence on civilians. Med Confl Surviv 21: 19–27.
18. Restrepo J, Spagat M, Vargas JF (2004) The dynamics of the Colombian civil conflict: A new data set. Homo Oeconomicus 21: 396–428.
19. Spagat M (2006) Colombia's paramilitary DDR: Quiet and tentative success. Available: http://www.cerac.org.co/pdf/UNDP_DDR_V1.pdf. Accessed 4 November 2008.
20. (2006) 'Atrocity statistics' and other lessons from Darfur. In: Totten S, Markusen E, editors. Genocide in Darfur: Investigating the atrocities in the Sudan. New York: Routledge. pp. 189–195. editors.
21. Totten S, Markusen E, editors. (2006) Genocide in Darfur: Investigating the atrocities in the Sudan. New York: Routledge. 284 p. editors.
22. Schmitt MN (2005) Precision attack and international humanitarian law. International Review of the Red Cross 87: 445–466.
23. Walzer M (1977) Just and unjust wars: A moral argument with historical illustrations. New York: Basic Books. 361 p.
24. Slim H (2007) Killing civilians: Method, madness and morality in war. London: Hurst & Company. 319 p.
25. Bilukha OO, Tsitsaev Z, Ibragimov R, Anderson M, Brennan M, et al. (2006) Epidemiology of injuries and deaths from landmines and unexploded ordnance in Chechnya, 1994 through 2005. JAMA 296: 516–518.
26. Smith R (2005) The utility of force: The art of war in the modern world. London: Allen Lane, Penguin Group. 428 p.
27. Grossman D (1995) On killing: The psychological cost of learning to kill in war and society. New York: Back Bay Books/Little, Brown and

Company. 366 p.

28. Coalition to Stop the Use of Child Soldiers (2008) Child soldiers. Available: http://www.child-soldiers.org/childsoldiers. Accessed 4 November 2008.
29. McKay S (2005) Girls as "weapons of terror" in Northern Uganda and Sierra Leonean rebel fighting forces. Studies in Conflict & Terrorism 28: 385–397.
30. (2008) Statistical thinking and data analysis: Enhancing human rights work. In: Asher J, Banks D, Scheuren FJ, editors. Statistical methods for human rights. New York: Springer. pp. 65–85. editors.
31. Kolbe AR, Hutson RA (2006) Human rights abuse and other criminal violations in Port-au-Prince, Haiti: A random survey of households. Lancet 368: 864–873.
32. Physicians for Human Rights (2002) War-related sexual violence in Sierra Leone: A population-based assessment. Available: http://physiciansforhumanrights.org/library/report-sierraleone-2000.html. Accessed 4 November 2008.
33. (2008) Obtaining evidence for the International Criminal Court using data and quantitative analysis. In: Asher J, Banks D, Scheuren FJ, editors. Statistical methods for human rights. New York: Springer. pp. 195–226. editors.
34. Appy CG (2006) Vietnam: The definitive oral history told from all sides. London: Ebury Press. 574 p.
35. Kalyvas SN (2006) The logic of violence in civil war. New York: Cambridge University Press. 485 p.
36. Bugnion F (2002) Just wars, wars of aggression and international humanitarian law. International Review of the Red Cross 84: 523–546.
37. Atran S (2006) The moral logic and growth of suicide terrorism. Wash Q 29: 127–147.
38. (2006) Dying to kill: Motivations for suicide terrorism. In: Pedahzur A, editor. Root causes of suicide terrorism: The globalization of martyrdom. London: Routledge. pp. 25–53. editor.
39. Richards P (2004) Fighting for the rain forest: War, youth & resources in Sierra Leone. Portsmouth (NH): Heinemann. 198 p.
40. Leites N, Wolf C Jr (1970) Rebellion and authority: An analytic essay on insurgent conflicts. Chicago: Markham. 174 p.

41. Harrison M (2006) Bombers and bystanders in suicide attacks in Israel, 2000–2003. Studies in Conflict & Terrorism 29: 187–206.
42. Zwi AB (2004) How should the health community respond to violent political conflict. PLoS Med 1: e14.
43. Transparency International (2008) About Transparency International. Available: http://www.transparency.org/about_us. Accessed 4 November 2008.
44. World Bank (2007) Governance matters 2007: Worldwide governance indicators, 1996–2006. Available: http://info.worldbank.org/governance/wgi/index.asp. Accessed 4 November 2008.
45. Gawande A (2007) Better: A surgeon's notes on performance. London: Profile Books. 273 p.
46. Lindner E (2006) Making enemies: Humiliation and international conflict. Westport (CT): Praeger Publishers. 224 p.
47. al-Oadah S (2007) A Ramadan letter to Osama bin Laden. Available: http://www.islamtoday.com/printmenice.cfm?cat_id=29&sub_cat_id=1521. Accessed 4 November 2008.
48. (2005) Ballistic trauma, armed violence and international law. In: Mahoney PF, Ryan JM, Brooks AJ, Schwab CW, editors. Ballistic trauma: A practical guide. 2nd edition. London: Springer-Verlag. pp. 122–134. editors.
49. International Committee of the Red Cross (2003) Children in war: Summary table of IHL provisions specifically applicable to children. Available: http://www.icrc.org/web/eng/siteeng0.nsf/html/5ffljj5/$file/ang03_04a_tableaudih_total_logo.pdf?openelement. Accessed 4 November 2008.
50. Spiegel PB, Salama P (2000) War and mortality in Kosovo, 1998–99: An epidemiological testimony. Lancet 355: 2204–2209.
51. Sutton M (2002) An index of deaths from the conflict in Ireland. CAIN Web Service. Available: http://cain.ulst.ac.uk/sutton/index.html. Accessed 6 November 2008.

CHAPTER 8

MEASURING HUMAN RIGHTS VIOLATIONS IN A CONFLICT-AFFECTED COUNTRY: RESULTS FROM A NATIONWIDE CLUSTER SURVEY IN CENTRAL AFRICAN REPUBLIC

Alina Potts, Kathleen Myer, Les Roberts

Program on Forced Migration and Health, Heilbrunn Department of Population and Family Health, Mailman School of Public Health, Columbia University, 60 Haven Ave B-4, Suite 432, New York, NY, USA

Citation: Alina Potts, Kathleen Myer and Les Roberts, Conflict and Health20115:4, https://doi.org/10.1186/1752-1505-5-4 © Potts et al; licensee BioMed Central Ltd. 2011 Received: 9 November 2010 Accepted: 7 March 2011 Published: 7 March 2011.

ABSTRACT

Background

Measuring human rights violations is particularly challenging during or after armed conflict. A recent nationwide survey in the Central African Republic produced estimates of rates of grave violations against children and adults affected by armed conflict, using an approach known as the "Neighborhood Method".

Methods

In June and July, 2009, a random household survey was conducted based on population estimates from the 2003 national census. Clusters were assigned systematically proportional to population size. Respondents in randomly selected households were interviewed regarding incidents of killing, intentional injury, recruitment into armed groups, abduction, sexual abuse and rape between January 1, 2008 and the date of interview, occurring in their homes' and those of their three closest neighbors.

Results

Sixty of the selected 69 clusters were surveyed. In total, 599 women were interviewed about events in 2,370 households representing 13,669 persons. Estimates of annual rates of each violation occurring per 1000 people in each of two strata are provided for children between the ages of five and 17, adults 18 years of age and older and the entire population five years and older, along with a combined and weighted national rate. The national rates for children age five to 17 were estimated to be 0.98/1000/year (95% CI: 0.18 - 1.78) for recruitment, 2.56/1000/year (95% CI: 1.50 - 3.62) for abduction, 1.13/1000/year (95% CI: 0.33 - 1.93) for intentional injury, 10.72/1000 girls/year (95% CI: 7.40 - 14.04) for rape, and 4.80/1000 girls/year (95% CI: 2.61 - 6.00) for sexual abuse. No reports of any violation against a person under the age of five were recorded and there were no reports of rape or sexual abuse of males. No children were reported to have been killed during the recall period. Rape and abduction were the most frequently reported events.

Conclusions

The population-based figures greatly augment existing information on human rights violations in CAR, and represent a step forward in quantifying the protection needs of Central Africans. Government, donors, and international organizations should make use of this data to better inform advocacy, prevention, and response programs, to assist in fundraising, and to develop surveillance activities to monitor child protection concerns.

Keywords: Sexual Abuse, United Nations, Sexual Violence, Security Council, Recall Period

BACKGROUND

Measuring human rights violations is difficult even in the best of circumstances, and particularly challenging during or after conflict, when populations are under extreme duress and the systems needed to support them have been disrupted or destroyed [1, 2]. While data derived from surveys or surveillance systems is crucial to informing the funding and planning necessary for an effective humanitarian and public health response, these systems often do not track violations of individuals' rights. Where documentation of human rights abuses in conflict is available, it is often based on individual case reports, which provide detailed descriptions but are likely to represent only a small portion of actual events [3].

To gain a more complete understanding of the extent and nature of human rights violations, case reports and qualitative situational analyses should be augmented with population-based estimates that provide data on the scope and magnitude of the problem [4]. In taking this mixed methods approach, qualitative reports that provide information about the experience of those affected and the context in which violations occur are complemented by quantitative methods, to determine approximately how many people are affected, which violations are most prevalent, with what frequency they occur, and where. Several rigorous, quantitative studies of the prevalence of human rights abuses and sexual violence in conflict have been undertaken in recent years [1, 3, 5, 6, 7, 8], and epidemiological methods [9] have increasingly been used to explore rights violations. Yet such studies remain rare and lack uniform methods. Thus, there exists a need to develop appropriate methods to capture these data in insecure, logistically challenging, and culturally and politically sensitive environments.

The United Nations (UN) has increasingly asked country programs in conflict areas to collect such data and to specifically address the care and protection of children. UN Security Council Resolution 1612 requested the immediate establishment of a monitoring and reporting mechanism (MRM) "to collect and provide timely, objective, accurate and reliable information" on "grave" violations against children affected by armed conflict [10]. The

MRM seeks to monitor the following six grave violations against children: killing and maiming; abduction; attacks against schools and hospitals; rape and sexual violence; denial of humanitarian access; and recruitment or use of child soldiers (now referred to as children recruited or used by armed forces or armed groups) [11]. While MRM processes differ among countries, they currently rely on "verified" cases. This refers to a passive surveillance system that relies on incident reports captured by NGO partners implementing programs, or by community-based monitoring led by civil society organizations. These incidents are then confirmed, normally by a UN agency, through other sources. The collection of population-based data would complement this process, and provide the UN and other actors accountable for the protection of children with broader estimates of both the scale and spread of rights violations in conflict. In December 2007, Columbia University, the U.S. Centers for Disease Control and Prevention, and UNICEF initiated collaboration on developing population-based methods to capture grave violations capable of complementing the current practice of case-based MRM monitoring.

Conflict in the Central African Republic (CAR) is one of 20 situations of concern in the UN Secretary-General's 2009 report to the Security Council on children and armed conflict [12]. One of the world's poorest and least healthy states, CAR ranks 179th out of 182 countries in the 2009 Human Development Index rankings [13]. Multiple armed actors are active in CAR, including relatively weak government armed forces, five formal and recognized non-state armed groups, and various other non-state armed elements, such as village self-defense groups and road bandits-known locally as Zaraguinas-who operate throughout the country with impunity [14]. Due to the meager humanitarian presence outside the capital city, little information is available on the human (or child) rights abuses occurring or on the full extent of the health and security crisis facing the country. Thus, in June and July of 2009, a Columbia University research team, with the support of the United Nations Children's Fund (UNICEF) in CAR, executed a national, stratified, four-stage cluster survey to obtain estimates of the rates of four of the grave violations committed against children: killing or maiming, abduction, recruitment, and rape or sexual abuse. Attacks against schools or hospitals and denial of humanitarian access for children were not included at this time, as they occur at the community level rather than at the individual or household level at which the survey was conducted.

METHODS

In the 1980s, the "sisterhood method" was developed as an efficient means of measuring maternal mortality through population-based surveys. With this method, adult respondents are asked questions about the survival of siblings sharing the same mother [15]. Since maternal deaths are a relatively rare phenomenon, the ability to capture information on multiple persons through one respondent expands the effective sample available for analysis given a fixed number of data collection contact points, making data collection more efficient and avoiding the prohibitive costs associated with obtaining very large sample sizes. Building on this and subsequent revisions, Columbia University developed the "Neighborhood Method" to measure sensitive events, such as rape and sexual abuse, in situations of humanitarian concern where security, logistical and financial constraints can make large samples difficult to obtain.

In this method, interviewers conduct one-on-one, in-depth, household-based interviews, asking about respondents' experiences as well as the experiences of all members of their household, and members of the households of their three closest neighbors. The neighborhood method reproduces the efficiency of the sisterhood method, while also allowing two lenses through which respondents can speak about sensitive topics: disclosure of their and their family's experiences, as well as anonymous disclosure of their neighbors' experiences. These lenses also offer potential sources of validation, such as the potential to examine under-reporting by interviewees of their own adverse experiences [16].

The survey in Central African Republic represented the fifth time the neighborhood method has been executed in a conflict or post-conflict setting, following pilots in northern Uganda (2006) [17] with Christian Children's Fund, in Liberia (2007) [2] and Ethiopia's Somali region (2008) [18] with the International Rescue Committee, and in Sri Lanka (2008) [16] with Save the Children.

Protocol and Ethical Considerations

The research protocol was developed building on published guidelines for working with sexual violence survivors [19], as well as operational guidelines utilized by members of the research team during previous work in gender-based violence response. First and foremost, consideration was given to the sensitive topics to be covered and possible negative repercussions arising from such discussions, for both respondents and interviewers. Interviews took place only with women 18 years of age or older, in a private space, and after obtaining informed consent and notifying the respondent that she could end the interview at any time. Information on health and social services available in the different areas of CAR was obtained to enable interviewers to refer respondents to services if needed; however, it should be noted that access to services in most areas of CAR is severely hampered due to insecurity, lack of public or private means of transport, and poor quality roads. During field research, if the survey team came across a person deemed to be in dire need of immediate medical assistance, the team would provide her or him with transportation to the nearest health facility.

Confidentiality of neighbor reports was enhanced by a revision to the method in which small objects were used to represent the aggregate number of individuals residing in neighboring households (see further discussion below). In order to monitor the safety of survey respondents, households in some villages were re-visited several days to a week after the initial interview, and respondents were asked about any positive or negative consequences following their interview. If a negative incident was reported, the survey team would be able to gain insight into the possibility of risk to future respondents. If more than one violent incident were reported, the survey would come to an immediate halt. Columbia University's Institutional Review Board approved the protocol.

Interviewer Training and Questionnaire

The survey team consisted of three researchers from Columbia University and six Central African interviewers. Training of the interviewers took place over five days. Most interviewers had past survey experience with non-governmental organizations or private companies. All were female, university-educated, and fluent in French and Sangho, a language spoken nationally. Many interviewers spoke other local languages as well. The training method included role play, didactic sessions, and practice interviews. Training began with an open discussion on child protection and gender-based violence issues in CAR, followed by extensive discussions on the meaning and definitions of the grave violations being measured. Other topics covered included working with survivors of violence, informed consent and maintaining confidentiality, surveying methods and data collection techniques, and referral protocols. One of the interviewers, a trained social worker, co-facilitated the session on gender-based violence. The questionnaire and data collection forms were revised throughout the training, and field-tested during two days of pilot interviews conducted in

Bangui.

The questionnaire was based on those used in previous iterations of the method. Interviewer input assisted in placing each definition within a local context and wording questions such that local populations would best understand what was being asked of them. For example, maiming was defined locally using a term translatable in English as injury, and defined so as to include incidents of killing. The definitions for each grave violation, as agreed upon by the research team, are as follows:

- **Injury**: Any type of injury to a person, accidental or intentional, including killing and other injuries that resulted in physical harm. Only non-fatal injuries recorded as intentional and non-self-inflicted were counted as an injury violation. Intentional, non-self-inflicted injuries resulting in death were counted as a killing violation.
- **Recruitment**: Being approached by or recruited to join armed groups, forcibly or otherwise (i.e. voluntarily).
- **Abduction**: Being forcibly taken or disappearing from a home or village.
- **Sexual Abuse**: Unwanted verbal harassment or attempts at touching; unwanted sexual advances such as kissing, groping, etc.; or attempted rape, defined as an attempt at non-consensual penetration of an orifice by an object or the body part of another person, without the actual act of penetration taking place.
- **Rape**: Penetration of an orifice by an object or the body part of another person, without one's consent.
- Questionnaires were written in French, and a Sangho version was verbally agreed-upon by the interview team.

Sampling

Sampling was based on 2003 census data from the *3ème Recensement Général de la Population et de l'Habitation de 2003 (RGPH03)*, obtained from the UN Office for the Coordination of Humanitarian Affairs (OCHA) in Bangui. Previous surveys in CAR [20] and the experience of colleagues indicated that there is generally better economic status and development indicators in Bangui and the southern areas of the country, and identified the majority of recent or current conflict zones lying in the northern half of the country, which is close to neighboring conflicts in Chad and Sudan.

To increase the survey's precision, the country was divided into two strata based on these differences (see figure 1). The "northern stratum" included Bamingui Bangoran, Nana Gribizi, Ouham, Ouham Pendé, Nana Mambéré, Haut Kotto, Haut Mbomou, and Vakaga prefectures. This area has an estimated population of 1,394 million people. Prefectures considered to be less affected by conflict and within closer reach of government services were Mambéré Kadéï, Sangha Mbaéré, Lobaye, Ombella M'Poko, Bangui, Kémo, Ouaka, Basse Kotto, and Mbomou. This area is referred to as the "southern stratum" and has an estimated population of 2,501 million people.

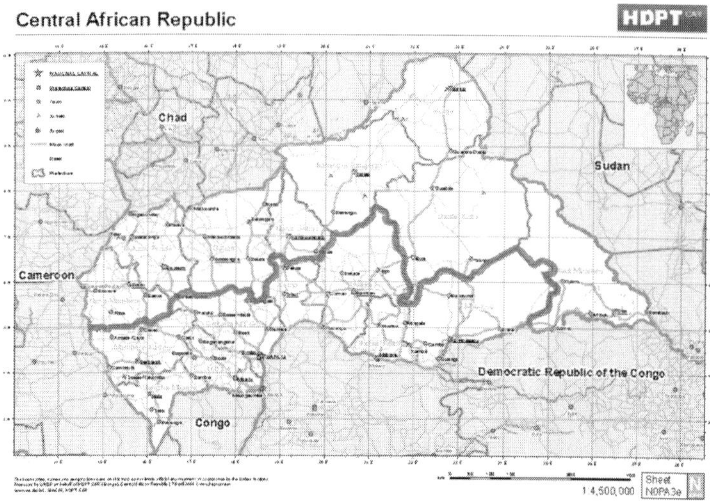

Figure 1: Map of the Central African Republic showing the delineation of the northern and southern strata.

A minimum effective sample size of 864 individuals (providing data on at least 6 female neighbors) in each stratum was required in order to estimate with 95% confidence the proportion experiencing rape to within 2% and assuming a true prevalence of 10% (calculated using Epi Info, Version 6, CDC Atlanta, 1993). A design effect of two was assumed, suggesting a sample of 300 households (30 clusters of 10 households) per stratum. A household was defined as people who eat together, and for the purposes of enumeration of the sample, included all members who had slept there the previous night.

Security and logistical constraints prevented the team from planning data collection activities in Vakaga and Haut Mbomou prefectures. Because of this, and the assumption that further logistical constraints and UN security regulations would arise during data collection, 36 clusters were selected from the northern stratum and 33 were selected from the southern stratum, with a goal of obtaining 30 clusters from each. Cluster selection was performed in four stages by sampling population proportional to size (PPS): first selecting the number of clusters per prefecture, followed by the number of clusters per commune (administrative district) within the prefecture, then the specific village or urban neighborhood, and finally the initial household. It was determined that by including the no-travel areas in the sampling frame, and then adding those missed clusters to the villages that were unreachable, the team could best articulate the fraction of the population missed because of security and logistical concerns. If, during surveying, a selected cluster was inaccessible not because of security but due to a damaged bridge, flooding, or some other logistical constraint, the nearest accessible town or village to that selected cluster was used as a substitute.

Within each selected cluster (either a village or urban neighborhood), permission to work was first sought from the locally identified leader, usually the village chief. The chief or a representative would accompany the research team to ascertain the village's or neighborhood's borders and create a rough map of the cluster. In small clusters, the team was able to count the total number of households, while in more populated clusters, the total was estimated by breaking the cluster into geographically distinct sections, counting the households along two axes of each section, and multiplying these together as an estimate of household density. The sampling interval was determined by dividing the total number of households by 10. The smallest interval used, regardless of the number of households in a given location, was six, guaranteeing that a selected household's neighbors would not then be re-selected as a household in the sample. If a village consisted of fewer than 60 households, interviewing would continue in the same direction, using the same sampling interval of six, into the nearest adjacent village. Because of the need to complete interviews and return to UN-approved overnight locations before curfew, the largest interval used was 20.

The first household to be interviewed was selected at random. In large villages and urban areas, this process sometimes occurred in two parts. First, the rough map of the cluster's layout and density was used to divide it in half, or for very large clusters, 3-5 distinct sections (of no more than 200 households each), and a coin flip or random digit generator (paper currency) was used to select the section in which surveying would begin. A random number between one and the sampling interval would then be selected from the numbers (beginning on the right) of a different piece of paper currency.

The next nine households were selected systematically in an attempt to have a sample that was spread evenly over the village or neighborhood. The ten households to be interviewed, and the three nearest neighbors of each, were identified by the team leader before interviewers approached the household.

Data Collection

On approaching the household, interviewers introduced themselves as members of a UNICEF team interested in learning about the situation of women and children, and asked to speak with the female head of household. After explaining the purpose of the visit and ensuring that the woman was at least 18 years of age, the interviewer would invite her to participate in an interview and ask to move to a private space in or near the home. The interviewer would then read an informed consent statement and record the respondent's oral consent and her age and marital status on the data collection form. If no eligible respondents were home or willing to participate, the interviewer would go to the next nearest neighbor of the three households previously identified by the team leader. If the interviewer encountered four refusals or unavailable households in a row, she would then proceed to the household at the start of the next sampling interval. In one cluster where many such "skips" occurred due to most of the village being away, several homes were revisited and the interviews conducted with those absent during the original day of data collection. This was done to determine the potential for absentee bias associated with the initial skips, and data from these revisits are not included in the analysis.

Interviewers were encouraged to collect information via semi-structured conversations rather than by a series of rigid questions. Questions regarding household composition, births, and deaths since January 1, 2009, were followed by a more general probe of the problems facing women and children in the respondent's village or neighborhood. In many cases, this would lead to a respondent-initiated discussion related to one or more of the violations under study, and the interview could be built on these initial concerns. The interviewer moved on to questions regarding the occurrence of each of the four grave violations since January 1, 2008; the longer recall period allowed for inclusion of events occurring before peace accords were signed in June and December 2008. At the end of the interview, women were asked what they thought would be the most helpful solutions to the problems discussed. If health or other services were available nearby, the interviewer would offer information on relevant services. Interviews typically lasted about 40 minutes.

Following the neighborhood method, all interview questions were asked both for the respondents' household and for those of her three closest neighbors. To facilitate this process, objects were used to represent the compositions of the three neighbor households. Different-sized bells or buttons of two different colors were used to denote both males and females above 18 years, males and females between 5 and 17 years, and children below 5 years of age. As each additional household was described, more objects were added to the pile that represented the combined composition of the three nearest households; grouping the objects in this way added a degree of anonymity to the neighbor's information, in that the specific neighboring household of someone experiencing an incident was not indicated to the interviewer. When events were discussed, interviewers could refer to the objects to ensure that the person experiencing the incident was one of the neighbors previously described. In the case of a death, an object could be placed in the collection to confirm that there was previously another person living among this group. If an interviewee did not know a household well enough to provide at least its crude composition, the interviewee was not asked about that household.

Analysis

In order to estimate the annual rate of each incident and provide a breakdown of these rates by age, each member of the sample population was analyzed individually, regardless of her or his status as belonging to a respondent ("self-report") household or a neighboring household. If an individual experienced multiple violations, for example rape and abduction, this would be counted as both a rape and an abduction. However, if the same individual survived repeat incidents of the same violation (i.e. multiple rapes), the first instance of the given violation occurring within the recall period is the only one counted.

Data were analyzed by strata. Annual incident rates and confidence intervals were calculated with software designed for Save the Children by Mark Myatt (Institute of Ophthalmology, UCL, London, UK), which takes into account the design effect associated with cluster surveys. Nationwide estimates were created using WINPEPI Describe version 1.44 (J.H. Abramson, 2004), which weighted strata proportional to their 2003 census population in making point estimates and confidence intervals. For confidence interval calculations, the entire sampling universe was assumed to have the same age and gender breakdown as the sample taken (for example, 16.7% of the sample in the northern stratum is <5 years old, so the entire population of <5-year-olds in the northern stratum was assumed to be 16.7% of the 1,394 million people comprising the entire 2003 census estimate for that area). The midpoint date of the interviewing process was used for a recall period of 18.1 months. A steady-state population, where the number of people entering the age category was equal to the number of people exiting over the recall period, was assumed as the denominator for each rate. Within-sample descriptive statistics were calculated with SPSS 16.0 (SPSS Inc, 2007).

RESULTS

In total, 599 women were interviewed about events in approximately 2,370 households across the two strata: 310 women in the southern stratum and 289 women in the northern stratum. The vast majority of women interviewed were able to report on the situations of the residents in all three neighboring households, with only 17 of the 599 respondents unable to do so. The population living in respondent households ("self-report households") and their closest neighboring households ("neighbor-report households") represented in the survey is 13,669 persons: 6,668 in the northern stratum and 7,001 in the southern stratum (Table 1). The median age of respondents was 28 years (range 18-80) and the majority (70%) was married, with 14% single, 12% widowed, and 4% divorced. Of the 69 villages or urban neighborhoods selected into the sample as clusters, 9 (7 in the north, 2 in the south) were inaccessible and could not be substituted with a nearby village or neighborhood. Of these, 3 were located in prefectures partly or wholly excluded from the survey due to both security and logistical constraints (Vakaga, Haut Mbomou, and Bamingui Bangoran). The total population represented by these missed clusters was approximately 19% in the north (7/36) and 6% in the south (2/33). On 9 other occasions (4 in the north, 5 in the south), the specific village selected could not be reached because of a logistical barrier, but a neighboring village was selected as a substitute.

Seven women (1.2%; 2 in the south, 5 in the north) refused to be interviewed for varying reasons. Two of the refusals occurred in a set of households where no neighbors were present to be interviewed either. No response was obtained on 63 occasions (9.5%), when the selected household and all 3 neighbors were not at home. On a separate 285 occasions (32%), no eligible respondent was home at selected households, but one of the other three neighbors was successfully interviewed about the same group of 4 households.

Table 1: Sample Population by Age, Gender, and Strata: Self-Report and Neighbor-Report Household (HHs)*

	Under 5		**5-17**				**18+**				**TOTAL**
	Self-Report HHs	***Neigh-bor-Report HHs***	***Self-Report HHs***		***Neighbor-Report HHs***		***Self-Report HHs***		***Neighbor-Report HHs***		
			Male	**Female**	**Male**	**Female**	**Male**	**Female**	**Male**	**Female**	
North	367	795	337	359	852.5	912	353	469	986.5	1236.5	**6668**
South	384	861	349	375	854	949.5	432.5	564	1030	1201.5	**7001**
	751	1656	686	734	1706.5	1861.5	785.5	1033	2016.5	2438	**13669**

* Non-integer numbers arose as the result of partial person-time being added for household members reported to have experienced one of the grave violations that resulted in their removal from the household at some point during the recall period. These numbers were always rounded to the nearest integer when totaled.

Self vs. Neighbor Reports

Information for each grave violation, broken down by respondents' reports of incidents in their own households and those occurring in their neighbors' households, are reported in Table 2. The annual rates (combined & weighted national estimates) of injury and rape were about twice as high among self-report households as among neighbor-report households. For abduction and sexual abuse, the rates reported among self-report and neighbor-report households were similar. Comparison between reports of killing, and of recruitment, is not possible due to the low number of incidents reported. By examining the confidence intervals surrounding the directly estimated difference in prevalence between self-report and neighbor-report households (among both strata combined), we noted no statistically significant difference between the occurrence of self-reported events and those reported to have occurred in neighboring households, except for reports of rape and intentional injury. Statistically significant differences (i.e. 80% confidence intervals do not overlap) between self-reported and neighbor-reported incidents exist for the reporting of rape in the northern and southern strata as well as the combined national estimate, and for the reporting of intentional injuries in the combined national estimate.

Table 2: Reported Violations Among Self-Report vs. Neighbor-Report Households (HHs)

		North		**South**		**Combined & Weighted National Estimate**	
		Incidents Recorded	***Annual Rate/1000 people (95% CI)***	***Incidents Recorded***	***Annual Rate/1000 people (95% CI)***	***Incidents Recorded***	***Annual Rate/1000 people (95% CI)***
Recruitment	Self-Report HHs	1	0.44 (0 - 1.35)	0	N/A	1	0.16 (0 - 0.49)
	Neighbor-Report HHs	17	2.83 (0.53 - 5.13)	0	N/A	17	1.02 (0.19 - 1.84)
Abduction	Self-Report HHs	26	11.36 (6.78 - 15.93)	1	0.39 (0 - 1.21)	27	4.32 (2.60 - 6.05)
	Neighbor-Report HHs	90	15.00 (10.19 - 19.81)	5	0.82 (0.03 - 1.61)	95	5.91 (4.11 - 7.71)

Rape	Self-Report HHs	41	32.83 (21.03 - 44.63)	32	22.59 (13.27 - 31.92)	73	26.29 (18.96 - 33.61)
	Neighbor-Report HHs	76	23.52 (17.16 - 29.88)	32	9.86 (6.84 - 12.89)	108	14.79 (11.79 - 17.79)
Sexual Abuse	Self-Report HHs	9	7.21 (3.14 - 11.27)	3	2.12 (0 - 4.57)	12	3.95 (1.81 - 6.10)
	Neighbor-Report HHs	30	9.28 (5.96 - 12.61)	8	2.47 (0.47 - 4.47)	38	4.92 (3.17 - 6.68)
Killing*	Self-Report HHs	4	1.75 (0.18 - 3.32)	0	N/A	4	0.63 (0.06 - 1.19)
	Neighbor-Report HHs	13	2.16 (0.99 - 3.34)	1	0.16 (0 - 0.47)	14	0.88 (0.42 - 1.35)
Intentional Injury*	Self-Report HHs	22	9.61 (4.89 - 14.33)	12	4.62 (2.29 - 6.96)	34	6.41 (4.15 - 8.67)
	Neighbor-Report HHs	30	4.99 (2.26 - 7.71)	12	1.97 (0.47 - 3.47)	42	3.06 (1.68 - 4.43)

* Killing and intentional injury are mutually exclusive categories.

Point Estimates

No reports of any violation against a child under the age of five were recorded and there were no reports of rape or sexual abuse of males. For this reason, all point estimates (Table 3) were calculated using the sample population five years of age and over, and using only females when calculating estimates of rape and sexual abuse.

Table 3: Reported Violations by Age Group and Strata

	North		South		Total Incidents Recorded	Combined & Weighted National Estimate	
	Incidents Recorded	**Annual Rate/1000 People (95% CI)**	**Incidents Recorded**	**Annual Rate/1000 People (95% CI)**		**Annual Number of Incidents (95% CI)**	**Annual Rate/1000 People (95% CI)**
Violation	**Children 5-17**						
Recruitment	10	2.70 (0.50 - 4.89)	0	N/A	10	1392 (252 -2520)	0.98 (0.18 - 1.78)
Abduction	21	5.67 (3.15 - 8.18)	3	0.79 (0 - 1.64)	24	3624 (2124 - 5136)	2.56 (1.50 - 3.62)
Rape	32	16.72 (10.44 - 23.00)	15	7.51 (3.67 - 11.34)	47	8172 (5640 - 10704)	10.72 (7.40 - 14.04)
Sexual Abuse	21	10.97 (5.96 - 15.99)	3	1.50 (0 - 3.53)	24	3660 (1992 - 5340)	4.80 (2.61 - 6.0)
Killing*	0	N/A	0	N/A	0	N/A	N/A
Intentional Injury*	3	0.81 (0 - 1.69)	5	1.31 (0.16 - 2.46)	8	1596 (468 - 2736)	1.13 (0.33 - 1.93)
	Adults >= 18						
Recruitment	8	1.74 (0 - 3.55)	0	N/A	8	1104 (0 - 2256)	0.62 (0 - 1.26)
Abduction	95	20.73 (13.94 - 27.51)	3	0.62 (0 - 1.32)	98	13908 (9516 - 18312)	7.77 (5.31 - 10.23)

Rape	85	33.12 (25.01 - 41.24)	49	18.40 (12.44 - 24.37)	134	23414 (18672 - 28164)	23.72 (18.91 - 28.53)
Sexual Abuse	18	7.01 (4.38 - 9.65)	8	3.00 (0.13 - 5.87)	26	4392 (2352 - 6432)	4.45 (2.39 - 6.52)
Killing*	17	3.70 (1.93 - 5.48)	1	0.21 (0 - 0.58)	18	2592 (1380 - 3804)	1.45 (0.77 - 2.13)
Intentional Injury*	49	10.67 (6.35 - 14.99)	19	3.90 (1.40 - 6.41)	68	11292 (7308 - 15288)	6.31 (4.08 - 8.54)
	Total Population >= 5						
Recruitment	18	2.17 (0.46 - 3.88)	0	N/A	18	2496 (528-4464)	0.78 (0.16 - 1.39)
Abduction	116	13.99 (9.71 - 18.27)	6	0.69 (0.10 - 1.28)	122	17532 (12456 - 22608)	5.47 (3.88 - 7.05)
Rape	117	26.11 (20.13 - 32.09)	64	13.73 (10.46 - 17.00)	181	31416 (26220 - 36660)	18.20 (15.19 - 21.20)
Sexual Abuse	39	8.70 (5.86 - 11.55)	11	2.36 (0.69 - 4.03)	50	8028 (5472 - 10584)	4.65 (3.17 - 6.13)
Killing*	17	2.05 (1.07 - 3.03)	1	0.12 (0 - 0.33)	18	2592 (1380 - 3804)	0.81 (0.43-1.19)
Intentional Injury*	52	6.26 (3.72-8.81)	24	2.77 (1.34 - 4.19)	76	12900 (8748 - 17040)	4.02 (2.73 - 5.31)

* Killing and intentional injury are mutually exclusive categories.

Looking within the sample at the confidence intervals around reported incidents among all persons over 5 years old, those living in the north consistently experienced violations at a rate significantly higher than those living in the south.

Recruitment

Eighteen incidents of forcible recruitment were reported, all in the northern stratum. Approximately 2.17 (95% CI: 0.46 - 3.88) people per 1000 in the north were forcibly recruited into armed groups each year over the recall period. It should be noted that only adults forcibly recruited by armed groups were included, while reports of both forcible and "voluntary" child recruitment were included. Both armed groups and Zaraguinas were responsible for recruitments. Of the 8 incidents among adults, 7 were males, with a median age of 21.5 years (range 18-32). All incidents were perpetrated by armed groups, except one man who was recruited by Zaraguinas. The median age among the 10 children recruited was 16 years (range 12-17). Six of the children were male and four were female. All incidents of child recruitment were perpetrated by armed groups, with the exception of two boys who were recruited as Zaraguinas. Two of the 16-year-old boys reportedly joined the armed groups "voluntarily". All incidents among females (1 adult, 4 children) involved an armed group first raping and abducting the victims.

Abduction

Abduction was one of the most frequently reported violations, with 122 incidents reported. The vast majority (95.1%, n = 116) of these occurred in the north, where the estimated annual rate of abduction during the recall period was 5.67 per 1000 children ages 5 to 17 years (95% CI: 3.15-8.18), and 20.73 per 1000 adults over 18 years (95% CI: 13.94-27.51). Most abductions (64.8%, n = 79) occurred among adult men. Overall, perpetrators included armed groups (70, all in the north), Zaraguinas (44, of which 40 were in the north), unknown actors (5), and government forces (3). Among 19 adult women, 10 were taken by armed groups and 8 by Zaraguinas; in 6 cases rape by the perpetrator(s) was also reported, and in 1 case in the north a 50-year-old woman was also killed by her captors.

The 24 children affected ranged in age from 8-17 years (median = 15); 21 lived in the north and two-thirds of all abducted children were male (n = 16). The largest perpetrator of incidents against children remained armed groups (12) and Zaraguinas (11), with Zaraguinas taking only boys and armed groups abducting both boys and girls. Among the 8 reported abductions of girls, 7 were taken by armed groups, of whom 6 were also raped. The parents of one girl paid for her release and 5 were still missing at the time of interview. Within abductions perpetrated by government forces, 2 adult males taken by gendarmes were later killed, and another adult male taken by the Central African army was released following payment by the family. Over half (56.1%, n = 64) of the 114 abductions perpetrated by armed groups or Zaraguinas ended in the return of the person abducted, after a period ranging from several days to 3 months. Of these returns, 27 (42%) occurred after payment of ransom by a family member.

Table 4 illustrates a trend that emerged from the data, of abducting people for periods of time varying from a couple of days to three months, and using them for labor or holding them for ransom. Men were frequently abducted to help carry goods pillaged from a village during a raid by armed groups or Zaraguinas, and then returned several weeks later. Three respondents noted exact ransom amounts up to $300-$400 USD, sums far beyond the reach of most Central Africans.

Table 4: Abductees, Returnees and Ransoms by Age Group, Northern Strata

	Children 5-17		**Adults >= 18**		**TOTAL**
	male	**female**	**male**	**female**	
Abducted	16	8	79	19	**122**
Returned (*Overall*)	13	1	40	10	**64**
Returned (*Ransom*)	6	1	16	4	**27**

Rape

Rape was the most frequently recorded incident within the sample, with 181 reports among women and girls (117 in the north, 64 in the south), allowing for a national estimate of 31,416 (95% CI: 26,220-36,660) rapes occurring each year during the recall period. The majority (74%, n = 134) were reported among adult women, ranging in age from 18 to 67 years (median = 22). The estimated annual rate of rape was 33.12 per 1000 adult women in the north (95% CI: 25.01-41.24) and 18.4 per 1000 adult women in the south (95% CI: 12.44-24.37). However, rape was also recorded among very young children: 47 rapes were reported against children ranging in age from 8 to 17 years old (median = 15). In the north, the estimated annual rate of rape was found to be 16.72 (95% CI: 10.44-23.0) per 1000 girls age 5 to 17. The rate in the south was less than half that found in the north (7.51 per 1000 girls per year, 95% CI: 3.67-11.34). Reported incidents allow us to estimate that 8,172 girls (95% CI: 5,640-10,704) across the country were raped in each year of the recall period.

Although the interviewer did not explicitly ask about marital rape, 80 incidents (44%) of women being raped by their husbands were reported, all among adult women except 2 incidents among married, 17-year-old girls. (While rape is illegal in CAR, the law does not specifically prohibit marital rape.[21]) Another 32 incidents were reportedly perpetrated by armed groups (17 among children), 26 by neighbors (16 among children), 16 by strangers (3 among children), 14 by Zaraguinas (2 among children), 5 by family members (4 among children), 4 by merchants (1 among children), 3 by "other" actors (including a 23-year-old raped by 5 people in a criminal gang, a 22-year-old raped by a man and later forced to marry him, and a 16-year-old raped by a 45-year old man in order to force her to marry him), and a 21-year-old female reportedly raped by a government soldier. With the exception of two incidents (1 by an armed group and 1 by Zaraguinas), the 25% of rapes perpetrated by armed groups or Zaraguinas (44) all occurred in the north.

Among all non-marital rapes (101), respondents reported that 9 resulted in pregnancy, and 4 occurred while the victim was pregnant. Four survivors were reported as sick following the incident, and a further 8 were said to be in the hospital. Eight gang rapes were reported, half perpetrated by armed groups and half by neighbors, usually in groups of 3-5 males. In two cases, the respondent noted that the survivor had been raped on multiple occasions. Four incidents resulted in talking to the chief, 2 in going to the police and 5 in the perpetrator's arrest. Forced marriage to the rapist was reported in 6 cases, and in 1 case the rapist paid the survivor's family 40,000 CFA but "refused" to marry her. Among rapes by family members, 2 were by the uncle, 1 by the aunt's husband's older brother, one in the aunt's household, and 1 reported as repeated forced sex by the husband's younger brother following the husband's death.

One rape also resulted in an intentional injury and another rape resulted in a killing. With 11 rapes (7 perpetrated by armed groups and 4 by Zaraguinas) the women or girls were also abducted, and among them 5 were also recruited into armed groups.

Sexual Abuse

The sample included 50 reports of sexual abuse (39 in the north, 11 in the south) against women and girls, of which 24 were among children. In the north, a higher annual rate was seen among girls, with an estimated 10.97 (95% CI: 5.96-15.99) instances of sexual abuse per 1000 girls each year and an estimated 7.01 (95% CI: 4.38-9.65) per 1000 women. However, the opposite was found in the south, with the rate among women (3.00 per 1000/ year, 95% CI: 0.13-5.87) twice that as the rate among girls.

Overall, 24 incidents (11 among girls) were classified as sexual harassment, 17 (7 among girls) as sexual abuse, 8 (5 among girls) as attempted rape, and 1 unknown (girl). Almost half of the incidents (42%, n = 21 including 10 among children) were perpetrated by neighbors. There were 11 incidents perpetrated by armed groups (8 among children), 6 by strangers (2 among children), 5 by husbands, 2 by other family members (1 among children), 2 by Zaraguinas (1 among children), 2 by merchants (both against children), and 1 by an additional perpetrator classified as "other." The ages of affected children ranged from 11-17 years (median = 15) and, for adults, the range was 18-55 years (median = 20).

All incidents perpetrated by members of armed groups or Zaraguinas occurred in the north, while only 1 incident perpetrated by a spouse was recorded against a 55-year-old female. Conversely, all incidents reported in the south were perpetrated by either husbands (36%, n = 4) or neighbors (64%, n = 7); all incidents perpetrated by a husband were against women over the age of 18. Among incidents of attempted rape, perpetrators included a husband (1 adult), a stranger (1 adult), armed groups (3, all children), Zaraguinas (1 adult, 1 child) and a neighbor (1 child).

Killing

Eighteen reports of violent deaths were recorded within the sample during the 18.1 month recall period, all among adults and all but 1 in the northern stratum. The ages of those killed ranged from 18-62 years (median = 34). Nearly half of perpetrators were armed groups (44.4%, n = 8), including one report of a man killed after being convicted of sorcery. Four killings were reportedly perpetrated by Zaraguinas, 3 by government forces (gendarmes or members of the military), 2 by other or unknown persons, and 1 by a stranger. Of those killed, 3 were females, including 2 women in the north killed by armed groups (ages 38 and 50 years, one of whom had been abducted) and 1 woman in the south (age 25 years) who was raped and then strangled to death by a stranger. Incidents recorded within the sample allow for an estimate of 2,592 (95% CI: 1,380-3,804) adults killed each year over the course of the recall period.

Intentional Injury

The survey captured 76 incidents of intentional injury, of which approximately two-thirds (68.4%, n = 52) occurred in the north. There, an estimated 6.26 per 1000 people per year (95% CI: 3.72-8.81) were intentionally injured over the course of the recall period. The rate is much lower in the south, at 2.77 per 1000 people per year (95% CI: 1.34-4.19).

Within both strata, the vast majority of incidents occurred among adults (89.5%, n = 68), and ages ranged from 18 to 57 years (median = 27.5). Among those injured in the north, over half (57.7%) were male while the opposite was true in the south, where 58.3% (n = 14) were female. The top 3 perpetrators were armed groups (n = 22), spouses (n = 17, all but one case involved the husband assaulting the wife), and family (n = 10) or neighbors (n = 10). Notably, all injuries perpetrated by armed groups and Zaraguinas (n = 7) occurred in the north. Spouses accounted for 20-25% of incidents reported within each stratum.

Among children, whose ages ranged from 7 to 16 years (median = 11), 6 incidents involved fights, often with knives and mostly with other children. Exceptions included a 7-year-old in the north, who broke his arm while fleeing an armed group, and a 15-year-old girl in the south, hospitalized and with broken teeth suffered during a gang rape.

Problems Facing Women and Children

At the beginning and end of interviews, respondents were asked general questions about problems facing women and children in their village or neighborhood. To analyze these responses, one researcher applied descriptive codes (using Excel) as they emerged from the data, and these codes were agreed-upon by the other members of the research team. In the northern stratum, the three most frequently raised issues related to health and health care (mentioned 176 times), food and nutrition (101), and water and sanitation (90). In the southern stratum, the most frequently mentioned areas of concern were health and health care (204), water and sanitation (109), and access to/quality of schooling (67), which was followed closely by support for agriculture and technology (including livelihood and income-generating activities) (66).

At the end of the interview, respondents were asked about what would help women cope with the problems facing them and their children in their village or neighborhood. In the northern stratum, the three most frequent responses related to support for health and health care (287), food and nutrition (182), and water and sanitation (157). In the southern stratum, the most frequently mentioned areas for support were health and health care (332), water and sanitation (192), and circulation of money (including support of microfinance projects and increased purchasing power) (132).

Ethical Checks

Six clusters were revisited several days after the initial interviews took place, to assess whether respondents had experienced any adverse consequences (such as anger or resentment from neighbors, abuse from a family member or spouse) as a result of speaking with the research team. Interviewers were able to speak with 33 of the respondents they had previously interviewed, none of whom reported adverse consequences. Many women reported being happy to have participated in the interview process and felt that the survey was good for their country, and the husbands of several respondents reported feeling proud when their wives told them they had represented their family and their village in the survey. Three women asked when development projects would be brought to their villages, and one woman expressed survey fatigue.

DISCUSSION

Considerable barriers exist in using population-based surveys to capture data on conflict-related violations throughout an entire country. Nevertheless, and despite reports of grave violations in only a small fraction of households, evidence suggests a significant difference between the experiences of both children and adults living in the northern areas of CAR compared to those in the south. The majority of incidents involved adults over the age of 18, with rates of abduction, rape, killing and intentional injury significantly higher among adults. This evidence points to the need for strengthened protection programs not only for children, but for entire communities.

Armed actors (armed groups, Zaraguina, or government forces) were reported as perpetrators in approximate4ly half of all incidents of killing, intentional injury, sexual abuse, rape, a4bduction, and forced recruitment among 5-17 year olds (55.8%) and person4s 18 years or older (52.0%). While rape was the most frequently reported violation, three-quarters of all reported incidents were perpetrated by non-armed actors (such as husbands, neighbors, and strangers), indicating that the need for protection against sexual violence extends beyond areas of conflict. Conversely, abduction was the second most commonly reported violation and almost exclusively perpetrated by conflict actors and Zaraguinas. While humanitarian response in northern CAR is limited, programs intent on responding to protection issues such as gender-based violence and the recruitment and use of children in armed groups do exist. The high rate of abduction among both adults and children is evidence on which the humanitarian community should extend services. The large number of violations reportedly perpetrated by Zaraguinas also highlights the need for security actors to mitigate harm inflicted on civilians by armed, non-state actors acting outside of traditional organized groups.

Overall, the minority of reported violations occurred among children. Among these, only incidents perpetrated by armed combatants can be classified as falling within the purview of Resolution 1612 and therefore reportable to the UN Security Council. In 2008, the UN documented 58 such incidents [14], using the current case-based reporting system. If instead one uses the total number of violations by armed actors reported in this survey (Table 5), an estimate of the total number of grave violations likely to have occurred in the north and south of the country can be obtained.

Table 5: Reported Incidents of Grave Violations Against Children Perpetrated by Armed Actors

	ARMED GROUPS	**ZARAGUINAS**	**CENTRAL AFRICAN MILITARY FORCES**	**TOTAL**
RECRUITMENT				
North	8	2	0	**10**
South	0	0	0	**0**
ABDUCTION				
North	12	9	0	**21**
South	0	2	0	**2**
RAPE				
North	16	2	0	**18**
South	1	1	0	**2**
SEXUAL ABUSE				
North	8	1	0	**9**

South	0	0	0	**0**
KILLING*				
North	0	0	0	**0**
South	0	0	0	**0**
INTENTIONAL INJURY*				
North	1	0	0	**1**
South	0	0	0	**0**
TOTALS	**46**	**17**	**0**	**63**

* Killing and intentional injury are mutually exclusive categories.

In the northern stratum, 59 grave violations perpetrated by armed combatants were experienced in a sample of 2,461 children (aged 5-17 years) between January 2008 and July 2009. This suggests that approximately 8,180 violations (95% CI: 4,500-11,800) against children occurred in the northern areas of the country each year during the recall period. The discrepancy between the 58 cases reported to the UN Security Council that were recorded in 2008 and the estimate drawn from this sample point to the vast difference between the two monitoring approaches. This highlights the intrinsic value of a complementary system that would allow for population-based monitoring of trends over time alongside a verified case-based reporting system, essential for negotiating with armed groups and armed forces, and for fulfilling the UN Secretary General's reporting needs.

As discussed above, several potential biases likely affect this survey's results. If the sampling frame used to identify clusters was not complete, or if some groups were systematically not included in the sampling frame-such as those living outside of the country in 2003-and experienced violations at a rate different than the rest of the population, this could result in estimates being biased either toward or away from the null. Since security and logistical constraints prevented the survey team from reaching 9 of the 69 selected clusters, survey results are also affected if those living in the clusters not reached experienced violations more or less frequently over the course of the recall period, as compared to those living in accessible areas. Given that excluded clusters were often in volatile security environments, it is thus likely that their inclusion would have increased the rates estimated here. The same can be said for clusters that were not reachable and substituted by the next nearest village or neighborhood.

In situations where a group of 4 households was skipped due to no available respondents, bias could have occurred if the experience of those households was systematically different than that of the households interviewed. In one cluster where several groups of 4 households were skipped on the day of surveying, interviewers returned a day later and conducted interviews with those previously absent. Data from these interviews suggests skipped households experienced similar rates of violations as those interviewed on the previous day. However, the small number of households revisited in this way (11) makes this finding inconclusive. In 32% of households, no respondent was available at the initially selected household, but a respondent was located within one of the three neighbor households. If neighbors can report successfully on their neighbors, then this 32% of households not at home creates no potential bias. However, a potential source of bias could exist if neighbors consistently report incompletely about other neighbors and those not at home differed from their neighbors.

Interviewer performance was closely monitored through the first several clusters, to take note of any obvious differences in the number and types of violations reported. However, time constraints, logistics and a difference in interviewers' language abilities required the research team to occasionally divide the interviewers into separate teams and work in different locations with different security situations on different days. Because the violations did not occur evenly across the population, the areas where each interviewer conducted the most interviews, which differed for all interviewers, greatly affects the number of violations each interviewer recorded. Therefore, an accurate assessment of inter-rater reliability is difficult to obtain.

As with any survey, results are affected by respondents' knowledge, willingness to report, and ability to recall which events truly happened within the period under study. The neighborhood method also assumes respondents have the ability to report on events within their own households and in all neighboring households with equal consistency and that any hostile or difficult relationships between households or household members would not bias accurate reporting. While it is always difficult to verify the integrity of information recorded through surveys, the lack of a significant difference between the rates found through self-reports and neighbor-reports (Table 2) indicates that we can make the assumption that neighbors can report on their neighbors. The similar prevalence in both strata between the two kinds of reports diminishes concern for gross under-reporting of violations in neighbor households. The notable exception is rape, in which estimates derived from neighbor-reports differ markedly from those reported among respondents' own households.

Rape is an extremely sensitive topic, and difficulties in documenting its prevalence arise repeatedly in studies from a variety of settings and contexts [22, 23]. In spite of slow, respectful interviews between two women, evidence of underreporting can be seen in this survey as well, and is particularly likely among neighbor-reports. The difference between the rates of rape reported is likely to have been influenced by the under-reporting of marital rape. We suspect that respondents might be unaware of marital rape occurring in neighboring households. In this survey, among 80 recorded marital rapes, 49 were self-reports and 31 were neighbor reports. As noted by Swiss, the true scale of violations can be suggested using additional means, including medical data such as the number of pregnancies known to be the result of rape [22]. Among the 181 incidents of rape reported in our data set, nine pregnancies are known to have resulted. Assuming that 1% of unprotected acts of sexual intercourse lead to pregnancy [22], and that this applies equally to all age groups, this would indicate a five-fold underreporting of rape within this sample.

Despite these difficulties, the survey instrument was sensitive enough to capture data that could be used to estimate the rate of most of the violations under study, and was able to detect a hundred times more incidents than those documented by the case-based MRM process. The use of a semi-structured, open-ended questionnaire is believed to be a main factor in allowing respondents to discuss difficult topics, including rape and sexual abuse. Clear differences in the rate of all violations for persons over 5 years of age (Table 3) indicate that the delineation between the northern and southern strata was a useful one that allowed for increased precision of the estimates obtained. The close supervision provided to the survey team also served to minimize the effect of interviewer bias on results, as all respondent and neighboring households were identified by a team leader. Interviewers reported that the women surveyed responded favorably to the use of buttons and bells to represent household members, and that it greatly assisted them in clarifying household composition as well as maintaining confidentiality.

The data provided through this exercise goes some way to building a base of comparison for future surveys and surveillance data from CAR. The method, which gleans information about four households through one interview, proved efficient in terms of both cost and time. The team was able to visit clusters in a large swath of the country while working under restrictive security constraints. At a cost of less than $50,000, it was possible to collect data despite limited funding, vehicles and personnel to do the work.

The emphasis on a need for health care, food, and water, identified through respondents' answers to two open-ended questions, points to the dire situation most Central Africans find themselves in, with even the most basic needs going unmet. Concerning health, many women spoke of the long distance to clinics and hospitals; the lack of qualified staff, equipment, and medicines once there; and the specific health needs of women and children. It is important to note that respondents were not asked to rank their needs and concerns, nor were they prompted to talk about more sensitive or personal topics. In addition to the most frequently mentioned areas, women also expressed needs and concerns related to insecurity; theft; lack of access to markets; transport and degraded roads and bridges; gender-based violence; support for vulnerable groups such as orphans and widows; lack of non-food items such as clothes and materials to build shelters; electricity; unemployment; single motherhood; difficulties cultivating due to rainfall, hazards from elephants, and attacks by armed groups; exploitation of natural resources and poaching; and the need for peace and reconciliation in CAR.

CONCLUSIONS

This experience shows it is possible to collect representative, population-based estimates regarding the occurrence of grave violations in difficult and politically unstable settings. However, it is exceedingly difficult to calibrate innovative approaches to measuring grave violations when no gold standards exist. While it is likely that all events suffer from under-reporting, there is evidence that these events are occurring, particularly in the north of the country. Furthermore, respondents' articulation of the problems they and their communities face suggests that the dire health situation throughout the country cannot be ignored.

The neighborhood method was employed to allow respondents two different contexts in which they could discuss sensitive events-either within their households or within neighboring households-and as a means of accessing a large sample while working with limited time and resources. While this method may be sensitive enough to detect incidents, rates of violations in CAR may be too low to be detected precisely with a household survey. Nonetheless, these population-based figures greatly augment those presently available from case-based reporting systems. This survey and other recent, population-based work provide evidence that a security crisis is underway in CAR [24]. Yet establishing conditions on the ground is only one step in the accountability process. Both the national government and international actors present in CAR must acknowledge these dire conditions and actively work to better monitor and respond to them. Specifically, the Central African government, donors, international organizations such as the United Nations, and humanitarian aid organizations should make use of these data to better inform prevention and response programs, to assist in fundraising and advocacy, and to develop surveillance activities, which could provide ongoing, community-based monitoring of vital health and protection concerns.

DECLARATIONS

Acknowledgements

The authors would like to thank Stéphane Pichette, Ana Maria Rodriguez, and Lara Scott of UNICEF New York for their vision and support in this collaboration, as well as their assistance in dissemination of results and feedback on our findings. We extend our appreciation to Joanne Csete, Patrick Ball and Jeannie Annan for their attentive and constructive editing of this manuscript. We also would like to thank Mahimbo Mdoe, Jeremy Hopkins and the staff and drivers at UNICEF CAR for the support they provided during field work, along with Nick Imboden and Bony Mpaka Nkubiri of OCHA CAR for their invaluable advice and assistance in Bangui. The authors are forever indebted to the six-woman strong interview team for making the research possible. Final thanks to the U.S. Centers for Disease Control, Columbia University's Program on Forced Migration and Health, and UNICEF for their financial support of this project.

Competing Interests

The authors declare that they have no competing interests.

Authors' Contributions

AP and KM participated in research design, data collection, analysis and drafting of the manuscript. LR supervised the research design, data collection and analysis. All authors read and approved the final manuscript.

REFERENCES

1. Shana Swiss M, Peggy J, Jennings P, Gladys V, Aryee R, Grace H, Brown C, Ruth M, Jappah-Samukai B, Mary S, Kamara R, Rosana DH, Schaack R, Rojatu S, Turay-Kanneh R: Violence Against Women During the Liberian Civil Conflict. Journal of the American Medical Association. 1998, 279: 625-629. 10.1001/jama.279.8.625.
2. Incidence of Violence against Women and Girls in Liberia: A Quantitative Study using the "Neighborhood Method". [http://www.forcedmigration.columbia.edu/research/documents/IRCReportonNeighborhoodStudy_10-1-07.pdf]
3. Vincent Iacopina M, Martina W, Frank M, Heidi M, Bauer M, Allen S, Keller M, Sheri L, Fink M, Doug Ford J, Daniel J, Pallin M, Ronald Waldmand M: A Population-Based Assessment of Human Rights Abuses Committed Against Ethnic Albanian Refugees From Kosovo. American Journal of Public Health. 2001, 91: 2013-2018. 10.2105/AJPH.91.12.2013.
4. Ellsberg M, Heise L: Researching Violence Against Women: A Practical Guide for Researchers and Activists. 2005, Washington, DC: World Health Organization, PATH
5. Lynn L, Amowitz M, Glen Kim M, Chen Reis J, Jana L, Asher M, Vincent Iacopina M: Human Rights Abuses and Concerns About Women's Health and Human Rights in Southern Iraq. Journal of the American Medical Association. 2004, 291: 1471-1479. 10.1001/jama.291.12.1471.
6. Leonard S, Rubenstein J, Doug Ford J, Ondrej Mach M, Burkhalter H, Ramin Ahmadi M, Michael Vassiliev M, Haq Nawaz M, Vincent Iacopino M: Endless Brutality: War Crimes in Chechnya. 2001, Boston: Physicians for Human Rights
7. Ascherio A, Biellik R, Epstein A, Snetro G, Gloyd S, Ayotte B, Epstein PR: Deaths and Injuries Caused By Land Mines in Mozambique. Lancet. 1995, 346: 721-724. 10.1016/S0140-6736(95)91501-X.
8. Hynes M, Robertson K, Ward J, Crouse C: A Determination of the Prevalence of Gender-based Violence among Conflict-affected Populations in East Timor. Disasters. 2004, 28: 294-321. 10.1111/j.0361-3666.2004.00260.x.
9. Ball P, Spirer HF, Spirer L: Making the Case: Investigating Large Scale Human Rights Violations Using Information Systems and Data

Analysis. 2000, American Association for the Advancement of Science

10. Resolution 1612 (2005). [http://www.un.org/Docs/sc/unsc_resolutions05.htm]
11. Office of the Special Representative of the Secretary-General for Children and Armed Conflict. [http://www.un.org/children/conflict/english/securitycouncilwg.html]
12. Children and Armed Conflict - Report of the Secretary-General. [http://www.un.org/children/conflict/english/reports.html]
13. Human Development Report 2009: Overcoming barriers: Human mobility and development. [http://hdr.undp.org/en/reports/global/hdr2009/]
14. Report of the Secretary-General on children and armed conflict in the Central African Republic. [http://www.un.org/children/conflict/english/central-african-republic.html]
15. The Sisterhood Method for Estimating Maternal Mortality: Guidance notes for potential users. 1997, World Health Organization, United Nations Children's Fund
16. Estimating the Incidence of Physical and Sexual Violence against Children and Women in Trincomalee District, Sri Lanka: The Neighborhood Method. [http://www.forcedmigration.columbia.edu/research/ar.html]
17. Stark L, Roberts L, Wheaton W, Acham A, Boothby N, Ager A: Measuring Violence against Women Amidst War and Displacement in Northern Uganda: Using the 'Neighborhood Method'. J Epidemiol Community Health. 2009, 64: 1056-1061. 10.1136/jech.2009.093799.
18. Using the Neighborhood Method to Measure Violence and Rape in Ethiopia. [http://www.forcedmigration.columbia.edu/research/ar.html]
19. WHO Ethical and Safety Recommendations for researching, documenting and monitoring sexual violence in emergencies. 2007, Geneva, Switzerland: World Health Organization
20. Résultats de l'enquête nationale à indicateurs multiples couplée avec la sérologie VIH et anémie en RCA 2006. [http://www.childinfo.org/files/MICS3_CAR_FinalReport_2006_Fr.pdf]
21. 2009 Human Rights Report: Central African Republic. [http://www.state.gov/g/drl/rls/hrrpt/2009/af/135944.htm]
22. Shana Swiss M, Joan E, Giller M: Rape as a Crime of War. Journal of the American Medical Association. 1993, 270: 612-615. 10.1001/

jama.270.5.612.

23. Heise LL, Raikes A, Watts CH, Zwi AB: Violence Against Women: A Neglected Public Health Issue in Less Developed Countries. Soc Sci Med. 1994, 39: 1165-1179. 10.1016/0277-9536(94)90349-2.
24. Vinck P, Pham P: Association of Exposure to Violence and Potential Traumatic Events With Self-reported Physical and Mental Health Status in the Central African Republic. Journal of the American Medical Association. 2010, 304: 544-552. 10.1001/jama.2010.1065.

CHAPTER 9

POLICE VIOLENCE AND SEXUAL RISK AMONG FEMALE AND TRANSVESTITE SEX WORKERS IN SERBIA: QUALITATIVE STUDY

Tim Rhodes[1], Milena Simic[1], Sladjana Baros[2], Lucy Platt[1], and Bojan Zˇikic[2]

[1] Centre for Research on Drugs and Health Behaviour, London School of Hygiene and Tropical Medicine, University of London, London WC1E 7HT

[2] Department of Ethnology and Anthropology, University of Belgrade, Serbia

Citation: Rhodes Tim, Simić Milena, Baroš Sladjana, Platt Lucy, Žikić Bojan. Police violence and sexual risk among female and transvestite sex workers in Serbia: qualitative study BMJ 2008; 337 :a811

ABSTRACT

Objective

To explore female and transvestite sex workers' perceptions of risk in the sex work environment in Serbia.

Design

Qualitative interview study.

Setting

Street based locations for sex work in Belgrade and Pancevo, Serbia.

Participants

31 female and transvestite sex workers.

Results

Violence, including police violence, was reported as a primary concern in relation to risk. Violence was linked to unprotected sex and the reduced capacity for avoiding sexual risk. Participants reported that coerced sex was routinely provided to the police in exchange for freedom from detainment, arrest, or fine, and was enforced by the perceived threat of violence, sometimes realised. Accounts contained multiple instances of physical and sexual assault, presented as abuses of police authority, and described policing as a form of moral punishment. This was largely through non-physical means but was also enforced through physical violence, especially towards transvestite and Roma sex workers, whose experience of police violence was reported as relentless and brutal and connected with broader social forces of discrimination in this setting, especially towards Roma.

Conclusion

Preventing violence towards sex workers, which can link with vulnerability to sexually transmitted infections, is a priority in Serbia. This requires monitoring perpetrators of violence, providing legal support to sex workers, and creating safer environments for sex work.

INTRODUCTION

Physical violence links with vulnerability to sexually transmitted infections through coerced unprotected sex and the reduced capacity to negotiate sexual risk.**1 2 3** Violence can be ubiquitous in street sex work.**4 5 6** The incidence of physical violence, including rape, is higher among sex workers than among the general population.**7**The emotional harms of sex work are often inseparable from the experience of violence.**6 8 9** Violence links with social stigma and discrimination,**10 11 12** and sex work is highly stigmatised.**5 8 11**

Preventing violence is a global public health and human rights priority.**13** Policing and police violence can impact adversely on health.**14** Street policing can displace sex work geographically as well as disrupt sex workers' informal helping networks, exacerbating the risk of sexually transmitted infections as well as violence from clients.**11 15 1617** Police contact with street populations can be pervasive and violent as well as stigmatising or discriminatory.**1718 19 20 21 22 23** Studies of injecting drug use suggest increased HIV risk behaviour linked to police contact and arrest.**24 25 26** Excessive force, including physical and sexual violence, can be a feature of police "crackdowns" targeting street populations.**14**

Serbia is characterised by social and economic uncertainty, which links to poverty, illegal economies (including sex work), corruption, and ethnic and gender inequalities.**27 28 29** Representations of violence linked to regional conflicts have been readily accessible through mass media, with uncertain long term consequences.**30** There is a history of violence used as a stratagem for policing social unrest, and reports of police violence targeting vulnerable groups.**31 32** A culture of intolerance to social diversity and vulnerability has framed institutional responses.**29 33**Roma populations in Serbia and regionally are subject to pervasive inequalities in health, living conditions, citizenship rights, access to services, and income, and were subjected to violence in recent conflicts.**34 35 36** In parts of eastern Europe most sex workers are thought to be Roma.**36** We report findings from a qualitative study of the risk involved in a sex work environment in Serbia.

METHODS

We undertook 31 qualitative semistructured interviews with sex workers in two street based locations for sex work in Serbia; Belgrade, the capital, and Pancevo, a nearby town in Vojvodina region. The study included female and transvestite sex workers living or working in Belgrade or Pancevo who had exchanged sex for money, drugs, or other goods in the past month. This non-probability purposive sample set minimum quotas of outdoor and indoor sex workers, those under and over 21 years, injecting drug users, and Roma. We selected these purposive sampling dimensions to ensure variation in relation to contextual factors theorised to determine sexual risk differentially.**37**Previous research highlights sex work environment, drug use status, and age as important determinants of risk related to sex work,**4 5 6 18 19 20 23** and Roma are subject to noticeable inequalities in health, including risk of HIV and sexually transmitted infections.**35 36** We recruited participants through collaborating outreach projects at five discrete sex work "hotspots" and supplemented through snowballing and chain referral within networks of sex workers. We set an a priori target of 30 interviews with a fixed period for data collection.

We generated data using an interview topic guide containing key questions with prompts for patterns and organisation of sex work, use of condoms, risk perception, and risk in the sex work environment. The piloted topic guide was generated through close consultation with local sexual health and HIV prevention services, including non-governmental organisations, and fostered participant led description of experience related to sex work. Interviews were done in Serbian (by MS and SB) in cafes and restaurants (n=14), at local projects (n=12), at participants' homes (n=4), and in quiet outdoor spaces (n=1). Participants were reimbursed €10 (£8; $16). Interviews were tape recorded after informed consent, lasted 60-90 minutes, and were transcribed verbatim by locally trained staff and the research team. Translated transcription was done through close collaboration with a translator, with translated text checked by bilingual members of the research team.

Coding of data was descriptive and thematic, with an emphasis on typological description.**37** Data were collected in two waves to enable provisional coding to inform ongoing recruitment and purposive sampling as well as refinement of topic areas for interview. This enabled findings and codes to emerge iteratively.**37 38** At the interim analysis, violence (as defined by participants) emerged as a key theme and was thus given greater emphasis in later interviews. Coding of data was undertaken by TR and MS in two phases, with first level codes identifying key topics and concepts on the basis of a combination of participants' accounts and a priori defined topics of interest (for example, violence), and second level codes breaking these into smaller units for analysis (for example, client violence, police violence, moral policing, non-physical violence).

The sample comprised 24 female sex workers and seven transvestite sex workers of average age 28 years. Most (n=25) were street based sex workers—that is, soliciting and negotiating sex with clients in street locations (beside busy roads, at railway and bus stations, at busy hotels). Street based sexual services were provided in nearby parking lots and woods, and in central Belgrade in street alleyways and rooms rented for 15 minutes. The remaining sex workers solicited sex through advertising their telephone numbers, and one was connected with a bar/club. Half were Roma (n=15), all of whom worked the streets, and among whom were all the transvestites. Two thirds of the women had children (n=15). Only five sex workers self reported sexually transmitted infections and eight reported injecting drugs, one of whom reported being HIV positive and another three hepatitis C positive. All street based sex workers reported having experienced some kind of violence linked to their work. Sex work is illegal in Serbia under article 14 of the Law of Peace and Order, and thus operates in a prohibitive environment.

RESULTS

Violence, and police violence in particular, was identified as a primary concern of sex workers in their descriptions of the risks involved in street based sex work in Belgrade and Pancevo, Serbia.

Environment for Sex Work

As found elsewhere,**5 6** sex workers placed strong emphasis on condom use in transactional sex encounters: "Not using condoms with a client, God forbid!" (case 2, female); "With clients, it has to be with a rubber" (case 23, female). Condom use, as well as hygiene more broadly, was linked with personal integrity and responsibility: "I take good care of myself. All that [HIV] comes from the lack of hygiene, to those who don't take good care" (case 8, female). A core strategy for regulating risk was "client sorting," whereby the "messy," "dirty," and "dangerous" were avoided in favour of the "married," "normal," and "clean." Judgments about hygiene influenced condom use, with unprotected sex said to occur discriminately and exceptionally under conditions of assumed low risk: "It happened, even without a condom, but he was married, clean, neat, spotless" (case 7, female). For some, economic necessity was a concomitant factor: "He paid more for the service" (case 7, female); "If he pays me extra, then I can do it without a condom" (case 6, transvestite).

Accounts thus emphasised the role of situational factors, and especially the risk of violence, in undermining a norm for condom use. The risk of violence seemed to be ubiquitous to this street setting for sex work, and was reported as a primary concern: "No kind of money is worth it when he beats you, when you are scared to death" (case 25, female). Violence was reported as linked to incidents during condom use or breakages resulting from rough or coerced sex: "If they push it in violently, then it [condom] breaks" (case 19, female). Violence was also described as being linked directly to unprotected sex through coercion: "I had to accept everything he asked for . . . without the rubber" (case 25 female). The perceived threat of physical violence also had indirect effects on sex workers' capacity for reducing risk by feeding a sense of pervasive insecurity and loss of control in sex work transactions: "I get scared every time I get in [a car] with someone I don't know, so that I am consumed with fear" (case 12, female); "I find it very difficult to get into someone's car . . . because life is at stake" (case 22, transvestite). Physical violence by clients was reported to be common, but it was violence by police that was perceived as the greater threat and as less open to risk management: "You can manage your clients somehow, but to be honest, the greatest threat to us is the police" (case 7, female).

Police Violence

Although some participants had not experienced physical violence perpetrated by the police—"I perhaps got two slaps one time, that's all, but other girls were hurt pretty bad" (case 16, female); "The police don't know me well here, so I can stand freely where they don't know me" (number 10 female)—the following forms of police violence seemed normative: deception and coercion (box 1), extortion (box 2), and discrimination (box 3).

Box 1 Sex by deception and coercion

Extract 1: sex by deception

- And at the end of the job he shows me his badge, and says like "Give me my money back now." That's what he does. And he's not on duty. But he's some cop. *What do you do?* Give the money back (case 14, female)
- He says "let's do it." I say, "Well, pay me, give me the money." And then he asks, "Have you ever been taken in to the police?" Like he's a cop and all. And I say, "Yes, I have." And he says "Do you want to go to the station, you and I?" You know, they try you out, ask for blowjobs, sex in return. It's just their thing (case 10, female)

Extract 2: sex in exchange for freedom from police attention

- They want blowjobs, fucking, if you want them to let you go. You've got to. The police like fucking us more than anyone. They don't pay. It's like this: they fuck us, and so they let us go (case 5, transvestite)
- And he pulled out a police badge and said "C'mon, you want me to take you in or screw you?" I was scared, and allowed him to screw me (case 18, female)
- They want for blowjobs, fucks. I work for free, just so they don't take me in (case 23, female)

Extract 3: sex coerced by violence

- He wants me to blow him for free. I don't want to. Later, when he gets me on my shift, he beats me silly. Beats me silly (case 20, transvestite)

He beat me up with a baton. Up in this park. He beat me up with the baton. And several times I had to be [have sex] with him. I really had to. I was forced (case 15, female)

Box 2 Extortion

Extract 1: extortion of money

- They are screwing around with us. Like we need fuel, we need money for this, we need it for that (case 2, female)
- Yesterday, or the day before, the patrol, they wanted money from us. First he says, "C'mon, get in the car." Nothing to it, I get in the car. Then he says, "Why don't you treat us?" And he says, "C'mon, sort it out among yourselves," how much money we are to give him (case 14, female)
- It's really pathetic taking money from us. I don't know how they don't understand I struggled for that. I sold my body. I worked. The man, for instance, pardon me, fucked me and everything, for the money. And they take the money. Why? I don't know, but so they say it goes into some fund, what do I know? (case 16, female)

Extract 2: extortion of information

The first time they beat me because I didn't want to admit who I worked for. They slapped me around. Like, "Gypsy, motherfucker, why don't you start talking?" I was pregnant, and he started beating me. Like, "You ain't going to say you're pregnant any more, now you're going to get beaten up at the station, and nobody's going to believe you, and if you report me, I beat you up" (case 8, female)

Box 3 Discrimination

Extract 1: moral punishment

- They [police] take us into their office, and one starts kicking you in the legs, the other one into kidney. Without any reason. They want to accomplish something, to prevent us from doing something. *From what?*From doing this work. "Why don't you find another job?" I say, "Come on, find me another job and I will do it" And he goes, "Why should I look for a job for you?" and so on. It's like that (case 2, female)
- He [policemen] is swearing at us, saying we're sluts, whores . . . Pancevo is forbidden grounds to us. We can't even move on the streets, nor in bars. If I had a boyfriend now, and went for a drink, and he came, he'd kick me out of the place (case 3, female)

Extract 2: public humiliation and shaming

- A few times I went out with my boyfriend. I would sit down, drink coffee, and they [police] come in. "Hey, do you know . . .?," I mean, it's the first thing they say, "Do you know what she . . .?" And he [my boyfriend] goes, "Well, can I not have a drink with her?" "You know, well . . . Do you know what, do you know what she does?" (case 15, female)
- Most of the women get arrested. The last time they arrested people it was on television. I saw it in person. Arrested, chased, and filmed on camera (case 1, transvestite)

Extract 3: extreme violence driven by contempt

- They [police] started going wild, only on us transvestites. They let the girls go. They just pick us up, and go to the woods, and go wild on us . . . First, they beat us in the woods, and then they take us to the station. And then they tell us at the station "Hey, freshen up," and they beat us up in the bathroom (case 5, transvestite)
- They [police] kicked, kicked, kicked the hell out of us. Just transvestites. They took me to the woods, down by the bridge . . . They stripped everything off me . . . Flashlight in the eyes. I said a million times, "Take me away. Did you come to arrest me? Arrest me then, but, do not beat me up." . . . That makes it worse. "Shut up, motherfucker, shut up!" (case 20, transvestite)

What's the reason for them [police] to beat me up? The fact I'm like this is my business. One squad came over, and they beat me senseless because of what I am. I came back all black and blue . . . I didn't know where the blows were coming from . . . They just have this hate. Whether it's towards prostitutes or specifically trannies. But it's terrible (case 22, transvestite)

Sexual services were described as being commonly provided to police without payment as well as secured by them through deception and coercion (box 1). Police reportedly presented sex workers with the option of providing services without payment as a means of avoiding possible arrest, detainment (varying from hours to one month), and a certain fine (in Belgrade, between €100 and €200). Sex workers described how in cases of deception, presumed clients would usually reveal their identity as policemen once services had been negotiated and exchanged, demanding the return of their money (box 1, extract 1). This was described as a no choice situation, which for some had become routine: "They're in power, and we are not, what can I do?" (case 2, female). Although exceptions were reported ("Let me tell you, I didn't work with none of them police"; "I don't do cops") (case 3, female),sex would normatively be provided in exchange for freedom from detainment or arrest (box 1, extract 2).

The risk of detainment, arrest, or fine or the threat of physical violence were given as the reasons why sex workers acquiesced to police demands for sex without payment. Attempts to resist such demands were said to incite violence (box 1, extract 3). We were given multiple examples of coerced sex involving violence perpetrated by those presumed to be police (box 1, extract 3), although condoms were reported to be used in most: "Leave off mate, not only am I doing you for free, but you're not jacking me up without a rubber" (case 1, transvestite). Accounts also indicated routine extortion of money from sex workers by police, as unofficial fines or as "negotiated" payments to secure freedom from detainment, arrest, or registration as a prostitute (box 2, extract 1). Extortion of money or information (particularly about pimps and when giving "statements by dictation") was also reported to be enforced by the threat of violence (box 2, extract 2).

A common theme therefore was a fatalist acceptance to the inevitability of everyday police violence ("I can't fight destiny"), borne out of the internalisation of police "rights" to victimise ("They have a right to beat us because we do this prostitution thing") and recognition that rights to police protection are unrealised and unrealistic ("I can't complain to anybody, I'm a prostitute").

A striking feature of sex workers' accounts was that police violence was presented as transgressing boundaries of legal acceptability or rationality, and thus was thought to be moral punishment (box 3, extract 1). Enforced sex and coerced payments to police, although outside the law, were experienced as discipline as if for moral wrongdoing, to "bring sex workers to their senses," and suggesting that they were matter out of place (box 3, extract 1). Policing thus extended into private life. A common tactic reported to be deployed was humiliation in the face of "normal others." This involved unwanted disclosure of a sex worker's identity to friends and family, thus disrupting the preservation of a dignified private self away from work (box 3, extract 2). A striking instance of public shaming included police collaborations with national media, whereby police crackdowns and arrests of sex workers would be televised (box 3, extract 2).

Moral punishments for selling sex overlapped with other forms of social discrimination, especially towards Roma and transvestites: “There is nothing [about me] that is normal for our people here, for our nation, here in Serbia” (case 1, transvestite). Police violence was described as especially brutal towards transvestites, all of whom in this study were Roma, and most Kosovo refugees (box 3, extract 3). Extreme violence reported towards transvestites and Roma was generally interpreted as driven by contempt for being of minority or deviant status (box 3, extract 3).

Taken together there was strong emphasis in sex workers’ accounts on the need for greater protection from police violence and corruption as well as for creating safer and regulated off-street environments for sex work, including through legislative change: “Legalise it. I’ll be the first to pay taxes” (case 2, female); “Make it legal, so that we have some papers and do not get messed with by the police” (case 8, female); “[Legalising] it would bring a proper solution. I could work freely. I would be up for HIV testing. I’m here to pay taxes. I’m here to fulfil my obligations to the state” (case 1, transvestite); “We need some building—I’m standing in the street—so that the police can’t touch us, some workplace” (case 12, female); “If it was legal, we’d go to doctors, we’d have medical records, it’d be much better” (case 15, female).

DISCUSSION

Violence was reported as a primary risk concern of street based sex workers in Serbia and linked to coerced unprotected sex, breakages of condoms, and reduced capacity to negotiate sexual safety. Moreover, sex workers described being coerced into providing sex to police in exchange for freedom from detainment, arrest, or fine, and this was reportedly enforced by perceived risks, sometimes realised, of physical violence by police. Reports of police violence, deception, coercion, and extortion towards street sex workers in Serbia seem to contravene the Serbian police ethics guidelines, ratified in 2003 and based on the European Union Code of Ethics for Police Forces (2001).

This study has limitations. It is an exploratory study generating findings for testing in future research. Generalisability is inevitably limited to this specific sample and setting. The study is an interpretative analysis of participants’ accounts and reflects the themes of these. Counter narratives are possible, and the study did not investigate accounts by the police. Also, what distinguishes excessive force from legitimate force in policing can be a fraught debate.[39]

Interviews contained multiple descriptions of physical and sexual assault, presented as abuses of police authority. Reported coerced sex by police usually involved condoms, but the pervasive risk of violence contributed to a reduced sense of control over the negotiation of sexual transactions. Sex workers largely adopted a fatalistic acceptance to reported police demands for money or sex without payment. This study extends concepts of sex in exchange for money or goods to include coerced sex in exchange for freedom from police detainment, arrest, or fine.

This study also identified possible policing practices with little basis in legal rationality but which acted as forms of moral punishment. These practices discipline and stigmatise, positioning sex workers as having waived rights to respect or protection on account of having transgressed. Such practices usually comprised bullying of a non-physical nature, such as humiliation and shaming involving the unwanted disclosure of a sex worker's identity to "normal others." But discriminatory policing practices were also embedded in physical violence, and much of it brutal, as in the case of the relentless violence reported by transvestite sex workers, all of whom were Roma. Previous studies have noted excessive use of force when policing female or transvestite sex workers[17 20] and drug users.[14 40]

Police violence may be disproportionately directed towards vulnerable groups.[39 41] It is shaped by organisational culture as well as social context.[41 42 43] Violence linked to sex work reflects institutionalised social inequalities and anxieties relating to gender, ethnicity, sexuality, and vulnerability.[12 44] In Serbia, Roma are subject to immense social discrimination and impoverishment,[33] and we found that Roma transvestite sex workers reported being subjected to extreme acts of police violence.

In conclusion, physical violence, enacted or threatened, links with unprotected sex and vulnerability to sexually transmitted infections[1 2 3 4 5 20] and can contribute to sex workers' diminished sense of volitional control.[10 1112 17] The prevention of violence tends to focus on reducing violence by clients, including through negotiation strategies of transactions.[8 23] A need exists to "design out" violence from sex work.[8] This requires interventions to monitor client and police perpetrators of violence and contraventions in police conduct, legal support protecting sex workers' health and human rights, and the creation of safer environments for sex work.

The criminalisation of sex work environments exacerbates the vulnerability of sex workers to violence by police and clients while limiting sex workers' access to protection.**18 23 45** Interventions creating licensed regulated premises for sex work and enabling legislative frameworks protective of sex workers' health, safety, and labour rights should be considered.

What is already known on this topic

- Violence can link with coerced unprotected sex and risk of sexually transmitted infections, but little is known about police violence towards female and transvestite sex workers

What this study adds

- In Serbia, coerced sex was reported to be routinely provided to police in exchange for freedom from detainment, arrest, or fine, and was enforced by the perceived threat of violence, sometimes realised
- Policing acted as moral punishment through non-physical means but was also reportedly enforced through physical violence, especially towards transvestite and Roma sex workers

Footnotes

- We thank those who participated in interviews or who helped by referring us to others, especially JAZAS, a non-government organisation working in HIV prevention. The views expressed here are those of the authors and do not necessarily represent the views of their institutions or those of the Republican AIDS Commission of Serbia who supported the study.
- Contributors: TR designed and coordinated the study, did the analyses, and wrote the paper. He is guarantor. MS and SB undertook the interviews and their coding for analysis. LP assisted with analysis. BZ oversaw local coordination of the study.
- Funding: Department for International Development (UK). The Department of Health (UK) provide core funding to the Centre for Research on Drugs and Health Behaviour at the London School of Hygiene and Tropical Medicine, UK. All authors declare independence from these funding agencies.
- Competing interests: None declared.

- Ethical approval: Riverside ethics committee (UK), with additional support from the Republican AIDS Commission of Serbia.
- Provenance and peer review: Not commissioned; externally peer reviewed.

REFERENCES

1. Ravi A, Blankenship K, Altice F. The association between history of violence and HIV risk: a cross-sectional survey of HIV-negative incarcerated women in Connecticut. Women's Health Issues2007;17:210-6.
2. Maman S, Campbell J, Sweat MD, Gielen AC. The intersection of HIV and violence: directions for future research and interventions. Soc Sci Med2000;50:459-78.
3. Choi YP, Chen KL, Jiang ZQ. Client-perpetuated violence and condom failure among female sex workers in Southwestern China. Sex Transm Dis 2008;35:141-6.
4. Church S, Henderson M, Barnard M, Hart G. Violence by clients towards female prostitutes in different work settings: questionnaire survey. BMJ2001;322:524-5.
5. Barnard MA. Violence and vulnerability: conditions of work for street-working prostitutes. Sociol Health Illn2003;15:683-705.
6. Sanders T. A continuum of risk? The management of health, physical, and emotional risks by female sex workers. Sociol Health Illn2004;26:557-74.
7. Potterat J, Bewer DD, Muth SQ, Rothenberg RB, Woodhouse DE, Muth JB, et al. Mortality in a long-term open cohort of prostitute women. Am J Epidemiol2004;159:778-85.
8. Sanders T, Campbell R. Designing out vulnerability, building in respect: violence, safety, and sex work policy. Brit J Sociol2007;58:1-19.
9. Jackson LA, Bennett CG, Sowinski BA. Stress in the sex trade and beyond. Crit Public Health2007;17:257-71.
10. Parker R, Aggleton P. HIV and AIDS-related stigma and discrimination: a conceptual framework and implications for action. Soc Sci Med2003;57:13-24.
11. Shannon K, Kerr T, Allinott S, Chettiar S, Shoveller J, Tyndall MW. Social and structural violence and power relations in mitigating HIV risk of drug-using women in survival sex work. Soc Sci Med2008;66:911-21.
12. Epele M. Gender, violence, and HIV: women's survival on the streets. Cult Med Psychiatry2003;26:33-54.
13. World Health Organization. *The third milestones of a global campaign*

for violence prevention report. Geneva: WHO,2007.

14. Cooper H, Moore L, Gruskin S, Krieger N. Characterizing perceived police violence: implications for public health. Am J Public Health2004;94:1109-18.
15. Blankenship KM, Koester S. Criminal law, policing policy, and HIV risk in female street sex workers and injection drug users.J Law Med Ethics2002;30:548-59.
16. Shannon K, Rusch M, Shoveller J, Alexon D, Gibson K, Tyndall MW. Mapping violence and policing as an environmental-structural barrier to health service and syringe availability among substance-using women in street-level sex work. Int J Drug Policy2008;19:140-7.
17. Choi SY, Holroyd E. The influence of power, poverty and agency in the negotiation of condom use for female sex workers in mainland China. Cult Health Sex2007;9:489-503.
18. Sanders T. The risks of street prostitution: punters, police, and protesters. Urban Stud2004;41:1703-17.
19. Wojcicki JA, Malala J. Condom use, power, and HIV/AIDS risk: sex-workers bargain for survival in Johannesburg. Soc Sci Med2001;53:99-121.
20. Cohan D, Lutnik P, Davidson P, Cloniger C, Herlyn A, Breyer J, et al. Sex worker health: San Francisco style. Sex Transm Infect2006;82:418-22.
21. Jayasree AK. Searching for justice for body and self in a coercive environment. Reprod Health Matters2004;12:58-67.
22. Blanchard JF, O'Neil J, Ramesh BM, Bhattacharjee P, Orchard T, Moses S. Understanding the social and cultural contexts of female sex workers in Karnataka, India. J Inf Dis2005;191(Supp 1):S139-46.
23. Rekart ML. Sex work harm reduction. Lancet2005;366:2123-34.
24. Werb D, Wood E, Small W, Strathdee S, Li K, Montaner J. Effects of police confiscation of illicit drugs and syringes among injection drug users in Vancouver. Int J Drug Policy2008;19:332-8.
25. Miller CL, Firestone M, Ramos R, Burris S, Ramos ME, Case P, et al. Injecting drug users' experiences of policing in two Mexican-US cities. Int J Drug Policy2008;19:324-31.
26. Rhodes T, Mikhailova L, Sarang A, Lowndes CM, Rylkov A, Khutorskoy M, et al. Situational factors influencing drug injecting, risk reduction, and syringe exchange in Togliatti City, Russian Federation:

a qualitative study of risk environment. Soc Sci Med2003;57:39-54.

27. Rhodes T, Simic M. Transition and the HIV risk environment. BMJ2005;331:220-3.
28. Gordy E. *The culture of power: nationalism and the destruction of alternatives*. University Park, PA: Pennsylvania State University Press, 1999.
29. Nikolic-Rastanovic V. *Women, violence and war: wartime victimisation of refugees in the Balkans*. Budapest: Central European University Press, 2000.
30. Olujic M. Embodiment of terror: gender violence in peace time and war time in Croatia and Bosnia and Herzegovina. Med Anthropol Q1998;12:31-50.
31. Djenovic D. Serbia: violence continues against religious communities. Forum 18 News Service. 2007. www.forum18.org/.
32. Human Rights Watch. Serbia: violence against students escalates. 2000.http://hrw.org/english/docs/2000/07/20/serbia711.htm.
33. Djilas A. A profile of Slobodan Milosevic. Foreign Aff1993;72:81-96.
34. Bogdanovic D, Nikic D, Petrovic B, Kocic B, Jovanovic J, Nikolic M. Mortality of Roma population in Serbia, 2002-05. Croat Med J2007;48:720-6.
35. Kabakchieva E, Amirkhanian YA, Kelly JA, McAuliffe TL, Vassielva S. High levels of sexual HIV/STD risk behaviour among Roma men in Bulgaria: patterns and predictors of risk in a representative community sample. Int J STD AIDS2002;13:184-91.
36. World Bank. *Roma and the transition in Central and Eastern Europe*. Washington DC: World Bank, 2000.
37. Miles MB, Huberman MA. *Qualitative data analysis*. London: Sage, 1994.
38. Silverman D. *Doing qualitative research*. London: Sage, 2000.
39. Westmarland L. Blowing the whistle on police violence. Brit J Criminol2001;41:523-35.
40. Rhodes T, Platt L, Sarang A, Vlasov A, Mikhailova L, Monaghan G. Street policing, injecting drug use and harm reduction in a Russian city: a qualitative study of police perspectives. J Urban Health2006;83:911-25.
41. Lersch KM, Mieczkoski T. Violent police behaviour: past, present, and future research directions. Aggress Violent Behav2005;10:552-68.

42. Skolnick JH, Fyfe JJ. *Above the law: police and the excessive use of force*. New York: Free Press, 1996.
43. Jacobs D. The determinants of deadly force: a structural analysis of police violence. Am J Sociol1998;103:837-62.
44. Bourgois P, Prince B, Moss A. The everyday violence of hepatitis C among young women who inject drugs in San Francisco. Hum Organ2004;63:253-64.
45. Goodyear MDE, Cusick L. Protection of sex workers. BMJ2007;334:52-3.

CHAPTER 10

BUNDLING OCCUPATIONAL SAFETY WITH HARM REDUCTION INFORMATION AS A FEASIBLE METHOD FOR IMPROVING POLICE RECEPTIVENESS TO SYRINGE ACCESS PROGRAMS: EVIDENCE FROM THREE U.S. CITIES

Corey S Davis[1] **and Leo Beletsky**[2]

[1]University of North Carolina, Gillings School of Global Public Health, Campus Box 7411, Chapel Hill, North Carolina 27599, USA

[2]Yale University, Center for Interdisciplinary Research on AIDS, 135 College Street Suite 200, New Haven, CT 06510, USA

Citation: Corey S DavisEmail author and Leo Beletsky, Harm Reduction Journal20096:16, https://doi.org/10.1186/1477-7517-6-16 © Davis and Beletsky; licensee BioMed Central Ltd. 2009, Received: 06 April 2009, Accepted: 14 July 2009, Published: 14 July 2009

ABSTRACT

Introduction

In light of overwhelming evidence that access to sterile injection equipment reduces incidence of injection-attributable bloodborne disease without encouraging drug use, many localities have authorized sterile syringe access programs (SAPs), including syringe exchange and pharmacy-based initiatives. Even where such interventions are clearly legal, many law enforcement officers are unaware of the public health benefits and legal status of these programs and may continue to treat the possession of injection equipment as illegal and program participation as a marker of illegal behavior. Law enforcement practice can impede SAP utilization and may increase the risk of needlestick injury (NSI) among law enforcement personnel. Many SAPs conduct little or no outreach to law enforcement, in part because they perceive law enforcement actors as unreceptive to health-promotion programs targeting drug users.

Case Description

We report on a brief training intervention for law enforcement personnel designed to increase officer knowledge of and positive attitudes towards SAPs by bundling content that addresses officer concerns about infectious disease and occupational safety with information about the legality and public health benefits of these programs. Pilot trainings using this bundled curriculum were conducted with approximately 600 officers in three US cities.

Discussion and Evaluation

Law enforcement officers were generally receptive to receiving information about SAPs through the bundled curriculum. The trainings led to better communication and collaboration between SAP and law enforcement personnel, providing a valuable platform for better harmonization of law enforcement and public health activities targeting injection drug users.

Conclusion

The experience in these three cities suggests that a harm reduction training curriculum that bundles strategies for increasing officer occupational safety with information about the legality and public health benefits of SAPs can be well received by law enforcement personnel and can lead to better communication and collaboration between law enforcement and harm reduction actors. Further study is indicated to assess whether such a bundled curriculum is effective in changing officer attitudes and beliefs and reducing health risks to officers and injection drug users, as well as broader benefits to the community at large.

Keywords: Harm Reduction, Public Health Actor, Public Health Benefit, Injection Equipment, Needle Stick Injury

INTRODUCTION

The spread of bloodborne disease through injection drug use is a longstanding problem in the United States and abroad, with syringe sharing as the primary modality for disease transmission among injection drug users (IDUs) [1, 2]. Many states and localities have implemented syringe access programs (SAPs) to reduce the sharing of syringes, including over the counter syringe sales and syringe exchange programs (SEPs) [3]. These interventions have been associated with decreased incidence of bloodborne disease and risky syringe-related behaviors among IDUs. They have also been shown to increase access to drug treatment and to reduce the number of improperly discarded syringes in the community [4, 5, 6, 7].

Injection-related disease transmission is largely an unintended consequence of laws aimed at curbing illicit injection drug use. Possession of injection equipment for the purpose of injecting illicit drugs is unlawful in many U.S. jurisdictions, severely restricting syringe access [8, 9, 10]. A recent study of 89 U.S. cities found that higher rates of three measures of legal repressiveness (hard drug arrests, police employees per capita and corrections expenditures per capita) were associated with higher HIV prevalence among IDUs [11]. Studies have repeatedly shown that laws restricting syringe possession raise street prices for injection equipment, lead to risky injection-related practices, and may contribute to improperly discarded syringes [9, 12, 13, 14]. These laws also may increase the risk of officer needle stick injury (NSI) [8].

Even where the law has been amended to make SAPs clearly legal, officers may not be aware of these changes, may not understand the public health rationale for them, or may simply choose to ignore them because they perceive them as misguided or counterproductive [10, 15, 16]. As a result, officers may continue to arrest IDUs for possession of legal injection equipment, confiscate or destroy this equipment, or treat participation in

SAPs as a marker of illegal behavior, thereby limiting the public health benefits of SAPs [11, 16, 17, 18, 19, 20, 21, 22]. Such practices may also discourage IDUs from informing officers that they are in possession of injection equipment, thereby increasing the risk of officer NSI.

Although the precise extent of this problem is unknown, it is clear that law enforcement interference with SAPs is widespread. In a 2007 survey of syringe exchange programs in the United States, 29% of respondent programs reported police harassment of participants at or near their access point, while 8% reported police arrest or harassment of program staff [23]. Recent data from an ongoing national survey of SAP respondents in the U.S. suggest that syringe exchange programs experience an annual average of 11 incidents involving police harassment of clients and at least one incident of staff harassment. Four out of 85 programs sampled to date report police arrest of staff members over the previous 12 months, and almost one in five report at least monthly uninvited police visits to syringe exchange venues. About one third report police confiscation or destruction of clients' legal injection equipment over the same period (unpublished data on file with authors).

Many law enforcement officers – police, deputy sheriffs, probation/parole officers and other sworn personnel – routinely come into contact with people who use drugs, those with mental illness and other groups perceived as likely to commit crimes and disturb public order. These encounters can lead to searches, inventory of personal effects upon arrest and other activities that may increase officer occupational safety risk through NSI and other communicable pathways [24, 25]. Although officers express significant anxiety about these risks, they typically have limited access to training and resources that can equip them to effectively reduce the risks and to navigate the complex set of mental health, addiction and other issues pervasive among IDUs and other marginalized populations. This can be a source of apprehension and miscommunication between these populations and officers, as well as a point of conflict between law enforcement and public health professionals [16, 26, 27, 28].

Disparate Cultures, Common Goals

Public health and law enforcement professionals tend to embody distinctly divergent views of drugs and drug users. Although there is a great deal of variation between and within members of each group, public health professionals are more likely to view drug addiction through a medical and social support lens that favors treatment and iterative approaches to illicit drug use [29]. Conversely, law enforcement officers tend to regard illicit drug use primarily as a legal and moral issue best resolved through rule-based, disciplinarian approaches rooted in deterrence, incapacitation, and punishment [10].

Both groups, however, have much in common. Both sectors take as their mandate the promotion and maintenance of healthy and safe communities. Both are predominantly comprised of people who chose the profession out of a sense of duty or desire to contribute to the health and welfare of society. From an institutional standpoint, both must compete for scarce public resources and are subject to often frustrating and competing directives from political leaders who may not understand or properly credit the complex realities faced by the organizations.

Despite the fact that public health and law enforcement professionals often work with the same populations in the same neighborhoods, there is relatively little formal institutional overlap between the two sectors [10, 30]. In many communities, officers form the first and sometimes only point of contact for chronic IDUs and other groups engaged in criminalized behaviors. Because of this reality, harmonizing policing practice with evidence-based public health programs such as SAPs is an essential element of successful public health efforts directed at these groups.

In recognition of the potential for synergy between the two sectors, public health practitioners are increasingly forging partnerships with law enforcement that are mutually beneficial to those organizations as well as society as a whole [31, 32, 33, 34, 35]. Perhaps because they largely believe that such activities would be futile or a poor use of scarce resources, it appears that many SAP operators and other public health actors have failed to identify and adequately address the concerns of law enforcement in planning and implementing SAPs, and rarely emphasize the positive health benefits such programs may have for officers.

Collaboration and Training to Change Police Response to Marginalized Populations

Even when they interpret a person's illegal behavior as stemming from a mental illness, officers may arrest that person if they perceive that no appropriate alternative to incarceration is available. This view may often be correct; in many jurisdictions, psychiatric treatment is more accessible in correctional settings than in the community [36, 37]. Similarly, police crackdowns aimed at people who use drugs are sometimes justified by public officials as a means of enrolling drug users into treatment [38]. Qualitative research suggests that officers often view arrest and incarceration as fundamentally flawed approaches to reducing chronic injection drug use, but consider these tools to be the only ones readily available to them in addressing drug-related crime and nuisance [16].

Many similarities exist between officer reaction to individuals with mental illness and individuals who use illegal drugs. Both groups are stigmatized by the larger community and are often seen by police as likely to commit crimes, and police are more likely to use force with both groups than with most other populations [39]. Research has shown that law enforcement officers are interested in receiving training in improving their interactions with people with mental illness. A number of collaborative efforts between mental health advocates and law enforcement have been implemented, with positive effects on officers' attitudes, beliefs, and knowledge [32, 37, 40, 41].

Collaborations between harm reduction and policing professionals, including officer training, have also shown promise. Internationally, Drug Action Teams (DATs) comprised of police, social services, and health providers that work to reduce drug-related crime while increasing access to effective drug treatment have been implemented in Great Britain and Australia to the benefit of police and IDUs [42, 43]. In China, international funding has been utilized to create teaching materials, conduct attitudinal research, and train professors at Yunnan Provincial Police Academy in public health and the role of police in implementing harm reduction programs. As a result of these efforts, over 6,000 cadets and many senior officers have received harm reduction training including the role of police in facilitating harm reduction programs, and regular meetings are held between police and harm reduction actors [44]. Harm reduction training for police has also been conducted in other parts of East and Southeast Asia as well as the Ukraine [45, 46].

Trainings directed at harmonizing law enforcement with public health activities have also been successfully implemented in the United States. In 2003, in response to an overdose epidemic among IDUs in San Francisco, a local harm reduction program initiated an intervention to distribute naloxone, a drug used to reverse opioid overdose, and train police and community members on its proper use. The program trained approximately 200 officers of all ranks about the goals and evidence base for the program and the chilling effect of the threat of arrest at overdose sites on the willingness of witnesses to intervene and summon emergency responders. After the training, no program participants reported being arrested for possession of naloxone or presence at overdose sites, although some participants reported having their naloxone confiscated by police [47]. Harm reduction and public health agencies in New York and New Mexico sponsor programs to train officers on SAP law and policy. These activities are not the norm, however; nationally, only about 20% of U.S. SEPs participate in police trainings (unpublished data on file with authors).

CASE DESCRIPTION

While some harm reduction agencies have conducted either one-time or ongoing trainings for police on the benefits of SAP, many programs are reluctant or unequipped to conduct such outreach. We could find no reports in the peer-reviewed literature as to what methods are employed, and what results are achieved, by such trainings. Based on evidence from the fields of police training and adult learning together with our interactions with law enforcement actors in a number of jurisdictions, we came to believe that officers might be receptive to information regarding SAPs when it is bundled with information about reducing officer occupational safety and is delivered by a trusted source [48, 49]. Our goal was to determine whether departments and officers would be receptive to such a bundled training in three diverse cities in the Eastern United States.

We identified and approached three departments (Pawtucket RI, Philadelphia PA and Wilmington DE) to conduct these feasibility trainings. As a point of departure for the design of the curriculum, modules used in training police in New York and New Mexico were utilized together with knowledge gained from informal discussions with officers and public health professionals. Curricula (available at http://www.policingforhealth.org) were designed to be brief and easily adaptable. They covered the evidence base for SAPs, the legal status of these programs in the jurisdiction, and the benefits of SAPs to the occupational safety of law enforcement personnel as well as the wider community. The curricula were tailored for the geographic, policy, and other contexts of each city.

The trainings were delivered sequentially beginning in summer 2006. While each training was adapted to the local situation, they adhered to the same general model: the training sessions lasted less than 30 minutes, emphasized occupational safety, were delivered to officers at either the police station or police academy, and included members of the local SAP, who were on-hand to answer questions, further discuss the program and reiterate the benefits of the two groups working together to reduce drug-related harm.

Site 1: Pawtucket, Rhode Island

In 2000, the Rhode Island Legislature decriminalized over-the-counter sales of hypodermic syringes. A qualitative study of police officers in the Pawtucket Police Department – a semi-urban setting – three years after passage of the law found that respondents were misinformed about the change, with a substantial proportion of officers self-reporting confiscating and destroying legal injection equipment in spite of the new law [16]. Interviews suggested that law enforcement personnel knew little of the syringe deregulation's public health underpinnings, which led to misinterpretation and a sense of hostility towards the law [16]. These data also highlighted the sense of anxiety and lack of training among the officers regarding infectious disease risk flowing from frequent contact with IDUs and occupational NSI events.

Using the demonstrated need from that study and the personal relationships that had been developed in the course of conducting the research, one of the authors (LB) approached the Pawtucket Police Department to suggest training officers about occupational safety, the law and SAPs. The findings were also presented to Rhode Island's Attorney General, who agreed to the need for training to address the disconnect between the law and police knowledge, attitudes and practices. With support from the department, LB applied for and received grant funding from the Rhode Island Foundation to conduct a pilot training for department personnel. LB then collaborated with the departmental training staff to design a training module to be delivered to the department's officers. The training module included a PowerPoint presentation, training evaluation forms, and presenter's notes.

Although funding was approved and the department agreed to participate in the training, the project was stalled for six months because the department's leadership had not filed a letter of agreement to serve as the site for the project, a key grant requirement. Once this requirement was cleared, LB met with personnel from the department's Planning and Training Division to finalize and pilot the curriculum. Based in part on the collaborative relationships that had been formed during the research phase, the Director of the Planning and Training Division agreed to engage his Division's staff in the implementation of the training program. The training was presented by the staff of the Planning and Training Division to about 140 street-level officers in the department through 6 sessions between March 2006 and February 2007. Each session lasted 30 minutes and was delivered as part of an hour-long session that also included training on another, unrelated topic to lower personnel costs to the department. All participants were later provided with tactical needle-resistant gloves at no charge to the department or officers.

Site 2: Philadelphia, Pennsylvania

SAPs were authorized in Philadelphia in 1992, and a legal syringe exchange program has operated for many years under contract with the city health department. However, a 2005 study found that use of the exchange fell significantly after the implementation of an anti-drug initiative launched by the city's police department in 2002 [50]. Although police management had issued an internal memorandum instructing officers not to target syringe exchange attendees, clients regularly reported that police officers impeded their efforts to reduce their bloodborne disease risk, and exchange staff (including author CD) had observed officers improperly discarding used syringes taken from exchange clients.

One of the authors (CD) together with other members of the SAP and county health department officials arranged meetings with supervisory police personnel in the area in which the SAP is located to discuss the ongoing negative impact of police action on access to the SAP and the connection between SAP access and reduced officer NSI risk. The feasibility of implementing a training similar to that conducted in Rhode Island was raised. The level of interest in participating in the initiative varied. One upper-level police official was unsupportive of the SAP, while another expressed wariness of possible negative repercussions he believed might occur if he was seen as collaborating with an organization that, while legal and receiving explicit governmental support, is still considered controversial and misguided among some officers and community members.

The Captain in command of the area in which the SAP office and largest outreach site are located, however, was supportive of the program and receptive to the idea of the bundled training. He suggested that CD contact the department's Infection Control Officer. The Infection Control Officer, a registered nurse and Sergeant in the department, was also receptive. It became clear through these interactions that many department personnel, both officers and command staff, were unaware that the SAP was legal, did not understand its role in community protection, and had not considered that it could reduce their risk of occupational NSI. We also became aware that officers received little training in reducing the risk of NSI, and were not provided with appropriate syringe disposal containers or barrier methods with which to handle and dispose of confiscated syringes.

Based on this information and with the support of the Captain and Sergeant, the SAP applied for and received grant funding from the Drug Policy Alliance to train officers in the police district in which the SAP is located, and to record the training for further dissemination. Trainings were conducted for all three shifts in the district over a single day in summer 2006 by a high ranking officer from the Albuquerque, New Mexico police department who had conducted similar trainings in New Mexico.

The training module was similar to that used in Rhode Island. Using a PowerPoint presentation, the New Mexico officer discussed the legality of the SAP and its ability to direct clients to treatment and other services and the direct benefits of the program to law enforcement. He also shared his personal experience of the positive impact SAP had on law enforcement in his department. As part of the training, the Infection Control Officer presented information on proper procedures for reporting and avoiding occupational NSI. Officers were provided with puncture-resistant gloves and approved syringe disposal containers to reduce their NSI risk. The SAP also provided the district office with a large syringe disposal container which is collected and replaced by the SAP at its expense. Approximately 90 officers and supervisory staff received the training.

Site 3: Wilmington, Delaware

In June 2006, Delaware state law was modified to explicitly permit SEPs. This change provided an opportunity to build on the previous two training initiatives by designing and implementing an integrated curriculum to be presented to police concurrently with the change in syringe access law. The program was designed in collaboration with local and state public health and law enforcement officials. The trainings were coupled with programs for prevention, monitoring and response to law enforcement-related problems, and were augmented by trainings for SAP clients on interaction with the police. Funding for curriculum development and program activities was provided by the Drug Policy Alliance.

A Wilmington non-profit contracted with the Division of Public Health to operate the first syringe exchange program authorized under the new law. Before the program opened, staff members from this non-profit and representatives of the state public health agency met with the Wilmington police chief to discuss the effect of the change in law on police practice, and to suggest that training modeled on that conducted in the previous two cities might be beneficial. The chief agreed to the Department's participation and assigned the Officer in Charge to hash out a number of practical questions relating to the change in law and its effect on departmental action in relation to the SEP.

The training portion of the initiative, which is ongoing, was developed in collaboration with public health and law enforcement officials. The sessions are administered by SAP personnel, often accompanied by a training officer. The trainings include information on the basic design of the SAP, its geographic scope, the authorizing legislation, and the legal immunities the law affords to clients. The curriculum stresses the public health goals of the program and the specific ways they shape the department's standard operating procedures, including changes in search, arrest, and referral activities. It also describes proper occupational safety procedures for handling syringes, communication techniques for prevention of NSI, and appropriate actions to be taken in the case of an NSI. To date, the training has been delivered to approximately 175 city police, 100 county police and 100 state police officers. The training has also become a part of the standard curriculum at the county and city police academies, with 2 county and 1 city police academy cohorts receiving the training to date.

The training was coupled with education for exchange clients on their rights under the law. This system was implemented both at the exchange and at the local public defender's office, which pledged to add exchange-specific questions to its standard client intake form. Officers are also provided with a wallet-sized information card, which includes guidelines on avoiding NSI, information about the authorizing law, and a phone number officers can call with questions or referrals to the SEP.

DISCUSSION AND EVALUATION

Simply changing the law to improve syringe access and reduce HIV risk may be insufficient to change key factors that shape such access, including police practice. Organizational inertia, lack of information and real or perceived lack of options can slow the dissemination, assimilation and implementation of new laws, policies and values [51]. Officers may not know about the policy change, or may simply ignore it as misguided [16]. Without alternative sources of information, officers rely on their superiors and peers – the workplace's implicit and explicit organizational values – for informational and attitudinal cues about drug use and drug users [51, 52, 53].

Without additional training, therefore, officers will tend towards the status quo. For training to be effective, it must be sufficiently tailored to change attitudes in the face of both inertia and oppositional organizational culture [51]. Trainings must clearly demonstrate to the officer why he or she should abandon the status quo in favor of novel procedures and practices. In the context of legal reforms to facilitate syringe access, this amounts to a new method of policing IDUs, one that may go against not only officer's existing beliefs but also organizational incentives (such as making arrests and appearing "tough on crime"). Although there is agreement that training is a vital element in changing officer behavior and attitudes, there is a lack of consensus as to the best method for achieving this change [54, 28]. Recent scholarship, however, has shown that police culture is "much more open to change than was once assumed [55]."

In the realm of bloodborne disease prevention among IDUs, policing represents a key structural barrier to service uptake. In spite of its prominence, most harm reduction organizations do not systematically address interactions with law enforcement. Based on previous models, we set out to ascertain whether trainings that bundle the public health rationale behind SAPs with an explicit focus on officer occupational safety were feasible and would encourage receptivity among both street-level and supervisory law enforcement personnel. We collaborated with local public health and law enforcement officials to design and deliver such training in three American cities.

At all three locations, the trainings went forward with the approval and cooperation of law enforcement management. Although not all members of the departments were supportive of the SAPs, none of the three departments that were approached turned down the opportunity to participate in the trainings. None of the departments were compensated for these activities, other than the information and provision of barrier and safe disposal supplies; rather, all made the decision to proceed after being approached by public health actors who expressed sincere concern for the safety of the officers, as well as for the public health implications of their practices. Feedback after the training sessions suggested that both officers and SAP personnel felt that the training had been a positive and valuable experience.

In all cases the interactions necessary to design and implement the trainings also led to stronger relations between law enforcement and public health actors, including discrete innovations that link the two sectors. In Wilmington, when enrolled IDUs are arrested on charges other than paraphernalia and found to be in possession of syringes, those syringes are placed in appropriate disposal containers, which are gathered periodically by SEP personnel. Officers then issue the arrestee a voucher that he or she can take to the SEP upon release from prison or the police station to be exchanged for new sterile syringes. This sensible procedure is, to our knowledge, unique to that program and would likely not have occurred without the training and associated outreach.

Although grant funding was utilized in these three cases, it is not a necessary component of similar interventions. Trainings in Wilmington are now continuing utilizing solely police department funds, and many sources of law enforcement training funding are available that might be utilized for trainings such as those described here [56].

CONCLUSION

Many harm reduction and public health actors in the U.S. remain hesitant to engage with law enforcement when planning and implementing SAPs. This reticence is understandable given the cultural and institutional differences between the two groups, but likely hampers the public health impact of these programs. Our experience has shown that police can be receptive to learning about harm reduction programs, particularly when that information is coupled with content directly relevant to the health of the law enforcement trainees and is delivered by a trusted source.

Although this feasibility work was not designed to assess the sustained impact of trainings on officer attitudes or behavior, evidence from other fields suggests that the beliefs and attitudes of officers are often heterogeneous and open to change. Properly designed training can effectively alter behavior and lead to positive effects for law enforcement and public health. The receptivity of officers to learning about harm reduction programs through this training framework supports further consideration of this model.

DECLARATIONS

Acknowledgements

This work was supported by grants from the Drug Policy Alliance and the Rhode Island Foundation. We thank the employees and volunteers of the public health, harm reduction and law enforcement agencies noted, Capt. Sonny Leeper (ret) of the Law Enforcement Training Institute, and Victoria Carroll, Greg Denham and Rachel McLean for their helpful comments on early drafts of the manuscript.

Competing Interests

Davis was employed within the past five years by one of the harm reduction agencies reported on in the article. Beletsky declares no competing interests.

Authors' Contributions

Both authors contributed to designing and delivering the intervention and drafting the manuscript for publication. Both authors read and approved the final manuscript.

REFERENCES

1. Garfein RS, Doherty MC, Monterroso ER, Thomas DL, Nelson KE, Vlahov D: Prevalence and incidence of hepatitis C virus infection among young adult injection drug users. J Acquir Immune Defic Syndr Hum Retrovirol. 1998, 18 (Suppl 1): S11-19.
2. Needle RH, Coyle S, Cesari H, Trotter R, Clatts M, Koester S, Price L, McLellan E, Finlinson A, Bluthenthal RN: HIV risk behaviors associated with the injection process: multiperson use of drug injection equipment and paraphernalia in injection drug user networks. Subst Use Misuse. 1998, 33: 2403-2423. 10.3109/10826089809059332.
3. Burris S, Finucane D, Gallagher H, Grace J: The Legal Strategies Used in Operating Syringe Exchange in the United States. American Journal of Public Health. 1996, 86: 1161-1168. 10.2105/AJPH.86.8_Pt_1.1161.
4. MacDonald M, Law M, Kaldor J, Hales J, Dore G: Effectiveness of needle and syringe programmes for preventing HIV. International Journal of Drug Policy. 2006, 14: 353-358. 10.1016/S0955-3959(03)00133-6.
5. Gollub EL: Human rights is a US problem too: The case of women and HIV. American Journal of Public Health. 1999, 89: 1479-1482. 10.2105/AJPH.89.10.1479.
6. Raboud JM, Boily MC, Rajeswaran J, O'Shaughnessy MV, Schechter MT: The impact of needle-exchange programs on the spread of HIV among injection drug users: a simulation study. J Urban Health. 2003, 80: 302-320.
7. Strathdee SA, Ricketts EP, Huettner S, Cornelius L, Bishai D, Havens JR, Beilenson P, Rapp C, Lloyd JJ, Latkin CA: Facilitating entry into drug treatment among injection drug users referred from a needle exchange program: Results from a community-based behavioral intervention trial. Drug Alcohol Depend. 2006, 83: 225-232. 10.1016/j.drugalcdep.2005.11.015.
8. Groseclose SL, Weinstein B, Jones TS, Valleroy LA, Fehrs LJ, Kassler WJ: Impact of increased legal access to needles and syringes on practices of injecting-drug users and police officers – Connecticut, 1992–1993. J Acquir Immune Defic Syndr Hum Retrovirol. 1995, 10: 82-89.
9. Burris S, Welsh J, Ng M, Li M, Ditzler A: State syringe and drug possession laws potentially influencing safe syringe disposal by

injection drug users. J Am Pharm Assoc (Wash). 2002, 42: S94-98. 10.1331/1086-5802.42.0.S94.Burris.

10. Small D: Two cultures passing in the night. Int J Drug Policy. 2005, 06: 221-222. 10.1016/j.drugpo.2004.11.002.
11. Friedman SR, Cooper HL, Tempalski B, Keem M, Friedman R, Flom PL, Des Jarlais DC: Relationships of deterrence and law enforcement to drug-related harms among drug injectors in US metropolitan areas. AIDS. 2006, 20: 93-99.
12. Koester S: Copping, running and paraphernalia laws: contextual variables and needle risk behaviour among injection drug users in Denver. Human Organ. 1994, 53: 287-295.
13. Maher L, Dixon D: Law enforcement and harm minimization in a street-level drug market. British Journal of Criminology. 1999, 49: 488-508. 10.1093/bjc/39.4.488.
14. Aitken CMD, Higgs P, Kelsall J, Kerger M: The impact of a police crackdown on a street drug scene: evidence from the street. International Journal of Drug Policy. 2002, 13: 189-198. 10.1016/S0955-3959(02)00075-0.
15. Maher L: Drugs, public health and policing in indigenous communities. DrugAlcoholRev.2004,23:249-251.10.1080/09595230412331293306.
16. Beletsky L, Macalino G, Burris S: Attitudes of Police Officers Towards Syringe Access, Occupational Needle-Sticks, and Drug Use: A Qualitative Study of One City Police Department in the United States. International Journal of Drug Policy. 2005, 16: 267-274. 10.1016/j.drugpo.2005.01.009.
17. Maher L, Dixon D: Policing and Public Health: Law Enforcement and Harm Minimization in a Street-Level Drug Market. The British Journal of Criminology. 1999, 39: 488-512. 10.1093/bjc/39.4.488.
18. Martinez AN, Bluthenthal RN, Lorvick J, Anderson R, Flynn N, Kral AH: The impact of legalizing syringe exchange programs on arrests among injection drug users in California. J Urban Health. 2007, 84: 423-435. 10.1007/s11524-006-9139-1.
19. Kerr TSW, Wood E: The public health and social impacts of drug market enforcement: a review of the evidence. Int J Drug Policy. 2005, 16: 210-220. 10.1016/j.drugpo.2005.04.005.
20. Bluthenthal R, Kral A, Lorvick J, Watters J: Collateral damage in the war on drugs: HIV risk behaviors among injection drug users. Int J

Drug Policy. 1999, 10: 25-38. 10.1016/S0955-3959(98)00076-0.

21. Case P, Meehan T, Jones TS: Arrests and incarceration of injection drug users for syringe possession in Massachusetts: implications for HIV prevention. J Acquir Immune Defic Syndr Hum Retrovirol. 1998, 18 (Suppl 1): S71-75.
22. Roe v. City of New York. 151 F. Supp. 2d 495 (S.D.N.Y. 2001).
23. Des Jarlais D, McKnight C, Goldblatt C, Purchase D: Doing harm reduction better: syringe exchange in the United States. Addiction. 2009,
24. Sonder G, Bovee L, Coutinho R, Baayen D, Spaargaren J, Hoek van den A: Occupational exposure to bloodborne viruses in the Amsterdam police force, 2000–2003. Am J Prev Med. 2005, 28: 169-174. 10.1016/j.amepre.2004.10.003.
25. Lorentz J, Hill L, Samimi B: Occupational needlestick injuries in a metropolitan police force. Am J Prev Med. 2000, 18: 146-150. 10.1016/S0749-3797(99)00137-3.
26. Brendan Dillon SA: Prison Officers' Concerns About Blood Borne Viral Infections. The Howard Journal of Criminal Justice. 2005, 44: 29-40. 10.1111/j.1468-2311.2005.00353.x.
27. Fowler G, Allsop S, Melville D, Wilkinson C: Drug harm minimisation education for police in Australia. A collaborative report by National Centre for Education and Training on Addiction (NCETA). 1999, Queensland Police Service
28. Edwards T: State police basic training programs: an assessment of course content and instructional methodology. Am J Police. 1993, 23-45.
29. McLellan A, Lewis D, O'Brien C, Kleber H: Drug Dependence, a Chronic Medical Illness: Implications for Treatment, Insurance, and Outcomes Evaluation. JAMA. 2000, 284 (13): 1689-1695. 10.1001/jama.284.13.1689.
30. Caulkins JP: Law Enforcement's Role in a Harm Reduction Regime. NSW Crime and Justice Bulletin. 2002, Sydney: New South Wales Bureau of Crime Statistics and Research, 64:
31. Green TM: Police as Frontline Mental Health Workers: The Decision to Arrest or Refer to Mental Health Agencies. International Journal of Law and Psychiatry. 1997, 20: 469-486. 10.1016/S0160-2527(97)00011-3.
32. Deane MW, Steadman HJ, Borum R, Veysey BM, Morrissey JP:

Emerging Partnerships Between Mental Health and Law Enforcement. Psychiatr Serv. 1999, 50: 99-101.

33. Keram EA: Commentary: A Multidisciplinary Approach to Developing Mental Health Training for Law Enforcement. J Am Acad Psychiatry Law. 2005, 33: 47-49.
34. Teplin LA: Criminalizing mental disorder: The comparative arrest rate of the mentally ill. American Psychologist. 1984, 39: 794-803. 10.1037/0003-066X.39.7.794.
35. DeBeck K, Wood E, Zhang R, Tyndall M, Montaner J, Kerr T: Police and public health partnerships: evidence from the evaluation of Vancouver's supervised injection facility. Subst Abuse Treat Prev Policy. 2008, 3: 11-10.1186/1747-597X-3-11.
36. Lamb HR, Weinberger LE, DeCuir WJ: The Police and Mental Health. Psychiatr Serv. 2002, 53: 1266-1271. 10.1176/appi.ps.53.10.1266.
37. Lamb HR, Weinberger LE, Marsh JS, Gross BH: Treatment Prospects for Persons With Severe Mental Illness in an Urban County Jail. Psychiatr Serv. 2007, 58: 782-786. 10.1176/appi.ps.58.6.782.
38. Maher L, Dixon DT: The cost of crackdowns: policing Cabramatta's heroin market. Current Issues in Criminal Justice. 2001, 13: 5-22.
39. Kaminski RJ, Digiovanni C, Downs R: The Use of Force between the Police and Persons with Impaired Judgment. Police Quarterly. 2004, 7: 311-338. 10.1177/1098611103253456.
40. Compton MT, Bahora M, Watson AC, Oliva JR: A Comprehensive Review of Extant Research on Crisis Intervention Team (CIT) Programs. J Am Acad Psychiatry Law. 2008, 36: 47-55.
41. Vermette HS, Pinals DA, Appelbaum PS: Mental health training for law enforcement professionals. J Am Acad Psychiatry Law. 2005, 33: 42-46.
42. Compton MT, Esterberg ML, McGee R, Kotwicki RJ, Oliva JR: Brief Reports: Crisis Intervention Team Training: Changes in Knowledge, Attitudes, and Stigma Related to Schizophrenia. Psychiatr Serv. 2006, 57: 1199-1202. 10.1176/appi.ps.57.8.1199.
43. Midford R, Acres J, Lenton S: Cops, Drugs and the Community: Establishing Consultative Harm Reduction Structures in Two Western Australian Locations. International Journal of Drug Policy. 2002, 181-
44. Lin D: Harm Reduction and Role of Police in China. 2007, New York: Social Science Research Council

45. Morrison E, Denham G: Building support with law enforcement to enable harm reduction programmes. Exchange on HIV/AIDS, Sexuality and Gender. 2007, 2007 Winter: 27-29.
46. Carey C, Cohen J, Wolfe D: Tipping the Balance: Why Legal Services are Essential to Health Care for Drug Users in Ukraine. 2008, New York: Open Society Institute
47. McLean R: Working with Law Enforcement to Implement Overdose Prevention Programs. Law Enforcement and Harm Reduction Meeting of the Open Society Institute. Bangkok, Thailand. 2007
48. Knowles MS: The Adult Learner: A Neglected Species. 1990, Houston: Gulf Publishing
49. Birzer M: The theory of andragogy applied to police training. Policing: An International Journal of Police Strategies & Management. 2003, 26: 29-42. 10.1108/13639510310460288.
50. Davis CS, Burris S, Kraut-Becher J, Lynch KG, Metzger D: Effects of an intensive street-level police intervention on syringe exchange program use in Philadelphia, PA. Am J Public Health. 2005, 95: 233-236. 10.2105/AJPH.2003.033563.
51. Engelson , Shockley-Zalabak P, Morley D: Adhering to organizational culture. Group and Organizational Studies. 1989, 14: 483-500. 10.1177/105960118901400408.
52. Engelson W: The organizational values of law enforcement agencies: The impact of Field training officers in the socialization of police recruits to law enforcement organizations. J Police and Crim Psych. 1996, 14: 11-19. 10.1007/BF02830064.
53. Hazer J, Alvarez K: Police work values during organizational entry and assimilation. J Applied Psych. 1981, 66: 12-18. 10.1037/0021-9010.66.1.12.
54. Quinet K, Nunn S, Kincaid NL: Training Police: A Case Study of Differential Impacts Of Problem-Oriented Police Training. Police Practice & Research. 2003, 4: 263-10.1080/1561426032000113889.
55. Chan JBL, Devery C, Doran S: Fair Cop: Learning the art of policing. 2003, Toronto: University of Toronto Press
56. USDOJ: Grants. [http://www.usdoj.gov/10grants/]

CHAPTER 11

REHABILITATION OF TORTURE SURVIVORS IN FIVE COUNTRIES: COMMON THEMES AND CHALLENGES

Helen McColl[1], Craig Higson-Smith[2], Sarah Gjerding[1], Mostafa H Omar[3], Basma Abdel Rahman[3], Mona Hamed[3], Aida S El Dawla[3], Miriam Fredericks[4], Nicole Paulsen[4], Gugu Shabalala[4], Carmen Low-Shang[4], Fernando Valadez Perez[5], Liliana S Colin[5], Aurora D Hernandez[5], Eliomara Lavaire[6], Arely PA Zuñiga[6], Lucia Calidonio[6], Carmen L Martinez[6], Yasser Abu Jamei[7] and Zeyad Awad[7]

[1]International Rehabilitation Council for Torture Victims, Borgergade 13, 1022 Copenhagen K., Denmark

Citation: Helen McColl, Craig Higson-Smith, Sarah Gjerding, Mostafa H Omar, Basma Abdel Rahman, Mona Hamed, Aida S El Dawla, Miriam Fredericks, Nicole Paulsen, Gugu Shabalala, Carmen Low-Shang, Fernando Valadez Perez, Liliana S Colin, Aurora D Hernandez, Eliomara Lavaire, Arely PA Zuñiga, Lucia Calidonio, Carmen L Martinez, Yasser Abu Jamei and Zeyad Awad, "Rehabilitation of torture survivors in five countries: common themes and challenges," International Journal of Mental Health Systems20104:16, https://doi.org/10.1186/1752-4458-4-16© McColl et al; licensee BioMed Central Ltd. 2010

[2]South African Institute for Traumatic Stress, 302 Ideal Village, 30 Hannaben Street, Johannesburg 2198, South Africa

[3]El Nadim Centre for the Management and Rehabilitation of Victims of Violence, 3A Soliman El Halabi Street from Rasmis Street, Cairo, Egypt

[4]Trauma Centre of Survivors of Violence and Torture, Cowley House, 126 Chapel Street, Woodstock 7925, Cape Town, South Africa

[5]Collective Against Torture and Impunity, Pitágoras 1210, 16 Col. Del Valle, 03100 Mexico DF, Mexico

[6]Centre for Prevention, Treatment and Rehabilitation of Victims of Torture and their Relatives, Col. La Reforma, Calle Principal 109, Contiguo a Centro IDEAL, Tegucigalpa M.D.C., Honduras

[7]Gaza Community Mental Health Programme, Sheikh Ejleen-El Rasheed

ABSTRACT

Background

Torture continues to be a global problem and there is a need for prevention and rehabilitation efforts. There is little available data on torture survivors from studies designed and conducted by health professionals in low income countries. This study is a collaboration between five centres from Gaza, Egypt, Mexico, Honduras and South Africa who provide health, social and legal services to torture survivors, advocate for the prevention of torture and are part of the network of the International Rehabilitation Council for Torture Victims (IRCT).

Methods

Socio-demographic, clinical and torture exposure data was collected on the torture survivors attending the five centres at presentation and then at three and six month follow-up periods. This sample of torture survivors is presented using a range of descriptive statistics. Change over time is demonstrated with repeated measures analysis of variance.

Results

Of the 306 torture survivors, 23% were asylum seekers or refugees, 24% were socially isolated, 11% in prison. A high level of traumatic events was experienced. 64% had suffered head injury whilst tortured and 24% had ongoing torture injury problems. There was high prevalence of symptoms of anxiety, depression, post traumatic stress as well as medically unexplained somatic symptoms. The analysis demonstrates a modest drop in symptoms over the six months of the study.

Conclusions

Data showed that the torture survivors seen in these five centres had high levels of exposure to torture events and high rates of clinical symptoms. In order to provide effective services to torture survivors, health professionals at torture rehabilitation centres in low income countries need to be supported to collect relevant data to document the needs of torture survivors and to evaluate the centres' interventions.

Keywords: Beck Depression Inventory, Post Traumatic Stress Disorder, Asylum Seeker, Beck Depression Inventory Score, Mental Health Research

BACKGROUND

Despite a range of international conventions and prevention instruments dating back to the end of the Second World War, torture is still practiced by at least 81 governments around the world [1]. The definition of torture is contested and different organisations define the concept more or less broadly. The most commonly used definition is that contained within the United Nations Convention Against Torture and Other Cruel, Inhuman and Degrading Treatment or Punishment (UNCAT) of 1985, which defines torture as, any act by which severe pain or suffering, whether physical or mental, is intentionally inflicted on a person for such purposes as obtaining from him or a third person information or a confession, punishing him for an act which he or a third person has committed, or intimidating or coercing him or a third person, or for any reason based on discrimination of any kind, when such pain or suffering is inflicted by or at the instigation of a public official or other person acting in an official capacity. It does not include pain or suffering arising only from, inherent in or incidental to lawful sanctions [2].

What is not in dispute is that torture includes both physical and psychological methods of causing pain, distress or harm. Common forms of physical torture include beatings, burning, suspensions and stress positions, suffocation and drowning and electrical shocks. Psychological torture is most commonly seen in the forms of threats of execution and torture, threats against family members, mock executions, extended solitary confinement, sensory deprivation or overload, sleep deprivation, humiliation, and the forced participation in torture of others. Of course, most forms of torture involve both physical and psychological components, of which rape and other forms of sexual violence are clear examples.

Given the absence of comprehensive torture treatment in most developing countries, some torture survivors turn to one of the many non-governmental torture rehabilitation centres around the world for assistance. These centres are typically founded and run by small groups of health professionals and human rights activists, often at great personal cost and risk. This paper reports on a collaborative study of torture rehabilitation undertaken by five such centres, namely:

- *El Nadim Centre for Psychological Management and Rehabilitation of Victims of Violence* in Egypt;
- *Gaza Community Mental Health Programme* (GCMHP) in the Palestinian Occupied Territories;
- *Centro de Prevención, Tratamiento y Rehabilitación de las Víctimas de la Tortura y sus Familiares* (CPTRT) in Honduras;
- *Colectivo Contra la Tortura y la Impunidad A.C.* (CCTI) in Mexico;
- *Trauma Centre for Survivors of Violence and Torture* (TCSVT) in South Africa.

These centres are all members of the *International Rehabilitation Council for Torture Victims* (IRCT), a global network of 144 torture rehabilitation centres. These centres represent a diversity of socio-political and cultural contexts and their varied resources mean that a standardized rehabilitation program is neither possible nor desirable. Services may include the following:

- Medical (for both physical and mental health needs)
- Physiotherapy
- Counselling and psychotherapy: Individual, family and group work
- Legal, including medical legal reports for those seeking restitution for torture and assistance with the asylum seeking process
- Prison visits
- Outreach work to rural areas
- Practical help with basic needs (food, shelter, language lessons)

- Further social care and integration, including living skills, education and employment training

The Socio-political Context for Torture Survivors

Knowledge of the social and political context in which torture and recovery occur is key to understanding the needs of torture survivors. For example, torture survivors construct and reconstruct the meaning of their experiences and this is an important component of their recovery. How this meaning is constructed depends in part on the socio-political context in which the torture and recovery occur.

In Egypt, the UN Special Rapporteur on Torture has reported that "torture is systematically practiced by the security forces, in particular the state security intelligence. In spite of denials of the government, the allegations of torture submitted by reliable, non governmental organizations consistently indicate that reported cases of torture are seen to be habitual, widespread and deliberate in at least a considerable part of the country." [3]

Torture in Gaza is closely related to the political situation which includes Israeli occupation and siege as well as a violent power struggle between the political factions Fatah and Hamas. Torture of Palestinians thus happens both during arrest by Israeli police and military, in Israeli prisons, as well as at the hands of the Palestinian political factions, and in the Palestinian prisons.

In Honduras, torture has been carried out as a mechanism of domination and social control since the time of colonialism. In the 1980s a US backed National Security Doctrine characterized by the use of death squads and military police to abduct, torture and murder political opponents as well as human rights and peace activists, was established. Violence was and continues to be legitimized from the highest levels of economic and political power.

Torture in Mexico is part of the structure of social inequity and responds to a doctrine of National Security similar to the one in Honduras. It is used for purposes of investigation, punishment, social demobilization and repression of ethnic minorities under the pretext of serving the purpose of counter insurgency in the continuous war against drug trafficking and organized crime. Political opponents of the government, syndicate members and leaders as well as leaders of lands rights, indigenous rights and other social movements, who openly criticize government actions, are targeted and "evidence" of their participation in drugs or arms trade is often planted on them or in their homes. During apartheid in South Africa, torture and arbitrary deprivation of liberty were widespread and institutionalized. South Africans were tortured for their political beliefs and their efforts to bring about a democratic society. Unfortunately, many attitudes, practices and habits from the apartheid time have survived. The debate on torture in South Africa today therefore focuses especially on places where people are deprived of their liberty: prisoners, detainees in police custody, asylum seekers and refugees, children in secure care facilities, and patients in psychiatric hospitals. South Africa is also currently home to several hundred thousand refugees and asylum seekers, many of whom have been tortured in their countries of origin.

Research on Torture Survivors

While the political contexts in which torture takes place may be very different, there is some evidence to suggest that the consequences for individuals and families are consistent across different settings. A recent meta-analysis of surveys on conflict affected persons from 40 different countries found torture to be endemic in countries affected by pervasive conflict and that torture is associated with mental disorder across these settings [4]. The severe and lasting negative consequences to the physical and emotional wellbeing of torture survivors have been well documented across different political contexts [5, 6] and [7]. Previous studies have often focused on specific populations, such as asylum seekers or post conflict persons, for example, Hyder et al [8] present work with Afghan refugees in Pakistan and Alexander [9] who writes about refugees from Burma living in very vulnerable circumstances in India and Malaysia. Some studies have shown elevated levels of depression, anxiety, Post Traumatic Stress Disorder (PTSD), somatic disorders as well as physical health needs [4, 10].

A small number of studies of treatment outcome with certain groups of torture survivors in particular contexts have been published. These studies tend to focus on short term international led programmes, rather than on the contribution of the ongoing work of permanent local torture rehabilitation centres. Bolton et al [11] have demonstrated the effectiveness of Group Inter Personal Therapy for adolescent survivors of war and displacement in Northern Uganda. Weine et al [12] demonstrated the effectiveness of testimony therapy with refugees from Bosnia-Herzegovina to the United States of America. Carlsson's study in an IRCT centre in Denmark following up survivors of torture after nine months of multi-disciplinary service interventions showed no change in mental health outcomes [13]. A study looking at the effects of brief multi-disciplinary treatment in Nepal showed effectiveness in treating somatic symptoms and disability and increasing subjective functioning, but no clear improvement in mental health measures [14]. Similarly, group treatments focussing on empowerment and support have shown positive results [15] and [16]. However, precisely because of the difficulties of conducting research in under-resourced contexts and emergency situations, few methods have been systematically tested in different contexts [17].

There is a lack of mental health research and research infrastructure in low income countries. The Global Forum and WHO mapped mental health research in Low and Middle Income Countries (LMIC) [18]. Their study identified that persons exposed to violence and trauma were a prioritised population group for mental health research and recommendations were made for improving mental health research capacity in LMIC. This research is designed and implemented by clinicians working in low income countries in permanent long standing rehabilitation centres for torture survivors. They aimed to see if it was feasible, despite the challenges of heavy clinical loads and extremely difficult working environments, as seen above, to collect useful data on:

- Demographics, torture exposure and clinical needs from the population of torture survivors attending their centres
- The recovery trajectories of torture survivors receiving care in the centres, and any differences between these patients and those who drop out of treatment

METHODS

Design and Statistical Analysis

Clinical Staff at the centres received basic training on research methods, and participated in the design and data collection in the course of their therapeutic work. They developed a standardized intake questionnaire, and then follow up questionnaires after three and six months. Data was collected on socio-demographics, trauma exposure and clinical needs of the torture survivors. Staff used a questionnaire previously developed for use with asylum seekers in the UK as a starting point to develop their own questionnaire [19]. Data collection took place from January to December 2008, both directly from patients and indirectly from patient records.

The selection of instruments by the five centres in the study was based on their acceptability, feasibility and language. They had to be brief, as staff and patient time was limited. The instruments used were the Beck Depression Inventory (BDI), the Harvard Trauma Questionnaire (HTQ) and the Camberwell Assessment of Needs, shortened version (CANSAS). The HTQ produces two scores of PTSD. HTQ (1-16) is a score derived from the first 16 items of the test which relate directly to the symptoms of PTSD as listed in the Diagnostic and Statistical Manual of Mental Disorders, 4th Edition Revised (DSM-IVR). HTQ (1-30) is a total score which derives from the symptoms and further signs associated with the diagnosis of PTSD.

The demographic and assessment data was captured in the five centres using a standardized spreadsheet. Qualitative data from the Honduran and Mexican centres was translated from Spanish into English. The data from all five centres was then combined, cleaned and analyzed using the Statistical Package for the Social Sciences (SPSS - Version 10). Data queries and problems of consistency were referred back to the five centres for comment and correction. Frequency distributions and descriptive statistics were calculated for all variables and scales. Differences in exposure, functioning and symptomatology were calculated between key groups (for example: men and women, exiles [refugees and asylum seekers] and citizens) using chi-square tests and one-way analysis of variance. Differences between participants who left treatment (and so the study) before six months were also calculated on all baseline variables using chi-square and Mann-Whitney tests. Finally, changes in the number of symptoms, depression and PTSD scores over time were examined for those subjects who remained in the study using repeated measures analysis of variance. (Where the sphericity assumption was violated, the Huynh-Feldt correction was applied).

The Sample

The sample comprised of 306 torture survivors presenting for individual treatment to the five rehabilitation centres during the period January to July 2008 (Table 1). These patients were followed up at three and six months following their initial presentation at the centres. Patients were excluded if they were under the age of 14 years or if the context prevented detailed individual documentation: those seen in remote settings which did not allow regular care and follow up, or where only group work was possible.

Table 1: Sample breakdown by country of treatment

Country	Number of Torture Survivors	%
Egypt	83	27
Honduras	79	26
Mexico	51	17
Palestine	33	11
South Africa	60	20
Total	**306**	**100**

Of the 306 torture survivors for whom baseline data was recorded, 148 (48%) dropped out before the three month assessment. A further 61 (20%) dropped out before the six month assessment. As a result treatment outcome analysis is based on the scores of 97 torture survivors who provided data at all three assessments (32%).

RESULTS

Demographic Information

Of the total sample of 306 torture survivors 172 (56%) were male. The mean age was 37.7 years (SD 14.2). 70 (23%) were exiles (refugees, asylum seekers or illegal immigrants). Virtually all exiles came from African countries and were included in the samples from Egypt and South Africa. The most prevalent religions in this sample were Christianity (55%), and Islam (38%).

40% of these torture survivors described themselves as single, while 42% were married or in a permanent relationship. 10% described themselves as divorced or separated, and a further 8% were widowed. The mean number of children was 2.1, although 35% had no children, and a few individuals had up to nine children. 14% of the sample (predominantly exiles) reported that they did not know where members of their immediate family were.

When asked to rate their level of social support the majority (52%) described themselves as having daily support from family or friends. However, 24% were isolated, not having a member of their social network who they saw at least weekly. While the majority of torture survivors in this sample were living at home (82%), 11% were in prison, 5% were living in camps or shelters for exiles, and the last 2% were homeless. The level of education of this sample of torture survivors is summarized in table 2.

Table 2: Education Level

Education level	Freq.	Percentage
Primary education not completed	63	(21%)
Primary education completed	81	(26%)
Secondary education completed	91	(30%)
Tertiary education qualification	32	(10%)
Unknown	39	(13%)
Total	**306**	**(100%)**

Whereas 65% of the sample described themselves as being entitled to work, only 45% of the total was employed. The others described themselves as retired (5%), taking care of the home and family (11%), studying (7%) or unemployed and searching for work (32%).

Experiences of Torture and Other Potentially Traumatic Experiences

These torture survivors reported having experienced an average of 5.4 (SD 4.1) of the different traumatic events listed in table 3 below. Approximately 10% of the sample had experienced more than 10 events. Men had higher levels of events than women (means of 5.8 events [SD 4.1] and 4.8 [SD 4.8]). Similarly exiles had higher numbers of different events than citizens (means of 6.9, [SD 5.0] and 4.9 [SD 3.7]). Table 3 summarizes the numbers reporting exposure to traumatic events. Where there are significant differences between the exposure of key groups (women, men, exiles, citizens), the group with higher exposure is noted.

Table 3: Prevalence of different types of traumatic exposur

Traumatic event	Number reporting event	% of total sample	Group with significant higher exposure
Torture	175	67	Men**
Being close to death	140	54	Men**
Forced separation from family	125	48	Women* & Exiles**
Serious injury	117	45	Men**
Ill-health without access to care	117	45	Men** & Exiles**

Imprisonment	110	42	Men** & Citizens*
Lack of food and water	99	38	Exiles **
Murder of family or friend	89	34	Exiles **
Unnatural death of family/ friend	86	33	Exiles **
Lack of shelter	86	33	Exiles **
Forced isolation from others	82	32	Exiles **
Lost or kidnapped	63	24	Exiles **
Murder of stranger(s)	52	20	Exiles **
Combat	49	19	Men**
Rape or sexual abuse	46	18	Women** & Exiles**
Brainwashing	22	8	

$p < 0.05$ *, $p < 0.01$ **

While the exiles from Africa are significantly more at risk for a broad range of traumatic events, citizens are more likely to have suffered imprisonment. Men are more likely to have experienced torture, being close to death, serious injury, imprisonment and combat. Women are more likely to have experienced forced separation from family, and rape or sexual abuse.

Head Injury

Data relating to head injuries sustained during torture was collected for 171 patients. Of these, 109 (64%) had sustained some form of head injury. 105 (61%) reported beatings to the head, 40 (23%) reported suffocation, and 18 (11%) reported drowning. 20 people (12%) reported losing consciousness during their ordeal.

Service Use

The rehabilitation centres participating in this study offer a range of different services, either directly or through referral to partner service providers. Table 4summarizes the services used by torture survivors following an initial assessment during the study period.

Table 4: Service utilization

Service	**Freq.**	**Percentage**
Legal services	110	(42%)
Employment services	56	(21%)

Counselling or psychotherapy	51	(19%)
Social services	39	(15%)
Interpretation services	29	(10%)
Inpatient care	25	(10%)
Medical outpatient -- adult	24	(9%)
Crisis or emergency response	15	(6%)
Educational services	10	(4%)
Medical outpatient -- child and family	9	(3%)
Substance abuse services	3	(1%)
Alternative medical services	2	(1%)

Physical Health Problems and Injuries at Initial Presentation

Ongoing physical health concerns were noted in 61 cases (20%). These are broadly categorized in table 5.

Table 5: Ongoing General Health Concerns

Type of disorder	Freq.	Percentage
Circulatory disorders	24	(8%)
Endocrine disorders	12	(4%)
Neurological disorders	7	(2%)
Gastro-intestinal disorders	5	(2%)
Reproductive disorders	3	(1%)
Parasitic infections	2	(1%)
Orthopaedic problems	2	(1%)
Pulmonary disorders	2	(1%)

62 patients (20%) also presented with torture related injuries that continued to cause pain or distress. Table 6 summarizes the types of injuries reported.

Table 6: Ongoing Concerns relating to Injuries

Type of injury	Freq.	Percentage
Contusions	22	(7%)
Scarring	12	(4%)
Fractures	10	(3%)

Internal Injuries	6	(2%)
Mutilation	5	(2%)
Sprains, strains, disloca-tions	4	(1%)
Cut and stab wounds	3	(1%)
Gunshot wounds	3	(1%)
Burns	3	(1%)
Nerve damage	1	(.5%)

Psychiatric Assessment at Initial Presentation

Not all centres have doctors working at them, so some centres prefer not to make medical or psychiatric diagnoses unless absolutely necessary (and then some may do so in consultation with external physicians), for example for a medical-legal report. This in part reflects the professional make up of the centres and beliefs about the usefulness of a diagnosis. 196 clients (64%) did receive a diagnosis and these are detailed below (Table 7).

Table 7: Psychiatric Diagnosis

Diagnosis	**Freq.**	**Percentage**
Post Traumatic Stress Disorder	123	(40%)
Major Depressive Disorder	83	(27%)
Generalized Anxiety Disorder	28	(9%)
Adjustment Disorder	14	(5%)
Psychotic Disorder	5	(2%)
Somatoform Disorder	4	(1%)
Substance Abuse Disorder	4	(1%)
Obsessive Compulsive Disorder	2	(1%)
Conversion Disorder	2	(1%)
Delusional Disorder	2	(1%)
Borderline Personality Disorder	1	(.5%)
Panic Disorder	1	(.5%)
Dysthymia	1	(.5%)
Acute Stress Disorder	1	(.5%)

Mental Disorder due to General Medical Condition	1	(.5%)

A more detailed clinical picture is presented by the results of the clinical interview summarized in Table 8.

Table 8: Symptom Prevalence at Intake

Symptom Categories	Freq.	Percentage
Anxiety related symptoms		
General anxiety	206	(68%)
Panic attacks	40	(13%)
Social phobia	14	(5%)
Agoraphobia	8	(3%)
Obsessive/compulsive	4	(1%)
Simple phobia	3	(1%)
Mood related symptoms		
Depressed mood	190	(63%)
Irritability and anger	163	(54%)
Somatic symptoms	124	(41%)
Emotional Numbing	69	(23%)
Suicidal thoughts	34	(11%)
Elevated mood	29	(10%)
Passivity	12	(4%)
Trauma related symptoms		
Re-experiencing/intrusion	159	(52%)
Hyper-arousal	153	(50%)
Avoidance	137	(45%)
Dissociative symptoms	17	(6%)
Symptoms relating to thought and perception		
Poor concentration	90	(30%)
Loss of insight	28	(9%)
Dissociative symptoms	17	(6%)
Conceptual disorganization	14	(5%)
Disorientation	11	(4%)
Delusions	8	(3%)

Hallucinations	5	(2%)

Not unexpectedly, the symptom categories associated with anxiety disorders, post-traumatic stress disorder and mood disorders are the most prevalent. On average participating torture survivors reported symptoms in 5.9 of symptom categories listed in table 8 above (SD 2.8).

The HTQ and BDI provided similar results. PTSD scores from part 4 of the Harvard Trauma Questionnaire were collected from 71 torture survivors (from Mexico and Gaza) (Table 9).

Table 9: Harvard Trauma Questionnaire (HTQ) Scores

	mean	**SD**	**Symptomatic for PTSD**	**Risk groups**
HTQ (1-16)	2.32	0.8	30 (42%)	Women*
HTQ (1-30)	2.16	0.7	24 (34%)	Women*

$p < 0.05$ *, $p < 0.01$ **

Although these results suggest that more than a third of this sample is symptomatic for PTSD, they should be interpreted with caution. The cut off score is taken from international norms and a single test like the HTQ cannot be used in isolation to make diagnostic decisions. However, what these results do tell us is that a significant group of torture survivors in this sample report that they frequently experience many of the symptoms associated with PTSD.

Similarly high levels of depressive symptoms were measured using the Beck Depression Inventory. In order to ensure the best fit with available normal data the BDI I was used in Honduras and Mexico, and the BDI II was used in Egypt, Palestine and South Africa. The results are summarized in table 10.

Table 10: Beck Depression Inventory (BDI) Scores

	n	**mean**	**SD**	**Moderate or Severe Symptoms**	**Risk groups**
BDI I	122	14.2	9.8	29 (24%)	Women**
BDI II	113	27.8	15.2	73 (65%)	Women*

$p < 0.05$ *, $p < 0.01$ **

A particularly high prevalence of depressive symptoms was recorded in Palestine and Egypt. Again, these scores should not be taken as diagnoses of major depressive disorder but as an estimation of the high levels of depression related symptoms in this sample.

The total number of symptoms reported in the clinical interviews is significantly correlated with the total number of events experienced ($r = 0.135$, $p = 0.024$). Similarly scores on the HTQ and BDI tests are highly correlated ($r = 0.840$, $p = 0.000$) to each other. However, the HTQ and BDI scores are not significantly correlated with the number of events experienced.

Recovery Trajectories

The results are for the torture survivors seen at both three and six months after initial assessment.

Torture survivors who left the study before the six month assessment were not different from those who completed all three measurements in terms of sex, marital status, number of dependents, level of education, employment status, baseline depression scores, number of unmet needs, or overall number of symptoms. However, those who stayed in treatment until the six month measurement tended to be younger ($z = -2.26$, $p = 0.024$) and to have fewer children ($z = -2.28$, $p = 0.023$). People who stayed in treatment long enough to complete all three measurements also reported a more traumatic experiences ($z = -6.046$, $p = 0.000$) and were more likely to report being raped ($\chi^2 = 15.4$, df = 1, $p = 0.000$) and/or being tortured ($\chi^2 = 21.16$, df = 1, $p = 0.000$). Refugees tended to stay in treatment longer ($\chi^2 = 9.99$, df = 1, $p = 0.02$) as did people who lived with fewer people ($z = -2.09$, $p = 0.037$), and who reported having less social support ($z = -2.91$, $p = 0.004$). Finally, people reporting more PTSD symptoms tended to leave treatment earlier ($z = -4.514$, $p = 0.000$).

The change in the total number of symptoms reported, the HTQ and BDI scores at initial assessment, three months and six months reveal in part the recovery trajectories of torture survivors.

The mean number of symptoms dropped significantly over time ($F[1.44, 126.78] = 25.86$, $p = 0.000$) as illustrated in figure 1 below:

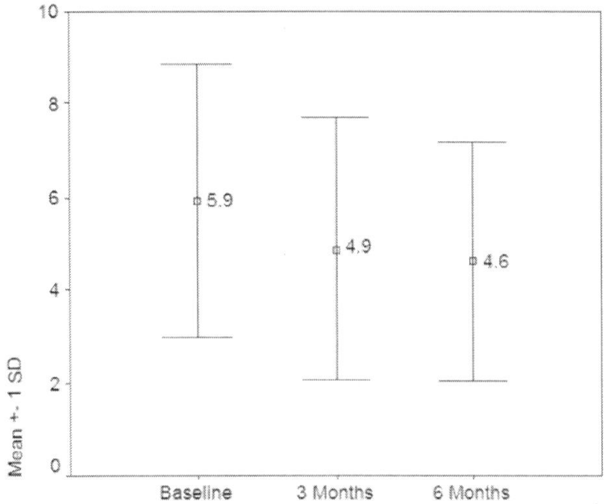

Figure 1: Mean number of symptoms over time (n = 88).

Measurements of depressive symptoms show similar significant drops for both the BDI-I (F[1.57, 48.78] = 13.349, p = 0.0000) and the BDI-II (F[1.17, 53.56] = 37.79, p-0.0000). These changes are presented in figures 2 and 3 below.

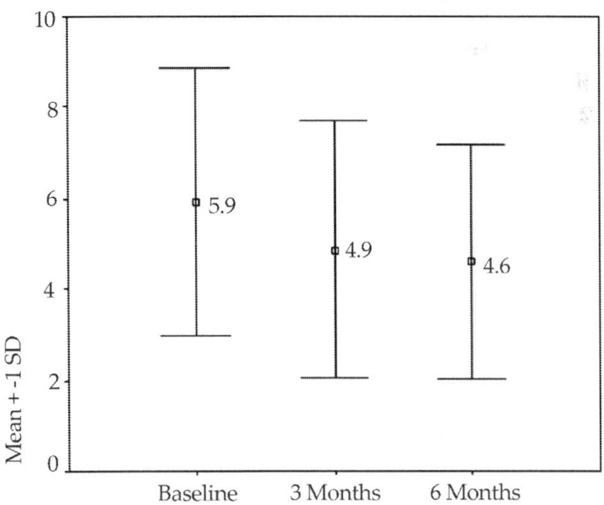

Figure 2: Mean BDI-I scores over time, Honduras and Mexico (n = 32).

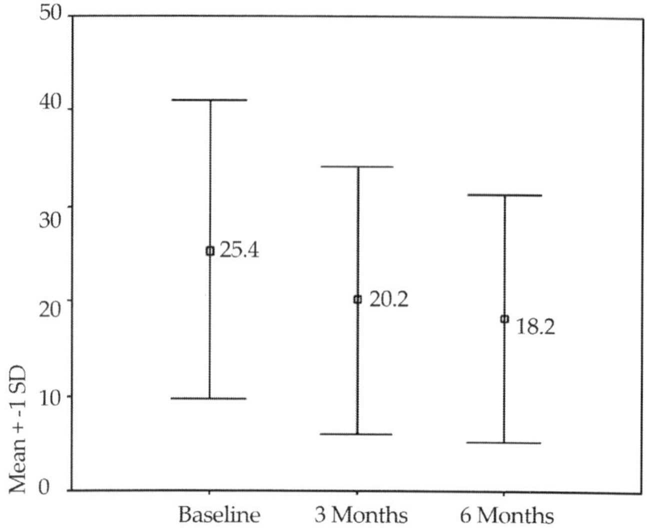

Figure 3: Mean BDI-II scores over time, Egypt and South Africa (n = 47).

Finally, although only the Mexican centre was able to collect HTQ data at all three measurement points, these results show significant improvement as illustrated in figure 4 below (F[2,30] = 5.097, p = 0.012).

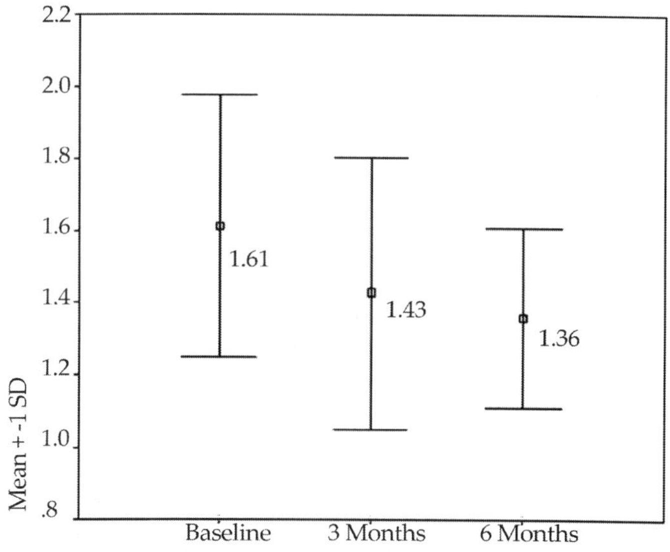

Figure 4: Mean HTQ scores over time (n = 16).

DISCUSSION

Medical and psychological care of torture survivors very often takes place in extremely difficult social, political, and economic contexts, which has effect on both staff and patients. Commonly clinicians working with torture survivors are managing large case loads with limited access to space, equipment, medicines, and technical and emotional support. This situation is often exacerbated by humanitarian crises such as war, when conducting research is understandably low on the priority list. For example, four of the five centres in this study suffered from attacks on their staff and/or premises during the research period; the centre in Gaza suffered from a war with Israel and the Honduran centre from a military coup. Nevertheless, it is important that centres providing care to torture survivors use research to identify needs and evaluate the effectiveness of their work. Data can also play a crucial role in the prevention of torture through documenting allegations and evidence of torture and advocacy work.

The study was a complex undertaking and there are many limitations to the data which must be kept in mind when interpreting the findings. In relation to the sample it is important to remember that this is a clinical sample of torture survivors who have received individual assistance at one or other of the centres. The patients described in this study are in no way representative of torture survivors in general, the vast majority of whom do not access health services.

The high dropout rate must also be considered when interpreting the results. Unfortunately it is not possible to determine the range of reasons that resulted in the majority of patients not completing six months of care. However, these reasons are likely to include a lack of resources such as transport to reach the centres, and changes in life circumstances (such as moving to a different town, finding employment, or being released from prison). Of course it is also likely that some patients left treatment because they felt that they had made sufficient recovery, or because they felt that the treatment was not meeting their needs.

Differences in language, culture, training and the professional backgrounds of staff presented many challenges to the study. Across the various centres service provision and data capture were conducted in Arabic, Spanish and English. Furthermore, service providers came from different disciplines including medicine, psychology, nursing and social work. These disciplines all have their own assumptions and technical language, and even within disciplines training differs enormously between different countries. As such this study provided important lessons in international and interdisciplinary work. Although the researchers went to great lengths to ascertain standard meanings and interpretations in the data, it is unavoidable that in some cases the quality of data was compromised.

Furthermore, the cultural applicability and standardization of the various instruments used was questioned. For example questions about substance use and sexuality are potentially insulting in some cultural contexts and health professionals decided to exclude them in many patient interviews, thus leaving too little data to analyze. Where possible the most glaring of these differences was allowed for in the analysis but it must not be assumed that the results were not influenced by cultural differences. Similarly, normal data and cut off scores have not been adequately tested for the varied study populations.

Finally, although the assessments conducted were extensive there are some areas of functioning which were not adequately documented. A larger battery of tests was not feasible given the contexts in which service providers are working and so some compromises were required.

While the high levels of symptoms are not unusual in a clinical sample such as this one, they do underline the enormous and lasting distress experienced by many torture survivors. However, it is surprising to note that the HTQ and BDI scores are not significantly correlated with the number of events experienced, a reminder that trauma and depression related disorders are a result of each person's appraisal of life events, rather than of the events themselves. The high prevalence of head injury (either due to beatings, drowning or suffocation) seen here is a particular challenge in the rehabilitation of torture survivors. Further research could investigate if head injury is adequately assessed and managed in torture survivors.

This study does provide an important picture of the demographic profile, living situations, experiences, and needs of torture survivors who seek assistance from treatment centres in these low income countries. This work also explores some of the difficulties of service provision (illustrated in part by the high dropout rate) and shows that where torture survivors are able to continue in care, modest but significant gains are likely, although whether due to treatment provided or external factors is not known. Finally, whilst carrying out this study we found enormous difficulties of collecting data on torture survivors where health professionals work in extremely taxing environments leading to recommendations of research networks to be formed.

CONCLUSIONS

The data collected showed that the torture survivors in the five centres had high levels of exposure to torture events and high rates of clinical symptoms. Data can be collected by clinicians working in torture rehabilitation centres in low income countries, despite their very difficult working environments. However in order to provide effective care for torture survivors further research needs to evaluate fully the interventions used. To do this the clinicians need to overcome the methodological and logistical challenges described above and to be supported by research networks.

AUTHORS' INFORMATION

Authors of this paper are a mix of psychiatrists, psychologists, social workers and anthropologists. All except CHS, HMC and SG work directly with torture survivors on a day to day basis in one of the five torture rehabilitation centres that have participated in this study. CHS is a South Africa based research psychologist, with a special interest in the rehabilitation of torture survivors. HMC is a psychiatrist and SG is a social anthropologist both were working at the IRCT secretariat as a medic and the project manager respectively.

Notes

Helen McColl, Craig Higson-Smith, Sarah Gjerding, Mostafa H Omar, Basma Abdel Rahman, Mona Hamed, Aida S El Dawla, Miriam Fredericks, Nicole Paulsen, Gugu Shabalala, Carmen Low-Shang, Fernando Valadez Perez, Liliana S Colin, Aurora D Hernandez, Eliomara Lavaire, Arely PA Zuñiga, Lucia Calidonio, Carmen L Martinez, Yasser Abu Jamei and Zeyad Awad contributed equally to this work.

DECLARATIONS

Acknowledgements

This study was made possible thanks to the financial contribution of the European Commission. This contribution covered the costs related to the design and coordination of the study, data collection and analysis, interpretation of data and writing of the manuscript. However, the EC played no direct role in the design and completion of the study. The decision to publish in the International Journal of Mental Health Systems was the independent decision of the authors. Alan Goss played an important role in cleaning and integrating the data from the five centres.

Competing Interests

The authors declare that they have no competing interests.

Authors' Contributions

MHO, BAR, MHA, AS, MF, NP, GS, CLS, FVP, LSC, ADH, EL, APAZ, LC, CLM, YAJ, ZA and HMC participated in the design of the study. MHO, BAR, MHA, AS, MF, NP, GS, CLS, FVP, LSC, ADH, EL, APAZ, LC, CLM, YAJ and ZA gathered the data for this study. CHS performed the statistical analysis of the data. HMC, CHS and SG participated in the coordination of the study and drafted the manuscript. All authors contributed to the outline of the manuscript. All authors read and approved the final manuscript.

REFERENCES

1. Amnesty International: Amnesty International Report 2008. The State of the World's Human Rights. London. 2008
2. United Nations Centre for Human: Rights Convention against torture and other cruel, inhuman, and degrading treatment or punishment. Methods of combating torture (Ed.). Geneva. 1989, 17:
3. United Nations High Commissioner for Human Rights: Report of the Committee Against Torture, Supplement no 44(A/51/44). Geneva. 1996
4. Steel Z, Chey T, Silove D, Marnane C, Bryant RA, van Ommeren M: Association of torture and other potentially traumatic events with mental health outcomes among populations exposed to mass conflicts and displacement: a systematic review and meta-analysis. Journal of the American Medical Association. 2009, 302 (5): 537-549. 10.1001/jama.2009.1132.
5. Quiroga J, Jaranson JM: Politically-motivated torture and its survivors: a desk study review of the literature. Torture. 2005, 16 (2-3): 1-111.
6. Quiroga J: Torture in children. Torture. 2009, 19: 66-87.
7. Johnson H, Thompson A: The development and maintenance of post-traumatic stress disorder (PTSD) in civilian adult survivors of war trauma and torture: A review. Clinical Psychology Review. 2008, 28: 36-47. 10.1016/j.cpr.2007.01.017.
8. Hyder AA, Noor Z, Tsui E: Intimate partner violence among Afghan women living in refugee camps in Pakistan. Social Science and Medicine. 2007, 64: 1536-1547. 10.1016/j.socscimed.2006.11.029.
9. Alexander A: Without refuge: Chin refugees in India and Malaysia. Forced Migration Review. 2008, 30: 36-38.
10. Alexander A, Blake S, Bernstein M: The staying power of pain: A comparison of torture survivors from Bosnia and Colombia and their rates of anxiety, depression and PTSD. Torture. 2007, 17: 1-10.
11. Bolton P, Bass J, Betancourt T: Interventions for depression symptoms among adolescent survivors of war and displacement in northern Uganda: a randomized controlled trial. Journal of the American Medical Association. 2007, 298: 519-527. 10.1001/jama.298.5.519.
12. Weine SM, Kulenovic AD, Pavkovic I, Gibbons R: Testimony psychotherapy with Bosnian Refugees: A pilot study. American Journal of Psychiatry. 1998, 155 (12): 720-1726.

13. Carlsson JM, Olsen DR, Mortensen EL, Kastrup M: Mental health and health related quality of life: a 10 year follow up of tortured refugees. Journal of Nervous and Mental disease. 2006, 194: 725-731. 10.1097/01.nmd.0000243079.52138.b7.
14. Tol WA, Komproe IH, Jordans MJD, Thapa SB, Sharma B, de Jong J: Brief Multi-Disciplinary Treatment for Torture Survivors in Nepal: a Naturalistic Comparative Study. International Journal of Social Psychiatry. 2009, 55: 39-56. 10.1177/0020764008091525.
15. Curling P: The effectiveness of empowerment workshops with torture survivors. Torture. 2005, 15 (1): 9-15.
16. Manneschmidt S, Griese K: Evaluating psychosocial group counselling with Afghan women: Is this a useful intervention?. Torture. 2009, 19 (1): 41-50.
17. Higson-Smith C, Bro F: Tortured exiles on the streets: A research agenda and methodological challenge. Intervention. 2010, 8: 14-28. 10.1097/WTF.0b013e3283387948.
18. Sharan P, Levav I, Olifson S, de Fransisco A, Saxena S: Research capacity for mental health in low- and middle-income countries: Results of a mapping project. World Health Organiation & Global Forum for Health Research (Eds.). Geneva. 2007
19. McColl H, Johnson S: Characteristics and Needs of asylum seekers and refugees in contact with London community mental health teams: a descriptive investigation. SPPE. 2006, 41: 789-795.

CHAPTER 12

HEALTH, HUMAN RIGHTS, AND THE CONDUCT OF CLINICAL RESEARCH WITHIN OPPRESSED POPULATIONS

Edward J Mills[1,2] **and Sonal Singh**[2,3,4]

[1]Programme in International Human Rights Law, University of Oxford, Oxford, UK

[2]Department of Pharmacy, Rhodes University, Grahamstown, Eastern Cape, South Africa

[3]Bloomberg School of Public Health, Johns Hopkins University, Baltimore, USA

[4]School of Medicine, Wake Forest University, Winston-Salem, USA

Citation: Edward J Mills and Sonal Singh , Globalization and Health20073:10, https://doi.org/10.1186/1744-8603-3-10 © Mills and Singh; licensee BioMed Central Ltd. 2007, Received: 23 April 2007 Accepted: 08 November 2007 Published: 08 November 2007

ABSTRACT

Background

Clinical trials evaluating interventions for infectious diseases require enrolling participants that are vulnerable to infection. As clinical trials are conducted in increasingly vulnerable populations, issues of protection of these populations become challenging. In settings where populations are forseeably oppressed, the conduct of research requires considerations that go beyond common ethical concerns and into issues of international human rights law.

Discussion

Using examples of HIV prevention trials in Thailand, hepatitis-E prevention trials in Nepal and malaria therapeutic trials in Burma (Myanmar), we address the inadequacies of current ethical guidelines when conducting research within oppressed populations. We review existing legislature in the United States and United Kingdom that may be used against foreign investigators if trial hardships exist. We conclude by making considerations for research conducted within oppressed populations.

Keywords: Malaria, Security Council, Artesunate, Global Compact, United Nations Global Compact

BACKGROUND

There is an overarching assumption that medical research, in general, is a good thing. Even those who don't subscribe to this arguably simplistic view would hold that medical research is absolutely necessary. This situation is made complex by a widespread expectation that science and technology are expected to be capable of curing all conditions. Society and the medical community have come to the conclusion that research on humans is both necessary and desirable. This poses urgent questions, however, when we consider the poor quality and poor outcomes of most clinical trials and basic science experiments [1, 2, 3, 4, 5, 6, 7] As clinical trials and sentinel data expand in number and location, the necessity and relevance of research's worth to participants represents both an ethical and human rights concern [8]. The recent globalization of international clinical trials highlights relatively new questions as to whether conducting research in marginalized or oppressed populations can or should be acceptable. The number and breadth of international and regional instruments displays the lack of clarity that exists within the biomedical fields of research. Declarations, by their very nature, are non-binding instruments that guide the conduct of research, but may hold mandatory rules within single institutions, not inter-state. Some have asserted that part of the problem is not that there is too little international standard setting but that there is too much of it [9]. We believe that issues arising in clinical trials are not limited to ethical concerns, but at times enter the world of international human rights law. We recognize the need for further discussion and the difficulties of conducting international research and the complexities of contemporary medical research in the developing world, particularly research amongst populations that are known to suffer systematic human rights violations- from here on called 'oppressed'. We recognize that in-light of existing cases of participation in rights and ethics violations, any new declarations or legal instruments must have the requisite teeth to bite when transnational companies and sovereign states engage in questionable foreign research with foreseeable negative consequences.

We have previously addressed the role of researchers in promoting vulnerable population participant rights in respect to HIV clinical trials [10]. Here, we present an overview of considerations for the conduct of research, whether clinical trials or sentinel data collection, when working with systematically oppressed populations. Using case-examples from Thailand, Nepal, and Burma (Myanmar), we recommend considerations regarding the protection of participants and local colleagues in settings with oppressed populations.

Thailand

Conducting trials within a population that is not just marginalized but is actually under direct threat from government action poses its own problems for researchers. The situation concerning those involved in the drug trade in Thailand remains of grave concern. During Thailand's 2003 'war on drugs,' over 2,500 alleged drug traffickers and users were extrajudicially killed [11]. The former Prime Minister, Thaksin Shinawatra (since ousted in a bloodless coup), publicly denigrated non-government organizations for reporting the human rights abuses internationally [12].

Given these conditions, conducting research that collaborates with Thai authorities and addresses drug user issues creates dilemmas that straddle ethics and international human rights law. Could participation in a state-authorized clinical trial of HIV prevention 'out' an intravenous drug user and potentially expose them to a risk of state-sanctioned violations? In these circumstances, what duties regarding privacy and confidentiality of information exist on the part of the researcher? Although medical records in a clinical trial are confidential, the security of the records is a serious concern, given the state history of behavior amongst this population. It is not unreasonable to suggest that lists of populations can be used to devastating effects when we consider the state-led violence in Rwanda's genocide, Chile's military rule, or China's crack-down on Falun Gong membership [13, 14].

A clinical trial that is currently being conducted in Bangkok amongst IDUs displays the complexity and challenges that exists when one examines clinical trials only as an ethics dilemma or only as a legal dilemma [10]. The trial, assessing the effectiveness and safety of oral tenofovir for HIV prevention in 1,600 IDU participants from the Bangkok area, is funded by the US Centers for Disease Control and prevention (CDC) and conducted by Thai research partners. This trial, like others around the world assessing tenofovir, has come under scrutiny for highlighting ethical questions rarely addressed. In this case, the study is funded by a US state transnational organization. US state funds are not permitted to cover the supply of drug paraphernalia and as a result, clean needles are not provided to participants. However, article 29 of the Helsinki Declaration states that '*benefits, risks, burdens and effectiveness of a new method should be tested against those of the best current prophylactic* ‹interventions [15]. Further, article 23 of the recent UNGASS Declaration of recommitment to HIV/AIDS, signed by both Thailand and USA [16], notes the affirmation of access to essential commodities, including sterile injection equipment and harm-reduction efforts related to drug use. This raises important legal and ethical concerns. Domestic laws, such as the US policy, are countered by international norms for provision of clean needles [16]. Should a foreign state's (US) laws override an internationally agreed upon standard of clinical trials, the Helsinki Declaration or the UNGASS Declaration, signed by both the Thai and United States Medical Associations?

Nepal

In autumn 1995, the United States Armed Forces Research Institute of Medical Sciences established the Walter Reed/AFRIMS Research Unit-Nepal field unit in Kathmandu, Nepal, for the study of Hepatitis E, a water-borne disease with a high maternal mortality rate.

In late 1999, plans for a Phase II/III clinical trial of a Hepatitis E vaccine were approved by the Nepal Health Research Council and the U.S. Army's Human Subjects Research Review Board[17]. The vaccine had been patented by California based biotech company Genelabs, and licensed by SmithKline Beecham (now GlaxoSmithKline). It was subsequently announced that the trial would begin in mid February 2000 with the screening of 8,000 volunteers in Lalitpur, 3,000 of whom would be enrolled in the trial receiving the vaccine or placebo. Following the trial's announcement Genelabs' share price nearly doubled, reaching their highest level in the nine year history of the company [18]. While shareholders were celebrating their good fortune, articles began to appear in Nepali newspapers suggesting that the Nepali population was being taken advantage of by Western pharmaceutical companies. Concerned about the controversy and possible political fall-out, local government officials from Lalitpur met to discuss the trial. They concluded that the trial should not continue as scheduled until the researchers satisfied the governing committee that relevant actions such as post-trial access had been accomplished.

During this intermission, the controversy heightened, with critics asking whether there had been adequate education to allow informed consent among the trial participants and why researchers would not contribute to the clean up the water supply – Thailand had been initially planned as trial site but the disease had been largely eradicated in the 80's and 90's due to advances in water sanitation. The Deputy Mayor had asked for a hospital to be built, as proposed profit sharing was considered out of the question. The prohibition against the trial was upheld and it was moved to a community that predictably did not raise any objections: recruits from the Royal Nepalese Army.

As with any army population, the use of serving members of the military as trial participants is dubious at best since questions of informed consent and undue influence must be asked in light of what is necessarily a highly ordered and authoritative community, even in developed nations [19]. Upon entering military service, soldiers necessarily give up certain rights enjoyed by private citizens and it is conceded that if a military is to be at all effective there must be some element of the destruction of individual autonomy. However, can there consistent informed consent in the RNA when there is only 44% literacy rate? [18] Nepal's military is also well known for torture, disappearances and inadequate and infrequent pay for its members [20]. Can conscripts ever be said to engage in any military activity voluntarily? How much coercion is involved by decision-makers? Can a participant withdraw? [21] When Sachit Rana, Chief of Army Staff at the RNA, claims "the army can do anything it wants – shoot at people, use bombs, arrest people" [22], it is difficult to imagine a more unsuitable population for such a trial. Surely institutions that are guilty of mass human rights abuses, such as the RNA or the Thai drug authorities, should be neither subjects nor partners for human subject research, yet in this case they were both – a sad state of affairs seeing as the trial had been approved by the National Institute of Allergy and Infectious Diseases and US Army IRBs.

Burma (Myanmar)

In the examples of Thailand and Nepal, we present cases of clinical research that could have been conducted in populations other than the oppressed participant populations. However, should research ever be conducted in populations with foreseeable oppression?

There are few countries in the world that can boast of such egregious human rights violations as Burma (Myanmar). A military government, since 1958, has ruled Burma. In 1988, a new military government, the State Law and Order Restoration Council (SLORC) took over and renamed the country Myanmar. SLORC would change Burma's name to Myanmar and impose martial law, repressing any democracy movements [23]. SLORC would begin a systematic train of human rights abuses including forced labour, rape, torture and murder [24]. Burma's present authoritarian military government, the State Peace and Development Council (SPDC), continues to operate a strict police state and drastically restricts basic rights and freedoms. Its military is estimated at 350,000 and as many as 70,000 are estimated to be child soldiers [25, 26]. Freedom of expression, assembly, and association are not respected and the arbitrary detention and incarceration of those expressing their political opinions continues [26]. As a result of the military violations, the United Nations appointed a country specific Special Rapporteur on the situation of human rights Myanmar since 1992. Most recently, the *Doe* versus *Unocal* case set important precedent [23]. This case, settled in 2005, addressed whether Unocal, a multinational oil company, could be held responsible for crimes against humanity committed by the Myanmar military, a business partner. The case was found admissible and demonstrates that multinational companies that partner with repressive states may be responsible for their partnering states actions. Given the widespread nature of the human rights violations, it is difficult to determine whether researchers should choose to conduct their work in such an atmosphere. We recognize that even in vulnerable populations, relevant research is necessary if the population has exception medical needs, as in the case of malaria, which is often geographically distinct in terms of drug-resistance and endemicity [27]. This may explain why so many malaria trials have been conducted in Burma.

When dealing with geographically specific diseases, we need to consider the importance of the research initiatives. Trials evaluating artesunate treatment for malaria have been successfully conducted in Burma amongst military recruits and their families. These clinical trials, approved by the University of Oxford ethics review committee in the UK, display the inadequacy of our current ethics frameworks. Regardless of actual human rights violations within the trial, it seems implausible that the ethics review committee members from Oxford have a through knowledge of the situation for Burmese recruits residing in Burma. The Oxford review committee insisted on a partnership between the Oxford researchers and the SPDC Ministry of Health (MOH). At this time it is worth noting the debacle last year between the SPDC and the Global Fund to Fight AIDS, TB, and Malaria resulted in the withdrawal of funding for HIV/AIDS programmes as the junta had prevented allocation of resources to the required programmes and suspected of using the money for military purposes instead [28].

Given the realities of research infrastructure, clinical trials conducted in Burma must partner with the relevant local authorities. These trials raise important and difficult questions. As illustrated in the Doe vs Unocal case, partnering with the Burmese government is against many state laws and may implicate a research body in crimes. We would argue that partnering with such an organization may be excusable in limited circumstances – where there are compelling and pressing reasons why such research cannot be conducted amongst another population. Indeed, several trials demonstrating the effectiveness of artesunate based therapies for severe malaria have instigated a national policy change regarding treatment within Burma, demonstrating that this research was necessary and in certain circumstances can result in important improvements for the populations at risk [29].

DISCUSSION

These case studies illustrate the complexities and potential pitfalls of examining research from simply an ethical or simply a human rights legal framework. As previously stated, there are many international instruments that confer and safeguard the rights of participants in clinical trials. The first widely-adopted instrument was the Nuremburg Code; followed in 1964 by the Helsinki Declaration (since revised 7 times by the World Medical

Association) [15]; the 1966 International Covenant on Civil and Political Rights (CCPR)(particularly Article 7 as it relates to consent for medical and scientific experiments) [30]; the Council for International Organizations of Medical Sciences (CIOMS) international ethical guidelines in 1993 (since revised) [31]; and, the 1996 International Conference on Harmonization of Technical Requirements for Registration of Pharmaceuticals for Human Use – Good Clinical Practice: Consolidated Guidelines [32]. On a European level [EU], the EU has issued its directive on good practice in clinical trials [33] and the Council of Europe has issued a Convention on Human Rights and Biomedicine on biomedical research [34]. Most recently, UNESCO has developed a Universal Declaration on Bioethics and Human Rights [35]. Although there is considerable overlap between these documents there are also dramatic differences between them, that no doubt contribute to general confusion and the possible conflation of discrete legal principles that has resulted in some pausing to question whether they can contribute to the development of a comprehensive international framework [9].

Given their brevity, the Nuremberg Code and the CCPR are of minimal benefit today in any discussion on human rights in clinical trials. Neither document recognizes the distinction between therapeutic and non-therapeutic research. This fundamental deficiency means that they have largely been ignored by the medical profession. A logical consequence of a strict construction of Article 1 of the Code and Article 7 of CCPR (both addressing consent) would mean that consent would be necessary in all circumstances: those who become unconscious due to an accident or disease or those who are mentally handicapped could not, if no standard treatment exists, be offered new therapeutic measures that might restore their health or save their lives. Such a rigid interpretation would mean that the respective provisions exclude many of those they were designed to protect. Furthermore, in the case of Article 7 CCPR it is obvious that the provision is to be read as a whole and that the caveat contained in the second sentence must be read in conjunction with the first.

"No one shall be subjected to torture or to cruel, inhuman or degrading treatment or punishment. In particular, no one shall be subjected without his free consent to medical or scientific experimentation."

The Article prohibits experiments that violate the integrity of the person by cruel, undignified or inhuman treatment. Clinical research carried out in accordance with general principles would not violate this provision. Yet the right to health argument confounds this. At the recent XVI International

AIDS Conference in Toronto, UNAIDS presented an ethical argument as to why trial participants that seroconvert during a trial do not require access to effective treatment [36]. UNAIDS representatives considered these ethical and not obligatory legal issues. We were dumbfounded to see a UN agency using an ethical argument to abstain from providing the highest attainable standard of health, a human right guaranteed in so many UN legally binding documents.

Although the ethics declarations themselves are not binding legal documents, they arguably represent customary law – law based on an established pattern of behaviour that can be objectively verified within a specific field. The Declaration of Helsinki is a respected document of long standing and esteemed pedigree that is cited in numerous international and national legal instruments, giving it force of law in certain jurisdictions and under certain well-established principles, such as voluntary participation and informed consent [37]. It is signed by all member-state medical associations. It is also subject to intermittent revisions approved by the General Assembly of the World Medical Association (WMA), and therein lies its vulnerability: the WMA is a non-governmental association and is subject only to private law while the rights of participants in clinical trials is increasingly being viewed through the prism of international human rights law [37]. There is little recourse for most Nepali rural dwellers or drug users who might have participated in a trial that conceivably constitutes a violation of Article 19 of the Declaration (access to effective interventions) or the RNA conscript whose participation is, on first appearance, a violation of Article 20 (informed and voluntary consent) if there has not been ratification by their respective national legislatures.

This shortcoming is even more pronounced with respect to the CIOMS since the method by which proposals are adopted is much less transparent. It was the covert nature of the deliberations that led some to criticize the 1993 version of the guidelines claiming that protection had been over emphasized and more pragmatism had been called for, reflecting much more the interests of the research community than the basic rights of the individual or official WHO policy [38]. However, the 2002 CIOMS guidelines do make reference to the Declaration of Helsinki and indeed claim it is "*the fundamental document in the field of ethics in biomedical research.*"[31] The updated version also enunciates the laudable goal that "*the research is responsive to the health needs and the priorities of the population or community in which it is to be carried out; and any intervention or product developed, or knowledge generated, will be made reasonably available for the benefit of that population or community.*"[39]' Nevertheless, as stated in the Declaration of Helsinki, human rights issues are coming to be seen as within the proper domain of public law and private law remedies such as negligence and the tort of trespass do not constitute a potent deterrent for unscrupulous researchers operating in under-developed countries where access to legal advice is scarce and/or prohibitively expensive. But if the long arm of civil law can reach them in their largest market there may be light at the end of the tunnel.

Alien Tort Claims Act

One potentially powerful tool in the rebalancing of rights within clinical trials in vulnerable populations is the United States' Alien Tort Claims Act [ACTA, 28 U.S.C., 1350] [40]. Considering that the majority of clinical trials conducted in developing nations are supported by US based organizations [5, 41], the ATCA is particularly relevant. It was originally part of the Judiciary Act of 1789 and was one of the first laws of the new American Republic. A federal law, it allows lower courts to hear cases in violation of international law or the "*law of nations*". There have been 3 modifications since its passing and now reads: "*The District Courts shall have original jurisdiction of any civil action by an alien for a tort only, committed in violation of the law of nations or a treaty of the United States.*" The statute had been invoked only five times in the first 200 years of its existence and was arguably a rather ineffective remedy [42]. There is renewed interest in the use of the tort as a tool for human rights litigation. One of the most important ATCA decisions, in 1980, the Second Circuit court addressing *Filartiga v. Pena-Irala* [43], held that the ATCA represented liability for torture committed using state authority as it found a Paraguayan police official that visited the US to be criminally responsible for his actions in torturing and disappearing a young man in Paraguay. Torture, in this case, was viewed as illegal under any international circumstances as no reasonable state should permit torture. In 1995, the tort was used to serve Radovan Karadzic for atrocities in Bosnia in the *Kadic v. Karadzic*[44] case, that expanded the statute's reach to private actors. These decisions put to rest (at least on the Second Circuit) questions regarding whether or not the Act conferred mere jurisdiction or an actual substantive cause of action [45]. It should be noted, however, that ATCA does not grant the federal courts jurisdiction over foreign governments or their agencies [46]. Nevertheless, it is clear now from a developing body of case law, and the recent case of *Doe I v. Unocal Corp*, a case that identified Unocal Oil Corporation responsible for atrocities committed in partnership with the Burmese junta, that the liability of multinational corporations falls squarely within the domain of ACTA. Most recently, in 2007 US Federal Prosecutors used the ATCA successfully against Chiquita Brands International for their funding of Colombian rebel groups resulting in fines [47].

For a claim to be successful under ATCA there are three requirements: (i) there must be alien plaintiffs; (ii) suing for a tort; (iii) committed in violation of international law [24]. The first two required elements are relatively straightforward; however, the third presents difficulties as it requires American courts to consider customary international law or treaties and attempt to give effect to customary law, where actual law had not previously existed. This task is simplified somewhat if the alleged violations concern international laws that are *jus cogens* – a violation of international norms from which no derogations are permitted. The *Unocal* case concerned forced labour which was likened to slavery – a blatant *jus cogens* violation. However, the court held that «a *jus cogens*violation is sufficient, but not necessary, to state a claim under the ATCA" [23]. With this in mind there is an argument to be made that a violation of a provision of the Helsinki Declaration resulting in foreseeable injury could found a claim under ATCA. Might a conscript in the Burmese Army or the Royal Nepali Army file a suit against SEAQUAMAT or GlaxoSmithKline respectively for their part in a trial alleging a lack of informed consent and therefore an infringement of Article 20 of the Declaration of Helsinki? Could the family member of a Thai IDU who was subject to extrajudicial execution sue a pharmaceutical corporation for retaining a Thai police officer as security by alleging a violation of the victim's right to confidentiality as expressed by Article 21?

These questions have recently been answered, to some extent, when the State of New York Federal Court permitted a Nigerian claim against a multinational pharmaceutical company, Pfizer Ltd, for the conduct of therapeutic research using an experimental antibiotic, Trovan, versus the on children without receiving informed consent during a meningitis epidemic in Nigeria [48]. In this clinical trial (n = 200), 11 children died and others were left blind or paralyzed. This case was dismissed from the US courts in 2002, finding on the grounds of that the case be completed in Nigeria, where able courts exist (*forum non conveniens*), but did identify Pfizer US as a state-actor, given its financial inter-dependence with the US government, and the approval of the US Food and Drug Administration for the trial. In Nigeria, criminal charges have been brought against Pfizer officials and a civil suit seeking billions in damages has been sought. The case is ongoing.

On June 29, 2004, in the case of Soza vs *Alvarez-Machain* [49], the US Supreme Court upheld the ATCA in recognition of serious human rights abuses. The court did however, limit these abuses to "specific, universal, and obligatory international norms (violations of safe conduct, infringement of the rights of ambassadors)." Nevertheless, courts may not be slow to accept new causes of action under ATCA as recent decisions on the concept of complicity and secondary liability differ. ATCA claims are generally held against private organizations that may be working independently or as state-actors. However, it cannot be applied to the state itself. In the Thai and Nepali trial examples, the trials were funded by the US state, with some involvement however peripherally with the drug manufacturer. The New York District Court has held that liability in international law "for knowing practical assistance or encouragement which has a substantial effect on the perpetration of the crime" is a core principle that forms the foundation of customary international legal norms [50]. Only time will tell which approach is ultimately adopted.

The arguments laid out towards the use of the ATCA and United Nations Global Compact [51] on good corporate responsibility are limited as they apply predominantly to multinational corporations and not to states. However, states are the largest funders of clinical research on neglected diseases in developing settings and in all case examples that we apply here, states have either funded or coordinated the clinical research. There are state laws regarding state behaviour when dealing with oppressive regimes. Without being extensive, we briefly describe relevant laws in the United States and the United Kingdom.

502B

The US government has issued communications to sitting judges claiming that ATCA should be given a narrow interpretation, arguing in support of limiting the role of ATCA to finding corporations liable for human rights violations. Such conduct should be seen in light of existing legislation designed to prevent the government from trading with known human rights abusers. Section 502B of the Foreign Assistance Act of 1961 (now coded as 22 U.S.C., 2304) as amended reads "*...a principal goal of the foreign policy of the United States is to promote the increased observance of internationally recognized human rights by all countries*." The law enforces that no state-funds made available by the Foreign Assistance Act should be dispensed to foreign military units with known human rights violations for weapons or training. In the spirit of the law, the provision of funding to Thai military or Nepali military seems specious. Although the statute addressing defense appropriations allows for derogation if such action is certified by the Secretary of State owing to "extraordinary circumstances", it is difficult to see why the jurisdiction of the US courts should be denied to victims of a corporate-foreign-regime-relationship when such a regime would not even qualify for US foreign aid by virtue of them being known human rights violators. This law, commonly known as the Leahy Law (after Senator Patrick Leahy) has most famously been implemented with regards to assisting specific units in Colombia's military, which was circumvented by units swapping out abusers to make specific units clear of abusers.

United Kingdom

There is not one exhaustive statute that deals with preventing government and the private sector partnering with rogue states or abusers of human rights. The UK has passed a number of statutes that authorize the imposition of trade or economic sanctions, providing some inference that illegal behaviour outside the UK is viewed with condemnation.

The United Nations Act 1946

This Act is essentially an enabling statute that brings UN Security Council resolutions into the law of England and Wales. Once again, under Chapter VII (Article 41) of the United Nations Charter, if the UN Security Council determines that a threat to the peace, a breach of the peace or an act of aggression has occurred, it may decide what measures shall be taken to maintain or restore international peace and security. A UN Security Council decision taken pursuant to Article 41 imposes a legal obligation on the UK (as a UN Member) to take all necessary measures to give effect to the decision domestically. When a resolution imposes sanctions, the UK must introduce them into domestic law. This is done by passing statutory instruments under the United Nations Act.

Section 1(1) of the Act enables Parliament to pass legislation in furtherance of Article 41. It provides:

"If...the Security Council of the United Nations call upon His Majesty's Government in the United Kingdom to apply any measures to give effect to any decision of that Council, His Majesty may by Order in Council make such provision as appears to Him necessary or expedient for enabling those measures to be effectively applied..."

The UN Security Council resolution will be enabled in domestic law by way of an Order in Council (a statutory instrument) made by the Foreign Secretary, and laid before Parliament. Such an instrument will have force of law and a violation of it could bring a term of imprisonment of up to 6 years.

Recent example of Orders in Council made under the Act include: The Sudan (United Nations Measures) Order 2006 [52]; The Lebanon and Syria (United Nations Measures) Order 2005 [53]; The Democratic Republic of the Congo (United Nations Measures) Order 2005 [54].

These Orders in Council are simply a mechanism by which UN Security Council resolutions are enacted and made enforceable in the UK under domestic law. They do not proscribe trade or aid with nations or organisations who are not subject to a Security Council sanction and who may be gross human rights violators. Further, they do not forbid all trade even with proscribed countries but only those items specified in the Security Council resolution (most often arms, aircraft, etc.).

The Export Control Act 2002

The *Import, Export and Customs Powers (Defence) Act 1939* provided the Secretary of State with a general power to impose import and export controls on goods. The 1939 Act was considered to be a temporary measure to deal with the emergencies of the time. However, the 1939 Act has remained in force (although it was amended by the Import and Export Control Act 1990 to allow it to continue in force without relying on the continued existence of «the emergency» that existed in 1939).

The Scott Inquiry into *Export of Defence Equipment and Dual-Use Goods to Iraq and Related Prosecutions* in February 1996 identified a number of limitations in the 1939 Act, including the lack of parliamentary scrutiny of secondary legislation made under the Act and the absence of any indication of the purposes for which export controls may be imposed. The 2002 Act was passed after a government white paper was circulated that took account of some of the concerns raised by Lord Scott.

In the absence of a UN Security Council resolution embargoing trade with a particular group or nation, the UK has the power to prohibit such trade by use of Orders in Council made under the *Export Control Act 2002*. But are clinical trials a trade issue? Section 5(2) of the Act states that " [c]ontrols of any kind may be imposed for the purpose of giving effect to any Community provision or other international obligation of the United Kingdom." This refers to bilateral and multilateral agreements which the

UK may have, notwithstanding their UN obligations. In practice it is most common for Orders in Council made under the Act to be in furtherance of European Union objectives, an example being under Title V of the Treaty on European Union (provisions on a common foreign and security policy).

Although there is guidance from the EU on trading and engaging with rogue states (for instance the European Union Code of Conduct on Arms Exports) the regulations are not all-encompassing. Matters of defence and foreign policy are still within the proper domain of member states and since both of these areas are governed to a large extent in the UK by the Royal Prerogative it is not difficult to see instances where partnering with questionable regimes would be possible since it had not been specifically proscribed by the EU.

The power of US 502B is that it requires the Secretary of State to justify why trade/aid should be allowed with such a nation despite its hideous human rights record. Whether or not 502B has had a positive impact on foreign trade and the ability to partner with rogue regimes is difficult to say, since exemptions can be made under it if they are certified by the Secretary of State. Although this is not an ideal safeguard, it does force politicians to publicly declare the reasons for partnering with such a regime.

Considerations for the Conduct of Research within Oppressed Populations

As the costs of research increase it is no wonder that pharmaceutical companies are looking to developing nations to conduct much of their research. Much of the marketing of multinationals is now trumpeting their commitment to human rights and the environment. Indeed many of the world's largest companies have apparently embraced guidelines drawn up by the United Nations concerning ethical conduct, such as the UN Global Compact and the UN Norms on the Responsibilities of Transnational Corporations and Other Business Enterprises with Regard to Human Rights [55]. Yet in the same breath these companies are lobbying in Washington in an attempt to have the Alien Tort Claims Act repealed by propagating the fiction that it will make it impossible for well-intentioned companies to know what conduct might subject them to liability or that it will stifle foreign investment. It is not cynical to suggest that this is the case because the Global Compact and the UN Norms do not contain a word about enforcement.

It is evident that in the absence of any effective international legal framework to address the dilemmas and complexities of research in vulnerable populations we are set to see the further abuse of human rights. Table 1 lays out necessary considerations for the conduct of clinical research in oppressed populations. It must be the case that if companies or states are going to reap the benefits of conducting research on vulnerable groups they carry out they requisite appropriate consultation. Ethical review boards cannot be a ‹one size fits all› but must take into account local concerns and address those concerns in liaison with local representatives and further in-roads must be made into the entrenched hostility on the part of drug companies to post-trial medical care. The greater the atmosphere of vulnerability the greater the level of consultation must be; in settings with foreseeable human rights violations, such violations much be captured. The time is ripe for an international legal instrument to address these concerns and upon ratification in national legislatures to provide a substantive cause of action without excessive restrictions on *locus standi* which result in companies never being brought to book as ‹victims› never make it to court. These are complex issues that demand attention, and in the absence of an international convention, it falls to creative and bold jurists to push for these issues in courts of law and various international fora.

Table 1: Considerations for conducting research in oppressed populations

Health Promoting	For clinical effectiveness interventions, interventions should be health promoting and address a clearly population relevant illness. There should be a clear plan for how research findings will assist community, based on *a priori* agreement on how findings will be used. This requires active engagement with target groups and plans for how findings should be interpreted with target group members.
Opportunities to avoid exposures should be afforded to participants	Exposures may include exposures to the target diseases or to human rights violations. This should include education (e.g. condom use, needle provision and needle cleaning); assistance with known human rights promoting activities or possible escape; and, the avoidance of remaining in exposed status.
Planned efforts to determine the human rights status of a particular population	This may include formative research and background reviews of human rights NGO literature.

Community participation commensurate with level of political oppression	There are few reliable ways to measure oppression. Due to the large geographical and cultural heterogeneity, there may not be a unified voice and so we need minimum standards for Community Advisory Boards (CABs).
CABs must include mixed levels of education, oppressive situations, age and gender	They should be able to inform on the importance of the research and therefore, acceptability. CABs may need to be outside target areas (i.e. Burma)
The more oppression, the more reason for research required	Assuming researchers cannot improve oppressive setting, the conducting research may be placing participants or colleagues at risks. Oppressive conditions may make population 'captive'
HR violations should be captured	Good research captures all health outcomes determined of interest in clinical event forms. In certain conditions we can anticipate HR violations. Case report forms should inquire of HR violations. This may allow for subgroup analyses.
Report an Ethical methodology	Ethics and human rights issues are not black or white issue (ethical or not ethical), but require explanation to determine challenges that exist in the research settings. It may well be appropriate to advocate for a limitations section of the article that addresses what could not be accomplished. This could be advocated by the Consolidated Standards for Reporting of Randomized Trials Group (CONSORT), a group that advocates minimum standards of reporting clinical research. It is only through acknowledgement of these issues that the field can be advanced.
Measure long-term impact, for informing "customary research"	We need to determine if the research has improved conditions, or worsened it? Has 'Western' research improved or reduced the quality/ expectations of indigenous research? Finally, we need to determine if post-trial access was accomplished and what care was provided for post-trial injuries related to participation.

Table 1 highlights issues for consideration of the conduct of oppressed populations. We have previously listed considerations for conduct in difficult to protect populations, and these previous recommendations are updated here. These recommendations recognize that research is often required within specific populations, but that research should be health promoting, rather than risking placing specific or large groups of a population at risk of violence, detention, or other state-led abuses. While no list is exhaustive and each setting is likely to be substantially different, these considerations address specific issues that are applicable to oppressed populations, where the likelihood of harm is impending. We predominantly argue that where oppression exists, the argument for conducting research in that population needs to substantially outweigh the negatives of not conducting the research. The central argument is the optimal balance between ensuring the safety of participants while advancing the needs of science. The "intentionality" of the research endeavour should not only be to advance scientific knowledge but also offer practical benefits, or at least the hope of future benefits for the oppressed population. Researchers need to bear the burden of proof and strive to minimize coercion. They need to identify representative leaders who represent the diversity of opinions, conduct public deliberations in the spirit of participatory decision-making and try to ensure decision making as much as possible at the local level. Some authors argue for a " modus vivendi " approach that favours decision-making via compromise rather than rational consensus. As we alluded to at the beginning of this paper, the assumption that research will necessarily lead to population benefits is naïve and is not supported by evidence. Good intentions alone are likely to be insufficient in protecting potential participants and so extra caution and planning is required.

CONCLUSION

As the medical research world becomes increasing globalized, there is a need to make research both methodologically valid and culturally valid. In the examples that we have highlighted, conducting research within oppressed populations stretches the current norms of medical ethics as well as stretching the current capabilities of international law. To rely simply upon minimum standards of non-binding and vague medical ethics instruments for conducting research within these populations is both naïve and culturally insensitive. Human lives are inherently complex and no single ethical framework, including ours can claim to capture the complexity of research and understand the ethical dilemmas that arise in these diverse settings. Paradoxically, legal course is least available to oppressed populations where the need is greatest. Ethical principals and legal approaches outlined above are not intended to be rigid inflexible pillars, rather as signposts along the way for researchers interested in grappling with this challenge of conducting research within vulnerable populations. In accordance with universal principals of justice, the “effective “ participation of oppressed populations in decision-making will be an instrumental step in combating the social, economic and political forces of globalization that constrain human capabilities.

REFERENCES

1. Constopoulos-Ioannidis DG, Ntzani E, Ioannidis JP: Translation of highly promising basic science research into clinical applications. Am J Med. 2003, 11: 477-484. 10.1016/S0002-9343(03)00013-5.

2. Ioannidis JP: Why most published research findings are false. PLoS Med. 2005, 2: e124-10.1371/journal.pmed.0020124.

3. Isaakidis P, Ioannidis JP: Evaluation of cluster randomized controlled trials in sub-Saharan Africa. Am J Epi. 2003, 158: 921-926. 10.1093/aje/kwg232.

4. Kavvoura FK, Liberopoulos G, Ioannidis JP: Selection in reported epidemiological risks: an empircal assessment. PLoS Med. 2007, 4: e79-10.1371/journal.pmed.0040079.

5. Kent DM, Mwamburi DM, Bennish ML, Kupelnick B, Ioannidis JP: Clinical trials in sub-Saharan Africa and established standards of care: a systematic review of HIV, tuberculosis, and malaria trial. JAMA. 2004, 292: 237-242. 10.1001/jama.292.2.237.

6. Kyzas PA, Denaxa-Kyza D, Ioannidis JP: Quality of reporting of cancer prognostic marker studies: association with reported prognostic effect. J Natl Cancer Inst. 2007, 99: 236-243. 10.1093/jnci/djk032.

7. Swingler GH, Volmink J, Ioannidis JP: Number of published systematic reviews and global burden of disease: database analysis. BMJ. 2003, 327: 1083-1084. 10.1136/bmj.327.7423.1083.

8. Trouiller P, Olliaro P, Torreele E, Orbinski J, Laing R, Ford N: Drug development for neglected diseases: a deficient market and a public-health policy failure. Lancet. 2002, 359: 2188-2194. 10.1016/S0140-6736(02)09096-7.

9. Gevers S: Medical Research Involving Human Subjects: Towards an International Legal Framework?. Eur J Health Law. 2001, 8: 293-298.

10. Mills EJ, Singh S, Singh JA, Orbinski JJ, Warren M, Upshur RE: Designing research in vulnerable populations: lessons from HIV prevention trials that stopped early. BMJ. 2005, 331: 1403-1406. 10.1136/bmj.331.7529.1403.

11. Anon: 'Thailand: Extrajudicial killing is not the way to suppress drug trafficking' (February 20th 2003) Amnesty International Press Release. 2003

12. Human Rights Watch: World Report 2006, pg. 314 [http://hrw.org/wr2k6/wr2006.pdf].

13. Beyrer C, Kass NE: Human rights, politics, and reviews of research ethics. Lancet. 2002, 360 (9328): 246-251. 10.1016/S0140-6736(02)09465-5.

14. Gourevitch P: We Wish to Inform You that Tomorrow We will be Killed with our Families: Stories from Rwanda. 1999, New York , Picador

15. World Medical Association: Declaration of Helsinki, 2004. http://www.wma.net/e/policy/b3.htm.

16. United Nations General Assembly Special Session Declaration of Committment, 2006. http://www.ungass.org/index.php/en/ua/ungass/declaration_of_commitment/ungass_declaration_of_commitment.

17. Shrestha MP, Scott RM, Joshi DM, Mammen MP, Thapa GB, Thapa N, Myint KS, Fourneau M, Kuschner RA, Shrestha SK, David MP, Seriwatana J, Vaughn DW, Safary A, Endy TP, Innis BL: Safety and efficacy of a recombinant hepatitis E vaccine. N Engl J Med. 2007, 356: 895-903. 10.1056/NEJMoa061847.

18. Andrews J: Research in the ranks: vulnerable subjects, coercible collaboration, and the hepatitis E vaccine trial in Nepal. Perspect Biol Med. 2006, 49: 35-51. 10.1353/pbm.2006.0001.

19. Miller RK: Informed consent in the military: fighting a losing battle against the anthrax vaccine. Am J Law Med. 2002, 28: 325-343.

20. Singh S, Dahal K, Mills E: Nepal's war on human rights: a summit higher than Everest. Int J Equity Health. 2005, 4: 9-10.1186/1475-9276-4-9.

21. Rosenau H: Legal prerequisites for clinical trials under the revised Declaration of Helsinki and the European Convention on Human Rights and Biomedicine. Eur J Health Law. 2000, 7: 105-121.

22. Khabarpatrika H: This is a different army: An interview with Sachit SJB Rana, former Chief of Army Staff. Repr. Nepali Times. 2001, http://www.nepalnews.com.np/ntimes/issue71/fromthenepalipress.htm.-

23. Doe v. Unocal Corp., 963 F. Supp. 880, 884 (C.D. Cal. 1997) (Unocal I) .

24. Zia-Zariki S: Suing Multinational Corporations in the U.S. for Violating International Law. UCLA Journal of International Law & Foreign Affairs. 1999, No 4 (97):

25. Human Rights Watch: Burma: Demobilize Child Soldiers. U.N. Committee Finds Burma in Violation of International Law, 2004.

http://hrw.org/english/docs/2004/06/04/burma8734.htm .

26. Human Rights Watch, World Report, 2006 pg 232-234.
27. Beyrer C, Suwanvanichkij V, Mullany LC, Richards AK, Franck N, Samuels A, Lee TJ: Responding to AIDS, tuberculosis, malaria, and emerging infectious diseases in Burma: dilemmas of policy and practice. PLoS Med. 2006, 3: e393-10.1371/journal.pmed.0030393.
28. Parry J: Global Fund withdraws grants to Myanmar. Bull World Health Organ. 2005, 83: 724-725.
29. Dondorp A, Nosten F, Stepniewska K, Day N, White N: Artesunate versus quinine for treatment of severe falciparum malaria: a randomised trial. Lancet. 2005, 366: 717-725. 10.1016/S0140-6736(05)67176-0.
30. Office of the High Commissioner for Human Rights: International Covenant on Civil and Political Rights. Adopted and opened for signature, ratification and accession by General Assembly resolution 2200A (XXI) of 16 December 1966 http://www.unhchr.ch/html/menu3/b/a_ccpr.htm.
31. Nilstun T: [New guidelines on research ethics from CIOMS (Council for International Organizations of Medical Sciences). A good example of balancing autonomy, benefits and human rights]. Lakartidningen. 1994, 91: 157-158.
32. The International Conference on Harmonisation of Technical Requirements for Registration of Pharmaceuticals for Human Use (ICH), 1996. http://www.ich.org/cache/compo/276-254-1.html.
33. European Union. Directive 2001/20/EC, 4th April 2001.
34. Council of Europe. Convention for the Protection of Human Rights and Dignity of the Human Being with regard to the Application of Biology and Medicine: Convention on Human Rights and Biomedicine,1997. http://conventions.coe.int/treaty/en/treaties/html/164.htm. 1997
35. UNESCO: Universal Declaration on Bioethics and Human Rights*. http://portalunescoorg/shs/en/file_downloadphp/46133e1f4691e4c6e57566763d474a4dBioethicsDeclaration_ENpdf. 2005
36. Weijers C, LeBlanc G. Revisiting the ethics of HIV prevention research in developing countries. XVI International AIDS Conference 2006. Toronto. TUAE0302 August 16 2006.
37. Schuklenk U: The standard of care debate: against the myth of an “international consensus opinion”. J Med Ethics. 2004, 30: 194-197. 10.1136/jme.2003.006981.

38. Legemaate J: The CIOMS guidelines for biomedical research involving human subjects. Eur J Health Law. 1994, 1: 161-165.
39. Council of International Organizations of Medical Sciences. International Ethical Guidelines for Biomedical Research Involving Human Subjects, 2002. http://www.cioms.ch/frame_guidelines_nov_2002.htm.
40. 28 U.S.C. §1350.
41. Hyder AA, Wali SA, Khan AN, Teoh NB, Kass NE, Dawson L: Ethical review of health research: a perspective from developing country researchers. J Med Ethics. 2004, 30: 68-72. 10.1136/jme.2002.001933.
42. Shaw C: Uncertain justice: liability of multinationals under the Alien Tort Claims Act. Stanford Law Review. 2002, 54: 1359-1362.
43. Filartiga v. Pena-Irala. 630 F.2d 876 (2d Cir.1980).
44. Kadic v. Karadzic. 70 F.3d 232 (2d Cir.1995).
45. Papa v. United States, 281 F.3d (9th Cir. 2002) at 1013; In re Estate of Ferdinand E. Marcos, Human Rights Litig., 25 F.3d (9th Cir. 1994) ("Marcos II") at 1474-75.
46. Argentine Republic v. Amerada Hess Shipping Corp., 488 U.S. 428, 434 (1989).
47. Cohen LP: Chiquita Ex-Officials Won't Face Charges. Wall Street Journal, Sept 12, 2007. 2007, online.wsj.com/article/SB118960240072225072.html?mod=googlenews_wsj (Accessed Sept 12, 2007)-
48. Abdullahi v. Pfizer, Inc., 2002 U.S. Dist. LEXIS 17436, at *1 (S.D.N.Y. Sept. 16, 2002), vacated and remanded by, 77 F. App'x 48 (2d Cir. 2003), dismissed at 2005 U.S. Dist. LEXIS 16126 (S.D.N.Y. Aug. 9, 2005).
49. Sosa v. Alvarez-Machain Et Al No. 03-339, 2004.
50. Presbyterian Church of Sudan v. Talisman Energy, No. 01 Civ.9882, 2005, 374 F. Supp. 2d at 340-341 .
51. United Nations Global Compact 2000. http://www.unglobalcompact.org/.
52. Resolution 1591 (2005) adopted on 29th March 2005 and resolution 1672 (2006) adopted on 25th April 2006.
53. Resolution 1636 (2005) adopted on 31st October 2005.

54. Resolution 1596 (2005) adopted on 18th April 2005.
55. U.N. Doc. E/CN.4/Sub.2/2003/12/Rev.2 (2003).

CHAPTER 13

CAN RIGHTS STOP THE WRONGS? EXPLORING THE CONNECTIONS BETWEEN FRAMINGS OF SEX WORKERS' RIGHTS AND SEXUAL AND REPRODUCTIVE HEALTH

Cheryl Overs[1], Kate Hawkins[2]

[1] Michael Kirby Centre for Public Health and Human Rights, School of Public Health and Preventive Medicine Monash University, Alfred Hospital Campus Melbourne, Victoria 3004, Australia

[2] Institute of Development Studies, University of Sussex, Brighton BN1 9RE, UK.

Citation: Cheryl Overs and Kate Hawkins, BMC International Health and Human Rights201111(Suppl 3):S6, https://doi.org/10.1186/1472-698X-11-S3-S6 © Overs and Hawkins; licensee BioMed Central Ltd. 2011 Published: 16 December 2011

ABSTRACT

Background

There is growing interest in the ways in which legal and human rights issues related to sex work affect sex workers' vulnerability to HIV and abuses including human trafficking and sexual exploitation. International agencies, such as UNAIDS, have called for decriminalisation of sex work because the delivery of sexual and reproductive health services is affected by criminalisation and social exclusion as experienced by sex workers. The paper reflects on the connections in various actors' framings between sex workers sexual and reproductive health and rights (SRHR) and the ways that international law is interpreted in policing and regulatory practices.

Methods

The literature review that informs this paper was carried out by the authors in the course of their work within the Paulo Longo Research Initiative. The review covered academic and grey literature such as resources generated by sex worker rights activists, UN policy positions and print and online media. The argument in this paper has been developed reflectively through long term involvement with key actors in the field of sex workers' rights.

Results

International legislation characterises sex work in various ways which do not always accord with moves toward decriminalisation. Law, policy and regulation at national level and law enforcement vary between settings. The demands of sex worker rights activists do relate to sexual and reproductive health but they place greater emphasis on efforts to remove the structural barriers that limit sex workers' ability to participate in society on an equal footing with other citizens.

Discussion and Conclusion

There is a tension between those who wish to uphold the rights of sex workers in order to reduce vulnerability to ill-health and those who insist that sex work is itself a violation of rights. This is reflected in contemporary narratives about sex workers' rights and the ways in which different actors interpret human rights law. The creation of regulatory frameworks around sex work that support health, safety and freedom from abuse requires a better understanding of the broad scope of laws, policies and enforcement practices in different cultural contexts and economic settings, alongside reviews of UN policies and human rights conventions.

Keywords: Reproductive Health, Sexual Exploitation, Human Trafficking, Policy Position, Forced Prostitution

BACKGROUND

The phenomenon of sex workers waving red umbrellas and shouting slogans about human rights is now a fixture at national, regional and international conferences and meetings on sexual and reproductive health and HIV. Yet it is only recently that the international community, and particularly the UN, have seriously embraced sex worker rights activists' logic about the connections between human and economic rights and public health goals.

"In many countries, laws, policies and practices against sex workers limit their right to basic social economic rights such as access to education, health care, housing, banking facilities, inheritance, property and legal services. They may also lack of [sic] citizenship or legal status, resulting from migration or unfavourable regulations." [1]

Shifts in thinking about criminalisation of sex work have happened primarily because of the recognition that programmes that have been proven to reduce HIV such as condom distribution and STI services are being thwarted by laws against commercial sex and the broader legal framework that affect sex workers lives. Health considerations have driven support for reform of the laws around sex work within the highest echelons of the UN system. At the International AIDS Conference in Mexico in 2008 Ban Ki Moon, Secretary-General of the United Nations, made a speech in which he explained that,

"In countries without laws to protect sex workers, drug users, and men who have sex with men, only a fraction of the population has access to prevention. Conversely, in countries with legal protection and the protection of human rights for these people, many more have access to services. As a result, there are fewer infections, less demand for antiretroviral treatment, and fewer deaths. Not only is it unethical not to protect these groups: it makes no sense from a health perspective."

In October 2009 the UN Human Rights Council adopted a resolution that urged States to eliminate laws that are counterproductive to HIV prevention, treatment and care including those that violate the rights of populations that are key to the dynamics of the epidemic and particularly affected by it. The

UNAIDS Joint Outcome Framework of the same year made the removal of laws, policies and practices that block effective action on HIV a priority. It also mentioned sex work as part of a broader human rights agenda [2]. 2010 saw the launch of the Global Commission on HIV and the Law which has had a remit to review the links between human rights, HIV and sex work. Most recently at a UN sponsored regional consultation on HIV and sex work in the Asia Pacific region [3], Purnima Mane, UNFPA Deputy Executive Director, stated that:

"Enabling sex workers to openly access prevention services with dignity must be part of every national HIV programme. Revising laws and policies and addressing attitudinal barriers will enhance the effectiveness of HIV prevention, improve access to health services, including reproductive health, and reduce violence against sex workers." [4]

That criminalisation of commercial sex limits access to health services is well documented. Anand Grover, the Special Rapporteur on the right of everyone to the enjoyment of the highest attainable standard of physical and mental health, comments:

"Criminalization represents a barrier to accessing services, establishing therapeutic relationships and continuing treatment regimes, leading to poorer health outcomes for sex workers, as they may fear legal consequences or harassment and judgement. This is particularly concerning given that HIV has been noted to disproportionately affect sex workers in many regions." [5]

That this is especially the case for migrants, transgender or drug-using sex workers as well as people who sell sex in conflict and emergency situations is also well acknowledged [6]. Despite this understanding of the link between criminal law and ill-health international law; national regulatory frameworks and the pronouncements and demands of human rights activists and policy makers at international level may not yet line up in ways that lead to effective solutions for sex workers in practice.

METHODS

The literature review that informs this paper was carried out by the authors in the course of their work within the Paulo Longo Research Initiative (PLRI). The PLRI is a collaboration of scholars, policy analysts and sex workers. Its aim is to develop, consolidate and disseminate ethical, interdisciplinary information about sex work to improve the human rights, health and well-being of women, men and transgenders who sell sex. PLRI is a collaboration between the Global Network of Sex Work Projects, the Institute of Development Studies at the University of Sussex, the Michael Kirby Centre for Public Health and Human Rights at Monash University Medical School and the Centre for Advocacy on Stigma and Marginalisation (CASAM) in India.

The review covered academic and grey literature such as resources generated by sex worker rights activists, UN policy positions and print and online media. Sex workers networks' email discussion groups, websites, blogs and other Internet communications were also tracked and analysed as they provide an important insight on the lived experience of sex workers in various different legal and cultural contexts.

The argument in this paper has been developed reflectively through extensive, long term research and advocacy involvement with key actors in the field of sex workers' rights. Burris et al. have stressed the challenge that researchers face in bridging the space between 'law on the streets' and 'law on the books' to achieve an accurate picture of the role of law in the health of marginalised groups [7]. By reviewing a variety of sources including; sex worker rights activist generated research and policy positions, academic literature, reports from UN agencies and non-governmental organisations (NGOs) and journalistic and online news we have been able to reflect on the connections and disconnections in various actors' framings of sex workers' sexual and reproductive health and rights. This article considers resources related to (1) government policy and national law, (2) international frameworks and conventions and (3) sex worker rights declarations and advocacy documents. The positions outlined in international frameworks and sex worker rights declarations are reviewed over time to demonstrate developments in the framing of sex workers' rights. We draw conclusions about the strengths and weaknesses in current framings of sex workers' rights, based on an assessment of these sources and suggest future pathways for a rights based approach to sex work and the law particularly as it pertains to sexual and reproductive health and the role of governments and public health organisations.

RESULTS AND DISCUSSION

Governments and National Laws

Historically, criminal law has addressed sex work through criminalising the selling of sexual services, with the imposition of penalties upon sex workers themselves and through criminalisation of various practices around sex work. These include keeping a brothel; recruiting for or arranging the prostitution of others; living off the proceeds of sex work; solicitation; and facilitating sex work through the provision of information or assistance. Although selling sex is not directly criminalised in many countries worldwide, there are widespread reports that sex workers are nonetheless treated as criminals where activities around sex work itself are criminalised, or through the use of pre-existing laws (not specific to sex work) to harass, intimidate or justify the use of force against sex workers [8]. In some settings, such as Sweden, the criminalisation of the clients of sex workers has been employed.

Some of the laws and policies that are designed to respond to matters unrelated to commercial sex have a legitimate purpose such as keeping public roads and pathways clear or protecting people from nuisance. But many are other discriminatory laws such as those against homosexuality and transgenderism. Transgender and male sex workers are often subject to laws against homosexuality or obscenity [9]. Drug-using sex workers in particular are subject both to laws about those activities and brutal enforcement [10]. Vagrancy laws are notoriously used to criminalise sex workers. For example, street-based sex workers in Malawi are arrested on the charge of "Rogue and Vagabond" a colonial-era legal term for what is more commonly known as loitering [11].

Executive orders and subordinate legislation (of varying degrees of legitimacy) often set out where and how the sex industry can operate. Such orders are often associated with 'crackdowns' and other forms of suppression that extend beyond the technical limit of the law. In 2010, all sex workers were ordered to leave the Nigerian capital Abuja by such an order [12]. However executive decrees may be also associated with toleration. For example, police may be instructed to ignore the law in relation to brothels in exchange for compliance with HIV prevention activities such as supplying condoms or ensuring that no HIV positive women sell sex. Executive orders were a central lever to secure the compliance of brothel keepers in Asia, such as in Cambodia, to comply with 100% Condom Use programmes [13].

In wealthier countries sex workers may be ordered by law to attend mandatory counselling or rehabilitation or subject to quasi-official "naming and shaming" by police and vigilantes. For example many US police forces publish pictures of sex workers , particularly those living with HIV [14] and the London Police issued Anti-Social Behaviour Orders to six street sex workers in London and published their full names, photos and dates of birth on their website because they were "persistent offenders" [15]. Sex workers and others associated with sex work are banned from entering several countries including Japan and the United States of America.

Increasingly offences related to sex work have been conflated in various combinations into the concept of "sex trafficking" or "trafficking and sexual exploitation" and given legislative expression, including in laws that criminalise buying sex. These can also stem from efforts to combat violence against women. Commercial sex may also be regulated and licensed, and these schemes take different forms. Some schemes permit commercial sex in certain areas in streets or in brothels, other schemes permit commercial sex that accords with prescribed standards, such as the licensing of managers and the registration of workers.

An increasingly prominent legal mechanism for addressing sex work is policies and directives that aim to reduce sex work, exploitation and human trafficking by removing women and children from brothels and other places in which they are deemed to be victims of trafficking and sexual exploitation. Sex workers have called this "Raid and Rescue" or "Rescue and Rehabilitation" and implicated it in serious human rights abuses against nationals and migrant sex workers [16]. In Cambodia, Human Rights Watch identified arbitrary detention in government rehabilitation centres as a result of the enforcement of the Law on the Suppression of Human Trafficking and Sexual Exploitation as a threat to both human rights and health. Human Rights Watch describe how detainees reported rape and missed medication among other consequences of their detention [17]. Sex workers report a variety of abuses including; rape by guards and other prisoners, beatings, deaths in custody, lack of medication or medical care (notably for HIV positive, mentally ill and pregnant inmates), abuse of disabled people, lack of hygiene facilities and toilets and food and water. Writing about raids by a Christian NGO in Sangli, India Rao and Sluggett explain,

"*At each stage of the intervention, women experience gross human rights violations. Their right to livelihood and their right to reside wherever they want is suspended; their right to privacy and their right to liberty and equality before the law is taken away because they are being 'taken care of'. Some sex workers sustain injuries in trying to escape being 'rescued'.*" [16]

Community violence against sex workers, as the public take "law enforcement" into their own hands, is also an issue of concern. For example, this year women in Nigeria threatened to create a "squad to apprehend and possibly prosecute call girls" who had moved to their area after the crackdown mentioned above [18] In India a mob burnt down a guest house in Naroda (Gujarat, India) reportedly to "teach a lesson" to criminals involved in law-breaking. Two women were injured and one died [19]. In Bolivia in 2007, sex workers were ejected from their homes by angry crowds who stormed the "red light" area and attacked them in protest at the sex industry. As a result sex workers refused to co-operate with the regulations that require them to submit to medical examinations if they are to work legally. Ten sex workers sewed their lips together and others fasted in a clinic demanding that the mayor reopen the area and secure their safety [20]. Negotiation with legislator Guillermo Mendoza led to the suspension of the protest [21]. Indeed, serial murderers of sex workers have sometimes invoked the anti-sex work aim of the law by claiming to be ridding society of such women. The 'Green River Killer' of sex workers in the US said to police "I thought I was doing you guys a favor, killing prostitutes… you guys can't control them, but I can" [22]. The Yorkshire Ripper in the UK said "The women I killed were filth, bastard prostitutes who were just standing round littering the streets. I was just cleaning the place up a bit." [23]

While health research concentrates on the important task of identifying levels of HIV among sex workers and measuring the impact of HIV interventions, much less is known about how law influences the sex workers' opportunities to avoid sexually transmitted infections, violence, unwanted pregnancies and access to sexual and reproductive health services and dual protection. Yet policy positions and statements from sex worker rights activists point to the intersections of sexual and reproductive health and law and their human rights.

What do Sex Workers Rights Statements Say?

An analysis of key position statements from sex worker rights groups on their rights shows that a concern with health and wellbeing is related to a host of rights claims that relate to the structural barriers – the socioeconomic, cultural and political factors – that limit sex workers' ability to participate in society on an equal footing with other citizens. The International Network of Sex Work Projects (NSWP) has long argued that the criminalisation of commercial sex inhibits sex workers' ability to realise their sexual, reproductive and other rights by rendering them vulnerable to exploitation, invisibilising abuses [24]; limiting access to health services and information and safe places to work [25] and denying them the economic, cultural and social rights conferred by citizenship. They argue that laws that try to abolish or limit sex work both limit access to services and create the unsafe working conditions that drive transmission of sexually transmitted infections, HIV, unwanted pregnancy and other threats to health. This happens, the NSWP says, because sex workers, especially women, in many settings face a choice between risking arrest and violence by working independently and working in venues that offer some degree of protection but which may be exploitative or abusive because they are operated beyond the reach of law and often by criminals.

At the same time sex worker rights activists have spoken about the effects of unfavourable laws that reach beyond health issues. They argue that states' protection of human rights is a matter of justice, not simply an instrument for reducing sex workers' role as vectors of disease. Networks of sex worker rights activists have vigorously claimed a space to link sex worker empowerment and health issues with human rights. Slogans such as "sex workers rights are human rights" [26] and "only rights can stop the wrongs" [27] capture the idea among activists that better health outcomes are a consequence of improved human rights.

Contemporary sex workers' positions on human rights were first documented in the World Charter for Prostitutes' Rights which was drafted as a result of the World Whores Congress of 1985 [28]. The Charter identifies stigma and discrimination as a key barrier to the realisation of rights. It has a strong focus on human rights from a feminist perspective and claims that sex work is an occupation that should be legal for sex workers, their employers, their clients and families. It calls for the decriminalisation of sex work and distinguishes between sex work and sexual abuse. It demands the regularisation of working conditions in the sex industry in line with other comparable businesses and calls for the creation of social services for sex workers. It opposes discriminatory mandatory testing but calls for universal access to sexual and reproductive health care (interestingly it does not mention HIV although the virus had been recently identified. This appears to be due to fear of stigma).

The Sex Workers' Manifesto from the First National Conference of Sex Workers in India, 1997 [29] echoes the Charter in its call for an understanding of sex work as a legitimate occupation. The Manifesto also explores how patriarchy and morality intersect in understandings of sexuality. It rejects the idea of sex as simply an instrument of reproduction which, in their analysis, leads to compulsory heterosexuality which curbs women's sexual freedom. It points out that such narrowly focused understandings of women's sexuality easily lead to the splitting of women into "madonnas and whores". Instead it calls for autonomous sexuality and mutually pleasurable safe sex, where people have the right to consent and sex is free of guilt and oppression.

This manifesto marks the important entry of sex workers from a poor country into a global movement that had previously focused on legal and policy issues as they apply in Europe and North America. Unlike the Charter, the Indian declaration challenges the role of choice in framing sex work as an occupation, "when do us women have access to choice within or outside the family? Do we become casual domestic labourer (sic) willingly? Do we have a choice about who we want to marry and when? The choice is rarely real for most women, particularly poor women". Its analysis places sex work in the context of a social and economic system where options for women are limited and where access to income generating activities of any sort is prized. Within this framework sex work is not necessarily seen as the worst option for women. The Manifesto rejects charitable interventions, rescue and rehabilitation, which it sees as the typical tools of those who seek to abolish the sex industry, and instead calls for the respect of human rights and improvement of sex industry standards.

The Taipei Declaration of Sex Workers' Human Rights was written at the 1998 World Action for Sex Workers Rights in response to a crackdown that revoked the licenses of Taipei sex workers [30]. Although a short document it is interesting in its use of reference to the Beijing Plan of Action and the Report of the UN Special Rapporteur on Violence Against Women in order to counter the city government's abolitionist interpretation of sex work as supported by international law on trafficking.

The Declaration of the Rights of Sex Workers in Europe was created in 2005 in response to what sex workers perceived to be a swing toward measures to constrain sex industries across Europe in order to safeguard public health and/or limit human trafficking [31]. It identifies human, labour and migrants rights that sex workers should be entitled to under international law as citizens and outlines specific measures that states should take to fulfil these rights. It does not call for special rights for sex workers but rather argues that to make sex work safe people engaged in the sale of sexual services should not be denied human rights. It hinges on the non-discrimination clause found in most human rights treaties.

The Declaration of the Rights of Sex Workers in Europe covers many of the topics that are explored in earlier statements on sex workers' rights including health, freedom from slavery and exploitation and associated labour rights. It also provides more detail on the right to seek asylum and to non-refoulement – protection from forced return to places where their lives or freedoms are threatened – reflecting the document's concern with migrant workers. The right to marry and found a family is also identified as an area of concern. The document calls upon governments to ensure that engagement in sex work does not restrict the ability of sex workers to obtain other employment or to marry, or lead to discrimination against sex workers' families by public authorities, "Current or former engagement in sex work should not be considered grounds for challenging a person's fitness to be a parent or have custody of his or her children". ([31]. p9)

The most recent call for sex workers rights which is considered by this paper is the Pattaya Draft Declaration on Sex Work in Asia and the Pacific (2010) (the Pattaya Draft Declaration) [32]. This Declaration was agreed by sex workers representing the Asia Pacific Network of Sex Workers and organisations and NGOs from the region. This draft is currently under consultation with the Asia Pacific Network of Sex Workers. This declaration is framed as a "unified and rights based approach to the reduction of HIV among adult sex workers" ([32]. p1). Unsurprisingly, access to services is a key theme – particularly efforts to counter stigma and discrimination on the grounds of occupation or HIV status. The document also calls for expanded economic and social opportunities; better health care for male and transgender sex workers, an end to the pressures for abortion and sterilisation, and protection from discrimination for sex workers of all genders living with HIV.

In contrast to some of the earlier statements, the Pattaya Draft Declaration focuses on all genders and does not refer to women's rights or have an overtly feminist analysis of oppression. Rather the unifying argument of the piece is the importance of the inclusion and the meaningful and active involvement of sex workers in decision making, programming, advocacy and action to address stigma and discrimination and capacity building.

"The starting point for a rights based approach to HIV and sex work is the formation of a partnership in which sex workers' contributions to policy and programme development is encouraged, supported, recognised and valued. This cannot occur in coercive environments...or where sex work is governed by laws that address trafficking" ([32]. p1).

Coercive efforts to control or reduce sex work identified by the document include mandatory medical treatment or procedures, raids, forced rehabilitation and programmes implemented by police or based upon detention of sex workers. The document states that in some circumstances these may constitute torture and other cruel, inhuman or degrading treatment or punishment.

What links all of these documents is a call for sex work to be recognised as a legal occupation to pave the way for commercial sex to be conducted in safe workplaces, for violence to be reduced and to enable universal access to appropriate health services. According to the sex workers' rights movement, removing criminal laws against sex work could provide an opportunity to reconfigure the way in which sex workers' sexual and reproductive rights can be realised. Where sex work is recognised as an occupation, SRHR could become a matter of labour, rather than criminal law. This would be linked to health and safety in the workplaces and environments within which the sale of sex takes place. In settings where they are recognised, the trade union movement could be harnessed to enforce positive norms and standards. In settings that are less conducive to unionisation – or where this is not a popular form of organising around labour issues – business regulations and workplace health regulations would still provide protection. Furthermore the recognition of sex work as an occupation would enable sex workers to access state and privately provided services and benefits such as education, pensions, welfare payment, healthcare and equal access to infrastructure such as housing, sanitation and transport.

Sex worker rights activist statements and policy positions make the argument that good health depends on sex workers having the same rights that protect other people in their roles as workers, business people, family members, tenants, patients, taxpayers etc. On this analysis it is not logical to aim to promote health in isolation from addressing the drivers of vulnerability through human rights.

The International Legal Framework and Its Interpretation in National Constitutions, Bills Of Rights and Legal Decisions

A plethora of international instruments addresses prostitution, trafficking and technical and medical ethical issues related to sex work. The Convention for the Suppression of the Traffic in Persons and the Exploitation of the Prostitution of Others (the Convention) was adopted in 1949 [33]. It grew out of "social purity" campaigns which were preceded by women's international organising around the "white slave trade" [34, 35]. The Convention describes prostitution as "incompatible with the dignity and worth of the human person and endanger(ing) the welfare of the individual, the family and the community" ([33]. p1). It frames prostitutes as "victims" and "fallen women" as tricked or exploited persons [33].

The Protocol to Prevent, Suppress and Punish Trafficking in Persons, Especially Women and Children, supplementing the United Nations Convention against Transnational Organised Crime, of 2000 [36], defines trafficking as

"the recruitment, transportation, transfer, harbouring or receipt of persons, by means of the threat or use of force or other forms of coercion, of abduction, of fraud, of deception, of the abuse of power or of a position of vulnerability or of the giving or receiving of payments or benefits to achieve the consent of a person having control over another person, for the purpose of exploitation." [p1]

Exploitation is further defined to include the prostitution of others or other forms of sexual exploitation. Additionally, the Protocol states that the consent of any victim of trafficking is deemed irrelevant where circumstances such as vulnerability or abuse of power exist.

Article 6 of the 1979 Convention on the Elimination of Discrimination Against Women (CEDAW) [37] calls on states to suppress "all forms of traffic in women and exploitation of prostitution of women." It does not require States to suppress consensual, adult sex work but calls for the suppression of "all forms of traffic in women and exploitation of prostitution of women". The term "exploitation of prostitution" has not been defined within the Convention; Article 6 is read to mean that prostitution is discriminatory in its impact on women and as such is an abuse under the premise of non-discrimination. However, Doezema [34] has argued that the inclusion of the word "exploitation" implies that the convention does not consider all prostitution inherently coercive and uses evidence from the negotiations around its drafting to support this point. Interpretation of the "exploitation of prostitution" is important as it goes to the heart of whether CEDAW considers prostitution itself exploitative or whether prostitution is a system and practice within which human rights abuses of women are prevalent.

The General Recommendation of the Committee on the Elimination of Discrimination against Women, 1993 [38] frames sex work as a practice that contributes to shaping the traditional attitudes that devalue women to help justify gender based violence as well as being a form of gender-based violence in and of itself. It continues to mirror the language of CEDAW in its use of the term the "exploitation" of prostitution. This led Balos [39] to interpret CEDAW as positing prostitution as a violation and inconsistent with human rights regardless of whether it is consenting. The Declaration on the Elimination of Violence Against Women (DEVAW), 1993, uses the term "forced prostitution" to refer to the "type of physical, sexual and psychological violence" that is "a violation of the rights and fundamental freedoms of women and impairs or nullifies their enjoyment of those rights and freedoms" [40]. This represents a shift in understanding from "prostitution" per se or "the exploitation of prostitution" to "forced prostitution" as a human rights abuse. By making a distinction between voluntary and forced prostitution the Declaration could be seen as a tacit admission that not all prostitution is an abuse of women's rights. This language was later used in the Beijing Platform of Action [41].

Lack of clarification of these terms is a key obstacle to State responses to adult sex work that protect health and human rights. As Grover points out, terms such as "vulnerability" and "abuse of power" remain undefined within the Protocol [5]. Indeed they have no independent legal meaning, and nor do concepts such as "dignity" and "exploitation."

Other conventions may contain provisions that can support efforts to reduce sex workers' vulnerability and improve sexual and reproductive health. These include the International Covenant on Economic, Social and Cultural Rights which protects the right to freely chosen, gainful work. The International Convention on the Protection of the Rights of All Migrant Workers and Members of Their Families applies to a significant number of sex workers who travel between States to engage in sex work [5].

In practice, the patchwork of ideas contained within these international instruments often manifest themselves as laws such as the Cambodian Law on the Suppression of Human Trafficking and Sexual Exploitation the enforcement of which was discussed earlier in this paper. The law deems all women who join the sex industry voluntarily to be victims of sexual exploitation and they have the same status as women who have been subject to kidnapping, rape, imprisonment and other crimes committed to force them to sell sex against their will. The legislation is aimed at preventing human trafficking and sexual exploitation, but the law actually prohibits all activities around sex work and effectively criminalises the sex sector in its entirety.

In some cases human rights as embodied in national constitutions, bills of rights and international conventions underpin legal decisions that have led to less punitive approaches to sex work. Although they remain rare they may provide an important signpost to resolving sex workers' human rights claims. A Canadian court recently accepted a constitutional challenge to three provisions of Canadian sex work law: keeping a common bawdy house, or brothel, communicating for the purposes of prostitution and living on the avails of the trade. The judge in the case ruled that even though the act of prostitution is not illegal in Canada, Parliament has seen fit to criminalise most aspects of prostitution and that these provisions violated sex workers' constitutional right by forcing sex workers to choose between their liberty interest and their right to security of person as protected under the Canadian Charter of Rights and Freedoms.

Some changes in legislation that recognise sex work as legitimate labour, and to safeguard sex workers from abuse, come from wealthy countries including the Netherlands, Germany, Australia and New Zealand. A recent evaluation of the reform in New Zealand showed that it has enabled people working in the sex industry to access protections through labour and anti-discrimination laws and that they are more able to access health services [42].

There have been similar developments in both legislatures and courts in developing and middle-income countries. In Brazil, sex work has been added to an official list of occupations that enable sex workers to claim social benefits. In South Africa, an industrial tribunal initially rejected a sex worker's right to bring a case for unfair dismissal against an illegal brothel on the basis that an employment contract between a prostitute and her employer cannot be recognised or enforced because it is unlawful and contrary to public policy. However an appeals court held that although the contract was unlawful, an employment relationship existed between them so the sex worker's claim fell within the scope of the Labour Relations Law [43]. Similarly national constitutions have been invoked in courts in Bangladesh [44] and Colombia [45] which have recently found in favour of recognising sex work as an occupation, clearing the way for sex workers to vote, pay tax and claim other civil rights.

In Taiwan, commitment to bring legislation into harmony with the International Covenant on Civil and Political Rights and the International Covenant on Economic, Social and Cultural Rights resulted in anti-sex work law being abolished in 2009 on the grounds that punishing commercial sexual transactions forces sex workers underground leaving them open to abuse. The government stated that while sexual transactions between consenting adults should be governed by personal, educational and religious considerations, rather than by laws, the sex trade should be regulated like any other occupation. Subsequent to this, the Constitutional Court declared the existing legislation unconstitutional, and ordered that it cease to be in effect within 2 years [46].

DISCUSSION AND CONCLUSION

Debates on how best to govern commercial sex and reduce its potential to generate health problems have a long and complex history out of which little consensus has emerged. These debates are often tied up with narratives about disease control and harm reduction; female virtue and empowerment; and migration and slavery [47, 48, 49]. In recent years attention to sex workers' sexual and reproductive health and rights has been prompted by a desire to control and reduce HIV. However, political framings of sex work within a paradigm of exploitation and slavery have also gained enormous political traction. In this paradigm the sex industry is imagined to be inherently abusive and those involved in it lacking agency. In this way sex work is conflated with "sex trafficking", which has the effect of creating a powerful force against public health or other initiatives aimed at making sex work safer lest it be considered as colluding with exploitation or even slavery.

Although some of those rights talked about by sex worker rights activists are mentioned in conventions, some are undermined or weakened by international law whose jurisprudence has traditionally constructed sex work as an affront to human dignity. The danger of a continuation of the status quo is that formal rights frameworks become even less relevant to sex workers. There is a significant tension between those who wish to uphold the rights of sex workers in order to reduce vulnerability to ill-health and those who insist that sex work is itself a violation of rights and human dignity and cannot therefore be regarded by law as a legitimate occupation.

There is much in the international human rights conventions and law that accords with sex worker rights activists' demands. However our analysis of international legislation and national legal responses highlights instances of difference and contestation. In some cases sex worker rights claims push up against the boundaries of conventional interpretations of human rights. Confused definitions and understandings of sex work, sexual exploitation and human trafficking are not merely a historical artefact. They are "live" issues that require informed debate and resolution if the UN and international law are to play a positive role in improving the health and human rights of women, transgenders and men who sell sex. Sex worker rights activists clearly have reason to be delighted about renewed attention to the idea that punitive laws against sex work should be removed. However the instrumentalist argument made by some public health professionals that sex workers' rights are necessary in order to ensure that sex workers' access HIV prevention services is quite different to the framing of sex workers' rights in the various declarations and position papers from activists that we reviewed. While both health authorities and sex workers stress the importance of access to HIV and STI testing and condoms as the key to good health outcomes, sex worker rights activists place equal or more weight on their ability to work in safe, clean and fair workplaces.

Simply removing criminal law is unlikely to be a solution in itself. Good regulations, effective health programmes and equitable policy do not automatically begin when criminal laws are removed even in rich and well governed countries, let alone where regulatory systems generally are not well organised. If criminal laws are replaced with discriminatory or inappropriate policy and law the health and safety conditions in the sex industry could actually be made worse and access to services denuded.

There are some clear gaps in the discourse around sex work. Most literature focuses on female sex workers and much of it on young women. Far less attention is paid to the health issues facing male, transgender, migrant, drug using or older sex workers. Better understanding of the broad scope of laws policy and enforcement practices that affect sex workers in the many very different cultural contexts and economic settings is needed urgently. The lived experience of sex workers is rarely the topic of ethical, methodologically rigorous examination and there is little systematic collection of data about law and its impact.

Careful review of UN policy and the international human rights conventions and related law is much needed too. Such a review should begin with recognition that the international legal framework is sometimes at odds with grounded understandings of entitlements and frequently at odds with itself. Sex workers' broad spectrum of claims is based on collective understandings of human rights grounded in justice rather than on sophisticated technical knowledge of international human rights conventions and laws and the various roles of the institutions and individuals upon whom they confer rights and duties. It is possible to create regulatory frameworks for commercial sex that support safe practice by recognising commercial sex as a legitimate activity. Only in this way does it become possible for sex workers to be accorded all of their human rights. To develop a formula for law, policy and enforcement practices that enables a safer sex industry, supports sex workers to claim human rights and protects health including reducing vulnerability to HIV, governments require three things:

- Precise language to describe the regulatory environments for commercial sex, the consequences of possible regulatory options, and the potential solutions;
- Accurate local data about the domestic laws, policies and enforcement practices to be remedied, and their impact, intended and unintended, on the health of male, female and transgender sex workers; and
- A commitment to human rights standards and norms, including the right to work, to equal protection under the law, to freedom of association, and a recognition of the right of consenting adults to form sexual relationships of their choice provided others are not harmed.

Health projects are well placed to gather information about law and its impact in much of the world. Those with policy and advocacy capacity can actively support sex workers' campaigns which are notoriously under-resourced. The best course for health agencies is to listen to sex workers and join with them to demand the fundamental changes locally, nationally and internationally that can make sex work safe, enable sex workers to realise their human rights and enable access to the sexual and reproductive services they need to stay healthy.

Notes

Cheryl Overs and Kate Hawkins contributed equally to this work.

DECLARATIONS

Acknowledgements

The authors would like to thank the members of community groups, non-governmental organisations and networks of sex workers who participated in the drafting of the declarations and statements on sex workers' rights which have been reviewed in this paper. The Network of Sex Work Projects and Asia Pacific Network of Sex Workers have contributed to our thinking in this area as have the other members of the Paulo Longo Research Initiative. We would like to express our gratitude to Bebe Loff of Monash University for her inputs. The Realising Rights Research Programme Consortium (2005-

10) provided the opportunity for the publication of this paper and financed some of the authors' time. This project is financed by the UK Department for International Development.

This article has been published as part of *BMC International Health and Human Rights* Volume 11 Supplement 3, 2011: Contextualising rights: the lived experience of sexual and reproductive health rights. The full contents of the supplement are available online at http://www.biomedcentral.com/1472-698X/11?issue=S3. Publication of this supplement has been supported by funding from the UK Department for International Development (DFID) for the Research Programme Consortium on Realising Rights: Improving Sexual and Reproductive Health in Poor and Vulnerable Populations.

Competing Interests

The authors declare that they have no competing interests.

Authors' Contributions

Both authors were involved in drafting the paper and contributed to the final analysis and recommendations.

REFERENCES

1. Thematic Task Team on Creating an Enabling Legal and Policy Environment: Creating an enabling legal and policy environment for increased access to HIV & AIDS services for sex workers. 1st Asia and the Pacific Regional Consultation on HIV and Sex Work. 2010, [http://www.plri.org/sites/plri.org/files/Enabling%20Environment%20discussion%20paper.pdf]
2. UNAIDS: Joint Action for Results, UNAIDS Outcome Framework 2009–2011. 2009, Geneva: Joint United Nations Programme on HIV/AIDS
3. APNSW, UNFPA, UNAIDS: Building Partnerships on HIV and Sex Work: Report and Recommendations from the First Asia and the Pacific Regional Consultation on HIV and Sex Work. 2011, Geneva
4. UNFPA, UNAIDS, APNSW: Press release: Sex Workers, Governments and UN Join Hands to Boost AIDS Response in Asia-Pacific Region. 2010, Thailand
5. United Nations General Assembly Human Rights Council: Report of the Special Rapporteur on the right of everyone to the enjoyment of the highest attainable standard of physical and mental health, Anand Grover. 14th Session, Agenda Item 3. 27 April 2010
6. UNAIDS: UNAIDS Guidance Note on HIV and Sex Work. 2009, Geneva: Joint United Nations Programme on HIV/AIDS
7. Burris S, Wagenaar AC, Swanson J, Ibrahim JK, Wood J, Mello MM: Making the case for laws that improve health: a framework for public health law research. Millbank Q. 2010, 88: 169-210. 10.1111/j.1468-0009.2010.00595.x.
8. Rekart ML: Sex-work harm reduction. Lancet. 2005, 366: 2123-2134.
9. UNAIDS: UNAIDS Guidance Note on HIV and Sex Work. 2009, Geneva: Joint United Nations Programme on HIV/AIDS
10. Commission on AIDS in Asia: Redefining AIDS in Asia Crafting an Effective Response: Report of the Commission on AIDS in Asia. 2008, New Delhi: Oxford University Press
11. Nyasa Times: Buying, selling sex not illegal in Malawi –lawyer. 8 September 2010
12. Agbo C: Nigeria government bans prostitution. AllAfrica.com. 13 June 2010, [http://allafrica.com/stories/201006140016.html]

13. Lowe D: Documenting the experiences of sex workers: perceptions of the Cambodian 100% Condom Use Program. Phnom Penh: Policy Project. 2003
14. Arner M, Neely L: Prostitutes' photos, case details put online. 30 October 2007, The San Diego Union-Tribune, [http://www.signonsandiego.com/uniontrib/20071030/news_1m30copsite.html]
15. Taylor D: Sex workers 'named and shamed' on Met police website. The Guardian. 6 August 2010, [http://www.guardian.co.uk/society/2010/aug/06/london-sex-workers-police-website]
16. Rao S, Sluggett C: Who Stole the Tarts? Sex Work and Human Rights. September 2009, Sangram: Sangli
17. Human Rights Watch: Off the streets. 19 July 2010
18. Oche M: Gwarimpa women ready for showdown with call girls. AllAfrica.com. 12 December 2010, [http://allafrica.com/stories/201012130519.html]
19. Daily News Analysis: Mob set Naroda guesthouse on fire. 3 November 2010, [http://www.dnaindia.com/india/report_mob-set-naroda-guesthouse-on-fire_1461500]
20. Reuters: Prostitutes sew lips together in protest. 25 October 2007, Reuters, [http://www.reuters.com/article/2007/10/25/us-bolivia-prostitutes-idUSN2436073120071025]
21. Australian Associated Press Pty Limited: Bolivian prostitutes suspend protest. 27 October 2007, Sydney Morning Herald, [http://www.smh.com.au/news/World/Bolivian-prostitutes-suspend-protest/2007/10/27/1192941371886.html]
22. Salvi SJT: The truth about the Green River Killer. 12 November 2003, AlterNet, [http://www.alternet.org/story/17171/]
23. Roberts N: Whores in History: Prostitution in Western Society. 1993, London: Harper Collins, 304-
24. Bindman J: Redefining Prostitution as Sex Work on the International Agenda. 1997, Anti-Slavery International and the Network of Sex Work Projects: London
25. NSWP: Only rights can stop the wrongs. Smart persons guide to HIV and sex work. 2010, [http://www.nswp.org/sites/nswp.org/files/Smart%20Guide%20to%20HIV%20and%20Sex%20Work_0.pdf]
26. La Rédaction: Mauritian sex workers demand rights. 3 January 2011, Le Matinal, [http://www.lematinal.com/news/local-news/9349-

Mauritian-Sex-Workers-Demand-Rights.html]

27. Matsamura Kiapi E: Inside the tough world of sex work. 15 December 2010, The Observer, [http://www.observer.ug/index.php?option=com_content&task=view&id=11398&Itemid=59]
28. International Committee for Prostitutes' Rights: World Charter for Prostitutes' Rights. A Vindication of the Rights of Whores. Edited by: Pheterson G. 1989, Seattle: Seal Press
29. Durbar Mahila Samanwaya Committee: Sex Workers' Manifesto. Theme paper of the First National Conference of Sex Workers, Calcutta, November 14-16. 1997
30. Taipei Union of Legal and Illegal Prostitutes for Self-help (TULIPS): The 1998 Taipei Declaration of Sex Workers' Human Rights. 1998
31. ICRSE: The Declaration of the Rights of Sex Workers in Europe. Agreed at the European Conference on Sex Work, Human Rights, Labour and Migration. 15-17 October 2005, Brussels, Belgium, [http://www.sexworkeurope.org/en/resources-mainmenu-189/declaration-mainmenu-199]
32. APNSW: Pattaya Draft Declaration on Sex Work in Asia and the Pacific. 2010, [http://plri.wordpress.com/2010/10/15/pattaya-draft-declaration-on-sex-work-in-asia-and-the-pacific-2010/]
33. UNGASS: Convention for the Suppression of the Traffic in Persons and of the Exploitation of the Prostitution of Others. Approved by General Assembly resolution 317(IV) of 2. 1949, December
34. Doezema J: Forced to choose: beyond the free v. forced prostitution dichotomy. Global Sex Workers: Rights, Resistance and Redefinition. Edited by: Kempadoo K, Doezema J. 1998, New York and London: Routledge
35. Fraser AS: Becoming human: the origins and development of women's human rights. Human Rights Quarterly. 1999, 21 (4): 853-906. 10.1353/hrq.1999.0050.
36. Protocol to prevent, suppress and punish trafficking in persons, especially women and children. Supplementing the United Nations Convention against Transnational Organized Crime. 2003
37. UNGASS: Convention on the Elimination of All Forms of Discrimination against Women. 1979
38. General recommendation No. 19 -- eleventh session, 1992 violence against women. [http://www.un.org/womenwatch/daw/cedaw/

recommendations/recomm.htm#recom19]

39. Balos B: The wrong way to equality: privileging consent in the trafficking of women for sexual exploitation. Harvard Journal of Law & Gender. 2005, 28 (137-175): 153-
40. UNGASS: Declaration on the elimination of violence against women. G.A. res. 48/104, 48 U.N. GAOR Supp. (No. 49) at 217, U.N. Doc. A/48/49. 1993
41. Beijing declaration and platform for action. Fourth World Conference on Women, 15 September 1995, A/CONF.177/20 (1995) and A/CONF.177/20/Add.1. 1995
42. New Zealand Ministry of Justice: Report of the Prostitution Law Review Committee on the operation of the Prostitution Reform Act 2003. 2008
43. South African Labour Appeal Court: Kylie v CCMA. Unreported Case No CA10/08, May 28. 2010
44. US Bureau of Democracy, Human Rights, and Labor: Country reports on human rights practices: Bangladesh. 2000, For example, Dhaka, 17 August 2010, http://www.bbc.co.uk/news/world-south-asia-11003199., [http://www.state.gov/g/drl/rls/hrrpt/2000/sa/692.htm]
45. Filipovic C: Sex workers have workers' rights. 4 October 2010, Colombia Reports, 14: 21-[http://colombiareports.com/colombia-news/news/12180-sex-workers-have-workers-rights-constitutional-court.html]
46. Hsiu-chuan S: Government moves to decriminalize sex transactions. 25 June 2009, Taipei Times, [http://www.taipeitimes.com/News/front/archives/2009/06/25/2003447087/1]
47. Global Sex Workers: Rights, Resistance, and Redefinition. Edited by: Kempadoo K, Doezema J. 1998, London: Routledge
48. Seshu M, Bandhopadhyay N, Overs C: How the development industry imagines sex work. Development. 2009, 52: 13-17. 10.1057/dev.2008.86.
49. Doezema J: Sex Slaves and Discourse Masters. 2010, Zed Books: London

CHAPTER 14

THERE IS SOMETHING ABOUT MARRYING... THE CASE OF HUMAN RIGHTS VS. MIGRATION REGIMES USING THE EXAMPLE OF AUSTRIA

Irene Messinger

Department for Political Sciences, Alumna University of Vienna, Vienna, 1090, Austria

ABSTRACT

States pursue various juridical strategies to prevent 'marriages of convenience' seen as undermining tightening migration regimes. This article examines how Austrian Alien Law constitutes entering into such a marriage

Citation: Irene Messinger, Department for Political Sciences, Alumna University of Vienna, Vienna, 1090, Austria Received: 9 August 2013; in revised form: 7 September 2013 / Accepted: 24 September 2013 / Published: 30 September 2013

as a criminal offense and looks at the legal proceedings in district courts in Vienna where most cases of alleged 'marriages of convenience' are being dealt with. It also studies the work of the Viennese branch of alien police investigating into this offense. These practices are often in conflict with Article 8 and 12 of the European Convention of Human Rights, granting the right to respect for private and family life and the right to marry.

Keywords: Austria, Alien Law Act, bi-national marriage, migration regulations, Article 8 ECHR, Article 12 ECHR, marriage of convenience

INTRODUCTION

The fundamental right to the protection of marriage and family life is laid down in various international human rights documents. This right encompasses family migration and family re-unification. Given that this issue of LAWS is about Human Rights and Migration, this article will show the tension between international human rights standards and state imposed migration regimes using Austria as an example. It will address how Austrian Alien Law seeks to prevent 'marriages of convenience', both in legislation and in legal practice, and how theses measure are in conflict with the right to marriage and to privacy enshrined in the European Convention on Human Rights (ECHR). Marriage and family rights, which are binding and enforceable, are written down in Article 8 and 12 of the ECHR, which is part of the Austrian Constitutional Law. The two articles define: the right to "private and family life, his home and his correspondence" (Article 8 ECHR) and the right "to marry and to found a family, according to the national laws governing the exercise of this right." (Article 12 ECHR) [1].1 Section 2 will describe the legal situation of bi-national couples in Austria with a special focus on the changes in the 2005 Alien Law Act that included a clause on 'marriages of convenience' for the first time. Section 3 and Section 4 will discuss article 8 and 12 ECHR in the light of legal exclusion mechanisms to the right to marry and will analyze the surveillance and control practices of the Austrian alien police and respective court decisions in regards to bi-national couples.

In recent years there has been a growing debate as to how the understandings and interpretations of Article 8 and 12 ECHR effects on governmental immigration policies [3,4]. Less in legal studies, but more in political practice, the question boils down to what is more important: international human rights standards that usually rank as constitutional law in most EU countries or national and European migration law and practice which tends to be harmonized on a European level on the strictest basis possible. The Viennese UN-Human Rights Expert, Manfred Nowak, states that one of the most severe and widespread violations of the right to family life derives from the restrictive asylum and migration policies of industrialized countries ([5], p. 374).

In several European states 'marriages of convenience' started to gain public and political attention in the 1970, when they came to be seen as a means to gain access to the labor market that states tried to close off for migrants [6] in the wake of oil crises. In recent years, again a growing number of EU states have introduced legal provision (e.g., income requirements) seeking to prevent 'marriages of convenience'. Some European research projects compare national developments between states [7,8,9], others focus on national strategies dealing with marriage migration e.g., in the United Kingdom [10,11,12], or in Norway [13,14,15]. As for the situation in Germany and Austria, the scholarly debate has mainly focused on bi-national couples in general, but very little research has been done on the situation of 'marriages of convenience'. German academic publications are mainly written by legal experts [16,17]. In Austria, the only work on 'marriages of convenience' is also a purely legal analysis dating from 1993 [18]. It was mainly NGOs (Non-governmental organizations) and journalists working and publishing their points-of-view in that field [19,20]. My publications [21,22,23] were breaking new ground in this field, not only by being the first in more than 10 years, but also by adding an inter-sectional analysis to a subject that was considered a purely legal matter.2

This article is based on my dissertation in political sciences that analyzes the construction of the phenomenon of 'marriages of convenience' by state authorities in Austria [22]. The empirical data used in this article are mainly based on questionnaires filled in by alien-police officers and on court records of Viennese proceedings regarding 'marriages of convenience'.

LEGAL SITUATION IN AUSTRIA

Since the early 1990s, Austria has been sharpening asylum and migration law [24]. The debate over the right to family life and marriage *versus* migration law has to been seen in that light. It is consequently a debate that has been dominated by a growing fear of abuse of the right to marriage by more and more migrants, allegedly entering into mere 'marriages of convenience' with willing Austrian, thus, undermining the tightening migration regime.

In 2000, the newly elected right of center government announced that it would take actions against bogus marriages [25]. This was the first time a government program would refer to this issue. After some delay, the Alien Law Act 2005 came into power on 1 January 2006 [26]. It proved to be a paradigmatic change in policy towards the families of Austrian citizens married to or wishing to marry a non-EU citizen [27]. As the rights of spouses of settled third country nationals (TCN) are similar to the ones of Austrians, I will use the term Austrians for referring to both groups. Some amendments have been made in 2009 and in 2011 to include same-sex couples but, in general, regulations have become more severe for bi-national couples seeking marriage.

Changes in the Alien Law

In Austria, during the last few years, between 35,000 and 39,000 marriages per year were contracted. Most marriages are between Austrians and EU citizens [28]. This has never been a political concern and spouses from other EU countries have not been affected by the new law. The Alien Law Act 2005 wishes to curb migration from outside the EU into Austria. With around 75% third-country-nationals family members, family migration forms the largest group of migration [27]. To restrict this type of immigration is one of the main objectives of the reorganization of the Aliens Law Act 2005. Indeed, in 2006, the number of Austrians marrying TCNs dropped by almost two-thirds compared to the years 2004 and 2005 [27].

Under the old legislation TCNs married to an Austrian citizen had a right to work and to stay and were entitled to apply for a residence permit within the country of Austria regardless their current legal residence status. With the Alien Law Act 2005 the Austrian government seeks to protect the institution of marriage from possible abuse by a range of measures. The newly introduced juridical term "residence marriage" indicates that the main interest of legislation is to prevent the evasion of residence regulations through 'marriages of convenience'. The equally new sanctions including court sentences and additional surveillance possibilities for the police [29] are accompanied by tightened provisions in the Settlement and Residence Act for the non-Austrian partner to obtain a residence permit [30]. The residence title "family relative" is issued for twelve months each only during the first two years of residency and, after this, will only be extended for three years if the couple is able to prove that necessary requirements are still being met. Since 2011, the knowledge of German has to be proven as well. In addition, the new legislation on income requirement poses an obstacle for many couples wishing to marry but whose monthly income does not reach a necessary minimum level of income.

The Alien Law Act 2005 has also led to the interesting, and somewhat absurd, situation that the TCN spouse of an EU or indeed EEC citizen living in Austria enjoys greater freedoms than the TCN spouse of an Austrian in the same situation [31]. Unfortunately, it is beyond the scope of this article to look into the legal repercussions of EU and EEA individuals who have enjoyed the European Union right to freedom of movement and wishing to marry a TCN.

"Residence Marriage"[3]

The Family Reunification Council Directive 2003/86/EC of the European Commission defines 'marriage of convenience' as a marriage "contracted for the sole purpose of enjoying the right of free movement and residence." ([32], p. 38) The Alien Law Act 2005, using a wider interpretation of the term 'residence marriage', defines "an Austrian or an TCN entitled to settle in Austria who enters into a marriage or a registered partnership with a TCN without the intention of leading a family life within the meaning of Art. 8 ECHR and knows or must have known that the TCN intends to rely on it to obtain or secure a residence title or residence rights secured by European Union law or to acquire Austrian nationality or to prevent measures terminating residence has to be sentenced by the court to a fine of up to 360 daily rates" ([29], my translation), *i.e.*, they are threatened to receive a criminal conviction.

In case of entering into a 'residence marriage' for a pecuniary advantage, the penalty is up to one year imprisonment. From 2006 to 2009, only the Austrian partner was punishable, the law changed in 2009. Now the TCN who wants to rely on such a marriage or registered partnership also has to be punished as a party to the offense. In addition, to these sentences under Administrative Penalty Law, the TCN will have to face residence terminating procedures taken by alien police (*i.e.*, non-issuance and termination of residence titles and the possibility of entry or return bans) [33]. An Austrian spouse who voluntarily cooperates with police and denounces him or herself before the state prosecutor has started investigations may remain exempt from punishment [29].

In political debates the 'marriages of convenience' are judged as an attempt to undermine the rigid immigration regime by illegal and almost offensive means. The general suspicion of being a bogus couple, that bi-national marriages have to face, displays the contradiction between a state promoted pro-family policy and a repressive anti-migration regime.

Numbers of Marriages/Registered Partnerships and Immigration

Since the early 1990s, the number of marriages between Austrians and people of other nationalities has more than doubled, rising from 14% of all marriages, contracted in 1995, to as much as about 28% in 2005 [28]. This rise is not only proof of a more globalized world, but also of a social phenomenon: the benefit of the right to stay, to work, and the possibility to gain Austrian citizenship more easily.

For the last few decades, Austrians have mainly married fellow Austrians and/or partners from European Union states. However, especially the group of TCNs grew until 2005, as it was one of the last options to enter the country legally and to profit from the benefits of family migration. A note-worthy gender gap can be observed during the last years among Austrians who marry TCNs: whereas Austrian men predominately marry Asian women, Austrian women mainly marry men from African countries [34]. Therefore, I will analyze whether these two groups show comparable figures of being suspected of 'marriage of convenience' and of being policed accordingly.

While in 2006 bi-national marriages between Austrian men and TCN women decreased by about 20%, the number of Austrian women and TCN husbands decreased even further by 34% [34]. A comparison with the marriage statistics for 2009 shows that this trend continues: the number of Austrian women who marry TCN partners is still dropping, more so than the number of Austrian men marrying TCN wives [35]. With a substantial decline of 84.8%, the number of marriages between Austrian women and partners from African countries illustrates who are the most affected of this change in law [35].

THE RIGHT TO MARRY

In Austria two individuals become a 'family' either through marriage (for heterosexual couples) or by entering into a registered partnership (for same-sex couples). Spouses are entitled to custody, the right to inherit, and a residence permit if required on family grounds. From a migration-control perspective gaining permission of residence due to a marriage or registered partnership allows for too many loopholes. As this perspective has become the mainstream discourse on migration, consequently most EU Member states have tightened their policies on marriage and same-sex partnership involving third-country nationals since the 1990s. It, indeed, conforms to human rights to declare marriages as null and void, which have solely been entered into in order to gain a residence status. However, it is incompatible to deny marriage merely because it would help one partner in obtaining a residence permit [36].

Family Rights for Married Couples Only?

The concept of 'family life' protected by Art 8 ECHR encompasses the right to close family relationships. This includes not only persons already related to each other through existing marriage but also to people planning to a build family [37]. At present, Austrian laws relating to foreigners only define the married spouse as a family member whereas the European Court of Human Rights (ECtHR) has ruled in constant jurisdiction that the marital partner-to-be also enjoys the protection of Art 8 ECHR [38]. Thus, the Austrian definition of the term family member is lacking and needs to be revised and broadened to be in compliance with the rulings of the ECtHR.

No Marriage for Partners without a Residence Permit?

In several EU Member States a legal residence permit of both marital partners is precondition for marriage or same-sex partnership, e.g., Germany, Denmark, Estonia, Greece, Lithuania, and Latvia [36]. In Austria, the same was discussed in parliamentary debate in preparation of the Alien Law Act 2005. The idea of simply barring illegal residents from the right to marry was dropped due to severe criticism, not only by many Austrian NGOs and Christian institutions, but also by the Office of the Federal Chancellor (the official constitutional law service of the government) and by the Association of Austrian Cities. This interesting example shows that drastic measures, *i.e.*, excluding a group of people from the right to marry altogether was opposed by a growing number of organization and, at least at that given moment in time, the right to marry for everyone was seen as more important than the prevention of a possible abuse.

Document Problems at Registry Offices

Most EU Member States require prospective marital partners to produce a 'certificate of no impediment to marriage'. This procedure seeks to prevent prohibited forms of marriages, e.g., polygamy, marriage of persons under marriageable age, or marriages between close relatives. In practice, such certificates have become an impediment to marriage for bi-national couples in general. In particular, citizens of less developed countries with inefficient and cumbersome bureaucracies fail to provide the documents needed. Austrian registry offices necessitate a considerable number of documents in order to register a planned marriage, all of which have to be presented in German and notarized, some of them becoming invalid after half a year. It requires a great deal of money and logistical prowess to have all papers ready at the same time, and not everyone is able to perform that task successfully in the preparations of the marriage. Fibel, an Austrian NGO representing bi-national couples, reports cases where Austrian embassies refuse to issue an entry (Schengen) visa for the prospective TCN spouse [39]. As a result, many Austrians must marry abroad. This poses a problem mainly for partners with low income or mothers of small children with limited options to travel.

Security Problems at Registry Offices

Since 2006, civil registry offices are required to pass on personal data of all fiancés from third countries to the alien police. This transfer of data occurs not only when there are tangible reasons for suspicion but is a general security procedure in all marriages with TCNs. Sometimes a marriage is prevented by alien police arresting one partner at the registry office [40,41]. Cases have been reported where fiancés, with precarious or no residence status, did not dare to marry because the registry office had become a highly unsafe place for them. It has been criticized that a civil act, such as marriage, is overburdened by potential police action [42].

Legalization with Marriage

Marriage alone does not guarantee a residence status for the TCN. Once being married he/she has to apply for residence permit. Those who entered Austria legally may apply for residence status as family member from within the country, all others have to apply from abroad [30]. For asylum seekers this often means going back to their country of origin, waiting for months, or even years until their application for family-reunification is dealt with. This option is quite expensive and also risky. For a newly wedded couple it is a heavy burden to be separated for such a long period, especially, if they have a child. In addition, it is also difficult to prove a family life when having to live apart. This is yet another feature of the Austrian migration regime, showing that security issues are considered more important than humanitarian matters.

Class-Exclusion via Income

Since 2006, the couple has to prove a regular income of more than 1,200 Euro per month, and 120 Euro, extra, per every child. It should be noted that, at this stage, the non-Austrian spouse is not yet allowed to work and, therefore, unable to contribute to the couple's income. The Austrian partner has to provide income for family alone. By comparison: Austria does not have a general minimum wage but welfare benefits provide a monthly minimum income of roughly 800 Euro which is considered enough to secure one's livelihood [43]. The gender pay gap in Austria is wider than in other EU member states, Women have about 25% less income than men [44]. Looking into recent statistics on working class women's income, it can be clearly seen that a woman in this wage bracket cannot earn these amounts of money, even with a full-time job [45]. The income requirement also excludes couples where the Austrian partner is working part-time or is only receiving child care allowance and, thus, cannot account for the required regular income. Again, this is, in particular, true for female Austrians. In consequence, the non-Austrian partner will not be granted legal residence status and is still not able to contribute to the required combined income. The individual consequences of these practices are dire: The husbands are denied a residence permit as a family member and families are separated simply on grounds of low income. This measure was devised to hinder poor people to enter into a 'residence marriage' for the sole reason of money. In practice, it works to the disadvantage of people already facing major discrimination in life and shows that family migration policies are highly gendered, in particular, with regard to dependency.

Measures on marriage restrictions as described and analyzed in this section do reflect concerns of states and their sovereign right to control immigration. However, as the Fundamental Rights Agency of the EU argues, states are meant to respect individuals' fundamental rights and must ensure that any measures adopted against the abuse of marriage do not endanger the fundamental right of each person to enter a marriage of his or her own free will [36]. As shown, some of these regulations are in stark conflict with

Art 8 and 12 ECHR, *de facto* excluding groups of people from their right to marry and to enjoy family life.

MARRIAGES UNDER SURVEILLANCE AND THE RIGHT TO PRIVATE LIFE

European states expend substantial effort to find ways how to prevent 'marriages of convenience' on the EU and on the national level. European Migration Network (EMN) was founded in 2008 to support policymaking in the European Union on migration and asylum with the aim of a common asylum and immigration policy. In 2012, the EMN published 24 national reports on the misuse of the right to family reunification that included marriages of convenience and false declarations of parenthood for migration purposes. It is the official response "to a growing concern that the right to family reunification may be misused as a route to settlement in the EU" ([7], p. 5) The report on Austria [46] is rather unsatisfactory as it is based on interviews with alien police authorities and representatives from the Federal Ministry of Interior only and refers to their point of views unreflectingly, focusing merely on the potential misuse. Possible tensions with human rights standards were not addressed.

To enjoy the protection of human rights, a marriage has to be considered as genuine. In this section I will look into the control practices of alien police and respective court rulings. I was given access to all documents of the Viennese court proceedings on alleged 'residence marriages' taking place in 2006 and in 2007. Hence, it was possible to work with a full survey of 57 Viennese court records of the first two years when the new Alien Law Act came into force. For comparison: in the years 2006 and 2007 in all of Austria about 120 procedures were heard at a court of first instance, which means about half of all procedures were allotted to Viennese courts [47]. The second source is 98 completed questionnaires, filled in by alien police officers specializing in the detection of 'marriages of convenience'. These set of data were combined for the analysis of the control practices using both quantitative statistical approaches and qualitative methods such as content analysis to reconstruct the timeline of being suspected, controlled, and possibly convicted. As mentioned already the registry offices send personal data of TCN fiancés to the alien police. The alien police decide and select cases that are investigated in detail. Similar as in most other European countries, alien police will investigate couples at home and invite them for separate interrogation sessions.

What are Reasons for "Suspicion"?

According to a 1997 EU council document [48], the following circumstances point toward a possible marriage of convenience: The couple does not live together or misses the "appropriate contribution to the responsibilities arising from the marriage"—this is taken to mean that they have not met before the marriage or do not know any personal details about the other person, maybe because of not speaking the same language. Other reasons are that money is involved or that one of them has already been married for immigration benefits. Not a lot has changed since then.

I was able to prove gender-related factors that may result in suspecting a marriage of being bogus: the difference in age is only decisive if the Austrian woman is older than her husband, not *vice versa*. What is distinct about Austria is that alien police relies on the family name system, which is patri-lineal. This singles out women who previously have been married to a foreigner. Men who may have been involved in previous 'sham marriages' thereby go undetected, which—strangely enough—is of no concern to alien police. A precarious legal status as asylum seeker or illegal status makes a couple suspicious, especially if the husband is from Nigeria or from Serbia [22].

Control Practices

Alien police investigations include on-the-spot checks in the house and at the work place, asking neighbors, colleagues, superiors, parents, apartment searches, and interviews with both partners. The central focus of alien police control practices is the couple's shared residence. It is checked for signs of cohabitation. Personal items such as clothes, shoes, cosmetics, documents, shared mementos, such as pictures, videos, letters, and even the couple's bed are searched and examined. Although the Austrian Marriage Act uses the term "conjugal life companionship" instead of "domestic community" [49], the cohabitation of bi-national couples is treated as the basis for credibility. This means that cohabitation is not a required characteristic of "conjugal life companionship", *i.e.*, marriage/same-sex partnership among Austrians, but is vital if one spouses or same-sex partners is a TCN. While the courts uphold the opinion that conjugal life companionship suffices, alien police regularly considers separate flats as an evidence for a 'marriage of convenience'. Investigating a couple's residence is a legal grey area [49]. In general, institutions have to respect ones intimacy and any state intervention into the private sphere has to be of due relevance. If the police carries out body searches or searches of a person's home, effective measures must be taken to protect the intimacy and dignity of the person searched. Furthermore, searches should be permitted only if absolutely necessary, such as to prevent a crime and always with a legally authorized search warrant [5].

Things are different when a TCN is involved and Austria's right of protected privacy becomes somewhat shaky. Although alien police officers do not have to be let into the apartment without a search warrant, there is the fear that this may easily be interpreted to the disadvantage of the persons concerned. The distinction between a tolerated house tour and a house search is debatable from a fundamental and human right's perspective [50]. Art. 36 Alien Law also provides for other circumstances where alien police may enter private houses without exigent circumstances or a legal warrant.

In addition to house searches, the couple's finances are investigated into. The financial data can be related to each other and compared with those made at the request for a residence permit. Moreover, financial transactions are easy to verify, and the necessary income levels can be checked for several months at a time [22].

The next step in alien police investigations is an invitation to separate interviews. If one person is abroad to apply for a residence permit, the interview often takes place at the embassy. These interviews include private questions about the relationship, the wedding, friends and family, future plans, and the daily life of the couple. It has to be criticized that these questions partly deal with very intimate matters of the relationship (e.g., questions concerning sexual preferences and frequency of intercourse, contraception, *etc.*). The questions asked frequently display Euro-centric notions, for instance, putting a large emphasis on celebrating Christmas together as a family.

For the affected couples, these inspections and interviews invade their private and intimate spheres and are frequently perceived to be very humiliating and highly distressing. Furthermore, this practice leads to delays in the family migration procedure. The investigations of the authority may take a period of three months, which can be prolonged by a further two months. These five months extra are a time of inquiries in which the spouses are sometimes separated and are unable to continue or build up their family life. The Austrian Ombudsman Board that independently monitors public administration reports cases where such alien police investigations were taking up to four years [51].

Who Defines What 'Family' and 'Marriage' is?

As already pointed out, the term 'residence marriage' is ill-defined. Alien police has numerous possibilities for interpretation. These interpretations are influenced by the moral ideals of alien police officers. The lives of bi-national families under scrutiny are less determined by their individual inter-cultural concepts of family live but rather by the often limited imagination of alien police using traditional concepts of what family is or should be as the following examples from police reports show:

Upon inspection of a very small apartment where also other family members had to live, the police officer stated "I cannot imagine how a marriage can be consumed here." ([22], p. 248, my translation) In another case, a police inspector described the lack of public display of affection during his observations at the registry office and concluded that the spouses "according to my subjective feeling are not behaving like a newlywed couple in love." ([22], p. 248, my translation). The assessments of whether a marriage is 'real or bogus' are based on subjective norms of Austrian alien police officers, commonly not speaking a foreign language, not trained in cross-cultural inter-action and with little knowledge of the living conditions of migrants.

How Do Courts Rule on 'Residence Marriage'?

If the alien police is confident of having identified a 'residence marriage', it proceeds as follows: first, the procedure of a residence or entry ban against the TCN will be initiated, and secondly, they file charges against the couple with the public prosecutor who will refer the procedure to the respective district court. Providing a formal proof that a marriage is indeed a 'residence marriage' is difficult in most cases. The court principle '*in dubio pro reo*' lead to a low number of convictions in the Viennese court cases in 2006 and 2007: in about one third of the cases the accused were found innocent or at least there was insufficient evidence for a conviction, in another third investigations did not produce any results and court procedures were stopped or given up on, and in a remaining one third, the accused couple was found guilty [22]. Analysis shows that only the ones who confessed of having entered into a 'residence marriage' were sentenced. The convicted couples were also mainly the ones where a monetary benefit was suspected or proven. The financial penalties were quite low as it affected mainly persons with a low income. (In Austria, law fines have to reflect the income situation of the convicted person.) Despite this low "success rate", the number of trials did rise: in 2009 there were 344 court cases in Austria [52], not counting all of those cases in which the suspicions were not sufficient to file a charge or the proceedings were later abandoned by the prosecution. Alien police is still trying through home searches and interrogations to provide evidence of a 'marriage of convenience'. However, the independent district courts apply different standards and judge more carefully: Out of the 344 procedures, only 53 were sentenced for having entered into a 'residence marriage'. This means that 84.6% of court proceedings were conducted without sufficient basis for a court conviction [52].

These low numbers in cases and even lower numbers in convictions indicate that the criminalization of 'residence marriages' serves merely as a threat scenario and gives alien police a powerful tool to control bi-national marriages. It should be noted that alien police may, and will, seek to terminate the residence of the TNC (either by deportation or refusing re-entry) irrespective a verdict of acquittal by a court. Both legal proceedings (court trial and granting or refusing residence permit by alien police) are independent and separate from each other. Court ruling affects only the criminal offence of 'residence marriage' but not the administrative procedures under Alien Law. Thus, a couple can be cleared of the suspicion of leading a 'residence marriage' by a court, yet, alien police may deport or ban the acquitted spouse.

Given that the concept of 'residence marriage' only affects TCNs and their families by definition, we can speak of institutionalized racism against this group. However, this discrimination has to be differentiated along the categories gender, class, nationality, and residence status. Chiefly couples with under-privileged Austrian women and their TCN husbands, mainly without legal status, were affected. They were inspected more frequently by alien police, but not convicted by the courts. Ironically, this group of Austrian women, discriminated against on several levels, is more likely to be suspected of having entered into a 'residence marriage' even though their marriages could not result in a later gained residence permit for the TCN spouse as this group of Austrian women do not meet required income levels in the first place.

The statistically by far more frequent constellation of the marriage between male Austrians and TCN women from Asia is not investigated into: neither in the construction of the group of the suspected ones, nor by alien-police or in judicial practices. This shows that not everyone is equal in front of the Alien Law but that there is a clear gender and nation bias.

The concept of 'marriages of convenience' is a flexible narration that can easily be adopted for various groups of migrants or otherwise marginalized persons.

Above examined control measures seek to differentiate between "real" and "fake" marriages—but whose marriage is "real"? Is it the romantic marriage where he goes down on his knees when proposing with no reasons at the back of anybody's mind other than enduring love? Leaving romantic notions aside, we can assume that in each marriage at least one person profits by, for instance, the legalization of children, tax, or other legal advantages, taking over a family business, and further strategic reasons. The state has shown no interest in verifying or ruling out any of such reasons and it would be seen as an inappropriate intervention of state policies infringing private matters. This changes when a foreigner is involved who might benefit from a marriage by gaining access to a residence and work permit and (facilitated) naturalization. Here the reasons for a marriage otherwise considered private become subject to state scrutiny. It highly questionable that the government in a secular state proscribes the morally "correct" reasons for marriage in this way [20]. These control measures result in arbitrary intrusion in the couples' private and intimate spheres, thus, violating Art. 8 ECHR.

CONCLUSIONS

Migration regimes of Western states are extremely eager to defend their sovereign right to regulate the entry and residence of foreigners on their territory. These aims are often in conflict with human rights standards. In Austria, the Alien Law Act 2005 and its implementation exacerbate or even hinder Austrians to marry a TCN and is effectively violating the human and constitutional right to the protection of marriage enshrined in Art 12 ECHR. Marriages between Austrian citizens and TCNs are strongly affected by the legal changes and their numbers have been in decrease since 2006. The ones worst hit are Austrian women with little income wishing to marry an Africa man who did not enter the country legally. Exactly, this group is the one suspected the most of having entered into a 'residence marriage'—although the future husband would not get a residence permit out of the marriage. On the contrary, the group of Austrian men marrying Asian women did not come under suspicion at all. This shows underlying gendered, classist, and racist structures. The criminalization of 'residence marriages' and the practices of the alien police trying to evaluate the "authenticity" of marriages by home visits, interrogations, and interviews violates human rights to private and family life laid down in Art 8 ECHR. The courts rarely follow the argumentation of the alien police and usually decide in favor of the accused couple. Acute police investigations lead to surprisingly low numbers of actual convictions.

Therefore, the following question has arisen: Can the intense invasion into the private life of bi-national couples and their right to marriage still be seen as proportional? Posing this question of balance between the interests of the individual rights and freedoms on the one hand and the interests of the states migration regime on the other hand, the result is sobering but probably not surprising: human rights lose out and are seen as less crucial than the fight against (alleged) 'marriages of convenience'. On one hand, the state is the guarantor of human rights, on the other hand, the very same state increasingly violates human rights of bi-national couples by effectively blocking them from living together or from marrying and by exercising a growing level of control into their private homes and most intimate relationships.

The case study of Austria leaves little hope that human rights will gain attention again in the near future. The current political discourse is dominated by xenophobic reflexes and the question remains open as to how human rights can take on greater significance, in theory and practice.

REFERENCES AND NOTES

1. European Court of Human Rights. "European Convention on Human Rights as amended by Protocols Nos. 11 and 14, supplemented by Protocols Nos. 1, 4, 6, 7, 12 and 13. Strasbourg." 2010. Available online: http://www.echr.coe.int/Documents/Convention_ENG.pdf (accessed on 10 June 2013).
2. Stuart Hall. "The West and the Rest. Discourse and Power." In *Formations of Modernity*. Edited by Stuart Hall and Bram Gieben. 1997, pp. 275–320.
3. Julia Woesthoff. "Romancing the Foreigner? 'Fictitious Marriages' and the Crisis between Immigration and Human Rights." In *Sexuality in Austria*. Edited by Günter Bischof, Anton Pelinka and Dagmar Herzog. New Brunswick: Transaction Publ., 2007, pp. 158–71.
4. Jari Pirjola. "European asylum policy—inclusions and exclusions under the surface of universal human rights language." *European Journal of Migration and Law* 11 (2009): 347–66.
5. Manfred Nowak. "Right to Privacy and Family Life." In *All Human Rights for All. Vienna Manual on Human Rights*. Edited by Manfred Nowak, Karolina Januszewski and Tina Hofstätter. Vienna-Graz: NWV Neuer Wissenschaftlicher Verlag, 2012, pp. 371–75.
6. Betty de Hart. "Introduction. The marriage of convenience in European immigration law." *European Journal of Migration and Law* 8, no. 3–4 (2006): 251–62.
7. European Migration Network. "Misuse of the Right to Family Reunification." In *Marriages of Convenience and False Declarations of Parenthood*. Luxembourg: Publications Office of the European Union, 2012.
8. Albert Kraler. "Civic Stratification, Gender and Family Migration Policies in Europe. Final Report." 2010. Available online: http://research.icmpd.org/fileadmin/Research-Website/Test_content/FINAL_Report_Family_Migration_Policies_Online_FINAL.pdf (accessed on 10 June 2013).
9. Eleonore Kofman. "Family-related migration: A critical review of European Studies." *Journal of Ethnic and Migration Studies* 30, no. 2 (2004): 243–62.
10. Katharine Charsley, and Michaela Benson. "Marriages of convenience, and inconvenient marriages: Regulating spousal migration to Britain."

Journal of Immigration, Asylum and Nationality Law 26, no. 1 (2012): 10–26.

11. Helena Wray. *Regulating Marriage Migration into the UK. A Stranger in the Home*. Farnham: Ashgate, 2011.
12. Helena Wray. "An ideal husband? Marriages of convenience, moral gate-keeping and immigration to the UK." *European Journal of Migration and Law* 8, no. 3–4 (2006): 303–20.
13. Anne Staver. "Family Reunification: A Right for Forced Migrants? " 2008. Available online: http://www.rsc.ox.ac.uk/publications/working-papers-folder_contents/RSCworkingpaper51.pdf (accessed on 10 June 2013).
14. Anne Britt Flemmen, and Ann Therese Lotherington. *Transnational Marriage Migration: Russian-Norwegian Encounters*. Saarbrücken: VDM Verlag, 2009.
15. Helga Eggebø. "The problem of dependency: Immigration, gender, and the welfare state." *Social Politics* 17, no. 3 (2010): 295–322.
16. Jens Eisfeld. *Die Scheinehe in Deutschland im 19. und 20. Jahrhundert*. Tübingen: Mohr Siebeck, 2005.
17. Kathi-Alexandra Hartmann. *Scheinehen mit Deutschen Staatsangehörigen. Struktur, Politik, (deutsch-)deutsches Ehebild*. Berlin: Wissenschaftlicher Verlag Berlin, 2008.
18. Ute Mayer. "Die Ehe als Scheingeschäft unter Besonderer Berücksichtigung der Namens- und Staatsbürgerschaftsehe." Diploma Thesis (MA), University Salzburg, 1993.
19. Antje Dertinger. *Schenk mir Deinen Namen. Scheinehen zwischen Menschlichkeit und Kriminalität*. Bonn: Dietz, 1999.
20. Association of Binational Families and Partnership. "Human rights infringements in the context of family migration policies in Germany." In Submission for the Second Cycle of the Human Rights Council Universal Periodic Review, 16th session, Frankfurt, Germany, 22 April–3 May 2013; Available online: http://www.institut-fuer-menschenrechte.de/fileadmin/user_upload/PDF-Dateien/UN-Dokumente/UPR_zu_Deutschland/UPR2013_germany_IAF_en.pdf (accessed on 10 June 2013).
21. Daniela Digruber, and Irene Messinger. "Marriage of residence in Austria." *European Journal of Migration and Law* 8, no. 3–4 (2006): 281–302.

22. Irene Messinger. "Verdacht auf Scheinehe. Intersektionelle Analyse staatlicher Konstruktion von, Schein- und Aufenthaltsehe' und ihre Auswirkungen im Fremdenpolizeigesetz 2005." Ph.D. Thesis, University Vienna, May 2011.

23. Irene Messinger, and Schein oder Nicht Schein. *Konstruktion und Kriminalisierung von "Scheinehen" in Geschichte und Gegenwart.* Wien: Verlag Mandelbaum, 2012.

24. Karin König, and Bettina Stadler. "Entwicklungstendenzen im Öffentlich-Rechtlichen und Demokratiepolitischen Bereich." In *Österreichischer Migrations- und Integrationsbericht. Demographische Entwicklungen—sozioökonomische Strukturen—rechtliche Rahmenbedingungen.* Edited by Heinz Fassmann, Irene Stacher and Helga Amesberger. Klagenfurt: Drava Verlag, 2003, pp. 225–61.

25. ÖVP-FPÖ. "Österreich neu regieren." Available online: www.bka.gv.at/2004/4/7/Regprogr.pdf (accessed on 10 June 2013).

26. "Fremdenrechtspaket 2005." Available online: http://www.parlament.gv.at/PAKT/VHG/XXII/I/I_00952/ (accessed on 10 June 2013).

27. Sebastian Schumacher. "Die Neuorganisation der Zuwanderung durch das Fremdenrechtspaket 2006." In *2. Österreichischer Migrations- und Integrationsbericht.* Edited by Heinz Fassmann. Klagenfurt: Drava Verlag, 2007, pp. 74–82.

28. Statistik Austria. "Eheschließungen seit 1970 nach Staatsangehörigkeit." Available online: http://www.statistik.at/web_de/static/eheschliessungen_seit_1970_nach_staatsangehoerigkeit_024813.pdf (accessed on 10 June 2013).

29. Bundesgesetz über die Ausübung der Fremdenpolizei, die Ausstellung von Dokumenten für Fremde und die Erteilung von Einreisetitel, Fremdenpolizeigesetz 2005 (Alien Police Law 2005), Para. 117. (1 January 2006).

30. Niederlassungs- und Aufenthaltsgesetz 2005 (Settlement and Residence Act 2005), Para. 21 (1 January 2006).

31. "Directive 2004/38/EC of the European Parliament and Council from 29 April 2004 on the right of citizens of the Union and their family members to move and reside freely within the territory of the Member States." *Official Journal of the European Union L229*, 2004, 35–48.

32. "Council Directive 2003/86/EC of 22 September 2003 on the right to

family reunification." *Official Journal of the European Union L251*, 2003, 12–18.

33. Niederlassungs- und Aufenthaltsgesetz 2005 (Settlement and Residence Act 2005), Non-issuance and termination of residence titles: Para. 11, Art.1 (4) NAG, and Bundesgesetz über die Ausübung der Fremdenpolizei, die Ausstellung von Dokumenten für Fremde und die Erteilung von Einreisetitel, Fremdenpolizeigesetz 2005 (Alien Police Law 2005), residence ban for TCNs who had legal residence: Para. 63 FPG, and entry ban for Asylum seekers Para. 54 FPG. (1 January 2006).
34. Verein Fibel. "Jahresbericht 2007." Available online: http://www.verein-fibel.at/images/stories/downloads/Fibel_JB_2007.pdf (accessed on 10 June 2013).
35. Verein Fibel. "Binationale Eheschließungen in Österreich 2009." Available online: http://www.verein-fibel.at/images/stories/Binationale_Eheschlieungen_in_sterreich_2009.pdf (accessed on 10 June 2013).
36. European Union Agency for Fundamental rights. *Fundamental Rights of Migrants in an Irregular Situation in the European Union*. Luxembourg: Publications Office of the European Union, 2011.
37. Rudolf Feik. "Recht auf Familienleben." In *Handbuch Menschenrechte. Allgemeine Grundlagen—Grundrechte in Österreich—Entwicklungen—Rechtsschutz*. Edited by Gregor Heißl. Vienna: facultas.wuv, 2009, pp. 176–92.
38. Sabrina Claudia Wittmann. "Binationale Ehen von ÖsterreicherInnen mit Drittstaatsangehörigen im Lichte der Judikatur des EGMR, VfGH und VwGH zu Artikel 8 EMRK." Master Thesis, Karl-Franzens Universität Graz, January 2010.
39. Verein Fibel. "Bi-cultural/bi-national partnership and Families in Austria 2010." Available online: http://www.verein-fibel.at/images/stories/Lnderbericht2010-englisch.pdf (accessed on 10 June 2013).
40. Irene Brickner. "Angst vor Festnahme beim Ja-Wort-Sagen." *Der Standard*. 6 June 2006. http://derstandard.at/2462716?sap=2&_seite=13.
41. "Eheleute am Standesamt durch Fremdenpolizei getrennt." *Der Standard*. 23 May 2007. http://derstandard.at/2892519.
42. Wolf Szymanski. "Fremdenrechtspaket 2005." *MigraLex, Zeitschrift*

für Fremden und Minderheitenrecht 3, no. 2 (2005): 68–75.

43. City of Vienna. "Mindestsicherung." Available online: http://www.wien.gv.at/gesundheit/leistungen/mindestsicherung (accessed on 10 June 2013).
44. Bundeskanzleramt Österreich. "Sozioökonomische Situation." *Frauenbericht 2010*. Available online: http://www.bka.gv.at/studien/frauenbericht2010/Frauenbericht_Teil1_4Soziooekonomie.pdf (accessed on 10 June 2013).
45. Statistik Austria. "Unselbständig Erwerbstätige nach Nettomonatseinkommen, Geschlecht und sozioökonomischen Merkmalen—Prozentwerte Jahresdurchschnitt 2011." Available online: http://www.statistik.at/web_de/static/unselbstaendig_erwerbstaetige_nach_nettomonatseinkommen_geschlecht_und_soz_057213.pdf (accessed on 10 June 2013).
46. European Migration Network. *Misuse of the Right to Family Reunification. Marriages of Convenience and False Declarations of Parenthood*. Vienna: IOM, Focussed Study Austria, 2012.
47. Claudia Bandion-Ortner. "Anfragebeantwortung 553J-NR/2009." Available online: http://www.parlament.gv.at/PAKT/VHG/XXIV/AB/AB_00661/imfname_153067.pdf (accessed on 10 June 2013).
48. EU Council. "Resolution 97/C 382/01 of 4 December 1997 on measures to be adopted on the combating of marriages of convenience." *Official Journal C 382*. 1997. Available online: http://eur-lex.europa.eu/LexUriServ/LexUriServ.do?uri=CELEX:31997Y1216%2801%29:EN:HTML (accessed on 10 June 2013).
49. Bea Verschraegen. "Entwicklungen des österreichischen Eherechts im 20. Jahrhundert. Zwischen Tradition und Wandel." In *Festschrift 200 Jahre ABGB*. Edited by Constanze Fischer-Czermak, Gerhard Hopf, Georg Kathrein and Martin Schauer. Vienna: Manz Verlag, 2011, pp. 667–90.
50. Walter Berka. *Lehrbuch Grundrechte*. Wien: Springer, 2000.
51. Volksanwaltschaft. "Missstandsfeststellung und Empfehlung des Kollegiums der Volksanwaltschaft." Available online: http://volksanw.gv.at/downloads/974tj/missstandsfeststellung-und-empfehlung-bmi-september-2010-1.pdf (accessed on 10 June 2013).
52. Claudia Bandion-Ortner. "Beantwortung der Parlamentarischen Anfrage 4305/J-NR/2010." Available online: http://www.parlament.

gv.at/PAKT/VHG/XXIV/AB/AB_04319/fname_183065.pdf(accessed on 10 June 2013).

53. The correct legal term for a person not holding an Austrian citizenship is "legal alien". The term "third country national" refers to any alien from outside the European Economic Area (*i.e.*, European Union member states plus Norway, Iceland and Lichtenstein) and Switzerland. These definitions have their basis in a problematic categorisation of human beings. By excluding "the rest" from Europe, it is assumed that Europeans share homogeneous norms, values and traditions which are being elevated from the "others" and therefore is a construct that fosters racist and nationalist notions. A critical analysis of such hierarchisations was first introduced by the cultural theorist and sociologist Stuart Hall in his work on "The West and the Rest" [2].

54. Intersectionality studies the relationships and interactions among multiple dimensions of oppression or discrimination. The theory maintains that different forms of inequality—which are based on categories—do not act independently from one other, but rather interrelate. For my intersectional analysis I have used the categories: gender, nationality/ethnicity, class and residence status.

55. In common debate the expressions "marriage of convenience" but also "sham marriage" or "bogus marriage" are being used. The Austrian Alien Law Act 2005 introduces the term "residence marriage". Whenever, I refer to the strictly legal practice I will use the latter.

CHAPTER 15

A MULTI-LEVEL BAYESIAN ANALYSIS OF RACIAL BIAS IN POLICE SHOOTINGS AT THE COUNTY-LEVEL IN THE UNITED STATES, 2011–2014

Cody T. Ross

Department of Anthropology, University of California, Davis, Davis, California, United States of America

ABSTRACT

A geographically-resolved, multi-level Bayesian model is used to analyze the data presented in the U.S. Police-Shooting Database (USPSD) in order

Citation: Ross CT (2015) A Multi-Level Bayesian Analysis of Racial Bias in Police Shootings at the County-Level in the United States, 2011–2014. PLoS ONE 10(11): e0141854. https://doi.org/10.1371/journal.pone.0141854

to investigate the extent of racial bias in the shooting of American civilians by police officers in recent years. In contrast to previous work that relied on the FBI's Supplemental Homicide Reports that were constructed from self-reported cases of police-involved homicide, this data set is less likely to be biased by police reporting practices. County-specific relative risk outcomes of being shot by police are estimated as a function of the interaction of: 1) whether suspects/civilians were armed or unarmed, and 2) the race/ethnicity of the suspects/civilians. The results provide evidence of a significant bias in the killing of unarmed black Americans relative to unarmed white Americans, in that the probability of being {black, unarmed, and shot by police} is about 3.49 times the probability of being {white, unarmed, and shot by police} on average. Furthermore, the results of multi-level modeling show that there exists significant heterogeneity across counties in the extent of racial bias in police shootings, with some counties showing relative risk ratios of 20 to 1 or more. Finally, analysis of police shooting data as a function of county-level predictors suggests that racial bias in police shootings is most likely to emerge in police departments in larger metropolitan counties with low median incomes and a sizable portion of black residents, especially when there is high financial inequality in that county. There is no relationship between county-level racial bias in police shootings and crime rates (even race-specific crime rates), meaning that the racial bias observed in police shootings in this data set is not explainable as a response to local-level crime rates.

INTRODUCTION

In 2014, Kyle Wagner began an open contribution campaign [1] to compile all records of police-involved shootings in the United States between 2011 and 2014 in an attempt to better record the use of lethal force by police [2]. The U.S. Police-Shooting Database (USPSD) collects information on the race/ethnicity of civilians shot by police, their status as armed or unarmed, the identity of the officer(s) involved, relevant geographic information, and citations to detailed descriptions of the events.

While other databases on police shootings have been published by the government, for example through the FBI's Supplementary Homicide Report [3], or the CDC's National Vital Statistics System [4], these records are often censored of critical information (such as the names of the officers involved), lack independent evaluation of the justification for the shooting, and are selectively published. The FBI data, for instance, are not only incomplete, but may be structurally biased by the reporting behaviors of police, as the majority of the 17,000+ police departments in the United States do not file fatal police shooting reports, or do so only selectively [5]. According to Gabrielson et al. [5], Florida departments have failed to file reports since 1997. The data collected thus far by the USPSD help to shed light on racial bias in police shootings in Florida, which has some of the most racially-biased police shooting rates in the nation. In Miami-Dade, for example, unarmed black individuals are estimated to be more than 22 times as likely to be shot by police than unarmed white individuals. Such patterns in police violence have been immune to public scrutiny until now.

The failure of the nation's police to critically evaluate their own use of force, has led the United Nations Committee Against Torture [6] to sharply criticize the ever growing militarization of police departments in the United States, especially as evidence of significant race-based and sexuality-based brutality and excessive use of force has been uncovered, including bonafide acts of torture (e.g., those committed by Chicago Police Commander Jon Burge and others under his command, between 1972 and 1991). The UN Committee Against Torture specifically noted that it: "regrets the lack of statistical data available on allegations of police brutality and the lack of information on the result of the investigations undertaken in respect of those allegations" (pp. 13, [6]). This paper provides a response to the first of these two concerns.

Moving Forward

The work of documenting police violence in the United States, has recently begun through several open-contribution, public-access projects in addition to the USPSD. The Stolen Lives Project started by the Anthony Baez Foundation and the National Lawyers Guild [7], the Fatal Encounters Database started by Brian Burghart [8], and the Killed By Police database [9] are examples, as is the Mapping Police Violence project [10], which emphasizes visualization of the raw data from the above-mentioned databases. Additionally, Wikipedia.org [11], the Washington Post [12], and the Guardian [13] have begun keeping rigorous statistics on police shootings in specific years. Unlike the censored data released by official sources, the data in the USPSD and other grassroots databases allow for fine-scale evaluation of the use of lethal force, including investigation of department-specific and even officer-specific patterns. It is, for instance, possible to identify police departments and officers who kill unarmed black individuals at disproportionate rates. With the previously-used SHR data, lack of reporting and/or selective-biases in reporting of police shootings, could have masked underlying racial biases in police shootings, or masked the rates at which unarmed individuals are shot by police.

USPSD data will provide the public and federal agencies within the United States with much needed information describing where external review of police procedures, training, and practices may be needed to protect the civil rights of American citizens. Additionally, the data may be of use to: 1) communities during local elections of mayors, city council members, and police chiefs, 2) organizations, like the United Nations Committee Against Torture, reviewing allegations of racially motivated homicide and torture, and 3) academics seeking to understand the structural drivers of race-based violence and homicide by police.

Towards Understanding the Racial Bias in Shootings by Police

Racial bias in police shootings in the United States has been widely noted in the sociological literature for many decades [5, 14–16]. Explanations range from implicit bias in the psychology of individual officers [17–19], structural biases established by the existing social order (the conflict theory of law, and the issue of 'minority threat' [15, 20–22]), proximate responses by police to areas of high violence and crime (community violence theory [14, 15, 23]), racial bias in profiling and encountering suspects [24], blatant racism [25–27], social dominance orientation [28], or other factors.

With the USPSD and a geo-referenced data set on racial animus [29], an additional hypothesis is tested that police officers embedded in more normatively racist cultural contexts show increased racial bias in killing of unarmed civilians. The motivation for this hypothesis comes from sociological literature on implicit racial bias in rapid responses decisions [18, 19], in the context of frequency-dependent and conformist social learning [30] and inter-ethnic interaction [31], especially when ethnicity is spuriously associated with 'being a threat' [32–34] in the mind of an individual with structural power, high social dominance orientation [28], and little accountability for excessive use of force.

Much of the theoretical debate on the topic of racial bias in police shootings is sidestepped until the discussion, as much of the quantitative data underlying previous attempts at theorizing may have been fundamentally biased by the behaviors of the very actors researchers hope to understand [2, 3]. Much previous research on police shootings is based on data released by police (see, for example, [15, 35–38]). The FBI [3] clearly notes the baises in the SHR, but many authors have attempted to use the data anyway, lamenting that it is the only data available with which one can answer research questions related to police killing of civilians at a finely-resolved geographic scale [15]. The USPSD aims to reinvigorate critical research on racial bias in police shootings by providing data for analysis that is not biased by the reporting behaviors of the police.

Research Objectives

In this paper, a multi-level, Bayesian approach is used to estimate the county-level risk ratios of being shot by police as a function of the race/ethnicity of a suspect/civilian and his/her status as armed or unarmed. As the data become more complete in the coming years, this methodology can be extended to estimate the absolute risk of being shot by police. For the purposes of this paper, however, the questions are more basic:

1. Shot by Police: Armed Versus Unarmed, by Race/Ethnicity
    a. What is ratio of the probability of being {black, armed, and shot by police} to the probability of being {black, unarmed, and shot by police}?
    b. What is ratio of the probability of being {hispanic, armed, and shot by police} to the probability of being {hispanic, unarmed, and shot by police}?
    c. What is ratio of the probability of being {white, armed, and shot by police} to the probability of being {white, unarmed, and shot by police}?
2. Armed and Shot by Police, Across Race/Ethnicity
    a. What is ratio of the probability of being {black, armed, and shot by police} to the probability of being {white, armed, and shot by police}?
    b. What is ratio of the probability of being {hispanic, armed, and shot by police} to the probability of being {white, armed, and shot by police}?
3. Unarmed and Shot by Police: Across Race/Ethnicity
    a. What is ratio of the probability of being {black, unarmed, and shot by police} to the probability of being {white, unarmed, and shot by police}?
    b. What is ratio of the probability of being {hispanic, unarmed, and shot by police} to the probability of being {white, unarmed, and shot by police}?
4. Shot by Police: Race/Ethnicity Across Armed Status

   a. What is ratio of the probability of being {black, unarmed, and shot by police} to the probability of being {white, armed, and shot by police}?
   b. What is ratio of the probability of being {hispanic, unarmed, and shot by police} to the probability of being {white, armed, and shot by police}?
5. County-Level Racial Bias in Police Shootings as a Function of County-Level Properties
   Using USPSD data, is county-level racial bias in police shootings associated statistically with:
   a. County-level absolute population size?
   b. County-level racial/ethnic composition?
   c. County-level inequality (Gini)?
   d. County-level median income?
   e. County-level race-specific crime rates (1. aggravated assault, and 2. weapons possession)?
   f. County-level norms about racism (via a proxy variable derived from use of specific racially-based expletives in Google searches [29])?

RESULTS

1. Shot by Police: Armed Versus Unarmed, by Race/Ethnicity

The median probability across counties of being {black, armed, and shot by police} is 2.79(PCI95: 1.72, 4.92) times the probability of being {black, unarmed, and shot by police}—the symbol, PCI95, indicates the lower and upper endpoints of central 95% of the posterior density; it is the Bayesian equivalent of a confidence interval. The median probability across counties of being {hispanic, armed, and shot by police} is 3.08 (PCI95: 2.05, 5.10) times the probability of being {hispanic, unarmed, and shot by police}. The median probability across counties of being {white, armed, and shot by police} is 3.33 (PCI95: 2.40, 4.70) times the probability of being {white, unarmed, and shot by police}.

There is, of course, variation across counties in the U.S. in these risk ratios. Figs 1, 2, and 3plot the posterior distributions of county-specific risk ratios, as well as the geographic distributions of the median estimates.

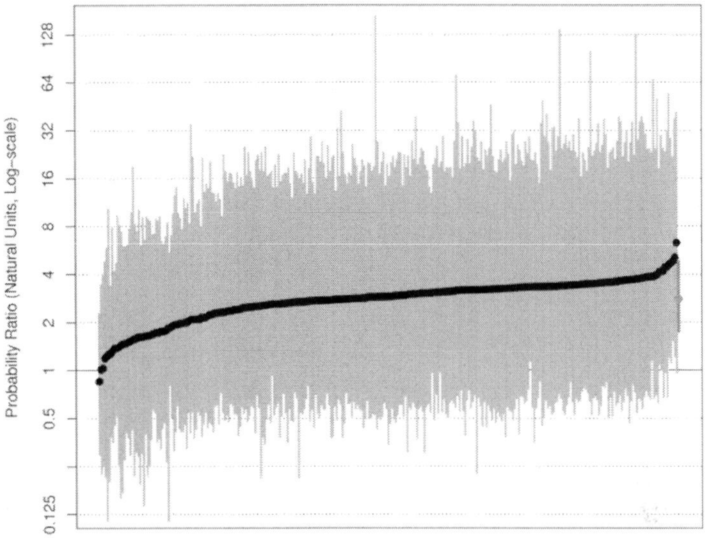

(a)

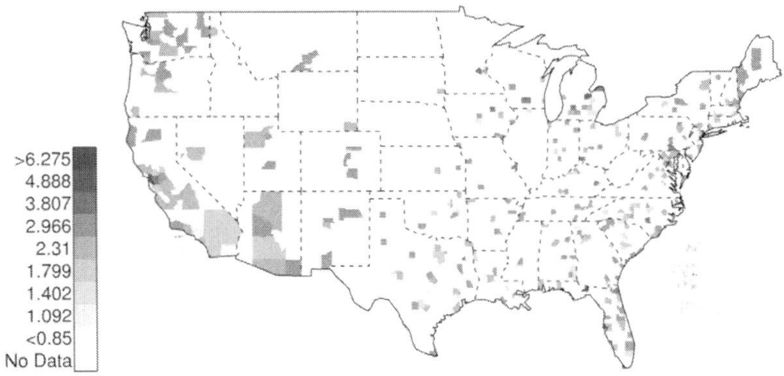

(b)

Figure 1. Posterior Random Effects Estimates: Risk Ratio Black, Armed-to-Unarmed. (a) County-by-county posterior estimates of the risk ratio of being {black, armed, and shot by police} to being {black, unarmed, and shot by police}. Grey bars are county-specific 95% PCI estimates. The blue bar is the nation-wide pooled 95% PCI estimate. The points on the error bars are posterior medians. Data are plotted on the log scale, but are labeled on the natural scale. (b) Map of county-specific posterior median estimates of the risk ratio of being {black, armed, and shot by police} to being {black, unarmed, and shot by police}.

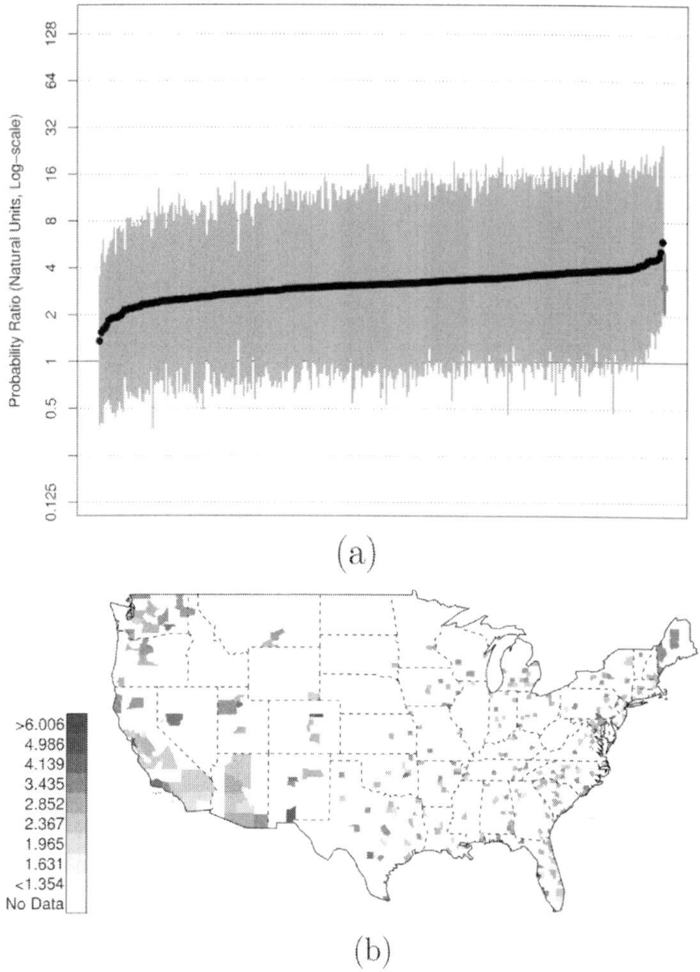

Figure 2. Posterior Random Effects Estimates: Risk Ratio Hispanic, Armed-to-Unarmed. (a) County-by-county posterior estimates of the risk ratio of being {hispanic, armed, and shot by police} to being {hispanic, unarmed, and shot by police}. Grey bars are county-specific 95% PCI estimates. The blue bar is the nation-wide pooled 95% PCI estimate. The points on the error bars are posterior medians. Data are plotted on the log scale, but are labeled on the natural scale. (b) Map of county-specific posterior median estimates of the risk ratio of being {hispanic, armed, and shot by police} to being {hispanic, unarmed, and shot by police}.

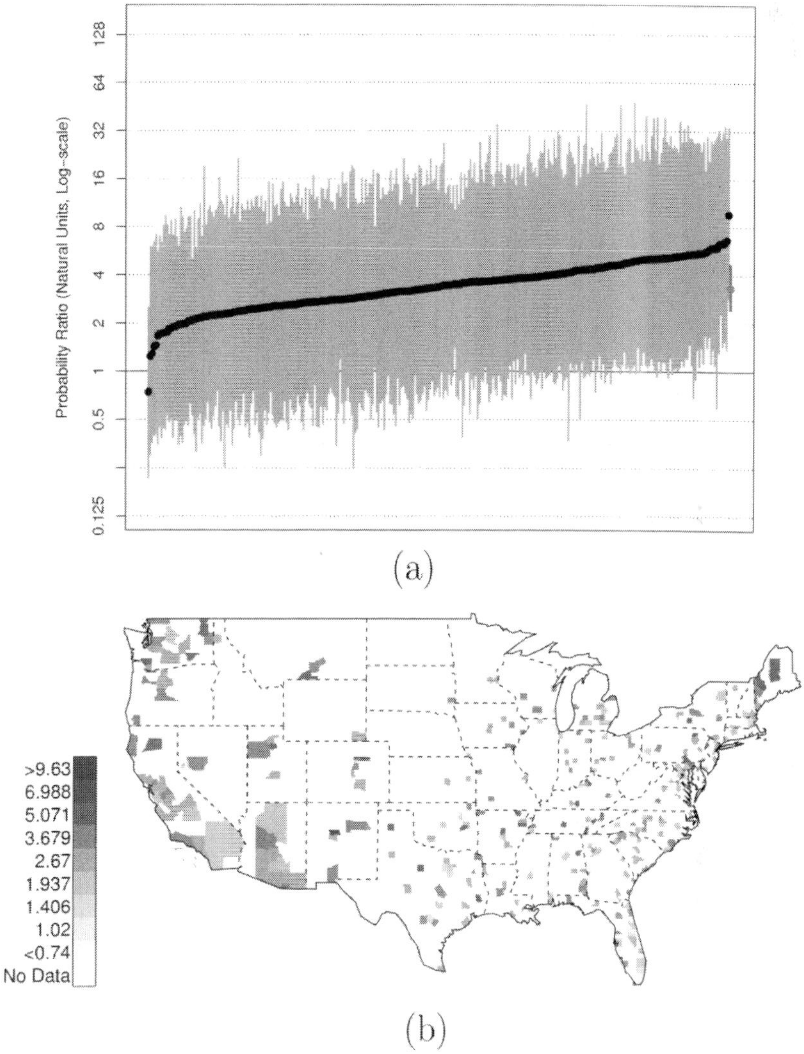

Figure 3. Posterior Random Effects Estimates: Risk Ratio White, Armed-to-Unarmed. (a) County-by-county posterior estimates of the risk ratio of being {white, armed, and shot by police} to being {white, unarmed, and shot by police}. Grey bars are county-specific 95% PCI estimates. The blue bar is the nation-wide pooled 95% PCI estimate. The points on the error bars are posterior medians. Data are plotted on the log scale, but are labeled on the natural scale. (b) Map of county-specific posterior median estimates of the risk ratio of being {white, armed, and shot by police} to being {white, unarmed, and shot by police}.

2. Armed and Shot by Police: Across Race/Ethnicity

The median probability across counties of being {black, armed, and shot by police} is 2.94(PCI95: 2.23, 3.86) times the probability of being {white, armed, and shot by police}. The median probability across counties of being {hispanic, armed, and shot by police} is 1.57(PCI95: 1.14, 2.09) times the probability of being {white, armed, and shot by police}.

As before, there is variation across counties in the U.S. in these relative risk ratios. Figs 4 and 5plot the county-specific results.

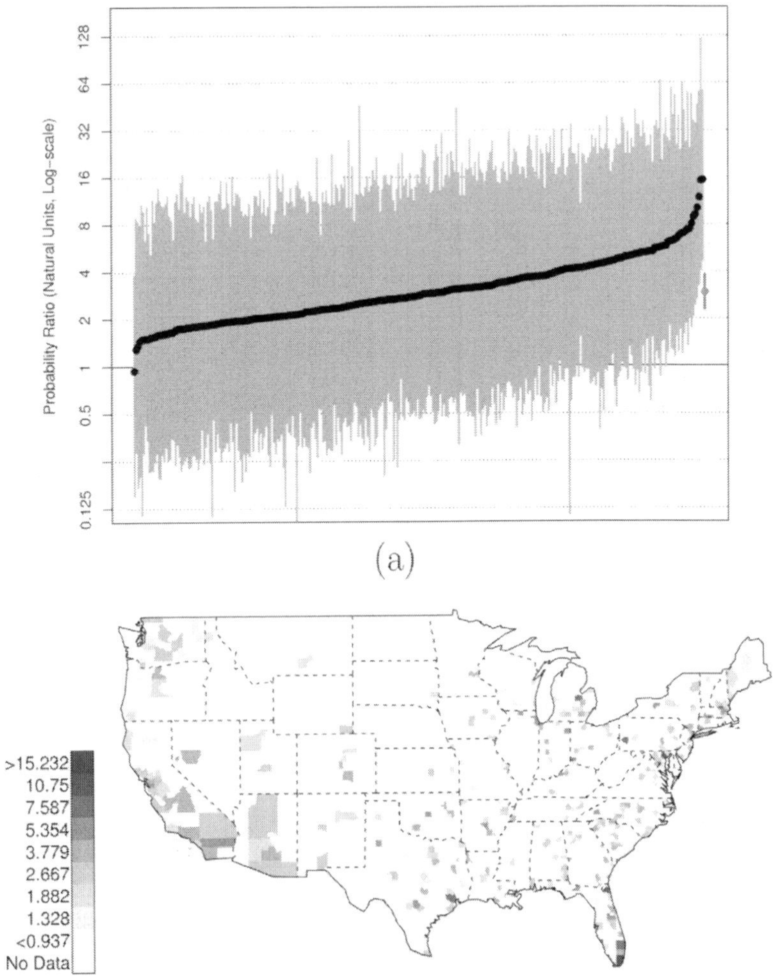

(b)

Figure 4. Posterior Random Effects Estimates: Risk Ratio Black-and-Armed to

White-and-Armed. (a) County-by-county posterior estimates of the risk ratio of being {black, armed, and shot by police} to being {white, armed, and shot by police}. Grey bars are county-specific 95% PCI estimates. The blue bar is the nation-wide pooled 95% PCI estimate. The points on the error bars are posterior medians. Data are plotted on the log scale, but are labeled on the natural scale. (b) Map of county-specific posterior median estimates of the risk ratio of being {black, armed, and shot by police} to being {white, armed, and shot by police}.

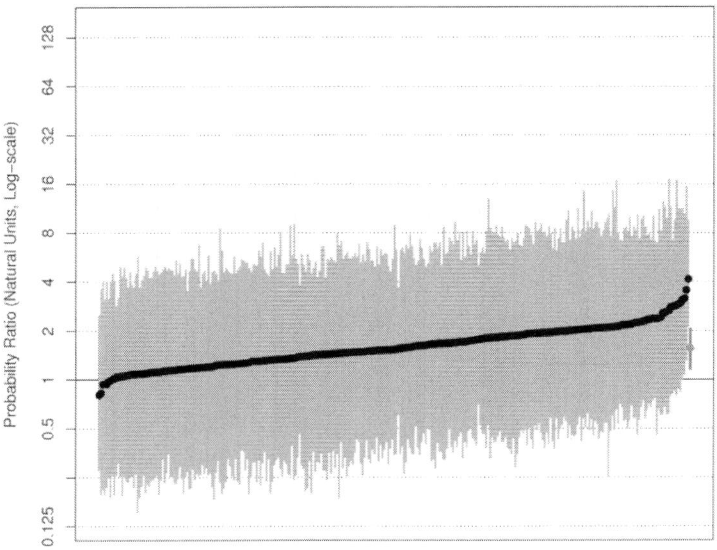

(a)

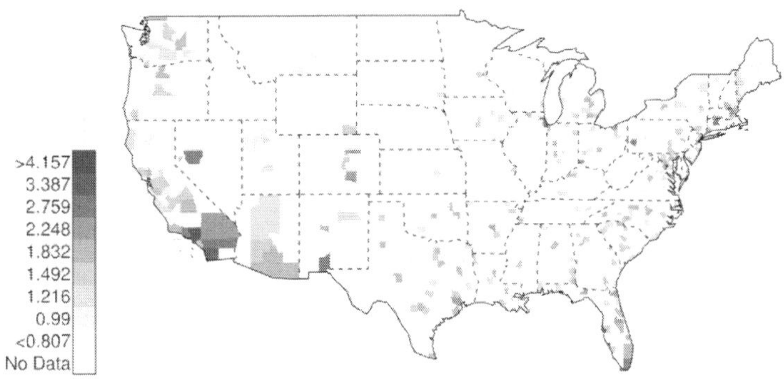

(b)

Figure 5. Posterior Random Effects Estimates: Risk Ratio Hispanic-and-Armed to White-and-Armed. (a) County-by-county posterior estimates of the risk ratio of being {hispanic, armed, and shot by police} to being {white, armed, and shot by police}. Grey bars are county-specific estimates. Grey bars are county-specific 95% PCI estimates. The blue bar is the nation-wide pooled 95% PCI estimate. Data are plotted on the log scale, but are labeled on the natural scale. (b) Map of county-specific posterior median estimates of the risk ratio of being {hispanic, armed, and shot by police} to being {white, armed, and shot by police}.

3. Unarmed and Shot by Police: Across Race/Ethnicity

The median probability across counties of being {black, unarmed, and shot by police} is 3.49(PCI95: 1.77, 6.04) times the probability of being {white, unarmed, and shot by police}. The median probability across counties of being {hispanic, unarmed, and shot by police} is 1.67(PCI95: 0.99, 2.68) times the probability of being {white, unarmed, and shot by police}.

As before, there is extensive variation across counties in the U.S. in these relative risk ratios. Figs 6 and 7 plot the posterior distributions of county-specific risk ratios, as well as the geographic distributions of the estimates. It is notable that Miami-Dade (FL, contains Miami), Los Angeles (CA, contains Los Angeles), and Orleans Parish (LA, contains New Orleans), stand out as counties where the ratio of {black, unarmed, and shot by police} to {white, unarmed, and shot by police} is elevated to 22.88 (PCI95: 6.25, 87.70), 10.25 (PCI95: 2.96, 76.05), and 9.29 (PCI95: 1.88, 105.54) respectively. See Data folder of S1 File for additional county-level results; there are several additional counties with highly elevated levels of racial bias in police shootings not listed here.

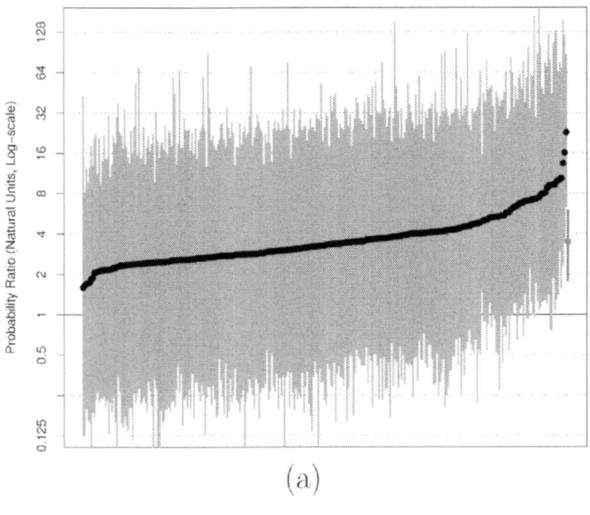

(a)

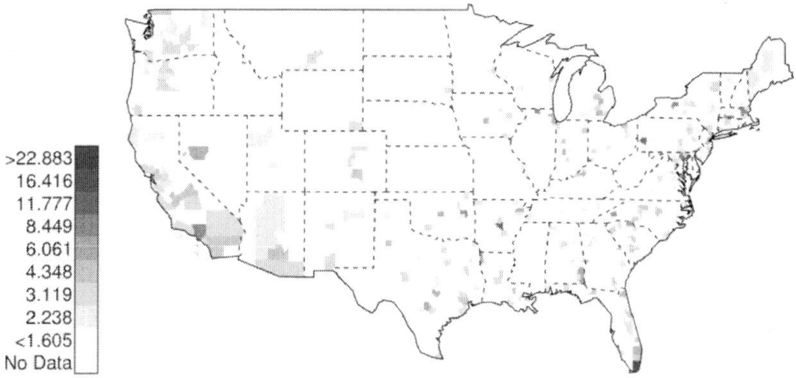

(b)

Figure 6. Posterior Random Effects Estimates: Risk Ratio Black-and-Unarmed to White-and-Unarmed. (a) County-by-county posterior estimates of the risk ratio of being {black, unarmed, and shot by police} to being {white, unarmed, and shot by police}. Grey bars are county-specific 95% PCI estimates. The blue bar is the nation-wide pooled 95% PCI estimate. The points on the error bars are posterior medians. Data are plotted on the log scale, but are labeled on the natural scale. (b) Map of county-specific posterior median estimates of the risk ratio of being {black, unarmed, and shot by police} to being {white, unarmed, and shot by police}.

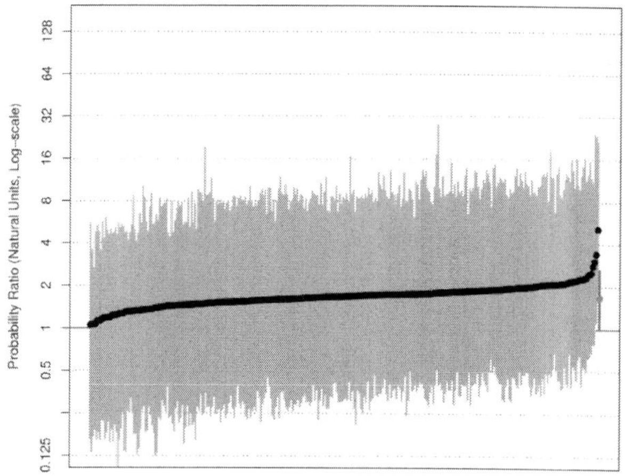

(a)

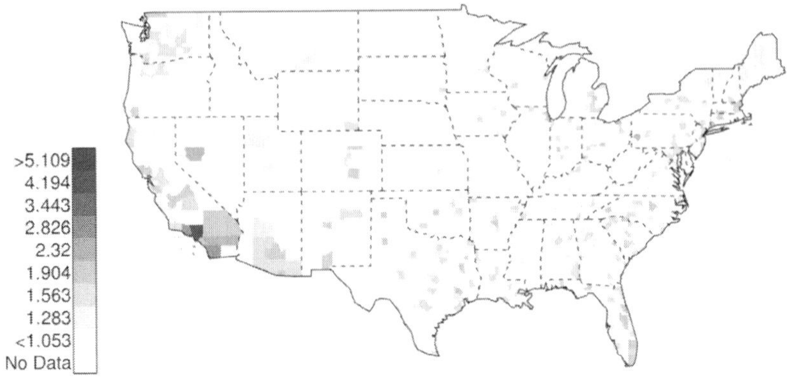

(b)

Figure 7. Posterior Random Effects Estimates: Risk Ratio Hispanic-and-Unarmed to White-and-Unarmed. (a) County-by-county posterior estimates of the risk ratio of being {hispanic, unarmed, and shot by police} to being {white, unarmed, and shot by police}. Grey bars are county-specific 95% PCI estimates. The blue bar is the nation-wide pooled 95% PCI estimate. The points on the error bars are posterior medians. Data are plotted on the log scale, but are labeled on the natural scale. (b) Map of county-specific posterior median estimates of the risk ratio of being {hispanic, unarmed, and shot by police} to being {white, unarmed, and shot by police}.

4. Shot by Police: Race/Ethnicity Across Armed Status

It is worth noting, that on average across counties in the United States, an individual is as likely to be {black, unarmed, and shot by police} as {white, armed, and shot by police}, with a median relative risk estimate of 1.04 (PCI95: 0.62, 1.61). The corresponding ratio for hispanics is 0.52 (PCI95: 0.32, 0.75).

Figs 8 and 9 plot the posterior distributions of county-specific risk ratios, as well as the geographic distributions of the estimates. It is notable that Miami-Dade (FL, contains Miami), Harris (TX, contains Houston), and Cook (IL, contains Chicago), stand out as counties where the ratio of {black, unarmed, and shot by police} to {white, armed, and shot by police} is elevated to 19.08 (PCI95: 4.46, 81.13), 6.71 (PCI95: 1.46, 26.77), and 5.60 (PCI95: 1.25, 21.97) respectively. As before, the Data folder of S1 File shows that there are several other counties with highly elevated relative risk ratios in addition to those discussed above.

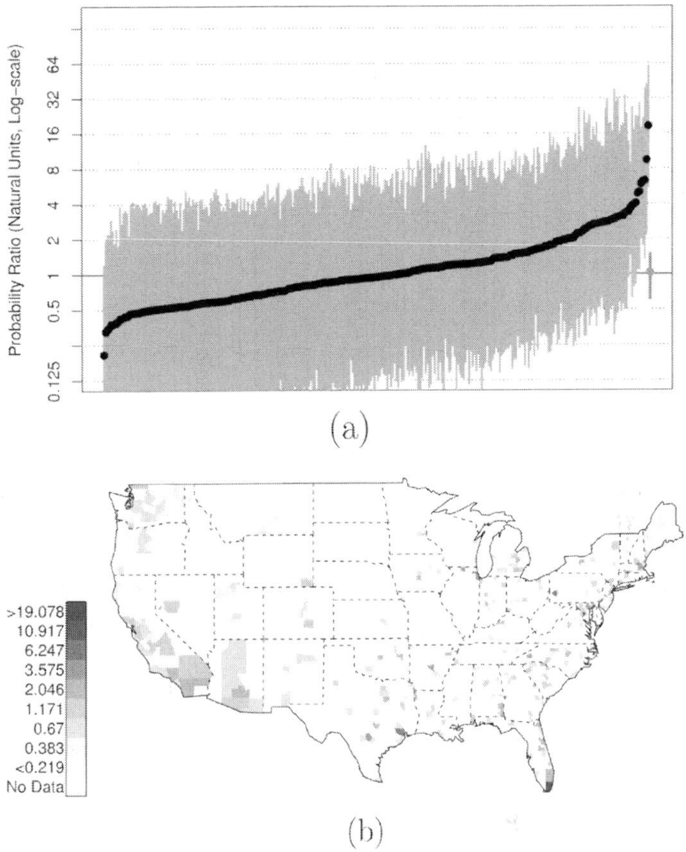

Figure 8. Posterior Random Effects Estimates: Risk Ratio Black-and-Unarmed to White-and-Armed. (a) County-by-county posterior estimates of the risk ratio of being {black, unarmed, and shot by police} to being {white, armed, and shot by police}. Grey bars are county-specific 95% PCI estimates. The blue bar is the nation-wide pooled 95% PCI estimate. The points on the error bars are posterior medians. Data are plotted on the log scale, but are labeled on the natural scale. (b) Map of county-specific posterior median estimates of the risk ratio of being {black, unarmed, and shot by police} to being {white, armed, and shot by police}.

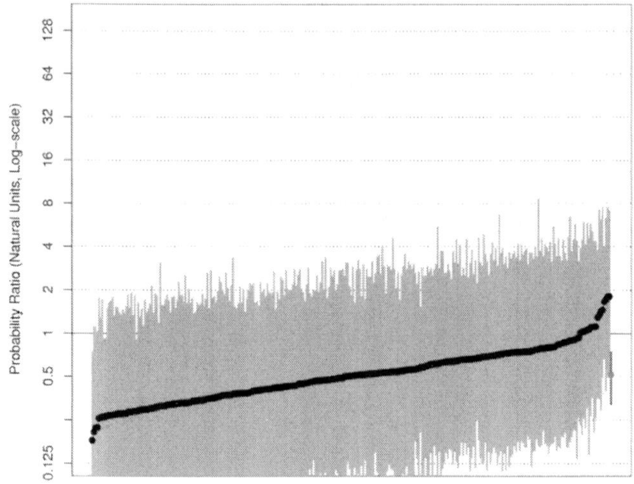

(a)

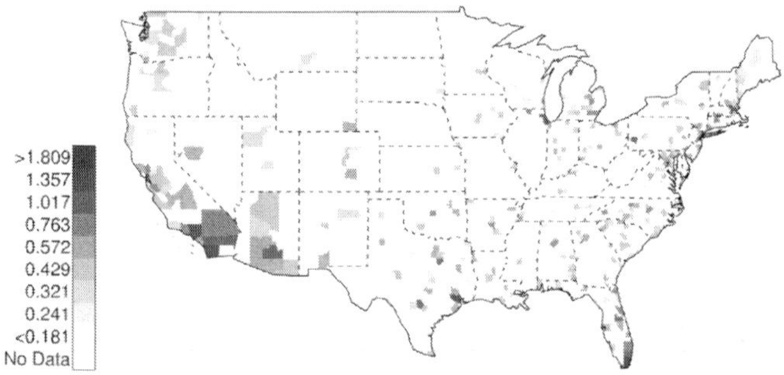

(b)

Figure 9. Posterior Random Effects Estimates: Risk Ratio Hispanic-and-Unarmed to White-and-Armed. (a) County-by-county posterior estimates of the risk ratio of being {hispanic, unarmed, and shot by police} to being {white, armed, and shot by police}. Grey bars are county-specific 95% PCI estimates. The blue bar is the nation-wide pooled 95% PCI estimate. The points on the error bars are posterior medians. Data are plotted on the log scale, but are labeled on the natural scale. (b) Map of county-specific posterior median estimates of the risk ratio of being {hispanic, armed, and shot by police} to being {white, unarmed, and shot by police}.

5. County-Level Racial Bias in Police Shootings as a Function of County-Level Properties

Understanding the source of racial bias in police shootings is difficult to do from county-level data, as the ecological inference fallacy can potentially obscure any results [39]. County-level data are far too coarse to use to reliably tease apart the conditions that drive racial bias in police shootings; more reliable findings will likely be based on rigorous, yet qualitative, investigations that are resolved to a more local level. Nevertheless, previous quantitative studies have used regression models on county-level data to compare theories about the county-level correlates of racial bias in police homicide [15, 35–38]. For comparability, this study uses similar models to analyze the USPSD data, contrasting the predictions from conflict and community violence theories, and testing a hypothesis about the possible association of community-level norms about racism and racial bias in police shooting.

Figs 10, 11, 12, 13, and 14 present the geographic distributions of the predictor variables used in the analysis; the outcome variables are: 1) the risk ratio of {black, unarmed, and shot by police} to {white, unarmed, and shot by police}, and 2) the risk ratio of {black, unarmed, and shot by police} to {white, armed, and shot by police}.

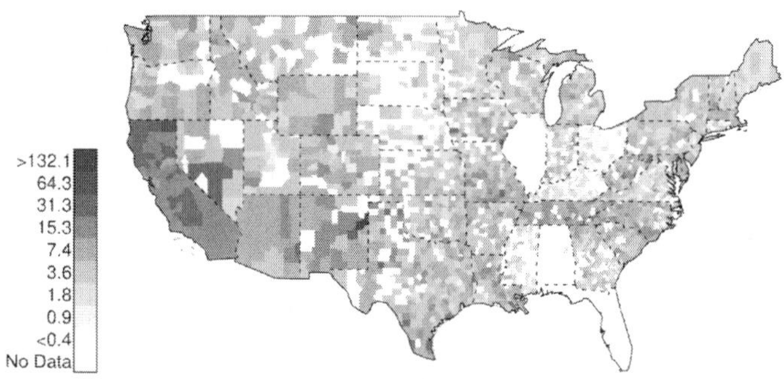

(a)

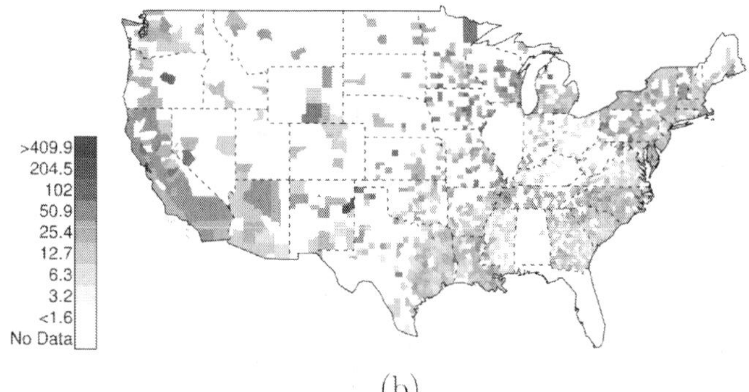

(b)

Figure 10. Data on Race-Specific Assault-Related Arrest Rates. In these figures, only counties with greater than one arrest are plotted. (a) County-specific Department of Justice data on assault-related arrests (White), per 10,000 residents (2012). (b) County-specific Department of Justice data on assault-related arrests (Black), per 10,000 residents (2012).

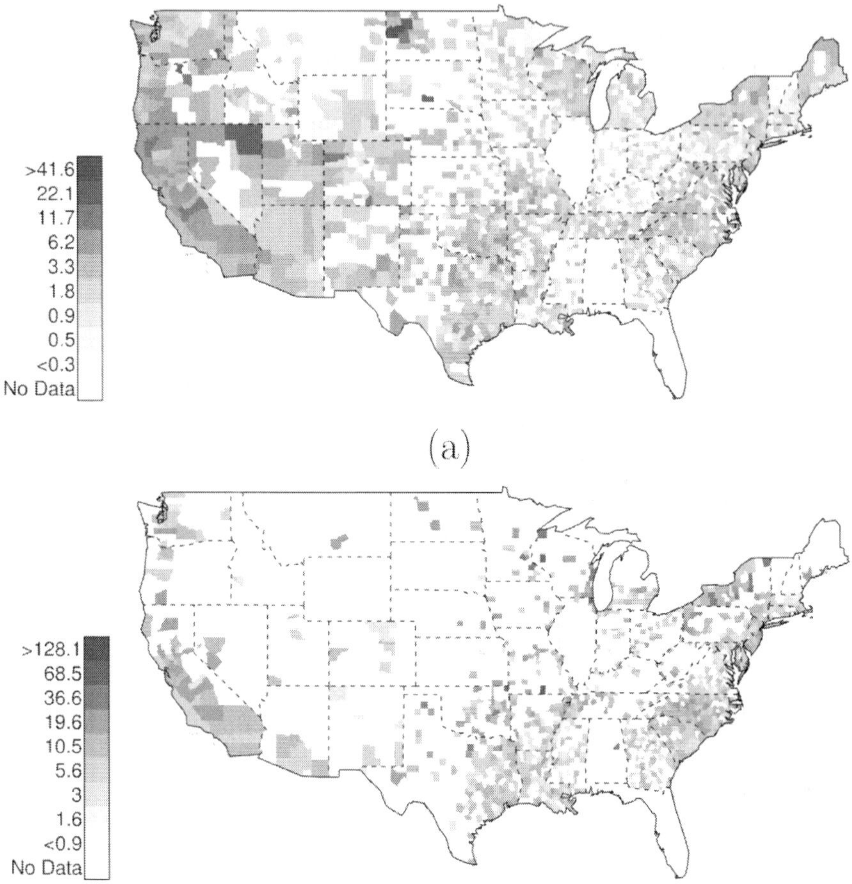

Figure 11. Data on Race-Specific Weapons-Related Arrest Rates. In these figures, only counties with greater than one arrest are plotted. (a) County-specific Department of Justice data on weapons-related arrests (White), per 10,000 residents (2012). (b) County-specific Department of Justice data on weapons-related arrests (Black), per 10,000 residents (2012).

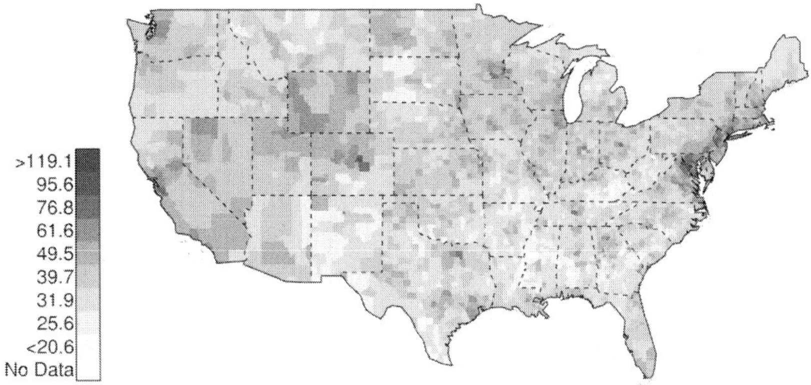

(a)

(b)

Figure 12. AIDSVu Data on Income and Inequality. (a) County-specific data on median income, in $1,000s. (b) County-specific data on inequality (Gini).

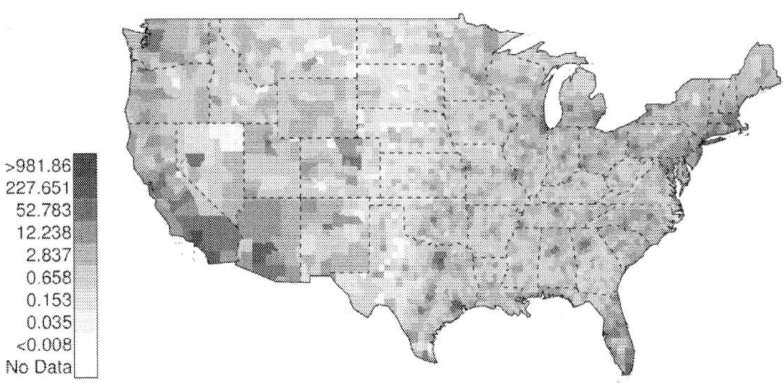

(a)

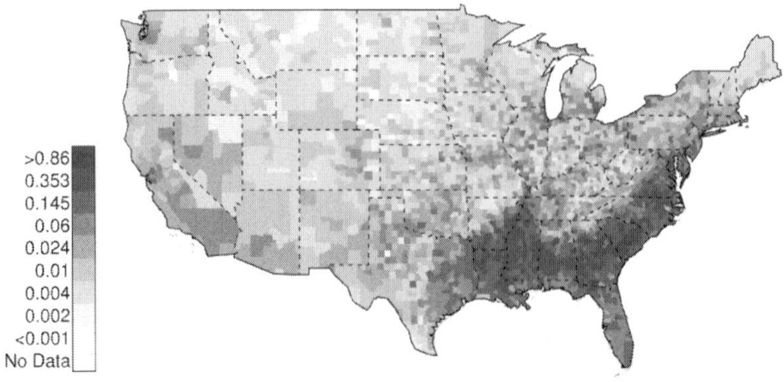

(b)

Figure 13. Population Data. (a) County-specific data on total population size, in 10,000s of residents. (b) County-specific data on the black-to-white population ratio.

(a)

Figure 14. Data on Proxy Measure of Local Norms Concerning Racism. (a) Designated Market Area-specific Google Search Racism Scores, 2004–2007.

Table 1 presents the results of modeling the risk ratio of {black, unarmed, and shot by police} to {white, unarmed, and shot by police}. Across models, there are some consistent trends: 1) population size is positively and reliably associated with the outcome, as is 2) the ratio of the black population size to the white population size; 3) median income shows a reliable negative association with the outcome; 4) the Gini index shows a reliable positive relationship with the outcome; 5) there is a consistently positive, though imprecisely estimated, relationship between the Google search data proxy of local-level racist norms and racial bias in police shooting; and, 6) there is no consistent relationship between the race-specific crime proxies (neither assault-related nor weapons-related arrest rates) and racial bias in police shootings.

Table 1. Predictors of an increased county-level risk of being {black, unarmed, and shot by police} relative to being {white, unarmed, and shot by police}

Model	Intercept	SD	log(Pop.)	log(Pct. B.)	log(Md. In.)	log(Gini)	log (GRP)	log(W. Ast)	log(B. Ast)	log(W. Wps)	log(B. Wps)
M1	1.29 (0.06)	0.07 (0.04)									
M2	1.4 (0.08)	0.07 (0.04)	**0.1 (0.04)								
M3	1.55 (0.13)	0.06 (0.04)	*0.09 (0.06)	0.06 (0.05)							
M4	1.99 (0.4)	0.08 (0.04)	***0.12 (0.05)		*-0.42 (0.28)						
M5	2.4 (0.73)	0.07 (0.04)	0.06 (0.05)			*1.29 (0.94)					
M6	0.53 (1.04)	0.08 (0.04)	**0.1 (0.05)				0.21 (0.25)				
M7	1.41 (0.08)	0.06 (0.04)	**0.1 (0.05)					-0.02 (0.08)	-0.01 (0.09)		
M8	1.39 (0.09)	0.07 (0.03)	**0.1 (0.05)							0.03 (0.07)	0 (0.08)
M9	2.01 (0.21)	0.06 (0.03)	***0.11 (0.04)	**0.05 (0.03)	**-0.35 (0.16)						
M10	2.42 (0.68)	0.07 (0.04)	0.05 (0.05)	0.05 (0.06)		*1.21 (0.91)					
M11	0.79 (1.25)	0.1 (0.03)	**0.08 (0.05)	0.05 (0.06)			0.18 (0.29)				
M12	1.5 (0.13)	0.11 (0.03)	0.06 (0.06)	0.06 (0.05)				-0.01 (0.08)	0.03 (0.09)		
M13	1.51 (0.14)	0.08 (0.03)	*0.07 (0.05)	0.06 (0.06)						0.02 (0.09)	0.01 (0.08)
M14	2.32 (0.61)	0.06 (0.04)	0.08 (0.07)	0.05 (0.06)	-0.27 (0.34)	0.58 (1.01)					
M15	1.8 (1.38)	0.12 (0.03)	**0.1 (0.06)	0.04 (0.07)	-0.38 (0.3)		0.05 (0.29)				
M16	2.02 (0.44)	0.06 (0.04)	**0.1 (0.06)	0.05 (0.05)	-0.37 (0.3)			-0.03 (0.08)	-0.01 (0.08)		
M17	2.07 (0.36)	0.09 (0.03)	*0.08 (0.05)	0.06 (0.05)	**-0.43 (0.26)					0 (0.07)	0.01 (0.08)
M18	1.83 (1.39)	0.08 (0.03)	0.07 (0.06)	0.04 (0.06)		0.99 (0.87)	0.1 (0.28)				
M19	2.26 (0.69)	0.06 (0.04)	0.06 (0.05)	0.04 (0.06)		1 (0.92)		-0.01 (0.09)	0.01 (0.08)		
M20	2.28 (0.67)	0.08 (0.03)	0.05 (0.05)	0.05 (0.06)		1.01 (0.89)				0.01 (0.09)	0 (0.08)
M21	1.39 (1.33)	0.1 (0.03)	**0.1 (0.06)	0.05 (0.06)	-0.33 (0.28)		0.14 (0.29)	-0.02 (0.08)	0.01 (0.07)		
M22	1.59 (1.31)	0.07 (0.03)	**0.1 (0.05)	0.04 (0.06)	-0.36 (0.31)		0.1 (0.28)			0.01 (0.08)	-0.02 (0.08)
M23	1.83 (1.42)	0.11 (0.03)	0.06 (0.05)	0.03 (0.06)		0.98 (0.89)	0.1 (0.28)	-0.02 (0.08)	0.01 (0.08)		
M24	1.68 (1.42)	0.07 (0.04)	0.06 (0.05)	0.03 (0.07)		0.67 (0.89)	0.13 (0.3)			0.02 (0.09)	-0.01 (0.08)
M25	1.62 (1.42)	0.08 (0.04)	*0.06 (0.06)	0.03 (0.07)	-0.27 (0.34)	0.64 (0.99)	0.06 (0.29)	-0.03 (0.09)	0 (0.09)	0.03 (0.1)	-0.02 (0.09)

Values are: posterior mean (posterior standard deviation) of the regression coefficients. The symbol log referes to the natural logarithm. Pop refers to absolute population size. Pct. B. refers to the percentage of the county population that is black. Md. In. refers to median income. Gini refers to the

Gini index of inequality. GRP refers to the Google search racism proxy. W. Ast and B. Ast refer to the white- and black-specific arrest rates for assualt, respectively. W. Wps and B. Wps refer to the white- and black-specific arrest rates for weapons violations, respectively. Posterior probabilty that a postive regression coeffcient is less than zero (or a negative one greater than zero) is coded as: * indicates a probability between 0.10 and 0.05, ** indicates a probability between 0.05 and 0.01, and *** indicates a probability of 0.01 or less.

Table 2 presents the results of modeling the risk ratio of {black, unarmed, and shot by police} to {white, armed, and shot by police}. In this case, there are much more reliable positive effects for: 1) population size, and 2) the ratio of black population size to the white population size. As before, 3) median income shows a negative association with the outcome, and 4) the Gini index shows a positive relationship with the outcome; 5) there is a consistently positive, though imprecisely estimated, relationship between the Google search data proxy of local-level racist norms and racial bias in police shooting; and, 6) there is no consistent relationship between the race-specific crime proxies (neither assault-related nor weapons-related arrest rates) and racial bias in police shootings.

Table 2. Predictors of an increased county-level risk of being {black, unarmed, and shot by police} relative to being {white, armed, and shot by police}

Model	Intercept	SD	log(Pop.)	log(Pct. B.)	log(Md. In.)	log(Gini)	log (GRP)	log(W. Ast)	log(B. Ast)	log(W. Wps)	log(B. Wps)
M1	0.15 (0.07)	0.11 (0.05)									
M2	0.4 (0.08)	0.09 (0.04)	***0.25 (0.05)								
M3	0.64 (0.15)	0.08 (0.05)	***0.21 (0.05)	**0.13 (0.06)							
M4	1.18 (0.43)	0.07 (0.05)	***0.29 (0.05)		**-0.57 (0.3)						
M5	1.78 (0.73)	0.1 (0.04)	***0.21 (0.05)			**1.77 (0.93)					
M6	-0.84 (1.15)	0.09 (0.04)	***0.25 (0.05)				0.3 (0.28)				
M7	0.41 (0.08)	0.07 (0.05)	***0.25 (0.05)					-0.07 (0.1)	-0.01 (0.1)		
M8	0.38 (0.1)	0.08 (0.05)	***0.25 (0.05)							0.01 (0.11)	0.03 (0.09)
M9	1.17 (0.44)	0.09 (0.05)	***0.24 (0.06)	**0.11 (0.06)	-0.39 (0.32)						
M10	1.6 (0.72)	0.08 (0.04)	***0.19 (0.06)	*0.1 (0.06)		*1.29 (0.94)					
M11	0.09 (1.26)	0.08 (0.04)	***0.21 (0.05)	*0.11 (0.07)			0.13 (0.29)				

Model	Intercept	SD	log(Pop.)	log(Pct. B.)	log(Md. In.)	log(Gini)	log (GRP)	log(W. Ast)	log(B. Ast)	log(W. Wps)	log(B. Wps)
M12	0.65 (0.15)	0.09 (0.04)	***0.21 (0.05)	**0.12 (0.06)				-0.06 (0.09)	0.02 (0.1)		
M13	0.62 (0.14)	0.08 (0.05)	***0.2 (0.05)	**0.12 (0.06)						0 (0.1)	0.04 (0.09)
M14	1.69 (0.69)	0.08 (0.04)	***0.21 (0.06)	*0.1 (0.07)	-0.3 (0.35)	0.88 (1.04)					
M15	0.93 (1.41)	0.09 (0.05)	***0.24 (0.06)	*0.1 (0.07)	-0.39 (0.33)		0.06 (0.3)				
M16	1.29 (0.45)	0.09 (0.04)	***0.26 (0.07)	*0.09 (0.07)	*-0.49 (0.32)			-0.07 (0.1)	0 (0.09)		
M17	1.22 (0.47)	0.08 (0.04)	***0.24 (0.06)	**0.11 (0.06)	*-0.43 (0.33)					-0.02 (0.1)	0.02 (0.09)
M18	1.54 (1.56)	0.11 (0.04)	***0.18 (0.06)	*0.09 (0.07)		*1.4 (0.96)	0.03 (0.31)				
M19	1.6 (0.75)	0.08 (0.04)	***0.19 (0.06)	*0.09 (0.07)		*1.29 (0.99)		-0.06 (0.09)	0 (0.1)		
M20	1.62 (0.72)	0.12 (0.04)	***0.18 (0.05)	*0.1 (0.07)		*1.33 (0.95)				0 (0.1)	0.03 (0.09)
M21	0.97 (1.46)	0.09 (0.05)	***0.25 (0.06)	*0.09 (0.07)	*-0.46 (0.33)		0.07 (0.31)	-0.06 (0.09)	-0.02 (0.1)		
M22	0.96 (1.54)	0.11 (0.04)	***0.24 (0.06)	*0.11 (0.07)	-0.41 (0.33)		0.06 (0.33)			-0.01 (0.1)	0.01 (0.09)
M23	1.39 (1.54)	0.12 (0.03)	***0.19 (0.06)	*0.09 (0.07)		1.2 (0.98)	0.04 (0.31)	-0.06 (0.1)	0.01 (0.1)		
M24	1.35 (1.55)	0.1 (0.04)	***0.19 (0.06)	*0.1 (0.07)		*1.24 (0.93)	0.05 (0.31)			0.01 (0.1)	0.03 (0.09)
M25	1.55 (1.58)	0.08 (0.04)	***0.22 (0.06)	0.08 (0.07)	-0.3 (0.38)	0.86 (1.08)	0.03 (0.31)	-0.07 (0.11)	-0.02 (0.11)	0.03 (0.1)	0.02 (0.1)

Values are: posterior mean (posterior standard deviation) of the regression coefficients. The symbol log referes to the natural logarithm. Pop refers to absolute population size. Pct. B. refers to the percentage of the county population that is black. Md. In. refers to median income. Gini refers to the Gini index of inequality. GRP refers to the Google search racism proxy. W. Ast and B. Ast refer to the white- and black-specific arrest rates for assualt, respectively. W. Wps and B. Wps refer to the white- and black-specific arrest rates for weapons violations, respectively. Posterior probabilty that a postive regression coeffcient is less than zero (or a negative one greater than zero) is coded as: * indicates a probability between 0.10 and 0.05, ** indicates a probability between 0.05 and 0.01, and *** indicates a probability of 0.01 or less.

In effect, larger county population size, a higher proportion of black residents in the population, lower median income, and greater disparities in income all appear to be reliably associated with an elevated ratio of police shooting rate against unarmed black individuals relative to unarmed—and even armed—whites.

In each model that considers them, race-specific crime rates are always entered as simultaneous predictors (see Tables 1 and 2). This model parameterization allows us to examine the effects of race-specific crime rates on racial bias in police shootings. However, there are questions that this model parameterization precludes. Most importantly, having an aggregated measure of crime rate would allow one to test the questions: 1) does racial bias in police shooting increase in areas where crime is generally more prevalent? And, 2) as the difference of black crime rate minus white crime rate increases, does racial bias in police shootings also increase?

As a robustness check, the results from two alternative model parameterizations in predicting the relative risk of being {unarmed, black, and shot by police} to being {unarmed, white, and shot by police} are presented. These models are based on including the sum and difference of race-specific crime rates in the regression; see Appendix.pdf in S1 File. The results of these supplementary models are qualitatively the same as those of the main models; racial bias in police shooting is not reliably associated with crime rate and not related to the difference in race-specific crime rates.

DISCUSSION

It is important to reiterate that these risk ratios come only from the sample of individuals who were shot by police and census data on race/ethnicity-specific population information. The USPSD does not have information on encounter rates between police and subjects according to ethnicity. As such, the data cannot speak to the relative risk of being shot by a police officer conditional on being encountered by police, and do not give us a direct window into the psychology of the officers who are pulling the triggers. The racial biases and behaviors of officers upon encountering a suspect could clearly be components of the relative risk effects observed in the data, but other social factors could also contribute to the observed patterns in the data. More specifically, heterogeneity in encounter rates between suspects and police as a function of race could play a strong role in the racial biases in shooting rates presented here.

Shot by Police: Armed Versus Unarmed

At face value, the data suggest that conditional on being of a given race/ethnicity and being shot by police, one was more-likely-than-not to be armed. It is interesting to note that the armed-to-unarmed risk ratio in whites is elevated relative to that of black or hispanic individuals (especially in a handful of outlier counties, see Data folder in S1 File). This pattern is consistent with police being more discerning of armed/unarmed status before shooting a white suspect than shooting a black or hispanic suspect.

At a broader level, conditional on being shot by police, the probability ratio of being armed rather than unarmed averages around 3 to 1, with variation depending on race/ethnicity and location. While it is true that vast majority of police contacts are presumably with unarmed people, and that police shoot only a small fraction of the unarmed people they encounter, the public, and even some police chiefs, still lament that the use of deadly force is probably avoidable in a non-negligible portion of police shootings, if for no other reason than the fact that the suspects/civilians are unarmed.

Chief of Police Chris Magnus of the Richmond Police Department in California, for example, details many ways in which use of force by police officers can be attenuated, while increasing the safety of both the officers and public [40]. Magnus argues that police often do not come from or live in the communities they police, and placement is not necessarily random—police can request the kinds of environments they prefer, even if such placements are not beneficial to the community; for example, underlying racial biases could lead certain kinds of white police officers to request work in predominately black neighborhoods. Magnus suggests that a way around creating conflicts of interest between the community and the police involves thinking:

"... about what kind of folks you want to attract to your department, and how you do that. You look at some departments' recruiting materials, and you see guys jumping out of trucks in SWAT gear and people armed with every imaginable weapon... My goal, at least, is to look for people who want to work in my community, not because it's a place where they think they're going to be dealing with a lot of violence and hot chases and armed individuals and excitement and an episode of Cops or something... I want them to be here because they're interested in building a partnership with the community" [40].

Following Magnus' line of logic, one might expect that some of the racial bias in police killings, as well as the rate of shooting unarmed civilians, could be attenuated by requiring police departments to adopt hiring and policing practices like those being used successfully in Richmond, where no civilians (armed or unarmed) were killed by police for more than five years in spite of Richmond having a large population size (107,000) [40].

Shot by Police: Across Race/Ethnicity

Across almost all counties, individuals who were armed and shot by police had a much higher probability of being black or hispanic than being white. Likewise, across almost all counties, individuals who were unarmed and shot by police had a much higher probability of being black or hispanic than being white. Tragically, across a large proportion of counties, individuals who were shot by police had a higher median probability of being unarmed black individuals than being armed white individuals. While this pattern could be explained by reduced levels of crime being committed by armed white individuals, it still raises a question as to why there exists such a high rate of police shooting of unarmed black individuals.

The posterior estimates of the relative risk ratios as a function race and armed/unarmed status are included for all counties in the Data folder of S1 File. From this data, one can identify the counties and police departments where racial bias in shooting rates is strongest. Counties like Miami-Dade (FL), Cook (IL), Los Angeles (CA), Orleans Parish (LA), Pulaski (AR), Harris (TX), Baltimore (MD), and Allegheny (PA), stand out as departments where police protocols may benefit from review.

County-Level Predictors of Racial Bias in Police Shooting

In predicting the risk ratio of {black, unarmed, and shot by police} to {white, unarmed, and shot by police}, there are effects of county-level population size, racial composition, median income, and Gini score. In predicting the risk ratio of {black, unarmed, and shot by police} to {white, armed, and shot by police}, there are more reliable effects for these same variables. These findings suggest that racial bias in police shootings is most common among police working in larger metropolitan counties with low median incomes and a sizable portion of black residents, especially when there is high financial inequality in that county. These results are consistent with much of the previous work outlined in the introduction.

It is sometimes suggested that in urban areas with more black residents and higher levels of inequality, individuals may be more likely to commit violent crime, and thus the racial bias in police shooting may be explainable as a proximate response by police to areas of high violence and crime (community violence theory [14, 15, 23, 35]). In other words, if the environment is such that race and crime covary, police shooting ratios may show signs of racial bias, even if it is crime, not race, that is the causal driver of police shootings. In the models fit in this study, however, there is no evidence of an association between black-specific crime rates (neither in assault-related arrests nor in weapons-related arrests) and racial bias in police shootings, irrespective of whether or not other controls were included in the model. As such, the results of this study provide no empirical support for the idea that racial bias in police shootings (in the time period, 2011–2014, described in this study) is driven by race-specific crime rates (at least as measured by the proxies of assault- and weapons-related arrest rates in 2012).

The methodology used in this paper does not allow one to speak with confidence as to the causal drivers of racial bias in police shooting; the source of racial bias in police shootings, however, can be logically decomposed into two parts: 1) racial bias in encounter rates between police and suspects/civilians, and/or 2) racial bias in use of force upon encountering these suspects/civilians. A racial bias in encounter rates could be unjustifiable (police engage in racist or ethnic targeting of blacks/hispanics irrespective of suspected criminal activity) or a proportional response to local-level, race/ethnicity-specific, crime rates. Under the assumptions that police express no racial bias in use of force upon encountering suspects/civilians, and also engage in interactions with suspects/civilians in direct proportion to race/ethnicity-specific crime rates (where crime rates covary with race/ethnicity), one would expect to see an association between racial bias in police shootings and race-specific crime rates—an association that is not found in these results. As such, the results of this study provide evidence that there is racial bias in police shootings that is not explainable as a response to local-level crime rates, and is related to either: 1) racial bias in police encountering suspects/civilians, or 2) racial bias by police in the use of force upon encountering suspects/civilians.

The geographically-resolved proxy of racial animus used in this study, however, did not show a reliable association with racial bias in police shootings, although the association was consistently positive across models. This finding does not rule out the possibility that racist norms within police departments themselves may potentially have much stronger associations with racial bias in police shootings than these more coarse ecological-level data. Many police, or former police, report of—or have been documented to engage in promotion of—extensive racist norms (e.g. see [41–49], and note that this list is far from exhaustive). Acquiring more systematic data on the extent of racist norms within police departments (as opposed to the counties in which they are clustered) will require more thorough qualitative and quantitative investigations of police departments themselves.

Conclusions and Future Directions

Completing the Police Shootings Database

While the USPSD already contains almost 2,000 records of police shootings, as many as 55% of the days to be screened for police shootings have yet to be scoured for incidents. While the currently available data are sufficient to investigate risk ratios across racial/ethnic categories, estimation of the absolute risk of being shot by police requires the completed data set. Furthermore, the completed data and absolute risk estimates will help to identify the departments and officers with disproportionately high: 1) absolute shooting rates, 2) rates of shooting unarmed civilians, and 3) rates of racially-biased shootings. Although an increased completeness of the data is unlikely to change the estimated mean effects presented in this analysis, since the sample used herein is a large and random subset of the to-be-completed data set, more data will allow for more precise estimates at the county-level, and may expand the number of counties that can be modeled at the ecological-level.

After data collection is complete, all new entries still require verification and archival of the primary sources of information. As with the data collection process until now, this phase of the project will require assistance from the public.

As new data are fact-checked and verified, it might be possible to expand the scope of variables included in the database. For instance, a qualitative assessment could be provided, indicating whether the shooting was clearly justified (for example, a lethal police response was immediately necessary and unavoidable to protect the lives of innocents), clearly unjustified (for example, a suspect was shot in the back while restrained, as was the case in the execution of Oscar Grant III [50]), or somewhere in between. To mitigate bias, the coding could be conducted by several individuals, and the suite of all responses could be used to construct confidence in the assessment.

Likewise, data could be classified on the basis of more direct empirical evidence. For example: was the suspect shot in the back? Was the suspect restrained when shot? Also, what were the circumstances surrounding the shooting? Were police called on report of a serious crime? Was the situation escalated by police prior to shooting? Does the race/ethnicity of a suspect vary by the circumstance surrounding the shooting? What was the race/ethnicity of the shooter? Are police more likely to escalate a situation when the suspect is black?

More Detailed Analysis of the Data

More detailed analysis of the data is needed. In the current analysis, county-specific risk ratios are estimated. In the future, these estimates could be extended in a Bayesian framework to include estimates unique to police departments, as clustered into counties, as clustered into states.

The analyses presented here are only a very rough first pass through the data. As the data become more complete, more nuance in analysis is needed. The estimated levels of unjustifiable racial bias in police shootings will likely change when reliable estimates of justification are included in the analysis, and when spatial correlations and ecological covariates are formally included in the model being used to estimate risk ratios.

In this paper, the relationship between race/ethnicity and status of a civilian/suspect as armed or unarmed on the relative probability of being shot by police is investigated, but there are differences between the categories of armed/unarmed and justified/unjustified, which should be taken into account in future research.

Higher Quality Covariate Data is Needed

Ecological regression on county-level characteristics is plagued by difficulties theoretically [39, 51]; issues with data quality make it even harder to use county-level data. In the analysis of county-level predictors of racial bias in police shootings conducted in this paper, some of the data were low quality. Notably, the crime data may be biased by the reporting practices of the police, and Florida, Alabama, and Illinois failed to fully release data, which led to the use Bayesian imputation for counties in these states.

Towards Attenuation of Racial Bias in Police Violence

Hopefully, a more transparent representation of police homicide and shooting data as a function of: 1) the race/ethnicity of suspects/civilians, 2) the status of suspects/civilians as armed/unarmed, and 3) the geographic location of the incidents will help the public, academic researchers, and federal agencies to better evaluate the practices of police in the United States. In addition to assisting in the testing hypotheses related to the structural drivers of racial bias in police homicide across the nation, these data can be used to justify more in-depth qualitative investigations by academics, journalists, and watchdog organizations of the subset of police jurisdictions with the most racially-biased police shooting rates.

Such in-depth investigations may help to identify the locally contextualized causes of racial bias in police homicide. Critically important in evaluating attenuation (or lack thereof) of racial bias in police violence are time series data on the extent of racial bias at the local level; hopefully, continued enthusiasm for citizen driven data collection will provide researchers with the data needed to study and publish results documenting temporal trends in racial bias in police shootings.

Much traditional academic work on the topic of police violence has focused on comparison of multiple theoretical causes as listed earlier. However, it is likely that all of the above-listed causes contribute to police shootings, but that the relative weight of each potential driver of racialized police violence may be heterogeneous over geography and time [52, 53]. As such, it may be valuable to transition from focusing on questions like: "What explains the racial bias in police shootings?" to questions like: "What explains the racial bias of police shootings in Miami-Dade county in 2011–2014?".

Attenuating the racial bias in police shootings in a given location requires a better understanding of the drivers of racial bias operating in that location. Databases like the USPSD cannot directly provide answers to such questions, but they can help identify where more detailed ethnographic investigations should be conducted. Perhaps police departments with disproportionate rates of racially-biased police homicide can provide justification for these patterns based on local context, or perhaps they are headed by individuals like Police Commander Jon Burge—the public needs to know which.

METHODS

Data

U.S. Police Shootings Data

Data on police shootings were accessed in December 2014, from the U.S. Police Shootings Database [1] compiled by Kyle Wagner. The data can be accessed and improved at http://goo.gl/Su60Cm.

From the total set of police shooting data, records were selected only when: 1) a suspect's status as either armed or unarmed was clearly described (sometimes by searching for subsequent media reports), 2) a suspect's race/ethnicity could be clearly assigned, 3) the year of the shooting was no earlier than 2011 and no later than 2014, and 4) a county name could be assigned. The data were then error-checked by removing listings for the same suspect/victim name; duplicates under spelling variations of suspect/victim name were found and eliminated by checking for multiple cases of police shootings with the same victim year, age, race/ethnicity, and county.

In total, 721 cases of police shootings were analyzed. About five percent (N = 35) of records were randomly spot-checked by using a random number generator to sort the cleaned Excel file containing the data; the urls cited in the USPSD were then checked to ensure validity of the data. In each case the urls were valid (but see below) and the data accurately described. In a small number of cases (N = 3) the original url returned an error and www.archive.org was used to retrieve the original web-page, which, in each case, was archived under the url provided in the USPSD and included a full event description. The raw data of the USPSD in its entirety can be found at http://goo.gl/QrylkY. Additionally, the cleaned data modeled in this paper are included in the the Data folder of S1 File. Finally, county-level raw data, covariates, and modeling results are included in the Data folder of S1 File in a geographically resolved format linked to a shapefile that can be used for geographic data visualization in the R software environment.

Methodologically, users are asked to adhere to the following protocol in data collection (see [1], direct quotation follows):

- Using Google's search tools, isolate a single day (e.g. Jan. 1, 2011, to Jan. 1, 2011) and search for the term "police involved shooting" (don't use quotation marks). Use Chrome's Incognito mode when searching to ensure you aren't getting local results.
- Read each link on the first 10 pages of results; for any instances of shootings involving a police officer, log them in the form.
- We're looking at 2011, 2012, [2013 and 2014], and tracking date, name, age, gender, race/ethnicity, injured/killed, and a number of other fields. Please be as thorough as possible with each incident, and provide links to where you found the information (this will be crucial during verification). Often, the first day of reports will not have personal details, and a second search of subsequent days will fill in more of the story.
- Before starting in, take a look at the submissions here and pick a day that no one has begun ("Not Checked" in the third sheet). Remember, we're starting off by looking at just the past three years.
- A later death, after a person is hospitalized in a police-involved shooting, is considered a death for our purposes.
- We are looking for any incidence of a police officer shooting and hitting another person. This can be off-duty if the officer was acting in a law-enforcement capacity.

- We are not looking for incidences of police officers discharging their weapons and hitting no one. In a perfect world these would be tracked, since often the only difference is that the shot missed, but these incidents are not as thoroughly reported and would probably bias the data.
- Please keep the data as neat as possible. Work within specific months, make sure you're in the correct year, keep the columns clean, add peripheral information in the "Summary" portion, etc.

Census and Covariate Data

County-level census population data and county-level covariates on income and inequality were accessed from AIDSvu [54], an open access database available through the Rollins School of Public Health at Emory University.

Google Racial Animus Data

The racial animus data were generously provided by Seth Stephens-Davidowitz [29] at the level of the DMA (designated market area), and were translated to county-level data using FIPS codes and a cross-walk provided by the ICPSR at http://www.icpsr.umich.edu/icpsrweb/DSDR/studies/22720.

Crime Rate Data

Race-specific assault- and weapons-related arrest data compiled by the United States Department of Justice were accessed from the Inter-University Consortium for Political and Social Research [55]. Arrests were summed within counties.

Geographic Data

Geographic shapefiles were downloaded from GADM [56], an open access database of Global Administrative Areas.

Bayesian Modeling

Estimating Risk Ratios for Police Shooting as a Function of Race and Arms Status

County-level police shooting rates are estimated using binomial probabilities, and a prior, estimated from the data, under hierarchical partial pooling.

Hierarchical pooling allows information collected in other counties within the United States to partially inform the parameter estimates in a focal county, which improves out-of-sample predictive inference globally [57], and regularizes otherwise undefined posterior predictive risk ratios. Prior to the introduction of multi-level modeling methods, relative risk ratios at local levels were very hard to infer. For example, if no unarmed whites but three unarmed black individuals were killed in a county, the estimated relative risk ratio would be:

$$\frac{\frac{3}{N^B_{[c]}}}{\frac{0}{N^W_{[c]}}} = \frac{\text{constant}}{0}$$

yielding some undefined relative risk ratio. The multi-level Bayesian methods used here, partially (rather than fully) pool information across counties, allowing for more stable estimates in relative risk ratios (by regularizing the denominator of the above equation away from zero and toward the global mean for that value), while still allowing for, and representing, heterogeneity across counties.

To begin the model, the race-specific probabilities of being shot by police at the county-level are estimated under two conditions (armed and unarmed), in all counties with at least a single incidence of a police-involved shooting between the years of 2011–2014. These probabilities are then used to estimate the relative risk of being the victim of a police shooting, conditional on being armed or unarmed, and race/ethnicity.

For example, the probability, $\theta^{B,U}_{[c]}$, in county c of a black (B) and unarmed (U) individual being shot by police can be estimated from the county-level census data, $N^B_{[c]}$, and the count of shootings, $S^{B,U}_{[c]}$, as:

$$S^{B,U}_{[c]} \sim \text{Binomial}(N^B_{[c]}, \theta^{B,U}_{[c]}) \tag{1}$$

Eq (1) serves as a template for each of the main probability statements in the model, where a probability unique to the interaction of race/ethnicity (B = black, H = hispanic, and W = white) and arms status (A = armed and U = unarmed) is estimated. Note that superscripts are labels, and do not indicate exponentiation. The subsequent main probability statements run as follows:

$$S^{B,A}_{[c]} \sim \text{Binomial}(N^B_{[c]}, \theta^{B,A}_{[c]}) \tag{2}$$

$$S_{[c]}^{H,U} \sim \text{Binomial}(N_{[c]}^{H}, \theta_{[c]}^{H,U}) \quad (3)$$
$$S_{[c]}^{H,A} \sim \text{Binomial}(N_{[c]}^{H}, \theta_{[c]}^{H,A}) \quad (4)$$
$$S_{[c]}^{W,U} \sim \text{Binomial}(N_{[c]}^{W}, \theta_{[c]}^{W,U}) \quad (5)$$
$$S_{[c]}^{W,A} \sim \text{Binomial}(N_{[c]}^{W}, \theta_{[c]}^{W,A}) \quad (6)$$

Thus, in each county, there are D = 6 probability parameters to be estimated. These parameters are organized into a vector:

$$\theta_{[c]} = (\theta_{[c]}^{B,U}, \theta_{[c]}^{B,A}, \theta_{[c]}^{H,U}, \theta_{[c]}^{H,A}, \theta_{[c]}^{W,U}, \theta_{[c]}^{W,A})' \quad (7)$$

The probability parameter vector $\theta_{[c]} \in (0,1)^D$ is transformed to a parameter vector on the unconstrained scale $\Theta_{[c]} \in \mathbb{R}^D$ using an inverse logit transformation:

$$\theta_{[c]} = \frac{e^{\Theta_{[c]}}}{1 + e^{\Theta_{[c]}}} \quad (8)$$

Then, vectors unique to each county c, are estimated from a higher-level distribution in a multi-level Bayesian framework:

$$\Theta_{[c]} \sim \text{Multivariate Normal Cholesky}(\mu, L) \quad (9)$$

The Cholesky factor, L, of the model's covariance matrix is formed from Cholesky decomposition of the correlation matrix ρ multiplied by a diagonal matrix of scale parameters, σ:

$$L = \text{Diag}(\sigma) \times \text{Cholesky Decompose}(\rho) \quad (10)$$

Each element of the mean vector, μ, is given a weakly regularizing normal prior:

$$\mu \sim \text{Normal}(-14, 4) \quad (11)$$

which places weakly regularizing prior support over the plausible range of values on the probability scale. Each element of the scale vector, σ, is given a vague half-Cauchy prior:

$$\sigma \sim \text{Cauchy}(0, 5)T[0, \infty] \quad (12)$$

The correlation matrix is given an implicit uniform prior over its support. The parameters of the model are estimated using Hamiltonian Markov Chain Monte Carlo simulation, implemented in the Stan version 2.5 C++ library [58].

The raw probability estimates at the county-level are surely underestimates, because the U.S. Police Shootings Database has still only documented a fraction of the police shootings since 2011. However, since the data are collected by users selecting a given day, and then recording information on police shootings documented on that day, the data are randomly collected with respect to the suspect's race/ethnicity, location, and status as armed versus unarmed. As such, the relative risk ratios of U.S. citizens to police shooting as a function of race/ethnicity, location, or armed status should not be especially biased. Relative risk ratios are notated as below:

$$R_{[c]}^{\substack{B,U \\ W,U}} = \frac{\theta_{[c]}^{B,U}}{\theta_{[c]}^{W,U}} \quad (13)$$

The symbol $R_{[c]}^{\substack{B,U \\ W,U}}$ reads as: "The relative risk in county c of being black, unarmed, and shot by police, to being white, unarmed, and shot by police."

Modeling Risk Ratios for Police Shooting as a Function of County-Level Covariates.

In each county, the relevant risk ratio, $R_{[c]}$, is modeled as a function of county-level covariates. To begin the model, each posterior sample of $R_{[c]}$ from the above described Bayesian model is log-transformed and the distribution is summarized by calculating the mean, $\mu_{R[c]} = \text{mean}(\log(R_{[c]}))$, and standard deviation, $\sigma_{R[c]} = \text{sd}(\log(R_{[c]}))$ over the MCMC samples. Uncertainty about these estimates is propagated using a Bayesian measurement error model:

$$Y_{[c]} \sim \text{Normal}(\mu_{R_{[c]}}, \sigma_{R_{[c]}}) \quad (14)$$

$$Y_{[c]} \sim \text{Normal}(\mu_{[c]}, \sigma) \quad (15)$$

where $\mu_{[c]}$ is defined for several candidate models (M1, M2, … M25), using a standard regression equation. The most basic, intercept only, model is defined as:

$$\text{I1}, \ \mu_{[c]} = {}_{\prime} \quad (16)$$

and various, increasingly complex, multivariate models are fit, up to the most complex:

$$\begin{aligned} \text{M25}, \ \mu_{[c]} &= \beta_1 + \beta_2 \log(N_{[c]}) + \beta_3 \log(P_{[c]}) + \beta_4 \log(I_{[c]}) + \beta_5 \log(G_{[c]}) + \beta_6 \log(H_{[c]}) \\ &\quad + \beta_7 \log(A_{[c]}^{W}) + \beta_8 \log(A_{[c]}^{B}) + \beta_9 \log(W_{[c]}^{W}) + \beta_{10} \log(W_{[c]}^{B}) \end{aligned} \quad (17)$$

where: $N_{[c]}$ is the total population in county c, $P_{[c]}$ is the percentage of black individuals in county c, $I_{[c]}$ is the median income of county c, $G_{[c]}$ is the Gini coefficient of county c, $H_{[c]}$ is the Google search data proxy for racist norms in county c, $A_{[c]}^{W}$ and $A_{[c]}^{B}$ are the assault-related arrest rates for whites and blacks, respectively, in county c, and $W_{[c]}^{W}$ and $W_{[c]}^{B}$ are the weapons-related arrest rates for whites and blacks, respectively, in county c. The covariates included in models M2–M24 are indicated in Tables 1 and 2 in the Results section.

Each element of the regression parameter vector is given a vague prior:

$$\beta \sim \text{Cauchy}(0, 5) \quad (18)$$

and the scale parameter is given a weakly regularizing prior:

$$\sigma \sim \text{Exponetial}(1) \quad (19)$$

ACKNOWLEDGMENTS

I would like to thank the editor and four anonymous reviewers for thorough commentary, feedback, and suggestions that improved the quality of this paper. Bruce Winterhalder and Sheryl Gerety provided additional guidance and suggestions, and helped edit the paper.

AUTHOR CONTRIBUTIONS

Conceived and designed the experiments: CR. Performed the experiments: CR. Analyzed the data: CR. Contributed reagents/materials/analysis tools: CR. Wrote the paper: CR.

REFERENCES

1. Kyle Wagner. U.S. Police Shootings Database, http://goo.gl/Su60Cm; 2014.
2. Klinger DA. On the Problems and Promise of Research on Lethal Police Violence: A Research Note. Homicide Studies. 2012;16(1):78.
3. U S Department of Justice, Federal Bureau of Investigation. Supplementary Homicide Report (OMB Form No. 1110–0002); 2014.
4. Centers for Disease Control and Prevention. National Vital Statistics System; 2014.
5. Gabrielson R, Grochowski Jones R, Sagara E. Deadly Force, in Black and White: A Pro Publica analysis of killings by police shows outsize risk for young black males. Pro Publica. 2014;.
6. United Nations Committee Against Torture. Concluding observations on the third to fifth periodic reports of United States of America. United Nations. 2014;.
7. Stolen Lives Project. Stolen Lives: Killed by law enforcement, www.stolenlives.org; 1999.
8. Brian Burghart. Fatal Encounters: A step toward creating an impartial, comprehensive and searchable national database of people killed during interactions with law enforcement, www.fatalencounters.org; 2014.
9. Killed By Police. www.killedbypolice.net; 2015.
10. The National Police Violence Map. www.mappingpoliceviolence.org; 2015.
11. Wikipedia. http://en.wikipedia.org/wiki/List_of_killings_by_law_enforcement_officers_in_the_United_States; 2015.
12. The Washington Post. Fatal police shootings in 2015 approaching 400 nationwide; 2015.
13. The Guardian. The Counted: People killed by police in the US, http://www.theguardian.com/us-news/series/counted-us-police-killings; 2015.
14. Jacobs D. The Determinants of Deadly Force: A Structural Analysis of Police Violence. American Journal of Sociology. 1998;103(4):837–862.
15. Smith BW. The Impact of Police Officer Diversity on Police-Caused Homicides. Policy Studies Journal. 2003;31(2):147–162.

16. Bergesen A. Race riots of 1967: An analysis of police violence in Detroit and Newark. Journal of Black Studies. 1982;p. 261–274.
17. Plant EA, Peruche BM, Butz DA. Eliminating automatic racial bias: Making race non-diagnostic for responses to criminal suspects. Journal of Experimental Social Psychology. 2005;41(2):141–156.
18. Correll J, Urland GR, Ito TA. Event-related potentials and the decision to shoot: The role of threat perception and cognitive control. Journal of Experimental Social Psychology. 2006;42(1):120–128.
19. Correll J, Park B, Judd CM, Wittenbrink B, Sadler MS, Keesee T. Across the thin blue line: police officers and racial bias in the decision to shoot. Journal of Personality and Social Psychology. 2007;92(6):1006. pmid:17547485
20. Harring S, Platt T, Speiglman R, Takagi P. The management of police killings. Crime and Social Justice. 1977;8(Fall-Winter):34–43.
21. Jacobs D, Britt D. Inequality and police use of deadly force: An empirical assessment of a conflict hypothesis. Social Problems. 1979;p. 403–412.
22. Holmes MD. Minority threat and police brutality: Determinants of civil rights criminal complaints in US municipalities. Criminology. 2000;38(2):343–368.
23. Fyfe JJ. Geographic correlates of police shooting: A microanalysis. Journal of Research in Crime and Delinquency. 1980;17(1):101–113.
24. Warren P, Tomaskovic-Devey D, Smith W, Zingraff M, Mason M. Driving While Black: Bias Processes and Racial Disparity in Police Stops. Criminology. 2006;44(3):709–738.
25. Goldkamp JS. Minorities as victims of police shootings: Interpretations of racial disproportionality and police use of deadly force. The Justice System Journal. 1976;p. 169–183.
26. Martinot S, Sexton J. The avant-garde of white supremacy. Social Identities. 2003;9(2):169–181.
27. Doane A. What is racism? Racial discourse and racial politics. Critical Sociology. 2006;32(2–3):255–274.
28. Sidanius J, Pratto F. Social dominance: An intergroup theory of social hierarchy and oppression. Cambridge University Press; 2001.
29. Stephens-Davidowitz S. The cost of racial animus on a black candidate: Evidence using Google search data. Journal of Public Economics. 2014;118:26–40.

30. Efferson C, Lalive R, Richerson PJ, McElreath R, Lubell M. Conformists and mavericks: The empirics of frequency-dependent cultural transmission. Evolution and Human Behavior. 2008;29:56–64. Available from: /rmpubs/efferson%20et%20al%20EHB%202008.pdf.
31. McElreath R, Boyd R, Richerson PJ. Shared norms and the evolution of ethnic markers. Current Anthropology. 2003;44(1):122–129. Available from:?p = 62.
32. Ezekiel RS. The Racist Mind Revisited: An Ethnographer Looks at Neo-Nazi and Klan Groups. American Behavioral Scientist. 2002;46(1):51–71.
33. Blascovich J, Mendes WB, Hunter SB, Lickel B, Kowai-Bell N. Perceiver threat in social interactions with stigmatized others. Journal of Personality and Social Psychology. 2001;80(2):253. pmid:11220444
34. Nesdale D, Maass A, Durkin K, Griffiths J. Group norms, threat, and children's racial prejudice. Child Development. 2005;76(3):652–663. pmid:15892784
35. Sorensen JR, Marquart JW, Brock DE. Factors related to killings of felons by police officers: A test of the community violence and conflict hypotheses. Justice Quarterly. 1993;10(3):417–440.
36. MacDonald JM, Alpert GP, Tennenbaum AN. Justifiable homicide by police and criminal homicide: A research note. Journal of Crime and Justice. 1999;22(1):153–166.
37. Smith BW. Structural and organizational predictors of homicide by police. Policing: An International Journal of Police Strategies & Management. 2004;27(4):539–557.
38. MacDonald JM, Kaminski RJ, Alpert GP, Tennenbaum AN. The temporal relationship between police killings of civilians and criminal homicide: A refined version of the danger-perception theory. Crime & Delinquency. 2001;47(2):155–172.
39. Freedman DA. Ecological inference and the ecological fallacy. International Encyclopedia of the Social & Behavioral Sciences. 1999;6:4027–4030.
40. Lind, Dara and Magnus, Chris. How not to shoot civilians: 9 community policing tips from a chief who got it right. Vox. 2014;Available from: http://www.vox.com/2014/9/18/6111457/example-good-police-relations-cops-killing-outreach-culture-training#interview.
41. Hudson R. Being a cop showed me just how racist and violent the police

are. There's only one fix. The Washington Post. 2014;Available from: http://www.washingtonpost.com/posteverything/wp/2014/12/06/i-was-a-st-louis-cop-my-peers-were-racist-and-violent-and-theres-only-one-fix/.

42. Hensley N. Ohio cops suspended for years of racist texts leaked to civil rights group. New York Daily News. 2014;Available from: http://www.nydailynews.com/news/crime/ohio-cops-suspended-racist-texts-leaked-nonprofit-article-1.2033713.
43. Murphy D. Michigan police suspend cop behind humiliating,'racist' footage of black man. New York Daily News. 2013;Available from: http://www.nydailynews.com/news/national/michigan-police-suspend-behind-racist-footage-black-man-article-1.1527387.
44. Swaine J. Ferguson: Officer relieved of duty after video of racist remarks surfaces. The Gaurdian. 2014;Available from: http://www.theguardian.com/world/2014/aug/23/ferguson-officer-relieved-duty-video-racist-remarks.
45. Alejandro R. Baton Rouge Police Officer Resigns after Sending Racist Text Messages. Afro. 2014;Available from: http://www.afro.com/baton-rouge-police-officer-resigns-after-sending-racist-text-messages.
46. Bankoff C. Two St. Louis–Area Cops Suspended After Racist Rants. NY Mag. 2014;Available from: http://nymag.com/daily/intelligencer/2014/08/st-louis-area-cops-suspended-for-racist-rants.html.
47. Post H. Earl Wright, LAPD Officer, Wins $1.2 Million After Enduring Vulgar Racial Harassment Within Department. Huffington Post. 2013;Available from: http://www.huffingtonpost.com/2013/03/27/earl-wright-lapd_n_2964467.html.
48. Stahl J. Off Duty Chicago Police Accused of Election Night Hate Crimes. Huffington Post. 2008;Available from: http://www.huffingtonpost.com/jayne-lyn-stahl/off-duty-chicago-police-a_b_142536.html.
49. Whaley N. Two Black Cops Write Statements About Racism in LAPD. BET. 2013;Available from: http://www.bet.com/news/national/2013/02/14/two-black-cops-write-statements-about-racism-in-lapd.html.
50. Antony MG, Thomas RJ. This is citizen journalism at its finest: YouTube and the public sphere in the Oscar Grant shooting incident. New Media & Society. 2010;.

51. Ross CT, Winterhalder B. A hierarchical bayesian analysis of parasite prevalence and sociocultural outcomes: The role of structural racism and sanitation infrastructure. American Journal of Human Biology. 2015;Available from: http://dx.doi.org/10.1002/ajhb.22757. pmid:26179238
52. Weitzer R. American Policing Under Fire: Misconduct and Reform. Society. 2015;52(5):475–480.
53. Ross C. Identifying the Drivers of the Exceptionally-High Rates of Lethal and Racially-Biased Violence by Police in the United States Requires Geographically-Resolved Data and Analysis. Sociological Forum. 2015;In Press.
54. Rollins School of Public Health at Emory University in partnership with Gilead Sciences, Inc. AIDSVu; 2013.
55. United States Department of Justice Office of Justice Programs Federal Bureau of Investigation. Uniform Crime Reporting Program Data: Arrests by Age, Sex, and Race, 2012. Inter-University Consortium for Political and Social Research. 2014;.
56. Hijmans R, Garcia N, Wieczorek J. GADM: Database of Global Administrative Areas. 2010;.
57. Gelman A, Hill J. Data analysis using regression and multilevel/hierarchical models. Cambridge University Press; 2006.
58. Stan Development Team. Stan: A C++ Library for Probability and Sampling, Version 2.5.0; 2014. Available from: http://mc-stan.org/.

INDEX

N

O

P

Q

R

S